The Fortification of Malta by the Order of St. John

frontispiece

Aerial view of the harbour area

The Fortification of Malta by the Order of St. John

1530-1798

Second edition

Alison Hoppen

Mireva
Publications

This edition first published in 1999
by Mireva Publications
of Tower Street, Msida, Malta, MSD 06.
(Mireva and logo are registered trade marks. Reg. no. 17998)
Phototypeset and electronically paged on
NewCentury SchoolBook 10/12pt and by MirevaSet.
Produced by Evan Cumbo.
Printed by Gutenberg Press,
Gudja Road,
Tarxien, Malta.

The first edition of *The Fortification of Malta by the Order of St. John 1530-1798*, (ISBN 07073 0241 2), was published by The Scottish Academic Press (Edinburgh) in 1979.

International Standard Book Number

1-870579-38-0

Contents

Illustrations

PLATES

Plates 2, 3, 4, 14, 18, 19 and 22 — © J. Quentin Hughes
Plate 11 — © The Vatican Library
Plates 1, 9, 17 and 24 — © The Malta Tourist Board

FIGURES

Figures 9 and 10 — © J.Quentin Hughes

to my
mother
and
father

Preface

This is a study of the fortifications built in Malta by the knights of St. John. Any visitor to Malta cannot fail to be impressed by the massive ramparts surrounding the harbour area, and, although less immediately obvious, quite as remarkable is the chain of defences which encircles the coast. For the student of European military history the Maltese fortifications, because of their concentration in so small an area, because of their compactness, because of the extensive survival of records connected with their construction, represent a unique opportunity for examining in detail the planning and building of large-scale defensive works. Such an examination, however, must range more widely than merely the minutiae of construction: the fortifications must be viewed against the political, diplomatic and economic situation of the Order of St. John. Equally important is the social context in which the Order found itself and in particular the effect of so massive an undertaking on a native population to which the Order represented an alien and foreign power. Without an examination of such wider issues a study of this nature is no more than a skeleton without flesh. But in order to elucidate such matters it is essential that they be placed within the firm and sturdy framework of a detailed account and description of when, how and why the fortifications were actually constructed. This is done in Part II, which, apart from the intrinsic importance of such an account, forms an essential preliminary to the more thematic treatment presented in Part III.

Although the Maltese fortifications erected between 1530 and 1798 are in some respects unique, they nonetheless constitute a representative example of contemporary European military architecture at its best. Their study is therefore of relevance to the wider field of European military history.

* * * * *

Many debts, both to individuals and to institutions, have been incurred while this book was in the making. Librarians and archivists, in particular those in the Royal (now National) Library of Malta, the Library of the Venerable Order of St. John of Jerusalem in Clerkenwell, and at the Vatican, answered my often importunate demands with unfailing courtesy and efficiency. The Countess Costanza Laparelli-Pitti of Florence kindly permitted me to work on papers in her family archives. The Carnegie Trust for the Universities of Scotland awarded grants which allowed me a final visit to Valletta to complete my research.

My interest in Malta was first awakened by Lionel Butler, then professor of medieval history at the University of St. Andrews and now principal of Royal Holloway College in the University of London, whose enthusiasm and knowledge have sustained me over bad times and good. Dr Quentin Hughes of the University of Liverpool both read the work in draft and with extraordinary generosity allowed me to plunder his collection of photographs and plans of Malta and the fortifications. Professor J.R. Hale of the University College London gave me encouragement at a time when I was much in need of it. My husband – with only sporadic complaints – undertook the task of reading the work in its various stages, of forcing me to defend my views against criticism, and of seeing to it that I did not lose heart. Those to whom I owe a debt which transcends all of these are those to whom this book is dedicated.

A.H.

The publication of this book has been assisted by grants from the Twenty-Seven Foundation and the British Academy.

Preface to the Second Edition

The years since the publication of the first edition of the Fortification of Malta in 1979 have seen a blossoming in the study of the development of the fortifications in the early modern period, both in Malta and in the wider European field. In English two books by Christopher Duffy, *Siege Warfare: The Fortress in the Early Modern World 1494-1660* and *The Fortress in the Age of Vauban and Frederick the Great, 1660-1789* provide a wide-ranging account of contemporary undertakings outside the islands, and allow the Maltese fortifications to be seen within a European perspective. On Malta itself various articles and books have appeared, the more important of which have been added to the greatly expanded bibliography. These more recent works have led to a modification of my views in some respects but I believe that the overall picture presented in the first edition remains substantially sound. Numerous minor changes have been made for this new edition as well as a number of substantial revisions and additions, especially in Chapters 9, 10 and 11.

Further study has enabled me to broaden the general context in which the building of the fortifications should be seen. In relating the Maltese defences to their overseas counterparts, a closer examination of the careers and backgrounds of the military engineers employed revealed the extent to which the works belong to a common European tradition. The list of visiting engineers who enjoyed a wide reputation is long and the list of those who were consulted at a distance even longer. (See appendices 2 and 3.) Overall the picture emerges of a lively interchange of personnel and ideas in which an association with the renowned Maltese fortifications could only enhance an engineer's reputation professionally and even, by admission to the Order, raise his social status. (See A. Hoppen, 'Military engineers in Malta, 1530-1798', *Annals of Science*, 38 (1981), 413-33.)

A rather fuller treatment of the ways in which the military activities of the Order impinged on the lives of the Maltese islanders can be found in my essay, 'Military priorities and social realities in the early-modern Mediterranean: Malta and its fortifications', in *Hospitaller Malta*, edited by Victor Mallia-Milanes. The change in the islands' strategic position following their occupation by a militaristic group of aristocrats bent on hostile activities towards the Moslems, ensured that military considerations were to play a more prominent part in the everyday life of the inhabitants. The Maltese paid a price, not always without protest, for their greater security through higher taxation, increased obligations to render labour service, and more generally through the subordination of their interests to those of the Order.

The history of the fortifications is more than a record of stone placed on stone: the construction of these works demanded commitment from both knights and Maltese. The defence of the islands was a matter of overriding importance to the Order and this concern pervaded its internal administrative policies and also its relationships with foreign powers and the local inhabitants. The fortifications are not only an enduring material legacy of the knights, but also epitomise the nature of the regime which for over two and a half centuries ruled the Maltese people. The newcomer can hardly fail to be overawed by the extent and beauty of the fortifications; they may no longer perform the military function for which they were designed but they cannot be disregarded or ignored. I hope that a fuller understanding of their history and purpose may lead to a better appreciation of their value and of their place in the common European heritage.

A.H.

Abbreviations

AOM	Archives of the Order of Malta, Royal Malta Library.
ASV	Vatican Secret Archives.
Barb. Lat.	Fondo Barberini Latino, Vatican Library.
BM	British Museum, London, (now the British Library).
Chigi	Fondo Chigi, Vatican Library.
Clerkenwell	Library of the Order of St. John, St. John's Gate, Clerkenwell, London.
Cod. Lap.	Codex Laparelli.
Col. doc. inéditos	*Colecciòn de documentos inéditos para la historia de España.*
PRO	Public Record Office, London.
RML	Royal Malta Library, Valletta, (now the National Library of Malta).
Tres.	Treasury manuscript, Royal Malta Library.
Univ.	Università manuscript, Royal Malta Library.
Urb. Lat.	Fondo Urbinate Latino, Vatican Library.
Vat. Lat.	Fondo Vaticano Latino, Vatican Library.

Part I

Introduction

Chapter 1

The Order of St. John in Malta

The military Order of St. John of Jerusalem, which, with the Order of the Temple, was to become one of the twin pillars of the crusader kingdom of Jerusalem, had decidedly unwarlike origins. A hospice, dedicated to St. John, was established in Jerusalem in the eleventh century to care for weary Christian pilgrims. After the conquest of the city by the crusaders in 1099 this hospice, or hospital, grew in importance attracting many pious gifts of land and money from laymen and clerics anxious to support its work. In 1113 Pope Paschal II recognized the hospital as an independent religious order and in the course of time the Hospitallers came to enjoy many ecclesiastical privileges such as exemption from episcopal jurisdiction, freedom from the payment of tithes, the right to have their own chaplains, churches and cemeteries, and the privilege of electing their own master free from outside interference.[1] The hospitaller activities of the Order continued unabated throughout its long history but very early the Knights of St. John assumed another role. Under the Master Raymond du Puy, in the early twelfth century, the Order began to take part in the military affairs of the kingdom although military officers, the marshal and castellans, do not appear among the officials until the late 1160s. This extension of the

---

1 This and most of the next paragraph is based on J. Riley-Smith, *The Knights of St. John in Jerusalem and Cyprus, 1050-1310* (London, 1967), pp. 376-89, 53-5, 237, 198-226.

knights' activities was probably brought about by a combination of circumstances. It has been suggested that the Hospitallers took up arms in emulation of the Knights Templar who had been founded in the early twelfth century as a military order. There is, however, reason to doubt whether the Templars were thriving in the 1130s, and, in particular, whether they were capable of arousing the Hospitallers to jealous rivalry. Undoubtedly there was a need to defend the pilgrim routes and the holy places from Moslem attack and this could be seen as an extension of their original duty, the care of the poor. By the thirteenth century the Knights of St. John were established as a hospitaller and a military order. It was, perhaps, not surprising that the military activities of the Order continued to expand when it is remembered that its members were drawn from the knightly families of Europe whose upbringing fitted them primarily for a military career.

After playing a long and, on the whole, an honourable part in the defence of the Holy Land the Hospitallers were finally expelled by the Egyptian Mamluks from their last stronghold at Acre in 1291 along with the remnants of the Christian forces. The Order withdrew to Cyprus, where it spent a troubled fifteen years before establishing itself in the island of Rhodes, which it had captured from the Byzantines together with Cos, Leros and other islands of the Dodecanese. In Rhodes the Order set up its own sovereign state independent of any secular prince. It continued its fight against the infidel making use of the efficient little navy which it had built up during its stay in Cyprus. In the fifteenth century, however, the position of the knights became increasingly more difficult as the Ottoman Turks consolidated their strength in the Near East: Byzantium fell in 1453; Serbia was conquered six years later; between 1458 and 1460 the greater part of the Morea was overrun; Bosnia was finally conquered in 1464. Rhodes itself was besieged in 1480 but did not fall. The death of Mehmed II in 1481 was followed by succession disputes among the Turks and the pressure on the knights was relaxed. Another attack seemed inevitable and the Order took the opportunity to strengthen the island's fortifications.[2]

---

2 A. Gabriel, *La Cité de Rhodes*, 2 vols. (Paris, 1921), I, 115; G. Bosio, *Istoria della Sacra Religione Militare di S. Giovanni Gerosolmitano*, 3 vols. (Rome, 1594-1602), II, 525; R. Vertot, *Histoire des Chevaliers Hospitaliers de S. Jean de Jérusalem*, 4 vols. (Paris, 1726), II, 411.

Despite these preparations, in 1522 the island succumbed after a siege of six months to the large army led by Suleiman II. The knights obtained honourable surrender terms and were allowed to evacuate, setting sail in their galleys with their most treasured possessions, and their archives, and accompanied by those Rhodians who preferred not to come under Ottoman rule. For a number of years the Order wandered from place to place, to Crete, Messina, Civitavecchia, Viterbo, Villefranche and Nice, hoping to find a base from which it could organize the reconquest of Rhodes. As early as 1523 Malta was offered by Charles V as a possible home but it proved unattractive: a barren, poorly fortified outpost, subject to raids by Barbary corsairs. Moreover, Charles expected the knights to occupy not only the sister island of Gozo, likewise inadequately defended, but also the fortress of Tripoli in North Africa, which had been a Spanish possession since 1510. The Order would thus provide the front line of defence in Charles's battle with the Turks for control of the central Mediterranean. The Grand Master de l'Isle Adam hoped in vain for something better. In 1524 a commission was sent to examine both the islands and Tripoli[3] and finally in 1529, in spite of its discouraging report,[4] it was decided to accept Malta and its dependencies as a temporary base. There was something to be said in Malta's favour: it possessed excellent harbours, which were essential for the seafaring activities of the knights. The islands were situated in the middle of the Mediterranean, about seventy miles from Sicily and two hundred from Tripoli (see figure 8). They could provide a useful centre for pursuing the naval struggle against the Moslems, especially against the North-African Regencies and the corsairs which they harboured. Although far from the Holy Land the knights could continue their crusading role. Charles V would remain the suzerain of Malta but the Order's neutrality was safeguarded by the provision that it was to be free from normal vassal services. Its only obligation was to present to the king of Sicily an annual fee of one falcon on All Saints' Day.[5]

---

3 Archives of the Order of Malta (hereafter referred to as AOM), 411, f. 202v. (28 June 1524).
4 Bosio, III, 29-30.
5 The grant of the island to the Order is set out in AOM 70.

If the knights were not overenthusiastic about Charles's gift, neither were the Maltese. They protested their wish to remain part of the Sicilian royal domain. In 1428, after suffering depredations at the hands of Aragonese noblemen who had been granted the islands as fiefs, the islanders had paid a considerable sum to ensure that they remained subject only to the crown.[6] The islands had enjoyed a measure of autonomy. Each had its own governing body known as the Università which raised taxes, administered justice, and regulated trade, the grain supply, public health and irrigation systems. The chief officer of the Università was called the *ħakem* or *capitano della verga*; under him were four *jurati* responsible for the day-to-day conduct of business; and there were other officials with specific duties such as the judge, treasurer, two *catapans* (market superintendents), a notary, a *marammero* (fortress-builder) and a *portolano* (port superintendent). Matters of importance were debated by a representative council, the *consiglio popolare*, which, although it depended to some degree on popular suffrage, was controlled by a closely knit body of churchmen, land-owners and lawyers. The Order swore to observe the ancient privileges of Malta and Gozo but, in practice, the Universitàs were soon divested of any real authority and tended to act as agents for the Order. An additional Università was established in Birgu, which enabled the knights to exercise even more direct control over the area around the harbours where their chief interests lay.

The Order was well aware of the disadvantages of Malta before it accepted the island as its new headquarters. The islands possessed practically no natural resources except an abundant supply of building stone. There were no rivers, and apart from springs the main source of water was the rain which drained off roofs to be collected in underground cisterns. The land was unable to grow sufficient grain to support the population of some 25,000 and the islands were dependent on grain imports from Sicily.[7] Practically everything in the way of raw materials had to come from abroad. Fortunately the knights could draw on their

---

6 There is no good general account of Malta in the Middle Ages. For a discussion of the problems facing a historian of medieval Malta see A.T. Luttrell, 'Approaches to medieval Malta', in *Medieval Malta: Studies on Malta Before the Knights*, ed. A.T. Luttrell (London, 1975), pp.1-70.

7 B.W. Blouet, *The Story of Malta* (London, 1967), p.89.

considerable possessions in Europe to supply what was lacking. Over the years, chiefly as the result of bequests, the Order had amassed estates and property, part of the revenues of which could be remitted to Malta as formerly they had been transferred to Rhodes, or, earlier still, to the Holy Land. Well before the early sixteenth century the European properties had been divided among the twenty-five priories which constituted the basic unit on which the territorial organization of the Order was founded. Within each priory the Order's possessions were divided into self-supporting subdivisions named commanderies. Although a member of an international body each knight of St. John belonged to one of the priories, usually that nearest his home, and when resident in Malta (or in the 'convent' as the knights called their headquarters), through his membership of the priory he belonged also to one of the eight langues. The langues – of Provence, Auvergne, France, Italy, Aragon, Castile, England and Germany – were geographical groupings of priories which were important constituents of the central organization in Malta but which had no standing in the European territories, so that the six priories of the French langue never operated as a single unit in France.

By the time of the Order's arrival in Malta it consisted of several clearly defined classes of members. The chaplains were the priests of the Order and could be found ministering in its hospitals, galleys and churches. To enter the Order as a chaplain a candidate had to prove that he was of legitimate birth, 'born of gentle and creditable parents, [and] that he had never followed any mean or servile art or business'.[8] Similar rules governed the admission of serving brothers, or servants-at-arms, who performed a variety of military, naval, administrative and household duties. Indeed two of the Order's resident engineers were serving brothers, Vittorio Cassar and Stephen de Tousard.[9] To become a knight of justice, however, strict proofs of nobility were required. The degree of proof demanded varied from langue to langue. Italy was satisfied if the four grandparents were noble, but Germany insisted that all sixteen great-great-grandparents be of noble

[8] From a statute of La Valette quoted in Vertot, IV, 78, second pagination.

[9] G. Mangion, 'Girolamo Cassar architetto maltese del cinquecento', *Melita Historica*, VI (1973), 197 (Cassar); and R. Cavaliero, *The Last of the Crusaders* (London, 1960), p.230; and Miège, *Histoire de Malte*, 3 vols. (Paris, 1840), III, 36 (Tousard).

birth. The chaplains, serving brothers and knights of justice were all fully professed members of the Order who took the three monastic vows of poverty, chastity and obedience. There were, in addition, several classes of associate members. Services to the Order could be rewarded by admission as a knight of grace for which no proofs of nobility were necessary. The painters Caravaggio and Mattia Preti, and the engineers Buonamici, Blondel, Colongues, Tigné and Mondion were all received as knights of grace.[10] On the other hand, those honoured by admission as knights of honour and devotion were always by birth eligible to become knights of justice, but chose not to take the full vows.[11] Confraters were lay associates attached to a particular house who swore to defend the Order and its property against ill-wishers, while donats were entitled to wear the half-cross in reward for services they had rendered and were noblemen who definitely intended to enter the Order some time before their death.[12]

The candidate wishing to enter the Order as a fully-professed member normally took his vows at the priory nearest his home. Once admitted it was customary to travel to Malta where the new recruit would live with his compatriots in the auberge of his langue. The auberge, or inn, was presided over by a senior member of the langue known as the pilier or conventual bailiff. The rules governing promotion within the Order were closely defined and were based on two principal criteria, seniority and service in the headquarters, or convent, in Malta. Before becoming eligible for promotion the newly professed knight had to undertake a number of tours-of-duty, called caravans. This could entail tasks such as serving aboard the galleys or performing garrison duty. Once such caravans were completed the knight would await eventual promotion to a commandery. Needless to say, popes, kings and princes were not averse to trying to exert pressure to ensure

---

10 V. Borg, *Fabio Chigi Apostolic Delegate in Malta (1634-1639)* (Studi e Testi no. 249, Vatican City, 1967), p.364 (Buonamici); AOM 477, f.233 (Mederico Blondel); Vertot, IV, 133 third pagination (Colongues); AOM 266, f.170v. (Tigné); AOM 522, f.162 and Vertot, IV, 143 third pagination (Mondion).

11 The engineers Floriani (AOM 111, f.264) and Grunenberg (AOM 263, f.63) were admitted as knights of devotion.

12 By the sixteenth century the distinction was becoming blurred. The engineer Girolamo Cassar was accepted into the Order as donat or confrater (AOM 432, f.253 and AOM 439, f.270v.)

that their relatives and favourites secured rich commanderies without too much delay. As a commander the knight (or indeed the serving brother or chaplain, as both these classes could hold commanderies) was expected to administer the lands and possessions of the commandery and remit a proportion of its revenues to Malta. This often entailed residence outside Malta, in the commandery itself. The knight would then participate in the annual provincial chapter of his priory which was presided over by the governor of the priory, known as the prior.

The prior was a senior member of the Order, one of the so-called grand crosses. Those grand crosses actually resident in Malta played an important part in the day-to-day government of the Order, and from among their number were chosen its chief officers and functionaries although selection to the highest posts was governed by strict and elaborate rules. The conventual bailiffs, for example, enjoyed as of right certain positions: thus the pilier of Provence was grand commander and controlled the common treasury; the pilier of Auvergne, grand marshal and thus senior military commander; the pilier of France, grand hospitaller administering the hospital; the pilier of Italy, grand admiral and commander of the sea-borne forces; Castile supplied the chancellor who headed the chancery; the pilier of Aragon as grand conservator was responsible for the upkeep of charitable foundations and the payment of subsistence allowances to knights resident in the auberges; the pilier of Germany occupied the position of grand bailiff and was in overall command of fortifications beyond the immediate harbour area; while the pilier of England, named the turcopilier – a title dating back to the thirteenth century when this functionary commanded the mercenary force of light horsemen, or turcopoles – controlled the militia and coastguard. After the demise of the English langue in the mid-sixteenth century, the seneschal, a nominee of the grand master, assumed these last duties. Equal in status to the conventual bailiffs were two churchmen, the bishop of Malta and the prior of the conventual church of St. John in Valletta. Both were drawn from the ranks of the Order's clergy, and their positions were the highest open to native-born Maltese who, although many entered the Order as chaplains, were never admitted as knights of justice and were thus debarred from the great majority of offices. The Order itself, however, enjoyed exemption from the bishop's jurisdiction and came under direct papal protection. The bishop, selected by the Sicilian king from three candidates nominated by the grand master and council, in time became the spiritual and, even on occasion, the political leader, of the Maltese, and as such often came into conflict with the order of which he remained himself a member. The highest dignitary actually within the Order's own clerical hierarchy was the prior of the conventual church, elected by the chaplains from among their own number. He performed on a more restricted scale many of the functions of a bishop and had spiritual oversight of the knights and control of the Order's churches and clergy.

The bishop, the prior of the conventual church, the piliers and the other resident grand crosses comprised the ordinary council which under the presidency of the grand master conducted the day-to-day government of the Order. The grand master, the head of the Order, was elected by representatives of the eight langues from among the ranks of the grand crosses.[13] In his government of the Order he was subject to its statutes and was expected to rule with the advice of the council. On the other hand, in his role as sovereign of Malta and the Maltese he was not so restricted and the ancient privileges and liberties of the islanders exercised little effective restraint over his authority. As the governing body of the Order the council managed a wide variety of business. It was responsible for the admission, training and promotion of all members, for the maintenance of discipline and the administration of justice, for the appointment of certain officials, for the auditing of the accounts of the common treasury, for the oversight of the navy and the military establishments, and for the conduct of diplomatic relations.[14] An appeal could be made from the decisions of the ordinary council to the complete council. This latter body consisted of the personnel of the former council supplemented by two senior knights from each langue.

---

13 Following the Reformation in England the English langue was virtually non-existent duing the period the Order was in Malta but representatives of the English langue were elected from the other langues and the election was theoretically carried out by the eight langues.

14 Until 1623 the council transactions dealing with both the internal administration of the Order and matters of state were recorded in the same registers, the *Libri Conciliorum*. In that year it was decided that the business of state should be recorded in separate registers, the *Libri Conciliorum Status*. The *Libri Conciliorum* for the period 1530-1793 are volumes AOM 85-167 and the *Libri Conciliorum Status*, 1623-1798, are volumes AOM 255-78.

The supreme legislative authority of the order was vested in the chapter general which comprised the grand master, the bishop, the prior of the conventual church, the conventual bailiffs, the priors, and certain bailiffs entitled to sit in the chapter general and therefore known as capitular bailiffs. This assembly thus brought together the two ruling elements in the order, those who controlled the convent and those who administered the European estates on the revenues of which the convent depended for its very existence. The chapter general was the only body empowered to sanction taxes on the European commanderies. During the early years in Malta chapters general were called regularly but the practice declined and not one was summoned between 1631 and 1776. Instead, the relevant functions were exercised by a committee of representatives of the langues. In practice the eclipse of the chapter general in the seventeenth and eighteenth centuries led to the increased power of the grand master, whose position was further strengthened by the development of the congregation of state.[15] This executive body, which consisted of the grand master's nominees, became responsible for the conduct of the affairs of Malta as a state rather than as a religious body. Thus, in the course of these two centuries the development of the Order as an independent sovereign state eventually grew to overshadow its origins as a religious order.

Despite the knights' vow of obedience the internal history of the Order was by no means smooth. Perhaps such turbulence was inevitable in a celibate community with a strong military tradition drawing its members from the ruling classes of Catholic states which were often at war amongst themselves. Undoubtedly, as the Order's military role in the defence of Europe diminished in the course of the eighteenth century, the grand masters were beset by frequent outbursts of insubordination both amongst the knights and the islanders.[16] Knights dabbled in freemasonry, joined republican clubs, indulged their high spirits in horse-play at carnival time, and when the occasion presented itself, in duelling, brawling and gambling. And, from time to time, for instance in 1771 and 1776, their unruliness and discontent erupted into open defiance of their sovereign's

---

15 Cavaliero, p.32.

16 Examples of protests are: Slaves' revolt, 1749 (Cavaliero, pp. 138-42); Cavalcabo's conspiracy, 1771 (ibid., pp.148-51); the priests' revolt, 1775 (ibid., pp.153-8); the formation of the Auvergnat club (ibid., p.165); Dolomieu's intrigues, 1783 (ibid., pp.169-70).

authority. However, these outbursts took place against a background of strong government and presented no real challenge to the grand master's position. Only after 1789 with the overthrow of the *ancien régime* in France and the questioning of those values on which the whole ethos of the Order was based, did the unrest assume a more serious direction. Other subjects of the grand master were, however, also showing signs of discontent. In 1749 the slaves on the island, incited by the Pasha Mustapha of Rhodes, then himself a captive, planned to conquer the whole of Malta with the aid of a Turkish fleet. The conspiracy was, however, betrayed some three weeks before the projected uprising, and forestalled. A decision by Grand Master Ximenes in 1775 to ban the hunting of game for a period of six months, in order to preserve the stocks of the chief game animal – the rabbit – precipitated a revolt of the local clergy who were passionately addicted to the hunt. But the deeper causes of unrest lay in the growing political resentment of the priests, as educated men and natural leaders of the community, at the exclusion of the Maltese from all positions of authority in the island and at the arbitrary rule of the grand master of which the hunting ban was but one example. This, combined with the failure of the Sicilian harvest in 1775, led a small band of priests, encouraged by Cavalcabo, an adventurer in the service of Catherine the Great, to attempt to capture the island and hand it over to a Russian fleet. The priests chose their time well. The Maltese navy was at sea assisting the Spaniards in a punitive expedition against Algiers, and with it had gone the majority of the fighting forces.

The insurgents captured fort St. Elmo and the watch-tower on St. James's cavalier in Valletta before the alarm was raised, but in the event no general uprising occurred, no Russian fleet appeared and the revolt was crushed within two days. It was, however, a sad reflection on the defences of the island that St. Elmo and part of St. James's cavalier could have been occupied with such ease. Although the revolt did not spread to the countryside, the Maltese were becoming steadily disillusioned with the rule of the knights, so that when Napoleon appeared in 1798, although he was not welcomed as a saviour, initially at least the Maltese were willingly prepared to accept from him what they thought to be republican liberation, and the Church authorities in particular adopted a conciliatory position.[17]

---

[17] G.V. Ellul, 'The French invasion of Malta: an unpublished account', *Hyphen*, III (1978), 4.

The Order of St. John when driven from Malta in 1798 was a supranational organization drawing its membership from the noble families of Catholic Europe. Its constitution provided for promotion based on seniority and service, and for government by the more senior knights. Its grand master was chosen by elected representatives from all levels of the Order. Despite protests from among the knights, the rule exercised by the eighteenth-century grand masters was essentially autocratic. Overwhelming financial problems were the principal exigencies which led to the calling of the chapter general in 1776. The sympathy of the Maltese and the loyalty of many of the knights had by then been lost, so that two decades later Napoleon was able to exploit these divisions to ensure an almost bloodless conquest.

Chapter 2

The Development of Gunpowder Fortifications

For over two and a half centuries, from their arrival in 1530, almost to the very time of their departure in 1798, the Order of St. John strove to improve and augment the fortifications of Malta and Gozo. Although removed from the eastern Mediterranean the knights' enthusiasm for the struggle against the Moslems had not waned, and they saw naval and military exploits as no less an essential part of their duties than hospitaller activities. The knights never disputed the principle that their fortifications should be as up-to-date and effective as resources of money, manpower and military expertise would allow. Their sojourn in Malta was virtually contemporaneous with the heyday of the bastion,[1] and the modern and popular method of fortification which they embraced was the bastioned system. The Maltese islands, therefore, show the application of this style of fortress design to a particular, geographically limited area, during the period when it was the accepted mode of fortification throughout Europe itself, and in colonial settlements around the world.[2] By 1530 the bastion was firmly established as the central element in fortifications designed to withstand artillery bombardment and at the same time to bring as much

---

1 For an explanation of this and other technical terms see the glossary.

2 Duffy, *Siege Warfare*, pp. 220-46; examples of such forts are Fort Jesus, Mombasa and Castillo San Marcos, St. Augustine, Florida (C.R. Boxer and A. de Azevedo, *Fort Jesus and the Portuguese in Mombasa* (London, 1960); and L.R. Aruna and A. Manucy, *The Building of Castillo San Marcos* (St. Augustine, Fa., 1977).

fire-power as possible to bear on the attackers. By the late eighteenth century the supremacy of the bastion was being challenged by the growing popularity of the tenailled system and of round forts advocated by, among others, Montalembert. Within these two hundred and fifty years, fortress design, although based on the bastion, did not ossify, but developed as new generations of engineers attempted to improve on the work of their predecessors. The Order, ever anxious that its defences should attain the best contemporary standards, tried to ensure that the fortifications of Malta were a worthy example of the modes of building then current in Europe. In the art of fortification, as in other matters, Malta under the knights may be considered 'an epitome of all Europe'.[3]

The bastioned system of defence was developed at the end of the Middle Ages in response to a new offensive weapon – the cannon. Although siege guns first appeared in Italy in the fourteenth century, it was not until the fifteenth century that, with the invention of cast bronze cannon and the increasing use of iron balls, they could inflict sufficient damage on contemporary fortifications to provoke innovations in defence. The medieval fortress was essentially a defensive structure which adapted itself in response to improvements in offensive weapons. Before the coming of gunpowder (early in the fourteenth century) the chief threats were from assault and, from the twelfth century onwards, mining; siege engines were too inaccurate to batter away consistently at one particular spot; the enemy could not launch an effective attack at long range, but was at his most dangerous close to, attempting to scale walls or batter down the gate. Thus the high walls of the medieval fort were designed primarily to prevent scaling; while the even higher towers placed at intervals on the walls enabled the defenders to fire at the attackers from the flanks; machicolations allowed them to rain a shower of missiles vertically onto the assault parties; and the narrow walk-way at the top of the walls permitted marksmen, protected by crenellations, to pick off individual enemies. In response to the threat from mining, engineers had thickened their fortifications at the base, but the high walls and towers still presented an excellent

---

3 Quotation from P. Brydone, A *Tour Through Sicily and Malta, in a Series of Letters to Wm. Beckford, Esq. of Somerly in Suffolk*, 2 vols. (London, 1791 ed.), I, 151, letter of 7 June 1770.

target to artillery. By the fifteenth century the attacker possessed a reasonably accurate gun which could deliver a long-range, powerful, horizontal blow, so that the primary threat to the fortress no longer lay in scaling but in bombardment and in mining made more effective by an increasingly skilled use of explosives. Walls became lower, thicker and more massive in order to withstand bombardment, and scarped so as to deflect cannon balls. Towers were first adapted to accommodate hand guns and small cannon; keyhole loops were introduced in the place of arrow-slits, but, as defenders recognized the potential of long-range cannon fire for the harassment of the enemy, it was found that the large guns required for this purpose could not be fired from within the towers: they produced too much smoke for an enclosed area and their arc of fire was restricted by the loophole. Instead the cannon were placed on platforms on top of the towers and the towers became, effectively, gun platforms and as such were soon to develop into bastions.[4]

The bastion is a solid platform projecting from the main line of the fortifications to provide as wide a range of fire as possible. Although retaining part of the tower's defensive function in affording flanking fire, it is essentially an aggressive form and it is this characteristic which distinguishes it from the tower.[5] The tradition of vertical defence was abandoned: walls were scarped to deflect cannon balls; machicolation was no longer a practical proposition for platforms which were to carry heavy guns. At first the bastion was round in shape, which had the advantage of deflecting shot from all angles and being relatively easy to construct as little squared masonry was needed, but at the same time had the disadvantage that there remained areas of dead ground which could not be covered by any flanking fire. Thus the angled bastion became widely accepted in the sixteenth century and in its most usual form came to be an irregular pentagon with two faces meeting at the salient angle, two flanks which abutted the curtain walls forming the re-entrant angles, and the fifth side, open to the interior of the fort, forming the gorge. An area of dead ground could still result where the bastion met the curtain; some

4 For the development of the bastion see J.R. Hale, 'The early development of the bastion: an Italian chronology, c. 1450 – *c*. 1534', in *Europe in the Late Middle Ages*, ed. J.R. Hale, J.R.L. Highfield and B. Smalley (London, 1965), pp. 465-94.

5 This is Hale's definition of a bastion – see 'The early development of the bastion', p. 475.

engineers covered this ground by batteries placed in the re-entrant angles and protected by the projecting orillion, or ear of the bastion; but by the seventeenth century this problem had been overcome by the realignment of the bastion and curtain.

The bastions were linked by the curtain walls, which with the coming of gunpowder artillery became lower and more massive. They were strengthened from the rear by the earth and rubble which formed the rampart. This backing of earth provided a wide passageway along which the guns could be moved with ease. The bastions themselves, unlike the towers, were the same height as the curtain walls which assisted the swift redeployment of artillery. Both guns and men were protected by pierced parapets presenting a more solid silhouette than the earlier crenellations which had been fine targets for the enemy gunner. The whole encircling ring of fortifications, the bastions and curtains, known as the enceinte, came to be regarded as a continuous gun platform from which the enemy could be attacked by horizontal aggressive fire power.[6] In order to give defenders additional height to dominate the countryside more effectively, at intervals along the enceinte, usually on the bastions, cavaliers – raised artillery platforms – were sometimes constructed.

The bastioned enceinte remained the principal mode of fortress construction until well into the eighteenth century but the design was subject to constant modifications and additions especially as regards the outworks. Outworks beyond the main enceinte proliferated in the course of the seventeenth and eighteenth centuries. Naturally as walls became lower the risk of escalade or scaling became greater should the enemy reach the main enceinte; outworks could keep the enemy at a distance, and, no less importantly, could shield the main walls from artillery fire. As offensive works they provided extra gun batteries with which to bombard the attacker, and carried the fire power of the fortress further forward. As they were often constructed later than the main enceinte they demonstrate the development in the ideas of fortification. Only in exceptional circumstances were rulers prepared to demolish a whole bastioned enceinte in order to rebuild it according to the latest design; it was too costly in

6 Hale, 'The early development of the bastion', p. 477.

money, time and resources. Instead, attempts were made to modernize fortresses by the addition of outworks which put into effect the latest practices, and which, thereby, corrected such old-fashioned features as had come to be regarded as faults.

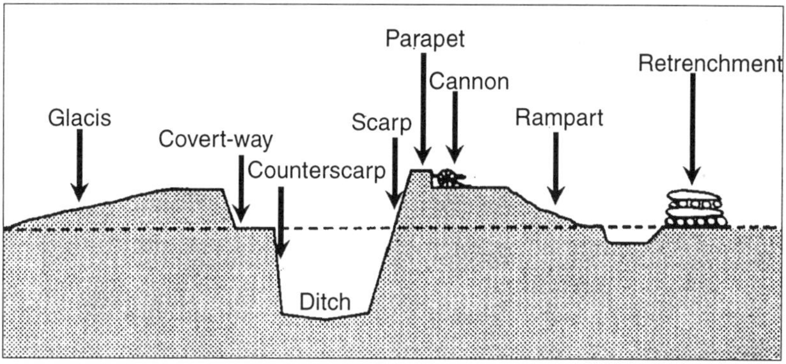

Fig.1. Cross-section of a defensive trace.

Outside the main enceinte was the main ditch, which could be either wet or dry. Where there were outworks the latter was often favoured because it simplified the task of supplying the outworks and allowed the defenders a safer retreat path into the main fort. The dry ditch also facilitated the assembly of troops for a sortie, and the entry of relief in time of siege. Along the top of the counterscarp, or the far side of the ditch, ran the covert-way which was protected from the open countryside by a parapet. Along this roadway troops could be stationed and assembled under cover before making a sortie, or withdrawing. At intervals, to assist the mustering of companies, there were assembly areas called places of arms. The parapet of the covert-way was normally hidden from enemy view by the slope of the glacis; the countryside immediately surrounding the fortress was cleared of all cover and sloped so that the guns on the ramparts could rake it with fire.

One of the earlier forms of outwork was the braye which was a continuous rampart shielding the base of the main wall and providing an additional tier of fire. The braye stood in the main ditch with ditches both in front and behind, thus distinguishing it from the fausse-braye which was not separated from the main enceinte in this way. Gradually it became customary to break the braye up into works of shorter length. The portion of a braye remaining in front of a curtain was known as a tenaille, that in front of a bastion as a counterguard. Extensive outworks beyond the main ditch were a later development, the most common form being a detached triangular work which by the seventeenth century could be called indiscriminately either a ravelin or a mezzaluna; a lunette was of similar shape but smaller. A hornwork consisted of a roughly oblong projection in front of the main ditch aligned to the faces of the bastions of the enceinte so as to be completely flanked by their fire. Its front presented two half-bastions, joined by a curtain beyond which was a ravelin; it was enclosed on each side by a straight curtain and ditch. More complicated was a crownwork which was formed of a double hornwork with a front of one bastion, flanked by two half-bastions (see figure 3). The choice as to which of these outworks to employ depended both upon the terrain and local conditions and also upon the inclination of the designer or engineer, for within the general system of bastioned fortification there were different schools of design and an engineer's work would naturally reflect the tradition in which he had been trained.

It has been customary to classify the different systems of bastioned fortifications under national schools.[7] This has given rise to competing claims on behalf of a specific nation, or even individual, for the credit of having introduced particular developments. The controversy over the invention of the bastion has been more or less resolved and it is now generally accepted that the transformation of the medieval tower into the bastion was not the concept of an individual, but a development which took place in Italy in the late fifteenth and early sixteenth centuries.[8] Within Italy there were considerable variations in the size and shape of bastions until eventually an optimum design emerged, but this was in no way standardized. The art of fortification was essentially practical, no two sites were the same, and the engineer had, above all, to adapt his design to suit local conditions. The great merit of the polygonal bastioned trace was its flexibility and ease of construction, and it was this above all which led to its adoption

---

7 See A. de Zastrow, *Histoire de la fortification permanente*, trans. Neuens (Liège, 1846); and [F. Engels], 'Fortification' in *The New American Cyclopaedia*, ed. A. Dana and G. Ripley, 16 volumes (New York, 1858-63).

8 Engels; Hale, 'The early development of the bastion', p. 467.

as an international style.[9] In the sixteenth century Italian engineers were to be found all over Europe, including Malta, disseminating the new methods of fortification but adapting them to local conditions. So great was the variety of such local conditions that the task of tracing precise lines of influence and interaction between generalized theories of fortification, on the one hand, and empirical solutions by individual engineers, on the other, is scarcely practicable, although some broad lines of development (and the reasons for them) can be pursued with comparative accuracy.

In fact, the division of engineers into different schools, the attempts to trace the influence of one on another, and the ascribing of credit for a specific innovation have often been based very largely on written works. Naturally posterity tends to know best those engineers who were authors of published works, and remains ignorant of the others. Many practising engineers were also writers of books which enjoyed wide popularity, but did this mean that their ideas were widely accepted or put into practice? Although the treatises by Marchi, Maggi and Castriotto were translated and read outside Italy, these men were never acknowledged as leaders in the art of fortification.[10] The fortifications designed by Floriani in Malta in 1635 bear little relation to anything found in his *Difesa et ofesa delle piazze* published only five years earlier in Macerata. The numerous Italian works written after 1550 were concerned with the controversies then raging over secondary problems associated with bastioned fortifications: the ideal distances between bastions, the geometric shape best suited to fortification, the relative advantages and disadvantages of mountainous sites, and the comparative merits of earth-built and masonry fortifications.[11] When faced with a situation in the field such theoretical considerations were, as often as not, irrelevant. Treatises were not in fact written as practical hand-books for engineers, but to enhance the reputation of their authors who

---

9 J.R. Hale, 'Armies, navies and the art of war' in *New Cambridge Modern History*, 'The Counter Reformation and the price revolution 1559-1610', ed. R.B. Wernham, III (Cambridge, 1968), p. 197.

10 F. Marchi, *Dell'architettura militare* (Brescia, 1599) [written about 1540]; G. Maggi and G. Castriotto, *Della fortificatione delle città* (Venice, 1564).

11 H. de la Croix, 'The literature on fortification in Renaissance Italy' in *Technology and Culture*, IV (1963), 38.

might one day find themselves in need of a patron or employer, and to explain the intricacies of the new system to the gentry of Europe whose education was incomplete without a smattering of military knowledge. In the sixteenth century one can see emerging the idea that war called for an acquaintance with mathematics;[12] many engineers such as Stevin, Pagan and François Blondel wrote treatises on mathematics, and others, who were primarily mathematicians, like Galileo, Marolois and Bélidor, concerned themselves with the art of fortification. However, as contemporary practice tended to lag well behind current scientific theories of the art of war,[13] too much emphasis should not be placed on the evidence of written works, uncorroborated by actual concrete fortresses.

It was the Italian engineers who, having effected a system of defence against artillery fire, were its leading exponents in the sixteenth century. They were employed throughout Europe and were responsible for fortifications at Vienna, Raab, Gratz, Comorn, Antwerp, Ghent, Utrecht, Spandau, Goletta and elsewhere and were especially active in France.[14] The Order followed the current practice and for a hundred and fifty years Italians such as Ferramolino, Bartolomeo Genga, Lanci, Laparelli, Serbelloni, Campi, Rinaldini, Floriani, Buonamici, Firenzuola, Giovanni de' Medici and Antonio Maurizio Valperga dominated the development of fortifications in Malta. The knights ensured that their fortifications kept abreast with modern developments abroad by engaging outside experts whenever a new project was to be undertaken. Thus the Catholic courts of Europe were regularly petitioned to lend their engineers to the Order for a few months. And generally the princes obliged, only rarely leaving the knights to rely upon the talent for original design of their little-esteemed resident engineers.

But the Italians, having provided the basic concept of the bastioned trace, failed to exploit their pre-eminence in the seventeenth century, and the lead in development was taken over by northern engineers. Already in the previous century the German

---

12 Hale, 'Armies, navies and the art of war', p. 178; and J.R. Hale, 'The argument of some military title pages of the Renaissance', *The Newberry Library Bulletin*, VI (1964), 91.

13 See A.R. Hall, *Ballistics in the Seventeenth Century* (Cambridge, 1952).

14 I. Zastrow, 42; P. Lavedan, *Histoire de l'urbanisme* (Paris, 1941), pp. 76-86; Duffy, *Siege Warfare, passim.*

Daniel Speckle had criticized certain aspects of the Italian method.[15] Although the Italians protected their curtains by small ravelins Speckle believed that these should be as large as circumstances might permit. However, protecting the curtains in this way laid the bastions open to attack and Speckle proposed various adjustments to enlarge and realign bastions to provide better mutual covering fire.[16] The Dutch engineer Simon Stevin also placed great emphasis on outworks such as fausse-brayes, ravelins, horn and crownworks, the addition of which made fortresses more aggressive. Instead of planning outwards from the place to be protected, as was the Italian method, the northerners planned inwards from a wide perimeter of outer defences, which were themselves appropriate to the surrounding terrain. All parts of the fortifications were to be mutually supporting with no length of wall or ditch not raked by the fire of an adjacent work. The systems of both Speckle and Stevin, however, required such meticulous surveying, and careful and costly contouring of the surrounding terrain that the simpler Italian system remained in common use.[17] The successful practical combination of the bastioned main enceinte and aggressive outworks was achieved by French engineers, above all by Vauban.

By the end of the seventeenth century the French had established a veritable corps of engineers led by Sébastien le Prestre de Vauban, and it was to France that the knights looked for their supply of engineers in the eighteenth century. The employment of men such as Colongues, Tigné, Mondion, Maigret, Folard, Bourlamaque and Pontleroy marked not only the eclipse of the Italians as the leading engineers of Europe, but also the transfer of the Order from the Imperial into the French sphere of influence.

Vauban himself was a practical engineer who constructed thirty-three new fortresses and remodelled about another three hundred, all of which, because he believed in adapting to local conditions, show considerable variation. Although he never published a treatise on the art of fortification, later writers have been

---

15 In *Architecture von Festungen* (Strasbourg, 1589).

16 In fact Zastrow (I, 57) claims that many of the innovations ascribed to later engineers such as Pagan, Vauban and Cormontaigne can be traced back to the writings of Speckle, but he may have been pleading a national cause.

17 Hale, 'Armies, navies and the art of war', p. 196.

tempted to deduce from the many concrete examples of his work, a set of theoretical rules providing the basis of his general approach. It has, accordingly, become customary to divide his work into three categories, or systems.[18] The first, which was employed for the majority of fortified places, followed closely the design advocated by an earlier French military architect, Pagan, although Vauban made more use of detached exterior works; wherever possible the outline was a regular polygon whose bastions were the key to the defensive system; in front of the curtains part of the fausse-braye (a Dutch innovation) was retained as a tenaille, and beyond the tenaille was a ravelin. After 1680 Vauban introduced two other methods which were intended to allow a more prolonged defence once the bastion had been breached.

The second system, examples of which are found at Belfort and Besançon, retained the polygonal structure, but the curtains were lengthened and the bastions replaced by bastioned towers protected by detached bastions in the ditch. The third method, of which the only example is at Neuf Brisach, was a development of the second. The shape of the curtain was modified to allow a greater use of cannon in defence, and the towers, detached bastions and ravelins increased in size. The bastioned towers and detached bastions permitted considerable flexibility in adapting to terrain, a function previously performed by horn and crownworks. However, the ideas of the eighteenth century were dominated by the disciples of Vauban, led by Cormontaigne, and later by the school of engineers founded about 1750 at Mézières, who chose to ignore these later systems in favour of the first. Vauban's first system, as modified by Cormontaigne, who enlarged the bastions, ravelins and the areas covered by crossfire, and strengthened the covert-way may be considered as the perfection of the bastioned trace. The second system was revived in the late eighteenth century by Montalembert, a Frenchman who rejected bastioned fortifications. His ideas were accepted by the Germans earlier than by the French, who were still bound by the Mézières tradition. In Germany, on the other hand, a tradition favouring a

---

18 On Vauban see P. Lazard, *Vauban* (Paris, 1934); and R.T. Blomfield, *Sébastien le Prestre de Vauban, 1633-1707* (London, 1938) and Duffy, *The Fortress in the Age of Vauban*, pp. 71-97.

tenaille as opposed to bastioned system stretched back to Georg Rimpler in the seventeenth century.[19] Malta in the eighteenth century followed the Mézières lead and no attempt was made to supersede the bastioned fortresses then in existence. Although at the very end of the century a round casemated fort, Tigné, was constructed, the last major fortress to be erected, Chambray in the 1750s, was built to a conventional bastioned design.

Although innovations were made in the offensive weapons directed against bastioned fortification no real break-through took place which demanded a drastic reappraisal of the methods of defence; iron was introduced as a gun metal in the mid-sixteenth century, the scale of cannon increased in the seventeenth, and in the eighteenth methods of boring improved.[20] But any application of theoretical ballistics was slow. Mortars continued to be used to crush and harass inhabitants and the standard method of breaching a wall was by the heaviest possible cannon at point-blank range.[21] Vauban is said to have been the first general to make effective use of ricochet at the siege of Philipsburg in 1688.[22] There is no reason to believe that the practical demands of warfare in any way stimulated the quest for scientific knowledge, nor did scientific advances lead to innovations in the art of fortification. Indeed, in the seventeenth century the practical man was a good fifty years behind the most advanced scientific knowledge.[23] The developments in fortifications and in military matters in general did, however, have an important impact on governments and society.[24] The new style in fortification in the sixteenth century was recognized not only as a more efficient defence against artillery, it also became highly fashionable. Rulers had a double incentive to remodel their fortresses: military necessity and the prestige demands of fashion. The military treatises of the Renaissance which inextricably linked the new defences with theories of town

---

19 Engels.

20 Hall, p. 8.

21 Hall, p. 53, quoting on the second point [-] De la Fontaine, *Les fortifications royales ou architecture militaire par une nouvelle practique* (Paris, 1666).

22 Blomfield, p. 110.

23 Hall, p. 51.

24 See G.N. Clark, *War and Society in the Seventeenth Century* (Cambridge, 1958); M. Roberts, 'The military revolution, 1560-1660', revised and reprinted in *Essays in Swedish History* (London, 1967), pp. 195-225; J. Hook, 'Fortifications and the end of the Sienese state', *History*, LXII (1977), 372-87.

planning which themselves reflected the current ideas of harmony and rational proportion, undoubtedly promoted the concept of the ideal city. Rulers were persuaded, either by military considerations or by the dictates of civic or national pride, to undertake extensive rebuilding programmes whose expense was immense. Apart from the actual cost of building material and labour, there were the associated expenses of clearing the ground, the payment of compensation to the owners of the land required, and, once the fortress was completed, the provision of guns and ammunition and the maintenance of a garrison. Not only could an ambitious building programme put a strain on the finances and administrative system of the government, it could also cause disruption and upheaval in the lives of its citizens, who were often required to shoulder heavy burdens of taxation, perform labour services, and to suffer eviction from their land and homes.

In Malta, perhaps even more than elsewhere in Europe, the compulsion to fortify persisted throughout the sixteenth, seventeenth and eighteenth centuries; the consequences of which both for the Order and for the Maltese will be considered in later chapters.[25] Although in the mainstream of European development, Malta as a small independent state drawing most of its wealth from beyond its own boundaries, is necessarily in many ways atypical, but the very scale of its involvement in relation to its size may only exaggerate and emphasise tendencies less clearly discernible in larger and more complex states. Even the fortifications themselves are in many ways unique, but in this Malta is no exception. The very essence of the bastioned system was its adaptability and flexibility, and all its greatest practitioners were renowned for attention to local conditions and their ability to adapt the basic principles to local terrain and building materials.

---

[25] See especially Part III, chapters 9, 10 and 11.

Part II

The Building of the Fortifications

Chapter 3

The Development of the Maltese Fortifications

The Knights of St. John assumed possession of the Maltese islands just at the time when the bastioned system of fortification was becoming widely accepted in Europe. As was so often the case elsewhere, their resources would not at first stretch beyond the modification of the existing defences. The near-disastrous siege by the Turks in 1565 did, however, prove fortunate in at least one respect: the terrible destruction wrought by the besiegers furnished an opportunity to rebuild in the modern fashion while avoiding the difficult and possibly controversial decision to demolish any well-built but obsolete fortifications.

After their arrival in Malta the knights continued their incessant struggle against the infidel. At first while Malta was regarded as only a temporary refuge, the navy continued to campaign in the eastern Mediterranean, hoping eventually to recapture Rhodes. Although some conquests were made in the Morea in the 1530s these were of no lasting significance to the knights whose attention was soon diverted nearer home. The sixteenth century saw the contest between the Spanish and the Ottoman Empires for control of the Mediterranean and North Africa and on its acceptance of Malta and its dependencies, the Order of St. John became directly involved in the struggle. Contingents of knights and their soldiers joined the armies of Spain in the various campaigns against Tunis, Goletta, Mahdiya, Algiers, Djerba and, after 1551, Tripoli, while the galleys assisted in the essential task of transporting men and war materials. By 1574 Spain had failed in her attempts to establish herself in Tripoli, Tunis and Algiers and thereafter focused her interests on

Morocco. Meanwhile as befitted its international composition, the Order assisted other Christian powers, notably the Venetian Republic, France and the Papacy. The ships of the knights also undertook forays on their own account, without allies. During the summer months the fleet usually undertook two or three cruises in search of Turkish and Barbary shipping hoping to capture rich prizes. In addition to the navy's activities Malta was a haven for freelance corsairs and was thus rightly regarded by the Moslems as a centre of Christian piracy.[1]

It was hardly to be expected that the aggressive activities of the knights would fail to provoke a hostile response from the Moslem powers, and the knights recognized the possession of a secure base as essential to their very survival. They therefore weighed up the defensive possibilities of Malta before ever they accepted it from Charles V. A commission sent to inspect Malta, Gozo and Tripoli was instructed to examine the principal city, the fortress and all the buildings. Its members were to visit the peninsula known as Sciberras and to assess its potential as a site for a fortress to serve as the headquarters, or convent, of the Order.[2] The commissioners' report was hardly encouraging:[3] the principal city, Notabile, situated on high ground in the middle of the island, was semi-deserted with half its houses uninhabited. Quite apart from its small size (its circumference was only 1303 paces), it was hardly appropriate as the headquarters of a seafaring Order. The commission could, however, report that on the east coast of Malta there were two spacious harbours where a whole fleet could anchor. The more southerly, or Grand Harbour, was inadequately protected by a small, half-ruined castle (St. Angelo) which could easily be stormed via the suburb of sailors' houses (the Birgu)[4] which had grown up on its landward side. Grand Harbour would provide an anchorage

---

1 For a general account of the knights' military activities see: A. Hoppen, 'The Knights Hospitallers and the defence of Malta', *Annales de l'Ordre Souverain Militaire de Malte*, XXXV (1977), 30-7 and for details of the activities of the corsairs operating from Malta see: P. Cassar, 'The Maltese corsairs and the Order of St. John of Jerusalem', *Catholic Historical Review*, XLVI (1960), 137-56; and P. Earle, *Corsairs of Malta and Barbary* (London, 1970).

2 AOM, 411, f. 202v. (28 June 1524).

3 Bosio, III, 29-31. The names of several of the towns and villages were changed during the knights' rule. After the building of Valletta, Notabile was usually referred to as Città Vecchia; however, throughout the period, and up to the present day, the name used by the Maltese was Mdina.

4 After the siege it was renamed Vittoriosa but the old name also remained in use.

safe from the sea and wind but not shelter from artillery bombardment. Sciberras, the tongue of land which divided this harbour from the second large harbour, the Marsamxett, would indeed, as had been conjectured from its appearance on a map, be a site eminently suited to the establishment of a fortress which would guard the entrances to both ports, but such an undertaking would require time and money. The island of Gozo possessed no harbour worthy of the name; the Castello, built to shelter the inhabitants from corsair raiders and situated on a hill, in the centre of the island, was weakly fortified. But if they were to take possession of Malta the knights would also have to occupy this nearby northern island lest it fall under enemy domination. The fortress of Tripoli might, likewise, prove a liability in defence. It was two hundred miles from Malta, surrounded by the lands of the corsair states: both the harbour and the castle were dominated by a neighbouring hill; the defences were weak and the sandy, water-logged foundations precluded any attempt at lasting improvement. Despite the near-derelict state of the defences, the Order decided, five years later, when no more congenial home had been offered to them, to accept the islands and the fortress of Tripoli. The sorry condition of the fortifications in 1530 can in part be attributed to the neglect suffered by the islands while subject to Aragonese rule. Overall responsibility rested with the Sicilian viceroy and council who delegated many of their powers and duties to the local Universitàs. From time to time the Sicilian council might issue a decree concerning the fortifications in Malta, but whether or not it was implemented was another matter. For instance, although in 1488 the viceroy had ordered a strong, well-fortified tower to be built on the tip of Sciberras, there is no evidence to suggest that it was ever constructed, and it was certainly not mentioned by the commission of knights which inspected the island in 1524.[5] The records of the Universitàs of Notabile and Gozo do, however, reveal their involvement in the defence of the islands. Although in the fifteenth century the militia was referred to as 'the walls of the island',[6] the

5 G. F. Abela, *Della descrizione di Malta* (Malta, 1647), Lib. IV, Not. I, Para. XVII, who cites as his authorities J. de Zurita, *Añales de la Corona de Aragón* (Çaragoça, 1580) IV, 358 and J, de Mariana, *Historia de España* (Madrid, 1608) II, 484.

6 S. Giambruno and L. Genuardi, *Capitoli inediti delle città demaniali di Sicilia approvati sino al 1458* (Palermo, 1918), I, 377 (1416); Royal Malta Library, Valletta, Università manuscripts (hereafter referred to as RML Univ.), 3, document 9 (1455).

Universitàs did also bear responsibility for building and maintaining stone and mortar walls. Each had among its officers a *marammero* or engineer who attended to the fortifications and a conservator of artillery and munitions.[7] The proclamations of the Università of Notabile reveal that the repair of the city walls was a major preoccupation in the fifteenth century,[8] and that it was on the islands themselves, and not the Sicilian royal treasury, that the burden of maintenance fell. The finance came from local taxation, either direct or indirect, and from the proceeds of judicial fines,[9] while the military obligations of the islanders included that of labour service in the fortifications.[10] To defend the coasts the Universitàs relied on a network of lookout posts backed up by a mounted militia, the *dejma*.[11] While they appreciated the value of lookout towers, the Universitàs did not embark on any systematic scheme of construction and the chain of militia posts was not linked to a cordon of coastal towers.[12]

The picture which emerges of fifteenth-century Malta is generally depressing.[13] The islands suffered from increasingly frequent corsair raids which disrupted both trade and agriculture. The population appears to have declined; many hamlets were abandoned and the area of land under cultivation diminished. The records of the Università reflect the demoralization of the inhabitants; they speak of Malta as 'a rock in the middle of the sea far from help and comfort'[14] and convey an impression of a poverty-stricken and insecure island. Whether simply because of lack of funds causing the collapse of the defensive organization, or because of a more intangible deficiency such as loss of morale, by the beginning of the sixteenth century the fortifications were no longer properly maintained, many of the houses in Notabile had been deserted and in 1524 the commission of knights could find only decaying and obsolete defences.

---

7 A. Mifsud, 'La milizia e le torri antiche di Malta', *Archivum Melitense*, IV (1920), 58; E.R. Leopardi, 'The island of Gozo, 1432-53', Part I, *Melita Historica*, III (1962), 78.

8 E.R. Leopardi, '"Bandi" of the XV century', *Melita Historica*, II (1957-9), 122-35, 186-195, 248-62. These 'bandi', or proclamations, are to be found in RML Univ. 11. See also Luttrell, pp. 56-9.

9 Leopardi, "Bandi", p. 254 and, on fines, pp. 126, 187, 189, 192 and 258.

10 Leopardi, '"Bandi"', pp. 189, 254, 259 and 'The island of Gozo, 1432-53', part II, *Melita Historica*, IV (1964), 70.

11 Mifsud, 'La milizia', pp. 55-65.

12 Mifsud, 'La milizia', pp. 68-70.

13 Blouet, pp. 46-8.

14 Quoted by Blouet, p. 47.

The Order fully appreciated the lamentable state of the fortifications when it accepted the islands and Tripoli and realized that these would have to be repaired and improved if the Order was to have a secure base.[15] But here the knights faced something of a dilemma: although they accepted the islands they were not resigned to the loss of Rhodes, and until well into the second half of the century there was talk of abandoning Malta and Gozo in favour of a more congenial, more fertile and less impoverished home. Only with the building of Valletta in the years after 1566 did the knights finally commit themselves to Malta as a permanent base. Consequently, in the intervening years, between 1530 and 1565, whenever the question of fortification was discussed the Order had to face a problem incapable of resolution until it had unequivocally decided on Malta as its headquarters: whether or not to invest money in the defences of what might be only a temporary base. Because the fortifications were dilapidated when they arrived, the knights had no option but to undertake repair work, and, because the existing works were old-fashioned at a time when developments in artillery were demanding defences resistant to cannon-fire, improvements were also soon deemed necessary.

Before the Order had actually taken up residence in Malta, an advance party was sent out in the summer of 1530 which included a large number of masons, carpenters and blacksmiths, who took with them a stock of mortar so that work could commence immediately on the restoration of the fortifications of Malta, Gozo and Tripoli.[16] On his arrival in the island in October of the same year, the Grand Master de l'Isle Adam took up residence in St. Angelo, considering the inland city of Notabile an inappropriate capital for a seafaring Order. This castle together with its suburb Birgu became the headquarters of the Order. St. Angelo was in origin an Arab fortress probably founded in the ninth century; it stood on a knoll of rock at the tip of a peninsula projecting into the Grand Harbour from the south-east. Although at first glance its position might have much to commend it, surrounded on three sides by water, guarding the entrance to the harbour, and providing more immediate cover for the ships which could shelter in

---

15 AOM, 410, f. 296 (1523); AOM 414, f. 262v. (1529).
16 Bosio, III, 85.

the creeks under its walls, the recent advances in artillery had rendered it insecure (see figure 2). It, and the peninsula on which Birgu stood, were surrounded on all sides by high ground from which they could be dominated and bombarded by enemy cannon. The site was such that even had all the modern techniques of fortification been employed it would not have been possible to erect walls which would effectively protect St. Angelo and Birgu. The knights were fully aware of the limitations of the site, yet decided that the alternative (already explored by the 1524 commission) of building a completely new city on the high ground of Sciberras peninsula lying to the north of St. Angelo was not a practical proposition in the then uncertain state of their fortunes. Instead, De l'Isle Adam, immediately upon his arrival in October 1530, ordered that Birgu should be enclosed by a wall.[17] Two years later it was decided that as far as possible the Order should make the most of the existing fortifications.[18] A Florentine engineer, Piccino, was employed to draw up designs for improvements and repairs to St. Angelo, Notabile and Tripoli.[19] He was also instructed to prepare plans for a tower to be constructed on the small island of Comino, and a bastion on Sciberras point.[20] It is possible that work on the latter project commenced in December 1533 but ceased shortly afterwards and no identifiable work remains which can with confidence be ascribed to this engineer.[21]

Less mystery surrounds the foreign engineer on whom the Order next called. He was Antonio Ferramolino, a Bergamese and

17 Bosio, III, 89.

18 The urgent necessity of improving the fortifications was stressed at the chapter general of 1533 (AOM, 286, f. 59).

19 Bosio, III, 110 and 124. This engineer is something of a mystery. The family name of the Florentine engineer Antonio da Sangallo the Younger was Picconi, which Bosio might have mistaken as Piccino, but there is no evidence to confirm that Sangallo was ever in the Order's employ. M. d'Ayala ('Degl' ingegneri militari italiani dal secolo XIII al XVIII' in *Archivio storico italiano*, IX (1869), 71-110) lists a Bernardo Puccini as working in Siena, Lucignano, Sartenna and Cetona in 1554. Neither Bosio nor the archival records (AOM, 415, f. 246) mention a Christian name.

20 Bosio, III, 128.

21 J. Q. Hughes, 'The defence of Malta', *Quaderno dell'Istituto Dipartimentale di Architettura ed Urbanistica*, Università di Catania, VIII (1976), 4-5, is less tentative in ascribing works to Piccino. Hughes's article has been reprinted in *Fort* [published by the Fortress Study Group and available from the School of Architecture, University of Liverpool], IV (1977), 13-52.

imperial engineer in Sicily.[22] Apart from undertaking various works in Sicily itself, he accompanied expeditions to North Africa in 1540 and 1550 when he met his death, advised on the defences of Ragusa in 1538 and twice visited Malta, in 1535 and 1541. On the first occasion he made recommendations regarding Birgu and St. Angelo which it is claimed were diligently carried out.[23] In 1541 Ferramolino once again advised on the fortifications of Birgu and St. Angelo.[24] As an experienced engineer, it is hardly surprising that he criticized the patently inappropriate site of these works. St. Angelo was cramped and restricted with no possibility of its being extended so as to become a haven for all who would wish to retire to its safety in time of siege; both were so overlooked that no amount of alteration or augmentation would make them secure against a strong army; in fact any money spent on such a project would be wasted. He recommended that once the Order had determined to remain in Malta, the solution was to build a fortress on the elevated site of Sciberras. But Grand Master Homedes was not prepared to undertake a scheme which was something of a gamble: undoubtedly, apart from the tactical and emotional question of committing the Order to Malta, he also had to consider the thorny problem of finance which was then in undeniably short supply, and the military danger if the Turks were to descend on the half-completed fort, capture it, and use it as an entrenchment from which to bombard Birgu and St. Angelo. In place of his grand scheme, Ferramolino was instructed to improve St. Angelo as best he could. Accordingly he designed a high cavalier to be built overlooking Birgu which was to be high enough to bombard the entrance to the harbour. He also deepened the ditch between the castle and its suburb so that it could hold a depth of water sufficient for the galleys to shelter there.[25] Ferramolino was never given his head in Malta, and the modifications for which he was responsible were mere tinkerings and,

22 See A. Ferramolino, *Le Fortificazioni di Palermo nel secolo XVI*, ed. V. di Giovanni (Società Siciliana per la Storia Patria: Documenti per servire alla storia di Sicilia, serie 4, Vol. IV; Palermo, 1896); C. Promis, 'Biografie dei ingegneri militari italiani dal secolo XIV alla metà del XVIII', *Miscellanea di storia italiana*, XIV (Turin, 1874), 369; F.W. Carter, *Dubrovnik (Ragusa): a Classic City State* (London, 1972), p. 519.

23 Claim made by Bosio (III, 140); there is no corroborative evidence concerning this visit or the later one.

24 Bosio, III, 198.

25 Bosio, III, 198-9, 213-14.

through no fault of his, did nothing to alleviate the fundamental weakness of the knights' position.

Ferramolino's successor as engineer in Sicily, Pietro Prato, who also followed in his footsteps by acting as adviser to the knights, was more fortunate in being less restricted in the work which he undertook in Malta.[26] The events of 1551 had alerted the Order to the dangers of a large-scale Turkish attack and had emphasized the inadequacy of its defences. In July a Turkish fleet had entered Marsamxett and had landed a force of men;[27] they were harried by a detachment of the Order's cavalry but their decision, after reconnoitring both the harbour forts and Notabile and ravaging the surrounding country, to withdraw rather than to lay siege to any of the forts, was based as much on the smallness of their force as on the strength of the defences. The Turks re-embarked and sailed off to descend on the even more ineffectual fortifications of Gozo. Within a few days the Castello capitulated and an estimated 5,000 of the inhabitants were carried off to slavery. From Gozo the Turks made for Tripoli; the fortress was inadequately supplied, no help was forthcoming from Malta, and in a short time it surrendered. With hindsight it is possible to regard the loss of Tripoli as a blessing in disguise: the fort was two hundred miles from the convent in Malta, situated in hostile territory and dependent on sea-borne supplies, and as such a drain on the Order's resources without in any way augmenting its security. The knights, however, did not see Tripoli in this totally unfavourable light; there had been suggestions in 1548 that Malta should be evacuated except for a garrison in St. Angelo, and the convent transferred to Tripoli.[28] Since the Turks' enmity was directed against the Order rather than Malta, it was unlikely they would attack the islands; if they did, Charles V would be bound to come to their aid as they were too close to his own possessions for him to allow them to be overrun with impunity; to fortify Tripoli so that it was impregnable would cost no more than the construction of the new city proposed by Ferramolino, and without this city it was impossible for the Order to survive in

---

26 This engineer's name is also found in a Spanish form, Prado. He wrote an unpublished account of the fortifications of Palermo entitled 'Ordinamenti per continuare le fortificazioni della città', cited in Ferramolino, p. 130.

27 Bosio, III, 296.

28 Bosio, III, 255-6; AOM 287, ff. 48 *et seq*.

Malta. The opposition of Grand Master Homedes and other senior knights was, however, sufficient to quash this proposal. But the loss of Tripoli was a blow both to the Order's prestige and to its morale, and left no doubt as to the serious nature of the Turkish threat; indeed, in September 1551 Pope Julius III went so far as to issue a brief commanding the grand master to withdraw to Syracuse or Messina leaving only a garrison in Malta which could undoubtedly expect a siege following the fall of Tripoli.[29]

The knights reacted to the danger in a fashion which was to form a recurring pattern over the years: they petitioned for the loan of an eminent engineer from abroad. On this occasion they approached the Sicilian viceroy De Vega, who released Pietro Prato.[30] In January 1552 the engineer and a commission of three knights, Georg Bombast, Louis de Lastic and Leone Strozzi, made a review of the fortifications.[31] In their final recommendations the view put forward by Strozzi prevailed: to build the proposed new city would be a lengthy undertaking, and was besides beyond the resources of the Order. As an alternative it was decided to build two forts, the oft-projected fort at the point of Sciberras to deny the enemy entry to the Marsamxett, and a fort on the Isola peninsula to the south-west of Birgu, now occupied by Senglea but at that time known either as mount St. Julian or St. Michael. This latter fort, it was hoped, would protect Birgu from attack on that flank, and in addition Birgu itself was to be strengthened. A sense of urgency was engendered by the fear that the Turkish fleet would reappear, this time to lay siege to Malta, as soon as the sailing season reopened. Work began almost immediately on 14 January;[32] workers were conscripted from the countryside, imported from Sicily, and even the galley crews were pressed into building service.[33] The grand master, stipulated that everything was to be in a defendable state by the time that the Turks might be expected. Already by March 1552, when its first captain was

---

29 S. Pauli, *Codice diplomatico del Sacro Militare Ordine Gerosolmitano, oggi di Malta*, 2 vols. (Lucca, 1733-7), II, 208.

30 AOM 422, f. 224v; Bosio, III, 370 and 323.

31 Bosio, III, 325; AOM 88, f. 106v. (8 January 1552). No copies survive in Malta of reports by Prato although some of his reports are found in the Archivo General de Simancas. (These were brought to my attention by Roger Vella Bonavita.) Unfortunately they add little to our knowledge of the fortifications.

32 Bosio, III, 323; AOM 88, f. 106v.

33 AOM 88, f. 107; Bosio, III, 323-4; AOM 88, f. 121; AOM 423, ff. 208 and 216v.

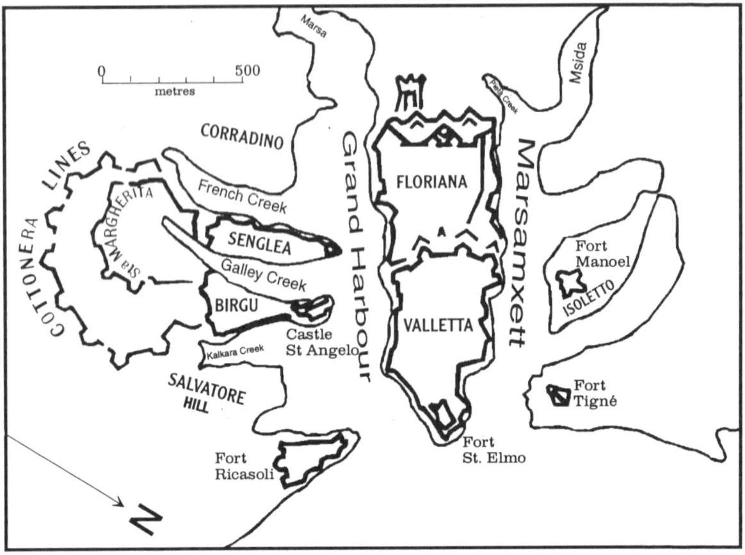

Fig. 2. The Harbour area.

appointed, the works on Sciberras, which were to be named after the chapel on the site dedicated to St. Elmo, were beginning to take on the appearance of a fort.[34] At this stage, when the harbour defences were well under way, Prato was dispatched inland to repair the Notabile fortifications.[35]

The haste with which fort St. Elmo was built probably accounts for the fundamental weaknesses in design, the remedying of which was to exercise the ingenuity of several engineers in the years to come. Because the grand master wanted the fort completed by June 1552 Prato restricted his design to a small star-shaped work with four very acute-angled bastions which was capable of being incorporated as a bastion in the enceinte of any city which might eventually be built on the site. The stellar form was very popular at this time for small-scale works, especially with the Spaniards, and St. Elmo was not intended to resist a full-scale siege, merely to defend the harbour entrances.

---

34 AOM 88, f. 112v.; Bosio, III, 325.

35 Bosio, III, 325.

Plate 1. St. Elmo and Valletta

Nonetheless Prato's fort has come in for much criticism on account of its size, its small bastions and its site which could be dominated from the higher ridge of Sciberras. However, once Prato had received his brief from the grand master regarding building time, it is difficult to see what alternative was open to him. He sited the fort on a raised knoll of rock at the tip of Sciberras which was indeed overlooked by higher ground, but to encompass these heights would have required a work outside the bounds of Prato's instructions. As it was, the fort was well situated to perform its primary task of guarding the entrances to the Grand Harbour and Marsamxett. It was not designed as a stronghold to withstand a prolonged siege; it had no magazines or storehouses, it depended on supplies ferried across Grand Harbour, and there was no keep to which the defenders could withdraw.[36]

[36] These deficiencies are pointed out by F. Balbi in his *La Vedadera relación de todo lo que este año de MDLXV ha sucedido en la isla de Malta* (Alcalá de Henares, 1567) translated by H. Balbi as *The Siege of Malta* (Copenhagen, 1961) – see p. 81. Balbi was present at the siege in 1565 as a soldier.

On two counts at least, however, criticism would appear to be justified. Prato included no outworks in his design. Within a few years, hardly time for the fort to become outdated through the normal process of design development, steps were taken to remedy this omission by building a high cavalier towards the sea.[37] Later, in the spring of 1565, another outwork – a ravelin – was hastily constructed outside the bastion of St. Elmo facing Sta. Maria point (later called Dragut point) on the northern shore of the entrance to the Marsamxett.[38] Both the cavalier and ravelin were poorly constructed,[39] a criticism which could, however, be levelled at the rest of the fort also, the walls of which were thin and made of poor material. The thinness of the walls, and the lack of traverses, may be accounted for by the restricted site. However, the normal practice was for the engineer to supervise the preparation of building materials, and the initial stages of construction, so Prato would seem to bear some of the responsibility for the poor quality of stone and lime used in the original fort. Despite the criticisms made of St. Elmo, the fort did withstand a determined Turkish onslaught for almost a month. Even allowing for tactical errors by the besiegers and the heroism of the besieged, the small fort must have afforded the defenders a fair amount of protection and its eventual structural collapse was by no means instantaneous.[40]

The construction of St. Elmo was but one of the measures taken in 1552, to improve the island's defences. The fortifications of Birgu itself were strengthened in 1552 and again in 1553, 1555, 1560, when the ditches were deepened and several of the bastions enlarged, and in 1563.[41] Attention was also paid to the Isola peninsula. Fort St. Michael, a high square-shaped tower, was

---

37 Bosio, III, 353. There is a contemporary copy of a plan of St. Elmo by Prato (Archivo General de Simancas [GA leg. 16] Mapas, Planos y Dibujos, XIX-107) which shows a regular star fort without either this seaward spur cavalier or the small cavalier on the landward front depicted in Laparelli's plan made in 1566 (Codex Laparelli – in the possession of Countess Laparelli Pitti in Florence, hereafter referred to as Cod. Lap. – ff. 79v.-80). The building of the latter cavalier seems to have caused the distortion of the regular star shape on the land front.

38 Bosio, III, 499.

39 Balbi, p. 27; Cod. Lap. f. 78v.

40 For a blow-by-blow account of the siege in English see E. Bradford, *The Great Siege: Malta 1565* (London, 1961).

41 Bosio, III, 343, 362, 395, 460.

built at the neck of the peninsula as part of the 1552 improvements,[42] and under the Grand Master de la Sengle it was decided to enclose by walls and bastions the shore not under the guns of St. Angelo.[43] In order to relieve pressure in Birgu which was seriously overcrowded following the influx of the knights and their various retainers, the grand master founded a new town on Isola, named Senglea in his honour. Senglea, like Birgu and St. Elmo, profited from periodic bursts of building activity in the years leading up to the siege, culminating in an effort in the early months of 1565 to complete the walls enclosing the town on the flank overlooked by Corradino Hill.[44]

The Order did all it could to strengthen its position in the island while appreciating that such improvements were not attacking the fundamental weakness of the existing fortifications. Nor was it allowed to forget its basically untenable position. The engineers called in to advise on fortification continued to extol the merits of Sciberras as the site of a modern fortified city. The knights themselves continued to regard the construction of this city as their long-term aim, if they were to remain in Malta.

With the election of La Valette as grand master the project took on a fresh impetus. A decision to build a new city on Sciberras was made by the council in June 1558, thereby implying that the Order had at last committed itself to residence in Malta, although later events were once again to put the issue in dispute.[45] The council had before it a design drawn up by Bartolomeo Genga, who had been released by the Duke of Urbino to serve the knights.[46] Work on the scheme, however, was not to begin until repairs to the existing fortifications, being carried out

---

42 Bosio, III, 323.

43 Bosio, III, 353; the work was undertaken by the engineer Niccolò Bellavanti, about whom I can find no more information.

44 Bosio, III, 494, 499; these walls were to link St. Michael and the bastion which had been built by the Order's resident engineer Evangelista Menga, a native of Brindisi.

45 AOM 90, f. 13v.

46 Bosio, III, 395; the report made by Genga does not survive although there is a summary by Bosio (III, 455). He proposed enclosing an area larger than present-day Valletta with a land front on the site now occupied by the Floriana lines. Genga had been trained by his father Girolamo. Bartolomeo was a well-known engineer of the time who had served the pope and the duke of Florence. For an account of his career see Promis, *Miscellanea*, XIV, 249 and G. Vasari, *Lives of the Painters, Sculptors and Architects*, ed. W. Gaunt, 4 vols. (London, 1927), III, 266-8. Hughes ('Defence of Malta', pp. 9-10) suggests that the engraving produced about 1563 by Nicolo Beatrizet, entitled 'Il porto dell'isola di Malta – Melita nunc Malta', may be based on Genga's scheme.

because a Turkish attack appeared imminent, were completed. In fact, the project never got off the ground. Genga died in Malta in the summer of 1558, but this was probably not the major reason for the scheme's postponement. Although the treasury was reported as having ample funds,[47] on the same day as Genga's proposals were approved the council ordered a tax on the Order's European property, which was confirmed and extended by a chapter general held in November.[48] The question of financing the work obviously loomed large in the knights' thoughts[49] and this, combined with an unwillingness to commence building while rumours of an impending attack continued, may account for the proposals not being implemented.

They were not, however, forgotten, and in 1560, the treasury again allegedly being full and the island thronging with gallant knights, the grand master's thoughts turned once more to the new city on Sciberras.[50] He was, however, unable to secure the services of an eminent engineer[51] and had to be content with improvements to the existing fortifications. In default of an engineer, La Valette addressed himself to the problem of finance which had proved a stumbling block during earlier attempts to found a new city.[52] However, when another engineer was employed in 1562, the Order still felt unable to implement his recommendations. Baldessare Lanci, who arrived in Malta on 18 March 1562, had been lent to the Order by Cosimo, Duke of Florence.[53] After inspecting all the forts, Lanci concurred with the opinion of earlier experts and recommended Sciberras as the best site for an impregnable city:[54] it was a healthier site than Birgu being more open to the winds; it was almost entirely surrounded by deep

---

47 Bosio, III, 398.

48 AOM 90, f. 13; AOM 288, f. 65v.

49 See AOM 427, f. 254v.; and Bosio, III, 403.

50 Bosio, III, 441.

51 AOM 428, f. 268v.; Bosio, III, 441.

52 AOM 429, ff. 210 and 240; Bosio, III, 450.

53 Bosio, III, 454. Lanci was a pupil of Gerolamo Genga (Vasari, III, 266). He served with the French armies in Italy and was employed by Pius IV in fortifying Ancona and Rome, and by Duke Cosimo at Siena and Livorno in the 1560s. He died in Florence in 1571. (See life by Promis, *Miscellanea*, XIV, 343.)

54 A copy of Lanci's report, lacking any plan, survives among the papers of the engineer Francesco Laparelli (Cod. Lap. ff. 21-25v.). It is summarized by Bosio (III, 455-6). Hughes ('Defence of Malta', pp. 10-12) suggests that the engraving made in 1572 by G. Braun and F. Hogenburg in *Civitates Orbis Terrarum* 6 vols. (Cologne, 1572-1618), I, folio 50, represents Lanci's scheme.

water, and the land front, which would only be about 200 canes long, would not require a large number of defenders; within the walls there would be room to accommodate all the islanders and their animals in time of siege; the larger area would permit a more gracious style of living for the knights than was possible in the cramped quarters of Birgu, which he hoped would attract more men of substance to join the Order. Lanci traced the outline of the front, which was to be closer to St. Elmo than that proposed by Genga probably about the line of the present Valletta front; he made various detailed calculations, the accuracy of which, if the experience of those schemes actually implemented is anything to go by, may well have been open to question. In four months at a cost of 20,000 scudi he believed the front could be raised to a defendable height, which thereafter could be increased at leisure. The lateral walls, which were unlikely to come under determined assault, did not need to be very high or thick, and should not therefore be too costly. Probably realizing the possibility that the building of the city would be deferred, Lanci included in his report suggestions for rendering Birgu more secure. Basically he was advocating a series of retrenchments so that the defenders could not be attacked in the rear by an enemy stationed on Salvatore hill to the north-east of the town, adjustments to the post of Castile on the left flank of the land front, which was recognized as being the weak spot in the enceinte, and better siting of cannon embrasures both in Birgu and on St. Michael.

Any doubts Lanci may have had as to whether his scheme would be accepted were fully justified. Both his plan and Genga's had points in their favour and each had its supporters. The grand master was unable to decide which to implement, but, as the season was too advanced for any work begun to be in a state of defence by the coming spring, the decision was postponed and Lanci was returned to the duke of Florence rewarded by a gold chain worth 200 scudi and 300 scudi in cash.[55] Strong rumours that a Turkish armada was sailing for Malta led to a further deferment of any new building projects and to a concentration on Birgu and Senglea.[56]

---

55 Bosio, III, 455-6.

56 Bosio, III, 460.

The sword of Damocles which for so long had been suspended over the Order and over Malta finally fell in 1565: a large Turkish fleet descended on the island and the forces of Suleiman II besieged the knights for four months from May to September. In April the viceroy of Sicily, Garcia de Toledo, visited the island accompanied by his engineers. He advised the building of the ravelin at St. Elmo, and the completion of the wall around Senglea, but was able to report that the fortifications were in good shape.[57] By September they were in ruins. Although only St. Elmo had fallen to the enemy, and only when it had become little more than a heap of rubble, the other fortresses, St. Angelo, Birgu, St. Michael and Senglea, had been mercilessly bombarded and mined by the Turks and were now virtually useless as protection or defences.[58] The Order had reached a watershed in its history: its treasury had been drained by the expenses of the siege; many of its members had been killed or wounded in the fighting; many of the islanders had suffered the same fate; others had fled to Sicily and were showing understandable reluctance to return; the island's agriculture and trade had been disrupted;[59] the fortresses were in ruins and there was every prospect that the Turks would return to the attack in the spring. In its present state the island could not be defended and the Order was in no state to remedy the situation. Without outside help it was unlikely that the Order could survive another year in Malta, for although it possessed extensive property in Europe it was no simple task to mobilize these resources, and in the autumn of 1565 it was imperative that some action be taken, and quickly.

In Malta itself the Order did what it could: immediately after the siege the knights busied themselves with the task which would be preliminary to any scheme of rebuilding – the clearing of debris from Birgu, Senglea and St. Elmo[60] – but the future was as yet undecided. After considerable diplomatic activity,[61] during

---

57 Bosio, III, 499; *Colección de documentos inéditos para la historia de España* (hereafter referred to as *Col. doc. inéditos*), ed. M. de Pidal, M. Salva et al., 112 vols. (Madrid, 1842-95), XXIX, 86-8.

58 There are numerous accounts of the siege but the standard modern work is still C. S. Zabarella, *Lo assedio di Malta* (Turin, 1902). See also Balbi and Bradford.

59 Blouet, pp. 126, 142-3.

60 Bosio, III, 710.

61 See the next chapter.

which plans for rebuilding and extending the fortifications proceeded, the Order finally made a momentous decision, at the very time when its fortunes were undoubtedly at a low ebb, to implement the oft-discussed and frequently postponed project to construct a fortified city on Sciberras, thereby finally resigning itself to the acceptance of Malta as its headquarters.

Once committed to Malta the knights strove whole-heartedly to make it both a capital worthy of so illustrious and noble a band of men, and a fortress that befitted a military Order whose *raison d'être* was its implacable enmity towards the infidel. Indeed, its military and naval exploits were such that the Order could not expect other than that the hostility of the Moslems would be a continuing fact of life. The construction of the new city of Valletta was the first link in what was to become an ever-expanding chain of defence, encircling first, by stages, the harbour area, but gradually extending outwards to embrace the whole island with supplementary systems in Gozo and even Comino. The major preoccupation in the years immediately succeeding the siege was the building of Valletta. Within ten years the city was more or less completed, but long before it reached that stage, the convent had been transferred there from Birgu in 1571. Despite the limitations of Birgu and Senglea which were only too well known, these towns and their fortifications were rebuilt, and because there was no convenient sheltered anchorage alongside Valletta, the naval headquarters of the Order remained in Birgu, and the galleys moored in the creek between Birgu and Senglea had to be afforded some protection. It was not until the late 1630s that a scheme was conceived which recognized the need to defend these harbour installations and which attempted by means of an outer ring of defences, the Sta. Margherita lines, to enclose the fronts of Birgu and Senglea and shield them from the neighbouring heights. This project had to compete for resources of men and money with the plans of Floriani and others for the updating of the Valletta defences, which as the capital, merited particular attention. In the event both the Floriana and the Sta. Margherita lines were built but as funds were sorely stretched work dragged on interminably and neither scheme was finished until the eighteenth century, by which time both had been subjected to frequent damning criticism and attempted improvements. In the late seventeenth century a crowned-hornwork and a fausse-braye were added to Floriana; Sta. Margherita suffered the indignity of being encircled by a far more impressive work, the Cottonera lines, whose function was identical to that of the earlier work. At the same time (1670) a fort, Ricasoli, was built opposite St. Elmo to defend the entry to Grand Harbour. The finishing touches were put to the defences of the harbours in the eighteenth century with the completion of the Floriana, Sta. Margherita and Cottonera schemes, and the construction of two forts to protect Marsamxett, Manoel on the Lazaretto Isoletto in the 1720s, and Tigné at the entrance to the port in the 1790s.

Meanwhile the Order's interest in fortification had spread beyond the immediate vicinity of the convent. A concern for the safety of the inhabitants had prompted a review of the Gozo Castello at the end of the sixteenth century; it was a fortress unsuited to modern warfare and schemes for its improvement or replacement recurred intermittently, finally bearing fruit in the construction of a new fortress, Chambray, in the mid-eighteenth century. Notabile, which after the building of Valletta was more usually known as Città Vecchia, was likewise outdated and despite various modifications was never satisfactorily adapted to the age of gunpowder artillery. In the seventeenth century the knights increasingly turned their attention to the maritime defences of the two main islands and Comino. A number of coastal towers were built, some to act merely as lookout and signalling posts, others to oppose any attempted enemy landing. This latter concept of defence, opposing the enemy on the beaches, was extended in the eighteenth century when a series of coastal entrenchments, batteries and redoubts was proposed, and some were even built. The system was further elaborated by the addition of inland entrenchments designed to prevent the free movement of enemy troops should they succeed in landing.

When the islands fell to Napoleon in 1798 there was therefore in existence an impressive system of fortifications which had grown up over the years from 1566. The destruction wrought by the siege had advantages in that it left the knights, for the most part, free to construct fortifications of their own choice unhampered by restrictions imposed by obsolete works. Where this was not the case, as at the Gozo Castello and Città Vecchia, the Order had to resort to adaptations which never corrected the fundamental faults of the forts. For all the wholesale destruction of the siege, the Order was to some extent restricted by its reluctance, for various reasons, to abandon the settlements on the southern shore of Grand Harbour. While fully cognizant of the military limitations of the sites of Birgu and Senglea, the Order was, nevertheless, prepared to defend them as best it could. Little trace remains of the fortifications erected during the Order's first thirty-five years in Malta; the post-siege fortifications, however, still dominate the islands, especially around the harbour area of Malta. The construction of these works erected during the centuries when the bastioned enceinte was the dominant system of fortification in Europe will now be examined in detail.

Chapter 4

Valletta and its Fortifications

I. The Building of Valletta

The situation which confronted the Order in September 1565 was far from encouraging: the defences were in ruins; the treasury empty; many men, both members of the Order and Maltese, had been killed or wounded; the islands' economy had been disrupted by the long siege; there was every prospect that the Turks would resume their assault in the spring, so that some provision had to be made for the defence of the island and the Order. The late siege had demonstrated all too clearly the vulnerability of St. Angelo, Birgu, Senglea and St. Elmo; although the obstacles which had previously led to the postponement of the project to build a new city, lack of time and money, had increased rather than diminished, this scheme, nevertheless, received close scrutiny in the autumn of 1565. However daunting the prospect of constructing a fortress *de novo* appeared, the alternative courses of action were hardly more attractive. To rebuild the old forts would solve nothing: they would never be impregnable; any attempt to defend them would again be costly in both manpower and money; any further outlay of resources in this manner could well cripple the Order and render meaningless its claim to independent sovereignty; besides, it was widely accepted that to construct the fortress on Sciberras would be hardly more expensive than to rebuild the old defences.[1]

---

1 This view was expressed by Don Garcia in a letter to Philip II dated 16 September 1565 (*Col. doc. inéditos*, XXIX, 531).

It was suggested that rather than risk another full-scale onslaught the main body of knights could withdraw to Sicily leaving garrisons in Malta, so that if the islands were overrun the heart of the Order would not be destroyed. The decision to build the new city was formally taken on 4 March 1566[2] but the preceding six months were filled with indecision and political manoeuvrings whose chief purpose was to ensure the assistance of foreign powers without which the Order was impotent.

Immediately after the retreat of the Turks Grand Master la Valette revived the plan to build a new city on Sciberras. Such a momentous undertaking demanded a worthy engineer, and various approaches were made through the Order's envoys in Europe to secure the services of a suitable man on loan from his princely employer.[3] Probably the grand master hoped that Lanci would return, but he was unwell, and it was the papal engineer Francesco Laparelli who, at the end of December 1565, arrived to take over the direction of the defences.[4] By this time the knights had already canvassed considerable support from the courts of Europe. The importance of refortifying Malta was recognized, and the need to build fortifications better suited to modern warfare appreciated;[5] help was promised both for the long-term project – the construction of a new headquarters – and for the immediate task of defending the islands against renewed Turkish attack. Soldiers were urgently required to protect the building workers and any half-completed defences, and to oppose the enemy in the field should he arrive before the fortifications were defendable. The pope and Philip II responded to the plea for troops by supplying between them some

---

2 Bosio, III, 741. For fuller detail than is possible here on the building of Valletta and Floriana see my Ph.D. thesis, A.M. Buchan (now Hoppen), 'The fortification of Malta by the Order of the Hospital of St. John of Jerusalem, 1530-1798, with special reference to Valletta and Floriana' (University of St. Andrews, 1970).

3 Bosio, III, 709; *Col. doc. inéditos*, XXX, 30.

4 Bosio, III, 720, 722; AOM 430, ff. 267, 268v. and 270. Laparelli was born in Cortona in 1521. In 1553 the Grand Duke of Florence sent the engineer Gabrio Serbelloni to fortify Cortona. Serbelloni met Laparelli and was impressed by his aptitude for military engineering. Laparelli was subsequently employed by Duke Cosimo in the construction of the fort of Girifalco at Cortona. Serbelloni introduced Laparelli to Pius IV and while in Rome he worked on the defences of Civitavecchia, Castello S. Angelo and the Borgo. Michelangelo nominated him as his successor to be in charge of St. Peter's.

5 See letter of Don Garcia to the grand master dated 26 October 1565 (*Col. doc. inéditos*, XXX, 27) and letter of Londano to Philip II dated 1 October 1565 (*Col doc. inéditos*, XXIX, 538); Bosio, III, 720-1.

6,000 men.[6] With the immediate defence of the island assured, with monetary donations now promised by the princes,[7] and with the arrival of the engineer, the Order could divert its main effort from clearing the debris of the old works to constructing the new fortifications. To a large extent, apart from some tidying-up work, the autumn of 1565 was wasted time, albeit unavoidably wasted, given the Order's dependence upon outside help and the time taken to mobilize its own resources.

Once in Malta, Laparelli lost little time in setting to work. He inspected the various defensive positions and on 3 January 1566 presented his first report.[8] Laparelli found that the fortifications of Birgu, Senglea and St. Elmo had been so badly damaged that it would be four months before 4,000 workmen, toiling day and night, could raise ramparts sufficient to present a serious obstacle to an enemy bent on scaling the walls. No attacker was likely in 1566 to attempt such a manoeuvre without first bombarding the ramparts, but the old fortifications had been so badly battered that, even after four months of intensive activity, they would still be unable to withstand fresh bombardment. In addition, Laparelli recognized, as did every other competent engineer employed by the knights, the total inadequacy of the sites on which they had been placed. He strongly opposed the suggestion, already being bandied about, that Malta should be abandoned, but supported the scheme to fortify Sciberras.

Laparelli proposed siting the land front of the new city 500 canes from the ditch of St. Elmo. Needless to say, the design would be adapted to the terrain, but no detailed planning had been possible in the short time available to him. He calculated that he would require 3,000 labourers, half employed in stone cutting, the rest transporting materials, plus 100 stone masons and 400 manual workers to assist the craftsmen. With such a work force in three months the city would be able to resist a siege if manned by a garrison of 3,000 well-provisioned infantry. A thousand workmen would be retained for a fourth month to carry out such work as could be undertaken even if they were under siege. Despite the fact that he had not drawn up a detailed plan, Laparelli estimated that

6 Bosio, III, 720-1.
7 See chapter 11, notes 31, 53 and 54.
8 Cod. Lap. f. 6.

to build the fortifications of the new city would cost less and be quicker than to rebuild Birgu and Senglea, although if one took into account the cisterns, mills and other essentials with which the city would have to be provided, it would prove more expensive in the long run.

No decision was taken on this first report so that on 13 January Laparelli submitted a second.[9] He had now had time to consider in more depth the scheme to fortify Sciberras, and was fully aware of the problems involved. It would, he argued, undoubtedly be a great mistake to begin a project which might not be finished in time and he feared that this might well happen as the knights had not the men, materials or tools for such an undertaking. The fifteen days which had elapsed since his arrival Laparelli regarded as wasted since neither workmen nor iron tools had been available to him. Every day the campaigning season came nearer, yet the artillery was for the most part out of commission and munitions in short supply. With each day's delay more workmen would be required to complete the project on time; he estimated that 5,000 labourers would now be needed before the end of January and by mid-March 5,000 infantry would be necessary to guard the works on Sciberras and the Città Vecchia. If the new city was not commenced because of the scarcity of workmen then 12,000 infantrymen and 200 light-horse would be needed to defend the island.

The report of 13 January furnished the grand master with further evidence, if any were needed, of the Order's dire need for aid from the princes. On the next day ambassadors departed for the courts of Spain, France and Sicily.[10] The ambassadors were to state unequivocally that the Order was unable to remain in Malta and undertake its defence unless an army was provided; a force of 15,000 infantry was considered essential and the Order itself could supply only a fifth of that number. The princes were to be acquainted with the possibility that the knights would if necessary abandon Malta, however reluctantly.[11] Pressure was to be applied to Philip II and the viceroy in the hope that some positive step might be

---

9 Cod. Lap. f. 9.

10 Bosio, III, 726; the ambassadors had been appointed on 5 January (AOM 91, f. 159) but their departure was delayed by bad weather. The instructions, although dated 5 January, clearly incorporate Laparelli's second report (AOM 430, ff. 267, 268, 268v.).

11 On 30 January Laparelli reported on the garrisons required to man St. Angelo, St. Elmo and Città Vecchia should the Order withdraw (Cod. Lap. f. 13).

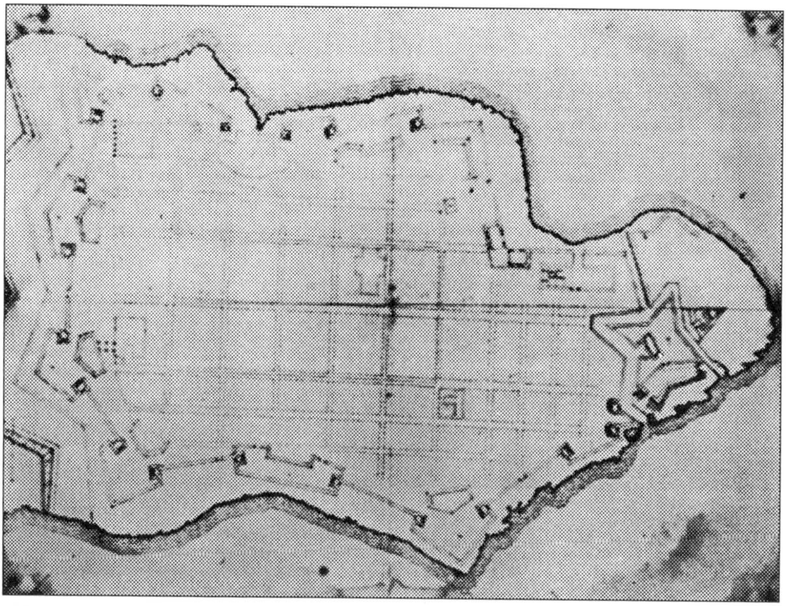

Plate 2 Laparelli's final plan for Valletta, June 1566.

taken to increase the flow of workmen, both Sicilians and Maltese refugees, from Sicily, as shortage of manpower was a major cause of the new city's having not yet been begun. As a result the viceroy decided to send Vincenzo Bosco, Count of Vicari, to Malta to inspect the situation at first hand and to report back.[12] Bosco submitted that the scheme to fortify Sciberras was the best solution to the Order's defence problems but that because of the shortage of workmen and time it seemed to him impossible that more could be done before the opening of the campaigning season than the repair of the old fortifications.[13] Just as Bosco was about to leave Malta further dispatches reached him from Sicily. He received intimation of Philip II's monetary subsidy to the Order, and Ascanio della Cornia's and the Duke of Alba's reports on the defence of the island.[14] Neither Della Cornia's suggestion to entrench 6,000 soldiers above Birgu,

---

12 Bosio, III, 727-8: *Col. doc. inéditos*, XXX, 93-5, copy of instructions given to Bosco on his departure for Malta dated 23 January 1566.

13 *Col. doc. inéditos*, XXX, 128 – Bosco's report.

14 Della Cornia, a maestro de campo of the Spanish king, had arrived in Malta with a relief force in September 1565; Alba's report is found in *Col. doc. inéditos*, XXX, 121.

nor that of Alba to establish an entrenchment rather than a new city on Sciberras, was well received by the Order. The knights insisted that Laparelli's plan could be executed in three months, but that as 235,000 scudi would be required to construct the front of the new city, and because there was a general lack of supplies and support, building could not be commenced that spring. Instead the Order proposed to abandon Malta on the arrival of any hostile fleet, leaving garrisons of 1,500 soldiers in St. Elmo and St. Angelo, and to return the following autumn to fortify the island.[15]

Quite a rift seems to have developed between the viceroy and grand master at this time which was only healed through the good offices of Gabrio Serbelloni, a well-known engineer and himself a member of the Order.[16] La Valette suspected that Garcia was far more concerned with the fate of Goletta, a Spanish possession in North Africa also under threat from the Moslems, than Malta, and that he was channelling the available resources in that direction. A formal decision was finally made by the grand master and council on 7 March that if the European powers did not supply an army in time the Order would retire to Sicily leaving garrisons in Città Vecchia, St. Elmo and St. Angelo.[17] Possibly the threat to withdraw was made in the hope of jolting the powers into action. Certainly the pope, Pius V, was alarmed when he learnt of the proposal and urged Philip to provide the aid which he had promised.[18] Although Philip and Garcia may have been dilatory in sending help they had no wish to see Malta evacuated, thus leaving the south-eastern flank of Sicily exposed.[19] Gabrio Serbelloni was therefore sent to the island on Philip's orders to examine Laparelli's fortifications. He arrived on 11 March, and on the 17th submitted a report to the viceroy,[20] in which he praised the decision to fortify St. Angelo, St.

15 *Col. doc. inéditos*, XXX, 132; Bosio, III, 728; Laparelli had reported on this possibility on 30 January (Cod. Lap. f. 13).

16 Bosio, III, 743; Serbelloni was a Milanese engineer and cousin of Pius IV, who used his influence to secure Serbelloni's entry into the Order and his appointment as prior of Hungary. Serbelloni was employed by Pius and also by the Hapsburgs in Italy, the Low Countries, Hungary and North Africa.

17 Bosio, III, 738; AOM 91, f. 162 (7 March 1566) notes the appointment of various commanders but not the decision to withdraw.

18 Bosio, III, 736; Pauli, II, 222 (brief to grand master, 22 March 1566), 224 (brief to Philip II); *Col. doc. inéditos*, XXX, 184 (brief to Don Garcia).

19 *Col. doc. inéditos*, XXX, 143.

20 Bosio, III, 739-4; *Col. doc. inéditos*, XXX, 205.

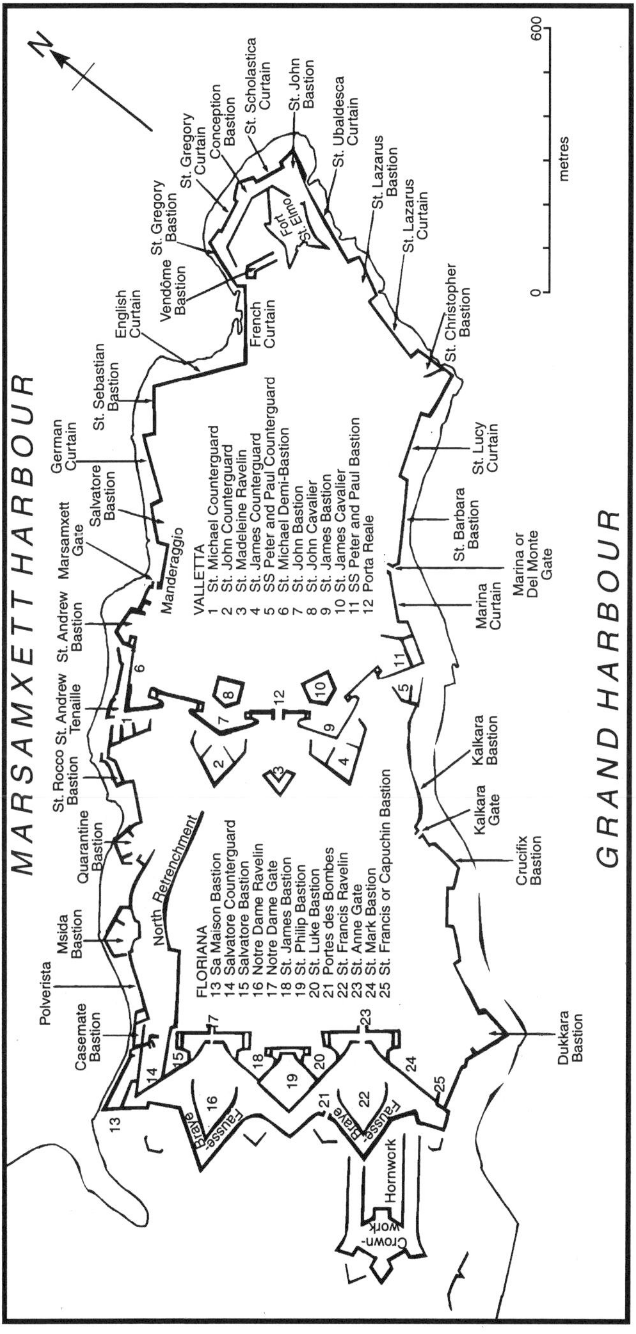

Fig. 3 Valletta and Floriana

Elmo and Città Vecchia on the grounds that if an army were sent, it would require a safe base in which to store munitions and provisions. The repairs already undertaken at these forts would be sufficient for this purpose and it seemed pointless to incur further expense in this connection. To satisfy Pius, Philip and the other benefactors it was essential, so Serbelloni believed, to start work on the new city immediately using whatever workmen were available. Serbelloni effectively flung his weight behind Laparelli's scheme and on 14 March the council sanctioned the building of the new city.[21] Two weeks later the official stone-laying ceremony of the city, to be named Valletta, took place,[22] by which time the land front had been marked out by rubble walls in accordance with Laparelli's designs.[23]

Serbelloni's support was invaluable to Laparelli, who had been criticized both for the concept of building a new city and for the actual design which he had produced. The former criticisms centred mainly on the point as to whether the Order should, at that particular time, commit itself to so large an undertaking rather than concentrate its resources by rebuilding, assembling a powerful army, or withdrawal. Laparelli firmly believed that Malta had to be defended as the heart of the Order and that the only practical way in which this could be done was by fortifying Sciberras. He was prepared to answer his critics with reasoned arguments and, as far as the design of the city was concerned, showed that he had given careful thought to the various positions at which the land front might be sited.[24] A front 1,500 canes from St. Elmo, although commanding the spring at Marsa, was dismissed as too grandiose, too costly, too large to defend and likely to be the target for large-scale assaults and bombardment. The site 800 canes from St. Elmo ditch was excellent in that it could not be attacked from the flanks, but was likewise rejected on the grounds of cost. Laparelli maintained that since the spring at Marsa could not be enclosed it was as well to make the front as far away as possible, so that the Turks could not site their artillery batteries around the spring. However, he considered a ridge only 180 canes from St. Elmo to be too close

21 Bosio, III, 741; Serbelloni had earlier acted as a patron to Laparelli and had introduced him to Pius IV.
22 Bosio, III, 744; Cod. Lap. f. 41v.
23 Bosio, III, 741; AOM 91, f. 164.
24 Cod. Lap. f. 10.

to the fort to allow anything approaching a city to be constructed within the walls. The site which Laparelli favoured was on the highest part of Sciberras, 500 canes from the fort; the front would not be exposed to excessive bombardment or assault, and although some had complained that the city would still be too small, it would nonetheless be three times larger than Birgu. The land front should, he argued, be so constructed that if an attack appeared imminent, it could be converted into a closed fort, but, if time permitted, its flanks could be extended to enclose St. Elmo. Despite opposition, there is no evidence that Laparelli significantly altered the design of the land front, details of which had already reached Sicily by 23 January.[25] The front he outlined in March 1566 consisted of four bastions with connecting curtains and two cavaliers – the basic design of the Valletta front to this day. Before work on the new city could finally get under way Laparelli had to clear one more hurdle. Early in April the viceroy arrived in person accompanied by various engineers to judge the merits of the proposed defences.[26] An on-the-site inspection was made and Laparelli explained his designs to a distinguished group of engineers and military experts which included Serbelloni, Chiappino Vitelli, Ascanio della Cornia, Fratino, possibly Scipio Campi,[27] and the ordinary engineers of the Order and the viceroy. Della Cornia and Fratino maintained that the land front should be withdrawn somewhat and consist of only three bastions. They criticized particularly the two bastions at the

---

25 *Col. doc. inéditos*, XXX, 93; a wax model had been examined in the Spanish court in the early months of 1566 (Bosio, III, 741).

26 Bosio, III, 746-8.

27 Vitelli, the Marquis of Cetona, had served in the forces of the Medici and had fortified Cortona, Port Ercole and the fortress of Castrocaro. He entered the service of Spain in the 1560s and first visited Malta in 1565 as a member of the relief force in September. He later saw action in Flanders under Alba. He was the patron of Maggi the author of *Della fortificatione delle città*. The engineer Il Fratino was employed by Philip II in North Africa where he was responsible for the forts of Melilla and Goletta (1566), and in Navarre (1571) and Majorca (1574) (F. Braudel, *The Mediterranean*, 2 vols. (London, 1972-3), II, 855-6, 1094, 1141). He also advised on the fortifications of Genoa between 1571 and 1576 (M. Giuffrè, 'Palermo città murata dal XVI al XIX secolo', *Quaderno dell'Istituto Dipartimentale di Architettura ed Urbanistica*, Università di Catania, VIII (1976), pp. 48, 50 and 51, who gives his name as Giorgio Palearo Fratino). There is some doubt as to whether Campi visited Malta in 1566; Bosio does not include him among the Spanish engineers. He certainly visited the island in June 1576 and compiled a report on the fortifications (Vatican Library, Fondo Chigi (hereafter, referred to as Chigi), Q III 69, f. 20). He was then in the employ of Spain and shortly afterwards served in Flanders. He also carried out some works of fortification in France for Catherine de' Medici (Zastrow, I, 105).

extremities of the front, St. Michael's and SS. Peter and Paul's. However, the rest of the company thought well of the design and the viceroy placed his seal of approval on the whole scheme.[28]

All Laparelli's surviving plans show that despite modifications over the years, the Valletta fortifications remain fundamentally as he designed them. Shortly after work had begun he prepared a report and plan which were circulated around the European princes whose continuing support was essential if the project was to be completed.[29] After explaining that Malta was not the ideal place in which to found a city, Laparelli, who no doubt saw this report as a vehicle for self-advertisement, then outlined how, following lengthy discussions, his plan, which was neither too grandiose nor too restricted, had come to be accepted. He described the four bastions of the land front which were to be cut from the living rock, and emphasized how very little masonry would have to be used except for building up those parts of the front where the terrain sloped away. The lateral walls of the city would link up with St. Elmo, and would be sufficiently high to protect the interior of the city, that is about twelve canes in height. By early April 1566, therefore, Laparelli had committed his designs to paper and was prepared to display his scheme to the European princes by way of a plan and explanatory report. His confidence was not misplaced and from that time on the new city proceeded under his guidance without serious interruption.

There are, however, certain discrepancies between Laparelli's designs, the various reproductions based on his plans published after 1566, and the work actually carried out. Thus there are features on the plans which were never executed. Although several cavaliers appear on paper, only two, St. James and St. John, were ever built. Laparelli himself confessed that he had no intention of constructing the others; they were included in the designs only to ensure that private buildings did not encroach on the platforms of the bastions.[30] Laparelli's original designs show a galley-pen, the manderaggio, and

---

28 Bosio, III, 747. Hughes ('Defence of Malta', pp. 14-15) suggests that the plan in the Uffizi (Florence), De Rocchi 4230A, may show Fratino's scheme.

29 There are four surviving plans in the possession of the Countess Laparelli Pitti. They probably accompanied a report drawn up in June 1566 (Cod. Lap. f. 40) and show changes in street layout. (See plate 2.) The form of the fortifications appears to have been fixed by this time. The plan which accompanied the report which was circulated around the princes in March or April (i.e. Cod. Lap. f. 124) has not survived. In August 1566 it was noted that Philip II had received plans of the new city (*Col. doc. inéditos*, XXX, 570).

30 Cod. Lap. ff. 40 and 124.

a ship repair yard, the arsenal, on the Marsamxett shore of Valletta. There were obvious advantages in having the naval installations sheltered by the Valletta fortifications but, unfortunately, Sciberras boasted no natural harbours or creeks. It was decided to excavate two valleys on the Marsamxett flank down to sea level to create artificial basins. Work started on the manderaggio and a gap of five canes for its entrance was left in the curtain between St. Andrew's and Salvatore bastions.[31] In 1569 it was decreed that all the stone to be used in building the houses of Valletta was to be quarried from the manderaggio,[32] but eventually a layer of stone unsuitable for building was encountered before sea level was reached. This, together with the realization that the Marsamxett did not afford sufficient shelter in rough weather, led to the abandonment of the project and an unplanned mass of slum dwellings sprang up in the old quarry. There is no evidence that work on the arsenal ever began; Laparelli made no provision for an entrance gap to be left in the enceinte. Although some of the early engravings portray the ditch as water-filled this must be accounted artistic fancy. Laparelli stated unequivocally that wet ditches were suitable only for small forts and Valletta was no small fort.[33]

Laparelli's reports after April 1566 convey an impression of steady progress, despite his repeated complaints about the shortage of workmen and money. He was particularly concerned lest the Turks should return before the city was in a defendable state. In August he wrote to Serbelloni lamenting that time was flying, that shorter days and wet weather were approaching, and that it was barely eight months before the enemy fleet might again be expected; there was, he emphasized, no substitute for completed fortifications, not even additional soldiers as some had seemingly suggested.[34] The princes had supplied funds but the urgent need was for workmen without whom the building rate could not be increased. Laparelli was not alone in ascribing the slow progress of the city to the chronic shortage of workmen. The Spaniard Don Sancho de Londono expressed the same opinion in a letter which he wrote to Philip II

---

31 Cod. Lap. f. 70; Vatican Library, Fondo Urbinate Latino (hereafter referred to as Urb. Lat), 833, f. 209v.
32 AOM 92, f. 141.
33 Cod. Lap. f. 31.
34 Cod. Lap. f. 41 (18 August 1566).

from Malta at about this time.[35] Laparelli undertook to engage 500 workmen in Italy and to bring them to Malta in an attempt to surmount this obstacle.[36] In the same month, June, the ambassador to the Spanish court was instructed to urge Philip II to command the viceroys of Sicily and Naples to assist the Order in its search for workers.[37] It was estimated that in the summer of 1566 between 1,000 and 1,200 men were employed. In October Laparelli expressed the fear that the Turks might actually break with normal practice and attack in the winter;[38] accordingly the knights must be constantly on the alert, and at the same time, press ahead with the building work. It seems likely that during this winter construction work continued whenever the weather permitted and that the usual winter closed-season for building was not observed.[39] The following May Laparelli listed the various items of work which remained to be carried out in Valletta.[40] The ditch on the land front had to be excavated to a uniform depth of forty palms below the cordon; at the flanks four pits were to be cut twenty palms deeper than ditch-level and forty palms square to collect rain water from the ditch; the material excavated from the ditch and pits was to be used to make the glacis; seven low platforms, twenty-four palms below the cordon, were to be hewn out in the flanks of the bastions of the front together with access passages; various gateways had to be made in the ditch and counterscarp; the material excavated in making the platforms, passages and gates could be used as infilling but not in places likely to be bombarded. Once the walls were raised they were to be backed by terrapleins of well-rammed earth which would protect the masonry from the effects of sun and wind; to prevent any damage to newly constructed walls through heat, it was necessary to keep them well moistened so that the mortar could dry out slowly and act as an effective binding agent;[41] it might be as well to cease stone-laying altogether during the next four months, the height of summer, and use the respite to build up supplies of mortar, sand and cut stone. Although the shape of the lateral walls had been marked out, as yet

---

35 *Col. doc. inéditos*, XXX, 338 (25 July 1566).
36 Cod. Lap. f. 42 (mid-August 1566).
37 AOM 431, f. 245v.
38 Cod. Lap. f. 43v. (21 October 1566).
39 See chapter 10 for the effect of the weather on building activity.
40 Cod. Lap. f. 45 (26 May 1567).
41 See chapter 10 for the effect of heat on construction work.

work had concentrated on the front; even so, trenches had been cut on those areas of high ground where the enceinte was to be carved out of the solid rock. When it was possible to do so without disturbing the building of the front, the material removed from the high ground was to be used to build up thick high walls in those parts where there was no natural rampart.

Very soon after writing this report Laparelli submitted another to the grand master, in which he outlined the work to be undertaken in the twelve months from 1 June 1567, assuming a workforce of 4,000.[42] This estimate was based on the volume of work carried out in the previous year. The ditch, which was still some sixteen palms short of the required depth of forty palms, was to be deepened. Laparelli proposed to allocate to this task half the workforce, who should be able to complete it in a year. The other 2,000 would be employed on the lateral walls, either in carving ramparts out of rock, or in building up masonry walls, according to the dictates of the terrain. No wall building was to take place in the immediately ensuing three and a half months, but the stone could be prepared for work to commence in mid-September. The construction of magazines to store artillery, munitions and victuals during a siege, and of bakeries, cisterns, corn and powder mills was also to be undertaken. With these 4,000 men Laparelli estimated that in twelve months the city would be in a defendable state; given a further year, the enceinte might be completed, but it would be many years before a fully-fledged city emerged. From this report and that of 26 May it is apparent that, as one might have expected, in the first year of construction the engineer had concentrated on building the land front of Valletta, while at the same time repairing St. Elmo.

Before the year required to render Valletta defendable was up, indeed after only four months, Laparelli was again expressing his fears that the infidel would appear before the fortifications were ready to receive him.[43] The reason for his alarm on this occasion was an eight-year truce between the Emperor Maximilian and the Sultan Selim. Laparelli cited five examples of places which the Turks had returned to capture after an unsuccessful first attack. Valletta was of course particularly vulnerable because of its unfinished state; once in enemy hands it could be turned against St. Elmo.

---

42 Cod. Lap. f. 47.

43 Cod. Lap. f. 49 (22 September 1567).

Despite the shortage of workmen, and the tight time schedule brought about by the Turks' impending return, Laparelli believed that the knights had no alternative but to proceed with Valletta if they were to fulfil their obligations towards the rulers who had so generously contributed to the building funds. He then outlined the current state of work in Valletta. The counterscarp was without either banquette or sally ports; the ditch had not been excavated sufficiently to allow the low platforms to be constructed and there were neither gates nor passages giving access to the ditch. All four bastions of the land front, but SS. Peter and Paul's and St. Michael's in particular, still required a considerable amount of attention. The progress on the lateral walls, and especially on the masonry walls in the low-lying sections of the site, was unsatisfactory. Those who sought to minimize the problem by suggesting that rubble walls would suffice were deluding themselves: on such sloping ground a wall of three or four canes with a small platform in the rear was essential to afford the defenders some protection. St. Elmo itself was in need of improvements including magazines for the storage of provisions. More mills and bakeries were necessary and the streets had to be cleared to allow for the free movement of artillery. Laparelli proposed that St. Angelo should be defended if the enemy mounted a siege but the provisions kept in that fort were to be strictly limited so that should it fall, the besiegers would gain little of value. He reckoned that 4,000 men working for seven months could get Valletta, St. Elmo and St. Angelo into order. These could then be defended by a force of 6,000, whereas to defend all the forts, old and new, would demand double that number.

A report compiled some three months later to acquaint some personage abroad with the progress adds further details to that of 22 September.[44] It is clear that the cavaliers of the land front were by this time completed apart from the parapets which were to be composed of earth. Laparelli expected that by the following May the bastions and their linking curtains should have been raised to the level of the cordon; already half of them had reached this stage of construction and in many places the cordon was being built directly onto the solid rock. The excavation work which was to shape the bastions, curtains and ditch was at various stages of progress, but nowhere were there more than twelve palms to be cut

[44] Cod. Lap. f. 54 (15 October 1567).

before the required depth of forty palms below the cordon was achieved. The low platforms, the covert-ways, gates and sally ports still remained to be excavated; the high platforms and passages to be levelled to facilitate the transfer of artillery and to allow soldiers room to manoeuvre. The terrapleins and parapets had to be constructed. The work of carving out and building up the bastions of the lateral walls was under way but progress was hindered because earth for the terrapleins had to be carted considerable distances by donkeys, then as always, in short supply. Storage magazines had been provided, and sites prepared for the construction of bakeries, flour and powder mills. Large cisterns had been excavated and the water supply problem further alleviated by the discovery of a fresh water spring on Sciberras.

Both the Order and Laparelli appreciated the importance of supplying up-to-date progress reports to interested foreign parties. Laparelli probably saw this as an excellent opportunity of acquainting prospective patrons with his work, while the Order was dependent on the princes' goodwill if the project was to be perfected. In December 1567[45] an account of progress was sent to the conservator of the Royal Patrimony of the Spanish king which differed in no essential points from the report dated 15 October. A further report[46] was submitted in the same month to that keen supporter of the building scheme, the pope; he had shown his support in practical terms by the appointment of a resident commissioner in Malta who disbursed regular sums of money to finance the work.[47] In the report prepared for the pope Laparelli revealed that he considered all the land front of Valletta to be already in a defendable state, but that he did not mean to imply the front itself to be complete. Since the written account was intended only as a supplement to a plan, now lost, Laparelli gave no details of the work outstanding beyond commenting that the most important undertakings were the construction of bakeries and mills. Because the city would still be in an unfinished state in the coming summer, 1568, extra soldiers would be required for its defence, in fact, double the number necessary once it was fully fortified.

---

45 Cod. Lap. f. 59 (17 December 1567).

46 Cod. Lap. f. 58 (12 December 1567).

47 Appointment of Girolamo Guidacci as commissioner – Vatican Secret Archives (hereafter referred to as ASV), Arm. XLII, 26, f. 118 (July, 1566). He supplied 5,000 scudi a month for several months (Bosio, III, 785 and 807).

Work continued steadily in the winter of 1567-8; so much so that by April 1568 Laparelli was confident that his assistant, Girolamo Cassar, if well briefed in what was to be done, could be left in command while he visited Cortona to attend to family business.[48] Although a harmonious working relationship appears to have existed between the two men, Laparelli had no doubts as to the subordinate position of his assistant, and the instructions given to Cassar allowed him little scope to display initiative.[49] These instructions provided that during Laparelli's absence work could proceed only to a predetermined point and no further. In particular, any matter involving the exercise of discretion or judgement was to wait the return of the expert. Thus, although Cassar could supervise the construction of the ramparts (following Laparelli's detailed directions) up to the level of the cordon, he was not permitted to add the parapet, the height of which was to vary according to the contours and nature of the surrounding terrain.

This memorandum confirms the picture conveyed by the earlier reports. Work on the front, to which Laparelli gave first priority, was more advanced than that on the lateral walls; St. Elmo had been reconstructed; the shape and form of the fortifications were by that time (spring 1568) settled, although details, such as the height of the parapets, were to be decided as work progressed. This is the final surviving account of the fortifications drawn up by Laparelli himself. He returned to Malta towards the end of 1568 and supervised the building works until his final departure from the island about a year later but left no report on the fortifications dating from this period. One of the reasons which he advanced for quitting the service of the Order was the desire to gain military glory, and he must have judged the scope for such an achievement while in Malta to have been strictly limited.[50] While pursuing this end in the service of the Venetians he died of plague in Candia on 26 October 1570. Cassar, who had

---

48 Cod. Lap. f. d (fourth page before start of foliation proper) – letter of the grand master to the pope announcing Laparelli's departure, 27 April 1568. Girolamo Cassar, born in Malta in 1520, studied under Menga and also in Rome, progressed through the ranks of the Order's engineers to become the resident engineer responsible for supervising much of the work on Valletta. He was received into the Order as a confrater and died in 1592 (V. Mallia-Milanes, 'In search of Vittorio Cassar', *Melita Historica*, IX (1986), 247-70). His son Vittorio also served as engineer and entered the Order as a serving brother. He designed coastal towers and worked extensively in Gozo. He probably died in 1607.

49 Cod. Lap. f. 70, instructions to Cassar.

50 Cod. Lap. f. 140.

Plate 3 SS. Peter and Paul's counterguard, Valletta, with St Angelo beyond.

visited Italy during 1569 to study architecture,[51] possibly in preparation for Laparelli's departure, took over the supervision of the fortifications. The fact that the Order entrusted this work to their resident engineer was in itself an indication of the progress which had been made. The implication is that no major design or conceptual problems remained to be overcome and that the work to be executed was regarded as, in the main, straightforward.

The development of Valletta in the years following 1568 cannot be traced through a first-hand account such as the Codex Laparelli. The picture must, instead, be pieced together from miscellaneous sources, often anonymous and undated. Such an anonymous report is that drawn up during the grand mastership of Del Monte.[52] After a general description of the island and the Order, the author went on to consider the fortifications. St. Elmo he judged to be impregnable because not only had all the damage incurred during the siege been repaired, but the high ground from which it had been bombarded on that occasion was now occupied by Valletta. The land front of the city

51 AOM 432, f. 253 (23 April 1569) – safe-conduct for Cassar.
52 1568-72; Urb. Lat. 833, ff. 137-221.

was well advanced; only where the ground sloped away steeply under SS. Peter and Paul's and St. Michael's bastions had any difficulties been encountered. Elsewhere the front was in good order – the bastions, flanks and curtains – apart from the bastions of St. John and St. Michael whose platform and terraplein respectively were unfinished because filling material was unobtainable. Work on the parapets was under way but only those of the low flanks were completed; these were twenty palms thick, cut from the solid rock. The greater part of the bastions of the front was also carved out of rock, and the walls made from stone excavated from the ditch. All four bastions had shoulders of ten canes with flanks of five canes. The low flanks were cut from the rock six canes wide, one cane of which was behind the flank. All the flanks had passages ten palms wide cut into the rock, and each passage had a vaulted magazine for the storage of munitions. The ditch was six canes deep, and, apart from some levelling work, was finished; in front of the salient angles of the bastions it was seven, and in front of the curtains twelve canes wide. The whole of the counterscarp could be viewed from the high flanks of the bastions. It was well supplied with places of arms, and those at either end, near the bastions of SS. Peter and Paul and St. Michael, could accommodate 200 arquebusiers. As planned, cavaliers had been built on the two central bastions only, and these rose to a height of three canes above the level of the bastions' platforms.

Plate 4 *Valletta: St. Andrew's bastion and tenaille, with St. Michael's demi-bastion behind.*

Situated in the curtain between these two bastions was St. George's gate (later known as Porta Reale), above which had been placed the arms of the Order's benefactor and supporter Pius V and of Grand Master la Valette. A sally port had been cut in the rock of each of the other two curtains of the land front and all three curtains had their cordons and terrapleins in position.

The lateral walls were gradually nearing perfection. St. Andrew's bastion incorporated three platforms, the highest of which protected St. Michael's bastion, and also the entrance to the Marsamxett. A passageway cut through fifteen canes of rock led down to the ditch. This high platform and the intermediate one were still about a cane short of their required heights. The lowest platform, on the other hand, was quite finished and terrapleined; underneath it was positioned a gate, the Marsamxett gate, into the city. The author noted the breach in the curtain between St. Andrew's and Salvatore bastions which was to allow entry to the proposed manderaggio. The Salvatore bastion and the curtains adjoining St. Elmo were more or less finished. The Grand Harbour flank appears to have been less advanced. The rock around St. Lazarus's bastion was being levelled off and stone cut near St. Christopher's bastion, but no work was being carried out on this latter bastion itself. St. Barbara's bastion had a gap of ten canes in its centre but at its corners the level had reached two courses above the cordon. The curtain between this bastion and SS. Peter and Paul had been cut out

Plate 5 Salvatore counterguard and Sa Maison bastion, Floriana.

of the rock and was three canes high except in the middle where the ground was too low to allow this method of construction.

At the time of this report almost 3,000 workers were employed continuously on the fortifications. The author thought that within a year the city should be encircled by walls; given a further year the parapets would have been constructed. However, even in its present state he believed the city to be impregnable if defended by 2,000 soldiers. This optimistic estimate of the completion date for the fortifications was in line with current thinking among the knights. The chapter general of November 1569 decided to move the convent from Birgu to Valletta.[53] After a delay of over a year the transfer was made in March 1571.[54] The knights undoubtedly passed their first few months in Valletta in some discomfort as there were few buildings ready for occupation. The first task of the builders had been to see to the fortifications and by concentrating their efforts in the first five years on the defences they had been able to ensure the Order a secure, if uncomfortable, headquarters.

The speed with which the fortifications had been built had not in itself given rise to the faults which were to arouse criticism in the years to come. The possibility of fortifying Sciberras had been under consideration since 1524 and various designs had been submitted before that of Laparelli. Laparelli's writings reveal that he had examined alternative sites and designs before deciding on the plan which was eventually executed. Even so, he had to endure criticism, which he rebutted both in speeches and in writing, before his design was finally sanctioned by the Order and the viceroy.[55] At the planning stage it was only natural that differing ideas should be expressed especially as, however much the mathematicians might strive for a regular bastioned trace, the engineer's skill was essentially practical and his solutions pragmatic. The criticism to which the defences were subjected in succeeding years could result as often from the changing fashions and theories of fortification and the improvements in artillery necessitating the adaptation of existing works, as from basic design faults which could conceivably have been avoided in the original construction.

---

53 AOM 289, f. 50.

54 AOM 93, f. 6v.

55 Bosio (III, 741-2) mentions that criticism was coming from various quarters. The Codex Laparelli (f. 15v.) contains Laparelli's answers to some of the points raised.

Despite lengthy discussion of the optimum number and size of bastions on the land front, the decision arrived at in 1566 would appear, in retrospect, to have had serious disadvantages. Della Cornia and Fratino had advocated a restricted front of three large bastions, thereby avoiding the necessity, inherent in Laparelli's plan, of siting the outer bastions on the precipitous slopes overlooking the Grand Harbour and Marsamxett.[56] The arguments of Laparelli, however, in favour of as large a fortified area as possible, bearing in mind the privations suffered during the late siege in the cramped confines of Birgu and Senglea, carried the day. The resulting bastions, SS. Peter and Paul and St. Michael, were subjected to repeated criticism:[57] the ground sloped away so steeply under them that there were areas of dead ground which could not be seen from the ramparts; it was impossible for the bastions to present a low profile on these flanks and consequently both they and the covert-way were very exposed and open to bombardment from the heights across the two harbours. All four bastions of the land front were alleged to be too restricted for the correct deployment of men and artillery; nor was there sufficient space to erect the earth parapets then coming into favour; the alignment of the bastions' flanks was also considered to be at fault. The earlier Italian designers were frequently criticized in later years for the small size of their bastions;[58] but short of demolishing the front there was no way in which those of Valletta could be enlarged or more advantageously sited. To diminish the areas of dead ground it was suggested that orillions might be added to the flanks of the bastions of the front and that the cavaliers of St. James and St. John be raised and enlarged, and there is evidence to suggest that this advice was probably followed in

56 Bosio, III, 747.

57 Criticisms can be found in (1) Vatican Library, Fondo Vaticano Latino (hereafter referred to as Vat. Lat.), 7776, f. 39 (1574).(2) Urb. Lat. 854, f. 182 (? 1570-80), of which copies can be found in Bodleian Library Tanner MS. 231, f. 94 and Western MS. 3031, f. 352; ASV Miscellanea, Arm II, 88, f. 401; British Museum, Harleian MS. 6794, f. 1; Lambeth Palace MS. 490, f. 90v. (3) Vatican Library, Chigi, Q III 69, f. 20 (Campi, 1577). (4) British Museum Additional MS. (hereafter referred to as BM Add.), 48133, f. 298 (G.B. Leone, 1582), of which copies can be found in ASV Fondo Pio 246, f. 260; ASV Miscellanea, Arm. XV, 53, f. 144; Vatican Library Fondo Trivulziano 1467; Chigi, N III 57, f. 225; Vatican Library, Fondo Barberini Latino (hereafter referred to as Barb. Lat.), 5325, f. 42; Trinity College, Cambridge, R 46, f. 298; BM Add. MS. 48146. See also *Archivio storico di Malta*, IV (1933), 1, for location of further manuscripts and a published copy of the report; the report was published again in *Archivio storico di Malta*, VII (1936), 280.

58 Zastrow, 1, 39-42.

Plate 6 Flank of St. John's bastion, Valletta.

the late sixteenth century.[59] The ditch was not fully protected, being too deep and narrow to be observed in all its parts from the ramparts. The widening work could, however, be undertaken gradually and did not involve major structural alterations to building already completed. In accordance with his desire to create a spacious city, Laparelli had sited the lateral walls on low land close to the shore. Short of erecting inordinately high ramparts, which would not accord with the increasing emphasis being placed on the advisability that as low a profile as possible be presented for fear of artillery bombardment, these lateral walls could not protect the higher ground within the city. Although it was suggested that the walls might be raised[60] or that cavaliers could be constructed on the bastions of St. Barbara and St. Sebastian and in the vicinity of St. Elmo,[61] no action was taken. There was general agreement that around St. Elmo too much fore-

59 Vat. Lat. 7776, f. 39; Chigi, Q Ill 69, f. 20; BM Add. MS. 48133, f. 298. The painting by M. Perez d'Aleccio (c. 1580) of Valletta now in the National Maritime Museum, Greenwich, shows the bastions of the land front with orillions.

60 Chigi, Q III 69, f. 20.

61 Vat. Lat. 7776, f. 39.

shore, where the enemy might establish himself, had been left. The obvious solution, to surround the fort by extending the Valletta enceinte, was eventually put into effect in the 1680s.[62]

Once the construction of Valletta had reached a certain stage the practical application of all but minor design improvements was no longer feasible, a fact recognized by the critics of the 1570s and 1580s. They accepted the fortifications as built but suggested possible modifications. Apart from the addition of the Vendôme bastion,[63] and the failure to complete the manderaggio or the arsenal, the fortifications of Valletta in the early seventeenth century were very much as Laparelli had intended. As such, despite their faults, they were renowned throughout Europe as a classic of the engineer's art, and eulogized in Speckle's *Architectura von Festungen* (Strasbourg, 1589). Those features which had already given rise to controversy in the sixteenth century continued to form the basis of the criticism levelled in succeeding years, and by the 1630s it was no longer possible to reconcile the works with contemporary views on fortification design. Rather than attempt any drastic alterations, new fortifications – the Floriana lines and the Valletta counterguards – in the more modern style were added beyond the Valletta front, enclosing it completely. The problem of the bombardment of the city's flanks was also solved by the construction of new defences, the Grand Harbour flank being protected by the Sta. Margherita lines, the Cottonera lines and fort Ricasoli built during the seventeenth century, and the Marsamxett flank by the eighteenth-century forts, Manoel and Tigné.

II. THE FLORIANA FORTIFICATIONS

Growing rumours of an impending Turkish attack in the 1630s finally prompted the knights to take positive steps to improve the fortifications of Valletta. These by then were over sixty years old, and, apart from the addition of the Vendôme bastion, no significant

---

62 The extension of the enceinte is suggested in Vat. Lat. 7776, f. 39 and Chigi, Q III 69, f. 20; for the execution of the work see AOM 1016, pp. 275-85 and 207-17.

63 Erected during the grandmastership of Alof de Wignacourt (1601-22), but there is no contemporary record of its construction. Blondel, writing at the end of the century, says it was named after Alexandre of Vendôme, Grand Prior of France, the illegitimate son of Henri IV, who took a great interest in its building (AOM 1016, p. 191); Vendôme is recorded as having been received into the Order in 1606 (Vertot, IV, 89 third pagination) and the bastion was probably built about 1614.

modifications had been made to the original design. News had already reached Malta in 1633 that a large Turkish fleet was being assembled, and, when the sultan and the Persian king, who had been at war for some years, concluded a peace in 1635, it appeared highly probable that an attack on Malta would materialize. Although the first step taken by the Order was to ensure that the existing defences were ready for action, and to summon knights to Malta,[64] it was also soon decided that there could no longer be further delay in a complete reassessment of the fortifications which, because of continuing development in design, were undoubtedly old-fashioned. Since it was likely that drastic alterations and additions would be deemed necessary the Order determined to procure the services of a respected engineer.[65] The negotiations took several months, and the Order was fortunate that on this occasion, as was so often to be the case, the Turkish threat never became a reality. The pope, having first sent an envoy to inspect the island fortifications, agreed in May 1635 to lend one of his own engineers, Pietro Paolo Floriani, who reached Malta on 1 September.[66]

Although the Order was still determined to proceed with the review of the fortifications some of the sense of urgency had been lost; a seven or eight months' respite could be expected before the new campaigning season; Floriani had taken ill on his journey to Malta and spent his first weeks on the island convalescing.

---

64 November 1633 (AOM 111, f. 14); a commission was appointed which recommended repairs to existing fortifications; similar recommendations were made by commissioners appointed on 16 February 1635 (AOM 256, ff. 126, 128v. and 131); the general citation was issued on 5 March 1635 (AOM 111, f. 119v.).

65 See the Italian letter of the grand master dated 2 March 1635 (AOM 1414, no foliation). A considerable amount of material on the construction of fortifications in the period 1634-9 is found in V. Borg, *Fabio Chigi*.

66 Letters of the Order's ambassadors to the Holy See to the grand master, 19 May 1635 (AOM 1264, no foliation). Floriani was the son of Pompeo Floriani, a well-known military engineer who had advised Don John of Austria on the fortifications of Goletta and Tunis and was the author of *Discorso interno all'isola di Malta* (Macerata, 1576). Among Pietro Paolo's instructors were Alessandro Pallavicini, Orzio del Monte di S. Maria, and Giovanni de' Medici. He entered the service of the Spanish king, reinforced S. Germano in 1617, repaired the defences of Tunis and Algiers in 1618 and saw action in Germany, Hungary and Bohemia. He returned to Italy in 1626 and in the following year was appointed castellan of the Castello S. Angelo in Rome. It was at this time that he is said to have been working on his treatise *Della difesa et ofesa delle piazze* (Macerata, 1630). In 1635 when he was ordered to Malta by the pope he was working on the fortifications of Ferrara. (The details of his career are taken from E. Clausetti, 'Pietro Paolo Floriani, ingegnere militare (1585-1638)' in *Palladio*, III (1939), 153-62.)

Consequently, it was not until 17 October that he presented his first report to the council.[67] Floriani asserted that the Valletta front could not be satisfactorily adapted to meet the needs of modern warfare. He believed the first essential of a defensive work to be that it should keep the enemy at a distance. But Valletta had no outworks to perform this task and the materials necessary to construct them quickly and easily – fascines and earth – were not available.[68] In addition he repeated the criticism earlier levelled against the Valletta front – that the flanks had a poor field of fire, the ditch was too deep and narrow, and the platforms of the bastions too restricted. Floriani recommended that a new line of fortification be built across the peninsula to enclose the old works. He proposed the line be sited approximately 800 canes from the ditch of St. Elmo on the escarpment of the plateau which overlooked Marsa. This site had been considered by Laparelli but rejected since the resulting city would have been too large; Floriani now considered it a positive advantage that the people of the countryside and their beasts could shelter within the new enceinte. The component parts of the front would be larger, *più reali*, than those of Valletta since the main line would consist of only one bastion and two demi-bastions. Two outer lines of defence were contemplated, a broken fausse-braye in front of the curtains and beyond that two ravelins. A modest number, three or four hundred, of extra soldiers would be needed to man these new works; the construction costs would not be excessive because the site would not have to be levelled and the building materials were ready to hand.

Floriani's proposals encountered instant opposition. It may be that his solution to the defects of Valletta was more radical than had been anticipated by some of the knights. Certainly his criticisms of the old front could hardly have come as a surprise since the faults which he detected had already been recognized in the late sixteenth century. Floriani was called before the commissioners of fortifications who examined carefully two models which he had given them, and

---

67 AOM 6554, f. 21; Barb. Lat. 6697, f. 63. Barb. Lat. 9905/3 I shows the land front of Floriana as executed whereas Barb. Lat. 9905/4 is an earlier incomplete version. These plans may be copies of those made by Floriani and may have accompanied this report. P. Marconi, 'I progetti inediti della Valletta: dal Laparelli al Floriani', *Atti del XV Congresso di Storia dell'architettura: l'Architettura a Malta dalla preistoria all'ottocento* (Rome, 1970), 353-86, incorrectly attributes all the plans in Barb. Lat. 9905/1-7 to Floriani.

68 In the *Difesa et ofesa delle Piazze* (libro primo, f. 44) written before his visit to Malta, Floriani described how outworks could be added to a fort using fascines and earth.

objected to the scheme on two grounds, the expense and the length of time it would take to complete. In the commissioners' opinion the old defences could be modified so as to overcome their defects. Floriani, however, rejected this suggestion.[69] He saw Valletta as the key to the defence of the whole island and, accordingly, felt that its fortifications must be as strong as possible; his scheme would offer the capital the best protection. To the chief objections – length of time and expense – he replied that with some 3,000 workmen the new fortifications, front and flanks, could be in a defendable state by the following May or June (1636); with only 2,000 workers the front alone could be ready. The cost, Floriani maintained, would be less than one supposed, although he did not commit himself to any precise figure. Although he asserted that one could not make a silk purse out of a sow's ear (referring to the Valletta front) he was prepared to carry out whatever project the grand master and council should decide upon. He did request, however, that his models be sent to the pope, emperor, kings of France and Spain, and the princes of Italy, both in order to obtain an expert opinion, and to protect his reputation should he be ordered to execute a lesser scheme. The dispute continued and on 10 December Floriani publicly defended his plans at a council meeting.[70] He outlined four major criticisms: that the Order could never raise the money required; that his works would be of no use in the siege which was expected; thirdly, the enlarged enceinte would require more defenders than the Order could provide; and lastly, and more specifically, that the ravelin dominated by the high ground near the Capuchin convent could not be defended. Floriani answered these points briefly. He asserted that the nature of the site was such that building costs would be very low and the use of slave labour would further reduce the expense; that the length of time taken to complete the fortifications was entirely in the hands of the Order, and that if 3,000 workmen were employed the front and flanks could be completed in eight to ten months; that only 400 extra soldiers would be required to man the new defences since the old and new fronts would not be manned simultaneously. While admitting that the ravelin in question was overlooked, Floriani insisted that since it was covered by the front the defenders would be protected. In conclusion he argued that the Turks were no ordinary foe, and that for this reason he had designed particularly strong fortifications.

---

[69] In a report dated 9 November (AOM 6554, f. 25; copies in Barb. Lat. 6697, f. 69 and Chigi, R I 25, f. 311).

[70] Barb. Lat. 6697, f. 72; a summary of his defence is given in a letter written by Chigi on 13 December 1635 (Chigi, A I 3, f. 435v.).

At the end of the council meeting Floriani's plan was approved by thirty-five votes to fourteen[71] and a decree was issued sanctioning the building at the Capuchin convent outside the walls of Valletta of a new town with ditch and fortifications according to the plan.[72] Opposition to the scheme did not die down once the council had reached a decision and authorized its implementation. Indeed, one of the commissioners in charge of the new fortifications, the Bailiff Gattinara, an opponent of Floriani's proposals, resigned his post in protest.[73] Work commenced without delay, although on this occasion, contrary to custom, there was no official stone-laying ceremony to initiate the new project. By the end of January Floriani could report to his patron Cardinal Francesco Barberini that he had finished marking out the fortifications and was ready to proceed to the next stage in their construction; in April he described the works as coming along splendidly.[74] Floriani and the papal delegate in Malta, the Inquisitor Chigi, between them ensured that Barberini was informed of all developments affecting the fortifications. Floriani himself wrote describing the outcome of the council meeting of 10 December and he enclosed with his letter reports and plans outlining the proposed scheme.[75] These Barberini passed on to Vincenzo Maculano da Firenzuola, a well-known expert in military architecture;[76] Firenzuola's written comments on the scheme were conveyed to Floriani, who, although they were in general favourable to his proposals, did not receive them kindly.[77] Firenzuola suggested modifications which, he believed, would make the scheme more compatible with the time and money available, but Floriani insisted that as the engineer on the site he could judge what was most suitable for Malta. Floriani undoubtedly took immense pride in his work and was reluctant to

---

71 Barb. Lat. 6697, f. 73. Floriani's letter to Barberini, dated 27 December 1635 (Barb. Lat. 6697, f. 74), described the dissension within the council. It is very unusual to have a record of the actual voting figures or even any indication of a dispute. The council minutes in the *Libri Conciliorum* and the *Libri Conciliorum Status* merely record final decisions.

72 AOM 111, f. 176v.

73 Barb. Lat. 6697, f. 74v.

74 Barb. Lat. 6697, f. 76 (28 January 1636) and f. 77 (8 April 1636).

75 Barb. Lat. 6697, f. 74.

76 Chigi, A I 4, f. 38v.; Firenzuola, a member of the Dominican Order, while inquisitor at Genoa (1627-9) helped in planning the fortifications of that city. In 1631 he was appointed vicar general of the Dominicans but he gave up this post in December of the following year to become commissioner general of the Holy Office. He carried out important restorations and fortifications at fort Urbano in Bologna and at Castello S. Angelo in Rome.

77 Firenzuola's report is headed 'Venuta di Roma a 15 marzo 1636' (Chigi, R I 25, f. 313); Borg (pp. 34, 200 and 203) describes Floriani's reaction to it.

admit that any improvement to his scheme might be possible. Indeed, from the moment of his arrival in Malta his haughty manner had given offence, and, although Chigi in particular had deplored this, he had been unable to persuade Floriani to modify his attitude.[78] A complicating factor in the various negotiations and discussions on the fortifications was the impending death of the Grand Master de Paule who was a keen supporter of Floriani.[79] A strong candidate to succeed as grand master was the Bailiff Signorino Gattinara, a vehement opponent, and the engineer did nothing to help the situation by declaring that he would at once depart were Gattinara to be elected. In the event his resolution was never put to the test as Jean Paul de Lascaris Castellar was chosen and continued to support Floriani's proposals. In any case, Chigi, quite apart from wishing to avoid trouble with the prima donna-like engineer, had by April 1636 judged that the work had progressed so far that an alteration in design was no longer possible.[80]

Criticism of Floriani's project continued to come, however, from various quarters, from both non-experts and professional engineers. Among the former was Saviour Imbroll, prior of the conventual church, whose views may be considered as representative of a fair body of opinion within the Order.[81] He accepted Floriani's assessment that the Valletta front suffered from five major defects: there were no outworks, the covert-way and ditch lacked any areas in which a sortie force could be assembled, the fire from the bastions did not cover the counterscarp adequately, the ditch was too deep and narrow, and the bastions were too small to allow a rearguard action to be fought. Imbroll questioned whether these faults were irremediable and argued that the old front could be modified to overcome them. Floriani had advanced several positive reasons as to why a new city beyond the walls of Valletta was necessary. His belief that the enemy would launch a very determined attack led him to insist on exceptionally strong fortifications. Valletta, he maintained, was too small to accommodate all who would wish to shelter there during a siege; the old glacis which was defective would be enclosed, as would the whole of the old front with all its faults; the new city could be reinforced and supplied from a strong base, Valletta; finally

---

78 See Borg, pp. 34 and 47.
79 Borg, p. 34.
80 Borg, p. 35.
81 Chigi, R I 25, f. 303 (1636); criticism along similar lines is found in AOM 6402, f. 365, an anonymous report dating from this time.

Floriani stressed that only three or four hundred additional soldiers would be needed, and the scheme would not be unduly expensive. Imbroll countered each of Floriani's points and proceeded to put forward what he considered valid reasons for not building a new city. Firstly, there was the cost which he estimated at 300,000 scudi if the necessary artillery and munitions were included; secondly, the new city would not be defendable until the enceinte was complete; this would take years and in the meantime the old front would remain unimproved and the harbour unprotected from the heights behind Birgu and Senglea; thirdly, it would be impossible to man the new enceinte as it would require a threefold increase in the size of the garrison; fourthly, the extra men would need extra food and munitions; fifthly, the forces of the Order would be divided and commands become confused; finally, it would give rise to contention among the langues over precedence when defensive positions were allotted. Imbroll concluded, therefore, that the new front should not be built but that Valletta should be improved.

Floriani may have viewed the criticism of the knight Lelio Brancaccio in a rather different light from that of Imbroll who had no particular claim to military expertise. Brancaccio, on the other hand, was the author of the work *I carichi militari* (Venice, 1620) and had a reputation as an expert on military affairs. At the time he compiled his report on Floriani's scheme, he was employed in Spain but had earlier served the Spanish crown in the Low Countries.[82] The criticisms advanced by Brancaccio were not original – the overreaching of resources, the merits of the old front, an overambitious design – but Floriani treated them with the respect due to the opinion of an experienced practical man and author, refuting the points raised by reasoned argument and often supporting his views by examples taken from the works of classical authors and from more recent campaigns. It is possible that Floriani hoped by this reasoned discourse to impress his patron Barberini. We know that it was forwarded to Barberini[83] and that the composition of learned treatises, often for publication, was a standard method whereby the engineers of the day publicized their talents.

Despite all the criticism Floriani continued with his original design. He enjoyed the full support of Grand Master Lascaris who

---

82 Summaries of his report together with Floriani's reply are to be found at Barb. Lat. 6697, ff. 78 and 85, and Chigi, R I 25, f. 315.

83 On 15 July 1636 (Barb. Lat. 6697, f. 95).

was most anxious that he should remain in personal charge of the building operations for as long as possible. Lascaris managed to obtain a three months' extension to Floriani's leave of absence, but on 1 October 1636 the engineer requested permission to leave the island and he departed on the 23rd of the month.[84] Floriani's estimate made in November 1635[85] that the fortifications would be finished in May or June 1636 was over optimistic, but progress must have been swift because after only eight months' labour the grand master was claiming that the new works were almost capable of being defended.[86] By the autumn of 1636 Floriani had decided that the final execution of his scheme, which he had guarded so jealously against all suggested alteration, could be safely left to his assistant Francesco Buonamici, who could be trusted to carry out the project faithfully. Buonamici had accompanied Floriani to Malta as his second-in-command, and was to remain in the island for over twenty years serving as the Order's resident engineer.[87] However, Floriani left nothing to chance, and to ensure that Buonamici knew exactly what was expected of him, he drew up full instructions as to how the work was to proceed.[88] To expedite the excavation of the ditch, and other parts of the new front Floriani suggested that all quarrying be restricted to the ditch and other sites as designated by the commissioner of works, so that all the waste material from stone cutting and the building work in general could be used to construct the terrapleins and parapets according to the method already in use. Although the completed work afforded examples of this process, Floriani nevertheless described it: a paste made from a moistened mixture of crushed stone and turma was to be pressed into position in the terrapleins and parapets and allowed to dry into a concrete-

---

84 30 July 1636 petition to pope for extension of Floriani's stay (AOM 1415, no foliation); 30 August request granted (Borg, p. 223); request by Floriani to depart (AOM 111, f. 258); actual departure (Borg, p. 49).

85 AOM 6554, f. 25.

86 Letter to grand duke of Tuscany dated 11 August 1636 (AOM 1415).

87 Francesco Buonamici, a native of Lucca, was active there in the early 1630s. In October 1650 he crossed to Sicily to carry out various civil commissions for the bishop of Syracuse (AOM 473, f. 274v. and S.L. Agnello, 'Michelangelo Buonamici architetto del secolo XVIII in *Atti del XV Congresso di Storia dell'Architettura: l'architettura a Malta dalla preistoria all'ottocento* (Rome 1970), pp. 465-7). On 25 May 1659 he was given permission to return to Lucca and in 1661 he was employed there as 'architetto primario', dying in 1677. There is no evidence that he worked on fortifications outside Malta (AOM 121, f. 17).

88 Chigi, R I 25, f. 329v. (29 September 1636).

like substance.[89] The positioning and size of sally ports and embrasures was laid down, as were the heights of various parts of the fortifications; the fausse-braye parapets were to be six feet lower than those of the lower batteries on the bastions so that the fire from the latter would not be obstructed; the covert-way was to be at least six feet high, and higher where the ground fell away towards the Marsamxett; it was to be thirty-five paces wide; the glacis, from which all the top soil was to be removed, was to extend for approximately 400 feet.

In the parting instructions Floriani was unable to confine himself to factual directions on the execution of the work, but also took the opportunity to justify his scheme yet again. In particular, he argued that his proposal to build houses within the new enceinte would in no way hamper the defence since they would be set well back from the fortifications, and that, moreover, the sale of building plots could raise many thousands of scudi and in constructing the houses good use could be made of the stone excavated from the ditch but not required for the defences. As to garrisoning the new enceinte Floriani adopted a somewhat different line of defence than he had earlier assumed. Instead of emphasizing how few extra soldiers would be required, he now claimed that there were ample men available in the shape of the islanders, 6,000 of whom he reckoned could be called to arms. As to the criticism that he had provided no defence for the harbours, Floriani had several lines of argument: once the new enceinte was finished the fact that the defences of Birgu and Senglea had not been improved would be irrelevant because no enemy would waste time attacking two such unimportant places; he dismissed the forecasts that the Turks would threaten the shipping in the Grand Harbour from a battery on Sta. Margherita hill; such an outpost would be too far from the enemy's main lines and would require a disproportionately large number of defenders ever to be established; the ships in the harbour could, in any case, be protected by materials like wool and sails; should the besiegers force a closure of the Grand Harbour the ships could be switched to the Marsamxett, and any attempt by the enemy to erect a battery on Dragut point would be frustrated by the over-whelming fire-power of

---

89 Turma is a mixture of stone and clay soil. The process described is very like that traditionally used in the construction of the flat roofs of Maltese houses – see H.D. Jones, 'Memoranda and details of the mode of building houses in the island of Malta' in *Papers on Subjects Connected with the Duties of the Corps of Royal Engineers*, V (1842), 196-205.

Valletta. Once Floriani had departed seeds of doubt began to grow in the minds of the knights as to the wisdom of pursuing his plans, and as to the merits of the whole project. Apprehension was expressed as to the cost and completion date of the undertaking, for Floriani seemed to have succumbed to a common fault among military engineers, over-optimism.[90] Accordingly the council decided to obtain a second opinion.[91] Their first choice, the engineer Gian Francesco Cantagallina, was unavailable and a Frenchman named Jardin, who had come to Malta in 1637 in the retinue of Frederick of Hesse Darmstadt, now assumed the direction of the fortification.[92] He drew up new plans recommending that Floriani's scheme be disregarded and that the Order concentrate on improving the Valletta fortifications.[93] But his professional qualifications were questioned by Buonamici and Floriani,[94] while both Inquisitor Chigi and Barberini resented his intrusion into what they regarded as a papal sphere of influence.[95] Despite all the objections, Jardin's plans were examined and approved by the council, which on 29 May 1638 decreed that the proposed fortifications outside the Valletta ditch be made to his designs, provided that expert advice on the plans was first obtained from further foreign engineers.[96] The knight Giovanni Battista Vertoa was therefore dispatched with reports and plans to

---

90 24 November 1636 a commission was appointed to review the cost (AOM 111, f. 274); it reported that 40,000 scudi had been paid out under contracts to craftsmen (AOM 111, f. 276v.; AOM 6554, ff. 8-13 and 15); on 19 January 1637 Chigi estimated that the fortifications might take another year to complete (Borg, p. 246).

91 AOM 256, f. 101 (17 January 1637).

92 AOM 256, f. 168 (8 April 1637). Cantagallina was a well-known engineer who had served the Spanish in the Low Countries before returning to Tuscany in 1626 or 1627. The fortifications of Livorno and Gaeta are attributed to him (Promis, *Miscellanea*, XIV, 85; *Dizionario biografico degli Italiani* (Rome, 1960-) – hereafter referred to as *DBI* – XVIII, 227). The exact identity of Jardin is not known; Floriani wrote of him that he was merely a teacher of mathematics and no engineer (Barb. Lat. 9296, f. 80). Among the French engineers of the time are Claude Dejardins, an architect who worked in Nancy between 1605 and 1646 and undertook some military work there and at Marsal and Stenay (*Dictionnaire de biographie française* (Paris, 1933-) – hereafter referred to as *DBF* – X, 1403) and Nicholas Desjardins an *ingénieur géographe du roi* who was serving at Blaye in 1665 (J. Coutura et al, *La Citadelle de Blaye*, Les cahiers du Vitrezais (Paris, 1978), p. 25).

93 Borg, p. 55.

94 Buonamici described him as a mere soldier (Chigi, A III 57, f. 58); Floriani was goaded into writing a book in defence of his scheme (Chigi, A III 57, f. 57); it was never published, perhaps because of Chigi's disapproval (Chigi, A I 4, f. 262v.) or Floriani's death (28 May 1638).

95 Borg, p. 55.

96 27 February a commission was appointed to examine the plans (AOM 256, f. 177); 29 May decree issued (AOM 256, f. 178v.).

tour the Continent and seek out expert opinion.[97] His journey took him to various Italian principalities and to the French and Spanish armies then engaged in conflict in northern Italy. Those engineers whom he consulted were unanimous in their criticism both of the design and of the siting of the Floriana front:[98] the work was, they believed, on too grand a scale for the Order's resources, and the site was overlooked from the surrounding hills so that it could be enfiladed from the Isoletto and Corradino hill. They advocated instead improvements to the old front, especially the strengthening of its flanks and the addition of outworks, and the construction of fortifications on Sta. Margherita hill. Although the council had sanctioned the execution of Jardin's plans, it lacked the courage of its convictions. Six months elapsed before Vertoa departed to seek approval abroad, and a full year between Jardin's initial proposals and Vertoa's return in February 1639,[99] so that by the time Vertoa submitted the reports he had collected the Order was no longer interested in Jardin's scheme, and the criticisms and suggestions of the distant experts, although interesting as further evidence of the controversy surrounding the Floriana lines, had no practical influence on the fortifications in Malta.

---

97 30 July 1638 Vertoa commissioned (AOM 256, f. 179).

98 The reports AOM 257, f. 6v. and AOM 6554, f. 27 are accounts of Vertoa's travels and consultations. The following engineers' reports have come to light: Chigi, Q III 69, ff. 25 Giuseppe Baracca (23 November 1638, Milan), 26 Giovanni de' Medici (25 December, Canese), 27 Giovanni de' Medici (same report as AOM 6554, f. 17), 31 Conte Ferrante Bolognino (8 December), 31v. Conte Ferrante Bolognino (4 November, Milan), 35 Giovanni de Garay (16 November, Alessandria), 37 François Lecamus (7 October, Pinarolo), 41 Orazio Grassi (Savoy). Baracca was a Milanese engineer and lieutenant general of artillery employed in the Spanish armies. He died in 1639. Giovanni de' Medici was the illegitimate younger brother of Grand Duke Francesco (1574-87). At the age of nineteen he was sent to Flanders and subsequently fought in Hungary and France. In 1610 he was employed by the Venetian Republic and rose to command its army in the War of Gradisca (1615-17) (M. Mallett and J.R. Hale, *The Military Organization of a Renaissance State: Venice c.1400-1617* (Cambridge, 1984), p. 309). The Genoese asked his advice about their fortifications in 1631 (L.C. Forti, *Le Fortificazioni di Genova* (Genoa, 1971), pp. 55 and 72) and in 1638 he was appointed general of artillery and superintendent general of fortresses in the Grand Duchy of Tuscany. Count Ferrante Attendola Bolognino was born in Milan, in 1594 and entered the Order in 1609, serving with the naval squadron. In 1617 he returned to Milan and saw action with the Spanish armies in the Low Countries and Italy, reaching shortly before his death, the rank of superintendent general of fortifications for the state of Milan in 1644 (*DBI*, XI, 356). Giovanni de Garay was a general of artillery in the employ of Spain. François Lecamus appears in the lists as an *ingénieur du roi* in the reign of Louis XIII. In 1638 he was superintendent of fortification in Pinarolo which was then in French hands. Orazio Grassi was born at Savona in 1583. He joined the Society of Jesus. A mathematician of repute, he took part in a famous dispute with Galileo and died in 1654.

99 AOM 257, f. 6v.

In general, the Order, although anxious to obtain the opinion of experts abroad, showed a reluctance to act upon the advice of men who had never visited the island, so that the engineer on the spot enjoyed an immense advantage over his rivals. Vertoa's mission had become redundant because during his absence the knights had secured the services of an engineer in whom they had confidence, Vincenzo Maculano da Firenzuola. Firenzuola was already acquainted with the Maltese fortifications, his advice on Floriani's proposals having been sought by Barberini,[100] although on that occasion Floriani had attached little weight to his opinion because Firenzuola had then been only able to work from maps. The latter was, however, able to remedy this defect in the course of a visit which he made to Malta in the winter of 1638-9. As early as April 1638 Barberini was contemplating sending Firenzuola to the island to counteract the influence of Jardin.[101] Firenzuola could not make the journey until October, but in the meantime Barberini forwarded a report, probably that dated 15 March 1636, which the engineer had already compiled on Floriani's plans. No action was taken on this although the grand master reacted favourably to the prospect of a visit by Firenzuola.[102] After some reluctance on the part of Pope Urban VIII, it was agreed to allow Firenzuola to make a three months' visit to the island, and he arrived on 10 November.[103]

After a detailed inspection of the various fortifications and sites he submitted a report to the council on 26 November.[104] He judged that the prime necessity was to fortify Sta. Margherita, Birgu and Senglea in order to protect the shipping entering the harbour, because in time of siege it was essential that relief ships could reach port with supplies and reinforcements. He did not condemn the Floriana lines out of hand; indeed, he said that the fortifications were of good design and well built, but he thought them of little use since the old front occupied the best site, the highest, on the peninsula. The justification for the new fortifications – that they would keep the enemy at a distance from Valletta – was hardly relevant, because the original glacis of Valletta, composed entirely of stone, afforded no cover under which an attacker could have approached

---

100 Chigi, R I 25, f. 313 (15 March 1636).
101 Borg, p. 55.
102 25 August 1638: he instructed the ambassador in Rome to request a visit (AOM 1417).
103 Letter of the ambassador to the grand master of 9 October 1638 (AOM 1266); Borg, p. 412.
104 AOM 256, f. 185; AOM 6554, f. 47.

the old enceinte. Firenzuola recommended the addition of three ravelins to the Valletta front in order to provide mutual defence. These ravelins would be so constructed, with parapets of solid material not earth, that if captured they could not be turned against the city. Firenzuola dismissed the assertion that Floriana was necessary to provide defending troops with a double line of defence, as the two existing cavaliers performed this function. He could not agree with Floriani's proposal to bring inside the new enceinte all the country dwellers and their animals, for these would merely obstruct the defenders and necessitate the carrying of a greater stock of provisions. His solution to the problem of the non-combatants was to send them to Sicily. On the question of the total cost of Floriana, he estimated that the amount so far spent would double before the work was finished. The council acted upon Firenzuola's recommendation and decreed that three ravelins be added to the Valletta front and fortifications be constructed on Sta. Margherita hill, while work on Floriana was to cease.[105] In accordance with custom, the Christian princes were informed of this important decision and sent plans to acquaint them with the proposals.[106] To take advantage of Firenzuola's presence to supervise the initial stages of the project, work started on 30 December with the laying of the foundation stone of the Sta. Margherita lines.[107] But the pope had released Firenzuola for a strictly limited period; and on 22 January 1639, exactly three months after his departure from Rome, he left Malta to return to Italy.[108] The Order was unable to persuade the Pope to allow a second visit,[109] and secured instead Giovanni de' Medici, Marquis of St. Angelo, on loan from the grand duke of Tuscany.[110]

The proposal to remedy the defects of the Valletta front by the addition of outworks was put forward by several engineers as an alternative to the more grandiose and costly scheme of a new enceinte, suggested by Floriani. Brancaccio, Imbroll, Jardin, Baracca, the Marquis of St. Angelo, Bolognino, Lecamus, Grassi and Firenzuola had all

---

105 AOM 256, f. 185 (26 November 1638); decree confirmed f. 186v. (9 December).

106 AOM 256, f. 185; B. dal Pozzo, *Historia della Sacra Religione Militae di S. Giovanni Gerosolimitano, detta di Malta*, 2 vols. (I, Verona, 1703; II, Venice, 1715), II, 29; Borg, p. 58.

107 AOM 112, f. 177v.; Dal Pozzo, II, 30.

108 AOM 1266 (letter of 22 October 1637); AOM 257, f. 4 (22 January 1638).

109 16 May 1639, the Order requested a return visit (AOM 257, f. 14); 23 May, it heard that he had departed for Lombardy (AOM 257, f. 15); 20 September it was still hoping for his return (AOM 257, f. 37v.).

110 AOM 257, f. 39v. (26 December 1639).

recommended outworks of some variety.[111] Who actually designed the counterguards which were added to the Valletta front in the 1640s is something of a mystery. The most likely contenders for the honour are the two engineers of international reputation who actually visited Malta, Firenzuola and the Marquis of St. Angelo. Firenzuola was first on the scene and in his report of 26 November 1638 proposed that three ravelins be built outside the old front which might suggest that he favoured a system of outworks in front of the three curtains rather than in front of the four bastions.[112] The council decree which authorized the construction of outworks stated that three ravelins or counterguards were to be added to the bastions of the Valletta front in accordance with a design which had been examined in the council.[113] In fact, four counterguards were constructed and when the Marquis of St. Angelo arrived in Malta early in 1640 he claimed that the works then in progress owed their origin and design to a model which he had sent from Italy the previous year.[114] Since this model is lost his claim cannot be substantiated but the decree of 14 September 1639 implemented Firenzuola's scheme, rather than that of the Marquis of St. Angelo. Although Firenzuola had the initial advantage of having presented his proposals in person, it is possible that after his arrival in the island the Marquis of St. Angelo was able to modify the original scheme to include four counterguards and also a small lunette, St. Madeleine, outside the main gate of Valletta, Porta Reale. No doubt the priority which he gave in his reports of 1 and 12 April[115] to finishing the counterguards helped to bring about their speedy completion within five years.[116]

---

111 Barb. Lat. 6697, f. 78; Chigi, R 1 25, f. 303; AOM 256, f. 178v.; Chigi, Q III 69, ff. 25, 27, 31v., 37, and 41; AOM 6554, f. 47 and also the anonymous author of AOM 6402, f. 365.

112 AOM 6554, f. 49v.; Barb. Lat. 9905/1 is a plan showing three ravelins outside the Valletta front which may have accompanied this report but the plan cannot definitely be attributed to Firenzuola. In time the term for an outwork in front of a curtain came to be 'ravelin', and in front of a bastion 'counterguard' but in the 1630s and 1640s there was no clear distinction.

113 AOM 257, f. 36v. (14 September 1639).

114 AOM 6554, f. 31 (1 April 1640); other copies at AOM 6402, f. 401, Barb. Lat. 6697, f. 96, Chigi, N III 61, f. 71, Chigi, N III 77, ff. 140 and 144. The plan which accompanied this report (copies of which survive at Barb. Lat. 9905/5 and Chigi, N III 77, f. 147) shows the Valletta front with four counterguards. St. Angelo's report brought by Vertoa (AOM 6554, f. 17) mentioned outworks but gave no indication of their form or number. For details he referred the reader to a plan and model, both now lost.

115 AOM 6554, ff. 31 and 35.

116 Dal Pozzo (II, 46) says they were finished by 1645.

The Marquis of St. Angelo did not wholeheartedly agree with Floriani's scheme for the defence of Valletta by a new enceinte, but his disapproval fell far short of that of Firenzuola who had proposed the demolition of the half-built Floriana lines. St. Angelo sought to convert the new enceinte into a large hornwork; the Floriana front would remain with slightly modified ravelins and demi-bastions, but in place of the lateral walls which Floriani had designed as bastioned ramparts running along the shore to link up with the bastions of SS. Peter and Paul and St. Michael, St. Angelo proposed the construction of two straight walls joining the counterguards of St. James and St. John to the modified demi-bastions. He did not intend the area enclosed to be anything other than a military position; no houses would be built there and he rejected Floriani's concept of a new city. In common with Floriani, St. Angelo believed that his front, being no larger than that of Valletta, could be defended by the garrison of the old city which, when the hornwork fell, could retreat within the old enceinte to continue its resistance.

When the plan of the Marquis of St. Angelo's proposed alterations is compared with the Floriana fortifications as they stand today, it is apparent that his modifications were not implemented. The present lateral walls are terraplained ramparts which hug the sea shore; the ravelins and demi-bastions of the front have remained true to Floriani's design. The knights indeed always displayed an understandable reluctance to destroy any fortification which was actually standing. And as St. Angelo left Malta after a brief visit of only five weeks he had no opportunity to supervise the execution of his plans.[117] After his departure the work continued under the direction of the resident engineer Buonamici, and the completion of the Valletta counterguards was considered the first priority, while the construction of Floriana, according to the original designs, proceeded in a dilatory fashion. By 1640 the Order had invested so much energy and resources in the building of Floriana that substantial alteration to the basic design, by then well established, was inconceivable. The knights' view of the merit of the Floriana lines was tempered by an appreciation of what was possible given the resources of the Order; military engineers continued to find fault with the fortifications but their advice, although sought by the Order, was rarely acted upon.

---

117 Dal Pozzo (II, 116) says he left on 21 April 1640.

The successful forays of the galleys in 1644, when among the infidel ships captured was one carrying a lady of the seraglio and her child, allegedly the son of the sultan, and the news of the fitting out of a fleet in the Constantinople arsenal, led the Order to fear a large-scale Turkish attack in the summer of 1645. Consequently a general citation, or summons that all able-bodied knights come to Malta and defend the convent, was issued.[118] In addition to members of the Order, volunteers also rallied to the defence of the island. Although it was soon apparent that the destination of the fleet of eighty Turkish galleys was Crete not Malta, the Order decided to take advantage of the skills of the assembled military experts to undertake a review of the fortifications.

Among the distinguished foreigners who visited Malta in the summer of 1645 were the Frenchmen Blaise François Count de Pagan, Louis Nicolas de Clerville and Louis Viscount de Arpajon,[119] whose presence reflected the fact that in the course of the seventeenth century the Order was moving gradually out of the orbit of Spanish influence into that of France. At the same time French engineers were supplanting the Italians as the outstanding designers of fortifications in Europe. Despite the eminence of these French military experts, their criticisms of Floriana and their suggestions for the improvement of both it and Valletta bore little fruit. The only modification executed was the addition of orillion batteries to the four bastions of the Valletta front, as proposed by Pagan.[120] Their criticism of Floriana and Valletta in 1645 followed well established

---

118 Citation AOM 257, f. 195 (24 January 1645); also the Maltese were ordered to work one day a week on the fortifications – AOM 257, f. 197 (7 February 1645) and AOM 6553, ff. 23 and 24v.

119 The Count Pagan, born 1604, had a distinguished career in the service of the French crown from 1616 until he was blinded in 1642. He was present at various sieges, Caen in 1620, La Rochelle in 1626, Nancy in 1633, Arras in 1640; he served under the Chevalier de Ville in campaigns in Picardy and Flanders. After losing his sight he continued work as a mathematician and published *Les Fortifications* (Paris, 1645). He died in 1665.

Clerville rose to prominence in the years after his visit to Malta, serving in Italy, the Low Countries and various parts of France itself. He was appointed field marshal in 1652 and in the 1660s was commissioner general of fortifications and had among his subordinates Sébastien le Prestre de Vauban who later occupied this position himself. Clerville became governor of the isle and citadel of Oléron in 1671 and died six years later.

Arpajon was created a field marshal in 1622; he was a soldier rather than a specialist engineer but he was present at many sieges and in 1642 was sent to Guyenne to prepare the defences against a Spanish attack. In 1657 he was appointed lieutenant of the royal regiment of infantry. He died in 1679.

120 AOM 6554, f. 88.

lines: the works could be overlooked and enfiladed from the surrounding heights; there were areas of dead ground which could be covered by fire from no part of the fortifications.[121] The engineers offered a variety of remedies to these defects. The general opinion, however, was that the construction of Floriana was so far advanced that the project should be completed with only minor modifications.[122] Pallavicino (an Italian knight), Pagan and Clerville all wished to strengthen the flanks of the Floriana front: the first by the addition of a low flanking post outside the Salvatore counterguard on the Marsamxett shore to protect against enfilade from an enemy battery sited on the Isoletto;[123] Pagan, also anxious to prevent bombardment from the Isoletto, recommended a realignment of the curtain between the centre bastion, St. James's, and the Salvatore bastion, and a realignment of the latter bastion itself; Clerville suggested alterations to the ravelins of the Floriana front, but declared himself strongly in favour of Floriani's design for lateral walls running along the shore, as he believed these would in part compensate for the weakness of the flanks of the fortifications and deny the enemy a foothold on Sciberras. Floriana, even when finished, was not considered the complete answer to the weaknesses of the old front of Valletta. Arpajon recommended that a hornwork be built to dominate all the area between Valletta and Floriana.[124] Clerville also proposed a hornwork to cover Porta Reale, and, to assist a retreat should Floriana fall, the construction of redoubts in the area between the old and new fronts; moreover Clerville approved the erection, already under way, of a low battery on the Marsamxett flank of St. Andrew's bastion.[125] Pagan favoured the addition of orillion batteries to the bastions of the old front.[126] Of all the proposals put forward in 1645 only this last one appears to have been implemented. The

---

121 AOM 6554, ff. 69 anonymous report presented to Luca Bueno the vice-chancellor; 75 report by knight Giovanni Bendinelli Pallavicino (8 July 1645); 83v. report by Pagan; 105 report by Arpajon (18 May 1645).

122 Only the author of AOM 6554, f. 69, suggested that work on Floriana be discontinued.

123 It is doubtful whether any such post was built. If it was it would have been incorporated in the Sa Maison bastion which forms part of the fausse-braye built in 1670.

124 AOM 6554, f. 69, suggested the addition of a hornwork to the Valletta front as an alternative to the completion of Floriana.

125 It is possible that the work referred to here is St. Andrew's tenaille. There is no record of the building of this tenaille but it appears on eighteenth-century plans.

126 AOM 6554, f. 88. Some plans made *c.* 1640 (Barb. Lat. 9905/4 and 5) show the Valletta front as having orillions and high- and low-level batteries, whereas another (Barb. Lat. 9905/1) shows only the orillions.

Plate 7 The central bastion, Floriana.

congregation of war decided that it was financially impossible to build the hornwork recommended by Arpajon which would require the labour of 2,000 men.[127] Instead it was suggested that the two walls proposed by the Marquis of St. Angelo be erected since they could be completed in a shorter time, would cost less, and have the same effect as a hornwork in covering a retreat and preventing an enemy attack from the rear.[128] The council of the Order accepted the congregation's decision and enacted several decrees to ensure that the workforce employed in the completion of Floriana was adequate.[129] In under a month's time, on 17 June, the langues were allotted their defensive positions in the Floriana enceinte, thereby implying that the fortifications were in a defendable state.[130] After hearing the report by Clerville the congregation, with the approval of the other engineers, decided to implement his recommendations

127 AOM 6554, f. 107 (20 May 1645).

128 Dal Pozzo (II, 141), probably basing his statement on the council decree of 20 May, says that it was decided to construct a hornwork outside Porta Reale but there is no evidence that such a work was built.

129 AOM 258, ff. 7 (20 May), 20v. (12 June), 24v. (18 June 1645).

130 AOM 258, f. 24v.

for Floriana, but there is no evidence either among the written records or in the fortifications themselves that this decree was in fact ever carried out.[131]

It appears that by 1650, although work was still in progress, the fortifications of Floriana were receiving their finishing touches and the massive building operations of former years were a thing of the past. In 1650 the front consisted of a large central bastion and two flanking demi-bastions with a ravelin in front of each of the linking curtains. The lateral walls, despite all suggestions to the contrary, seem to have been built according to Floriani's original plan, and this remains their present line. The counterguards of Valletta were said to be complete by 1645,[132] which there is no reason to doubt because the visit of the Marquis of St. Angelo in 1640 served to give impetus to the project. The same engineer also deserves credit for hastening the work in Floriana which had lost its momentum after Firenzuola's departure in 1638.

III. Additions and Alterations to Valletta and Floriana in the Late Seventeenth Century

Interest in the defences of the islands revived again after the fall of Crete to the Turks in 1669, for the Order had good reason to believe that Malta might be the next target. The knights had sent what aid they could to the Venetians and had played a valiant part in the defence of the island.[133] Believing themselves threatened by a full-scale invasion, the knights, who in the intervening years of comparative peace had contented themselves with routine tasks of maintenance and the gradual completion of work in hand, once again embarked on an ambitious programme to improve and extend the fortifications.

The level of activity in the two decades before 1670 can be gauged to some extent by the average annual expenditure of the commissioners of fortification during these years. The total sum spent on the fortifications of Valletta, Floriana, the Three Cities – Birgu (Vittoriosa), L-Isla (Senglea) and Bormla (Cospicua) – and Sta. Margherita was only 3,000 to 4,000 scudi a year in contrast to the

131 AOM 6553, f. 63 (7 June 1645); the fact that the lateral walls designed by Floriani remained unchanged may be ascribed to the forces of inertia rather than to Clerville's approval.

132 Dal Pozzo, II, 46.

133 See E. Eickhoff, *Venedig, Wien und die Osmanen* (Munich, 1970).

67,000 scudi which had been expended in the two and a half years immediately prior to June 1642 on the Valletta counterguards.[134] By 1657 the task of completing Floriana was considered sufficiently important for the common treasury to allocate 200 scudi a month for this specific purpose, which was later raised by 100 scudi for a limited period of four months, and in 1666 500 scudi a month was assigned for the building of a ravelin at Floriana.[135] Although this latest allocation was originally intended as of a six-months' temporary measure, it was later extended indefinitely.[136] In 1668 the level of grant was once again raised, to 1,000 copper scudi a month.[137] The incomplete state of Floriana was obviously considered a weak point in the defences of the convent, yet despite such regular supplies of funds from the common treasury, 1669, the year in which Crete fell to the Turks, still found the Floriana fortifications unfinished.

In the face of what appeared to be an emergency, the knights followed their customary practice and decided to summon an expert engineer from abroad, hoping that he could advise as to how the Floriana enceinte might be completed and also judge whether any new fortifications might be required. On this occasion the Order selected as visiting expert the chief engineer of the duke of Savoy, Count Antonio Maurizio Valperga.[138] After a delay of nearly a year, Valperga arrived in Malta in February 1670.[139] Two months later, on 2 April, the council approved his plan to correct and finish the Floriana fortifications, and decided to implement his design for new

---

134 AOM 257, f. 114v. (13 June 1642). This document and those referred to in notes 135-7 below are accounts rendered by the commissioners to the council.

135 AOM 260, f. 20 (8 November 1657); AOM 261, f. 42v. (15 March 1666).

136 AOM 261, f. 59 (29 October 1666).

137 AOM 261, f. 105 (27 August 1668).

138 AOM 261, f. 131v. (27 March 1669); Antonio Maurizio Valperga came from a family of engineers from Turin. His father Maurizio and his brother Andrea were also well-known engineers. Antonio Maurizio served in the French army led by Thomas of Savoy Carignan and Henry of Guise which intervened in the Neapolitan revolt of 1647. He was captured and spent many years imprisoned in Naples during which time he published *Esssercitio militare a beneficio del nuovo soldato* (Naples, 1653), and *Indirizzo del nuovo soldato* (Naples, 1655). Following the peace between Spain and France in 1660 he returned to Turin and was appointed professor of mathematics at the Accademia de' Nobili. After his visit to Malta in 1670 he returned to his native city and the employ of the duke of Savoy. His last connection with Malta appears to have been in 1680 when he wrote a letter from Turin concerning the Cottonera ravelins (AOM 6551, f. 60). There is a brief biography by C. Promis in 'Gl'ingegneri militari che operano o scrissero in Piemonte dal 1300 al 1650' in *Miscellanea di storia italiana*, XII (Turin, 1871), 635.

139 Dal Pozzo, II, 387.

works on Sta. Margherita hill.[140] Valperga proposed supplementary outworks to correct the long acknowledged faults of the Floriana front. The high ground to the left within musket-range which was not visible from the main works was to be occupied by a crowned-hornwork; the demi-bastions were to be strengthened by the addition of two bastions, one overlooking Grand Harbour, the other Marsamxett, and the whole front to be enclosed in a braye which would act as an extra enceinte.[141] Work on the new fortifications began in the summer of 1670 while Valperga was in Malta. Before he departed in November of that year, he drew up a further report which dealt with Floriana, the new works on Sta. Margherita hill known as the Cottonera lines and the new fort Ricasoli at the entrance to Grand Harbour.[142] The resident engineer, the Frenchman Mederico Blondel,[143] was left in charge of the general conduct of the building work and this detailed report was probably intended as a guide to assist him in this task. Unfortunately Blondel was enjoying sick leave in Rome while Valperga was in Malta outlining and initiating his schemes, and in the event he and his more famous brother, François, were highly critical of Valperga's ability, Mederico obviously resenting the lack of consultation which resulted in his having to execute designs of which he did not approve.[144] But despite his complaints, Blondel seems to have carried out Valperga's designs faithfully.

In his report of 15 October Valperga was chiefly concerned with modifications to the right demi-bastion of the Floriana front. Its

140 AOM 261, f. 161v.

141 Dal Pozzo, II, 387; AOM 6554, f. 115 – a summary of Valperga's proposals, other copies of which can be found in AOM 1011, f. 8 and AOM 6551, f. 44. The actual report submitted by Valperga has not come to light. Valperga and subsequent engineers referred to the Floriana fausse-braye, although, strictly speaking, since it has a ditch both in front and behind, it is a braye.

142 AOM 6554, f. 119 (15 October 1670); with other copies at AOM 6402, f. 312 and AOM 6551, f. 45.

143 Mederico Blondel arrived in Malta early in 1659 and was employed by the Order as resident engineer. He was the son of Louis Blondel de Croisettes, ordinary architect in things military to the French king, and brother of François Blondel, a well-known mathematician and member of the Académie des Sciences who rose to the rank of field marshal in the French armies and was the author of *Nouvelle manière de fortifier les places* (Paris, 1683) and *L'Art de jetter les bombes* (Paris, 1683). Mederico remained in the Order's service until his death in 1698 but was absent from the island on sick leave for prolonged periods in the late 1660s and 1670s.

144 Public Record Office, London, War Office Collection (hereafter referred to as PRO WO), 55, 1555/11, p. 106; F. Blondel, *Nouvelle manière*, p. 11.

weakness had been recognized by earlier engineers; its salient angle was too acute, and, because of the steep slope of the terrain, expanses of dead ground remained which could not be covered from the demi-bastion. Valperga ordered that a bastion (which he named La Vittoria, but which is now known as Sa Maison) be built along the Marsamxett shore linking up with the fausse-braye and equal to it in height. He also proposed retrenchments in the demi-bastion itself, the Salvatore bastion and the counterguard. The height of the fausse-braye was to be adapted to the level of the site, rising twenty-one palms, in three steps of seven palms, from where it abutted the Sa Maison bastion to the Capuchin demi-bastion on the opposite flank. Two sally ports were to be made, one in the re-entrant angle outside the Salvatore bastion, the other to give access to the crowned-hornwork. The crowned-hornwork was to be constructed according to the design which had been traced out in earth, taking care that it remained one cane lower than the fausse-braye. The principal gate of Floriana was to be in line with that of Valletta. Despite all previous orders and decrees on the subject, it appears that the parapets and terrapleins, especially those of the lateral walls linking Floriana to Valletta, were still incomplete. Valperga instructed that they, together with the ditches, should be finished. He recommended, in accordance with Floriani's original proposal, the building of houses in the area enclosed by the Floriana enceinte, a suggestion not, however, acted upon until the eighteenth century. He also recommended the construction of a round tower, larger than a sentry tower, in the re-entrant angle of the Capuchin bastion overlooking the Grand Harbour, but there is no evidence that such a work was in fact ever executed. Whatever his original intention in his proposals of 2 April, Valperga did not construct a low defence post on this flank to correspond to the Sa Maison bastion.

When Valperga left in November 1670 work was already well under way in building the fausse-braye and in modifying the right flank of the Floriana front. Work progressed without major interruption and by 1681 it was finished. The construction of the crowned-hornwork, whose design had been traced out by Valperga, was undertaken in 1671 following a donation for the purpose by Juan Galdiano, Prior of Navarre.[145] In recognition of his generosity the crowned-hornwork was named *La Galdiana* and graced with the donor's coat of

[145] AOM 261, f. 176v. (14 May); Dal Pozzo, II, 394. It was not uncommon for knights to make such donations: see chapter 11.

arms and a suitable inscription. The Order, although it had cast Valperga in the role of visiting overseas military expert and had entrusted to him the revision of the islands' defences, still felt obliged to seek second, third and further opinions on his proposals. As had been the case in 1637-8 when Vertoa had been sent round the courts of Italy, the knights in fact implemented Valperga's recommendations before they had received the advice sought from abroad. This pattern of behaviour repeats itself time and again, and one wonders whether the amassing of expert opinion represented no more than an exercise in public relations.[146] The Order, because so many of its assets were located outside Malta, depended heavily on the good will of the European rulers, and publicity given to fresh fortifications might have been presumed to reassure the powers that the Order continued to perform a useful role as the bastion of Christendom and had not degenerated into an association of fainéant aristocrats. Whereas other states might be reluctant to reveal the secrets of their defences, the Order, mistakenly as it happened, believed it had nothing to fear from the Catholic powers, and could even hope that some financial aid might be forthcoming. It may also be possible that the decision to send abroad for advice was a political manoeuvre designed to silence opposition to a scheme from within the Order. The bitter quarrels over the relative merits of Floriani's and Firenzuola's proposals show that feelings could undoubtedly run high, aggravated by the rivalry of different nationalities.[147] The promise to submit a scheme for outside assessment allowed tempers to cool, while ensuring that long before any reply was received the attention of the ever-factious knights had been diverted to some other burning issue of the day.

Criticism centred on Valperga's proposal for Sta. Margherita hill, but Venetian engineers, who examined the plans and reports sent from Malta at a conference held in the house of Montbrun Marquis of St. André, also found fault with his suggestions for the improvement of Floriana. Montbrun, disclaiming any theoretical knowledge and basing his opinion on practical experience, criticized some aspects of the design of the fausse-braye.[148] The report from the Count Verneda,

---

146 For other examples see chapters: 4, ii (Firenzuola, 1636, and Vertoa, 1638); 5, i (Vertoa, 1638, and Riccardo, 1639); 5, ii (Beretta and Verneda, 1671); 8, i (Chambray, 1753).

147 The decision to employ the papal engineer Floriani was probably an attempt to appease both the French and Spanish factions, each of which were insisting that a fellow countryman review the fortifications (Borg, p. 28).

148 AOM 6551, f. 49v.; Montbrun had served in Crete where he commanded a French contingent (Eickhoff, p. 244).

chief engineer of the Venetian Republic, was critical of the crowned-hornwork;[149] he considered that it would fall to the enemy relatively quickly and could then be turned against the defenders. He also commented upon the weakness of the flanks of the Floriana front, proposing that the dead ground to the right, in the valley of the Madonna di Pietà, should be covered by a large mezzaluna and a fort towards the shore. Despite these unfavourable comments, and the disapproval of Blondel, Valperga's proposals for Floriana seem to have been carried out more or less as he intended.

In 1681 Blondel submitted a report on the state of the fortifications in which, while anxious to dissociate himself from any shortcomings in the fortifications designed by Valperga, he nevertheless made it clear that these works had been executed.[150] Against the general run of engineers' opinions, Blondel was full of praise for the original Floriana front, going so far as to describe it as 'the strongest and best part of the fortifications and the most easy to sustain, defend and hold'. This being the case, he could hardly have been expected to approve Valperga's 'improvements'. The fausse-braye had been constructed to the latter's design and as a result the re-entrant angles were not covered by flanking fire. Blondel suggested that this fault could be remedied by removing the re-entrant parts of the fausse-braye so that the remains of the work would form counterguards around the bastions and ravelins. He criticized the crowned-hornwork as too small to accommodate the number of men necessary for its defence; a defect, he believed, which could be corrected by the addition of a retrenched ravelin flanked by the tenailles of the hornwork in the place of arms of the crownwork, and by the addition of two ravelins in front of the crownwork. Not unnaturally, since they were substantially as Floriani had designed them, Blondel found nothing to criticize in the lateral walls linking Valletta and Floriana. However, for added protection, he recommended that, where the terrain permitted, ditches and a parapet be cut on the steep Grand Harbour shore. Work had in fact started on such ditches but had not progressed far. As on the Marsamxett flank it was impracticable to construct ditches, he advised that a parapet be built supplemented by low attached ravelins in front of the curtains. Although Blondel acquired certificates from leading French

---

149 AOM 6551, f. 55v. (30 July 1670); Verneda had served in Crete for twenty-nine months as chief engineer and superintendent of artillery and fortifications, so that he could be regarded as an expert in siege warfare against the Turks.

150 PRO WO 55, 1555/1, 'Dévis général des fortifications de Malte'.

engineers of the day attesting the merits of his proposals,[151] there is no evidence that any of his suggestions were implemented. Modification of the Floriana front had to await the summoning of another expert from abroad in the 1680s.

By the end of 1680 unsolved problems and difficulties in the execution of Valperga's designs had reached such a level that Grand Master Carafa decided that the task was beyond Blondel, who was at the time in any case dogged by ill-health and on sick leave in Rome, and that it was necessary to obtain the advice of an outside engineer of standing.[152] Accordingly it was arranged that Carl Grunenberg, a Flemish engineer in charge of the fortifications of the Sicilian kingdom, should visit Malta. He arrived in January of the following year and on 15 March submitted his first report on the island's defences to the council.[153] Grunenberg reiterated the familiar criticisms of the Floriana front: that the salient angles of the demi-bastions were too acute and that the front had been constructed on a straight line from harbour to harbour without regard to the nature of the terrain. He suggested adjustments to the heights of the fausse-braye and of the demi-bastions, a widening of the covert-way of the hornwork so that it could be covered from the main defences, and the construction of caponiers in the ditch to provide a secure means of communication between the main enceinte and the outworks. As the ditches themselves, together with the fausse-braye and glacis, were still unfinished, he recommended their completion. The lateral walls for the most part lacked terrapleins, and even

151 PRO WO 55, 1555/1 after the main foliation, certificates from Sébastien le Prestre de Vauban, Alain Manesson Mallet, François de Vendôme Duke of Beaufort, De la Boissière, Pierre Mallel, François Houssaye and François Blondel. Mallet (1630-1706) entered the Portuguese service in 1660 as an engineer and on his return to France was appointed a professor of mathematics to the pages of the Petite-Ecurie. He published *Les Travaux de Mars* (Paris, 1671), *Description de l'univers* (Paris, 1683), and *La Géométrie pratique divisée en quartre livres* (Paris, 1702). Charles de Sauvage de la Boissière, born before 1625, was a long-serving *ingénieur du roi*. Dasfeld, who had become director of fortifications in 1715, tried unsuccessfully in 1716 to retire him on a pension, but he died in office aged ninety-one. Pierre Mallel and François Houssaye were described as *ingénieurs ordinaires du roi*.

152 AOM 262, f. 124 (29 October 1680).

153 AOM 262, f. 128v; report dated 14 March – AOM 6554, f. 167 with a copy at AOM 6551, f. 62v. Before he came to Sicily Grunenberg had worked with his brother on a scheme to render the river Mazanarre navigable from Aranjuez to Toledo. He was responsible for the building of the citadel of Messina, the most important Spanish fortification in seventeenth-century Sicily. He played a large part in the redesign of Catania and Messina after the earthquake of 1693. (S. Boscarino, 'Catania: le fortificazioni alla fine del seicento ed il piano di ricostruzione dopo il terremoto del 1693'. *Quaderno dell'Istituto Dipartimentale di Architettura ed Urbanistica*, Università di Catania, VIII (1976), 69.

where these were in position, he realized that it would be necessary to construct traverses to protect the demi-bastions of the front from attack from the flanks and rear. In so far as the council decreed that the completion of Floriana was of utmost importance, and the work on other projects was suspended,[154] Grunenberg's report can be seen as giving impetus to the long-drawn-out task of perfecting Floriana, although it is not actually possible to identify particular modifications resulting from the recommendations of 1681.

Grunenberg probably returned to Sicily soon after making his report. In the absence of Blondel, the knight Ugo de Vauvilliers was appointed to supervise the construction of the fortifications.[155] On his return Blondel resented the intervention of Vauvilliers, whom he considered an inexperienced amateur, and the relationship between the resident engineer and Vauvilliers, then under-commissioner of fortifications, was not a harmonious one. The situation was not helped by Grunenberg's continuing interest in the fortifications, as when he wrote a letter from Messina in August 1682 expressing his confidence, despite the grand master's misgivings, in Vauvilliers's ability to carry out the necessary adjustments to the covert-way.[156] In the following year the grand master had actually come to believe that the difficulties encountered were such that Grunenberg's presence was again required in Malta. However, on this occasion the viceroy was unwilling or unable to release him.[157]

Grunenberg's second visit to Malta eventually took place in 1687. He arrived in January in answer to a request from the grand master, and some six weeks later, having examined the progress of the fortifications, reported to the council.[158] His recommendations regarding Floriana did not differ substantially from those of 1681, for he continued to insist that the first priority should be the completion of the work modifying those parts known to be weak. The Capuchin convent, which predated that front, obstructed the gorge of the left demi-bastion and would have to be re-sited elsewhere.[159] Alterations were

154 AOM 262, f. 128v.

155 AOM 262, f. 129v. (16 April 1681). Vauvilliers was, by virtue of his position as commissioner of posts, deputy ordinary commissioner of fortification. See chapter 9 for a description of the duties of this official.

156 AOM 6554, f. 185 (10 August 1682); copy at AOM 6551, f. 65v.

157 AOM 262, f. 160 (12 October 1683).

158 AOM 262, f. 289v. (18 January 1687); AOM 6554, f. 187 (26 February 1687); presented to the council on 1 March, AOM 262, f. 292v.

159 Grunenberg subsequently submitted a memorandum suggesting an alternative site (AOM 6554, f. 197). The advisability of demolishing the convent had been considered as early

necessary to the main ditch, counterscarp and covert-way of the crowned-hornwork. The details of these modifications were given in a later report but even then Grunenberg did not propose any drastic amendment of the Floriana fortifications.[160] When he turned his attention to the protection of the mouths of both Grand Harbour and the Marsamxett a more radical approach was however necessary. He proposed that low-level batteries should be constructed on the rocks surrounding St. Angelo, Senglea point, Ricasoli and St. Elmo. Around the last, these batteries would form a fausse-braye of three nonsymmetrical bastions and curtains which would guard the entrances of both ports.[161] In a later report Grunenberg gave more detailed specifications for the new enceinte, and suggested that the exterior walls which would be exposed to salt spray should not be built of the common building stone, *franka*, as this weathered very badly, but of *żonqor* which was far more resistant under such conditions.[162] Further protection was to be afforded to the walls by the use of mortar and pozzolana in the construction of the more exposed parts.

As before, Grunenberg did not remain in Malta to supervise the execution of his plans; that task was left to Blondel. After considering the report of 26 February the council decided that work on the completion of Floriana could continue at no great cost, and that by advancing some money allocated to the fortifications, work on the new enceinte around St. Elmo could commence immediately.[163] Work continued on Floriana but it dragged on for so many years that Grunenberg cannot be given much credit for hurrying its completion. On the other hand, possibly because the Grand Master Carafa took a fancy to the scheme as a fitting monument to perpetuate the memory of his name, the new enceinte was begun without delay and speedily completed.[164] Blondel obviously approved of the additions to St.

---

as 1636 (AOM 111, f. 268) but no action had been taken and the convent still stands in the midst of the Floriana lines.

160 AOM 6554, f. 199 (13 March 1687).

161 Starting from the Vendôme bastion these new bastions are St. Gregory's bastion, Sta. Toscana's or St. Gregory's curtain, Conception bastion (renamed Ball's in the nineteenth century), Sta. Scholastica's (or Ball's) curtain, St. John's (or Abercrombie's) bastion and St. Ubaldesca's curtain which links up with St. Lazarus bastion. Grunenherg did not use these names but they were in current use shortly afterwards in the 1690s (AOM 1016); the design of the Marsamxett flank of the new enceinte can be seen in a now-damaged stone model, displayed in the Palace Armoury, Valletta, which originally accompanied Grunenberg's report.

162 AOM 6554, f. 199 (13 March 1687), and see chapter 10 on building materials in Malta.

163 AOM 262, f. 292v. (1 March 1687).

164 The foundation stone was laid on 28 May 1687 (AOM 263, f. 11; Dal Pozzo, II, 632) and the project complete by December 1689 (AOM 263, f. 62v.); its progress is recorded in AOM 1016.

Elmo. He had already in 1681 commented on the vulnerability of the fort and in the summer of 1687 he drew up a report which was not an account of the progress of the scheme but a further exposition of the whole plan.[165] In it he outlined six reasons for undertaking this building programme. The first four were military: to complete the enceinte of Valletta by enclosing St. Elmo; to deny the enemy access to the rocks at the foot of the fort; by converting St. Elmo into virtually a third cavalier on the city walls, to remove any threat posed to Valletta by its weakness which might result in its loss and use against the city; to flank and defend the entrances to both harbours. The fifth reason Blondel classified as one of propaganda – the new enceinte would confront visitors with a view of the island worthy of its claim to be the bastion of Christendom. Finally, the scheme would benefit the public by providing more level space of which there was little enough in Valletta because of the precipitous nature of the site. Blondel confirmed that *żonqor*, pozzolana and mortar were being used in accordance with Grunenberg's instructions; that the internal walls supporting the terrapleins were to be perpendicular but the outer ones were to have an incline of one in six, and that the new building was to be of the same height as the existing ramparts of Valletta, with which it would thus form a continuous enceinte.

The construction of the new bastions had not left the original fort St. Elmo entirely untouched, for the spur of the old cavalier had to be rebuilt as it protruded into the new enceinte.[166] Blondel was unable, owing to illness, to supervise this operation and he later complained so bitterly of the incompetence of Vauvilliers (to whom it had been entrusted) in demolishing a platform which should have remained intact, that the platform was re-erected conforming, so Blondel claimed, to the design sanctioned by the council.[167]

A further dispute arose over the question of the Vendôme bastion. Vauvilliers had suggested that it be dismantled. But just as Blondel was writing a reply to the proposal, Grunenberg was hourly expected from Sicily to ratify Vauvilliers's recommendation. Blondel stoutly defended the bastion:[168] Vauvilliers claimed that it was an eyesore, an obstruction, and that it had outgrown its usefulness. Blondel refuted all these criticisms. It was, he said, built to the same pattern

---

[165] PRO WO 55, 1555/1 (1681); AOM 1016, p. 277 (6 July 1687).
[166] Decree sanctioning the rebuilding passed 19 February 1689 (AOM 263, f. 49v.).
[167] AOM 1016, p. 207 (23 November 1689).
[168] AOM 1016, p. 183 (14 November 1689).

as the other Valletta bastions and although somewhat weathered, could easily be made good; it in no way impeded passage between the French curtain in the old enceinte and the St. Gregory bastion in the new; it was still of strategic value against Dragut point as it was higher than either of the adjoining bastions. In addition, so as to increase the fire power which could be brought to bear on the point, Blondel suggested that St. Sebastian's bastion should be raised and converted into a double platform.[169] But there was yet another proposal made in his absence to which Blondel took exception.[170] It had then been decided to build a low platform to defend the rock at the foot of the left face of St. Christopher's bastion. The preliminary levelling work was complete and had there not been a delay in obtaining *żonqor* the building of the actual platform would have been well under way. However, as Blondel had indicated, Grunenberg was awaited to give his expert opinion on the island's defences yet again. Soon after his own arrival in December 1689 Blondel submitted Vauvilliers's schemes for the Vendôme and St. Christopher's bastions to Grunenberg, who joined him in his opposition to the proposals.[171] On this occasion Grunenberg, while emphasizing the need to finish Floriana and the Galdiana crowned-hornwork, concentrated his energies on ensuring that the batteries which he had recommended in 1687 were indeed added to St. Angelo.[172]

During Blondel's final years as resident engineer, from 1690 until his death in the late 1690s, no major new works were undertaken in Valletta and the activity in the city was entirely routine.[173] The Order was, for example, dissatisfied with the state of the Galdiana crowned-hornwork which was held to be the weakest point of the Floriana front. Accordingly, in 1692 it was decreed that a braye designed by Blondel should be added, in front of the crownwork, but if this scheme was ever implemented no trace of it now remains.[174]

---

169 AOM 1016, p. 192. There is no evidence to show whether or not this was done.

170 AOM 1016, p. 189.

171 AOM 1016, p. 189.

172 AOM 263, f. 62v. (17 December 1689); AOM 6554, ff. 205 and 209.

173 1698 is given as the date of his death in Clerkenwell, MS. O 1, item 16 (MS. entitled 'Notes on the fortifications of Malta' in the Library of the Order of St. John, St. John's Gate, Clerkenwell, London), which is a brief outline of the various schemes proposed for Sta. Margherita hill written after 1761; the final dated report by Blondel in the Order's archives is of 26 October 1695 (AOM 1016, p. 291). See AOM 1016 *passim* for routine activities.

174 Decree issued on 21 April 1692 by congregation of fortification and war (AOM 1016, p. 55) which visited the site shortly afterwards; apparently work on Floriana had completely ceased prior to this decree. Blondel's report which accompanied a plan of the braye, or fausse-braye

Work on the Floriana defences in the 1690s followed the same pattern as that in Valletta: routine maintenance and desultory progress towards the final completion of the grand design.

Early in 1696 the Order once again felt itself in need of an engineer, although it is not clear whether he was to be a replacement for Blondel as resident adviser, or an outside expert invited for a brief visit. The French engineers, headed by Vauban, had by this time established a leading reputation in military architecture and it was to France that the Order turned in its search. After some abortive enquiries in the late 1690s[175] the Frenchman Claude de Colongues arrived in March 1703, and on 17 April it was decided to implement his proposals for the completion of the Galdiana crowned-hornwork and the covert-way on the right flank of the Floriana front.[176] However, before his plans could be put into effect Colongues left Malta taking with him copies of his proposals to show to Vauban in the hope of winning his approval. As he was about to embark on his return journey to the island he died, and the knights were again left without an engineer, a situation which, despite protracted negotiations, was to remain the case for several years. Although the names of various engineers were bandied about in the correspondence between the grand master and the Order's ambassadors in Paris, none actually materialized from this quarter.[177]

In the spring of 1708 the knights believed a Turkish attack to be imminent.[178] As France and thus most French engineers were fully committed to campaigns in Italy, Catalonia, Germany and Flanders, they approached the grand duke of Tuscany and the pope in the hope that one or other might release an engineer.[179] In the event the papal engineer, Johan Hecker, was in Malta by the end of April hard at work inspecting the defences.[180] He made various recommendations including instructions for the completion of the crownwork[181] and

---

as he called it, is dated 31 August 1692 (AOM 1016, pp. 101-8) and embodies the proposals outlined in April, which he repeated orally to the congregation on 24 August (AOM 1016, p. 79). On this last date he was instructed to put his plans in writing.

175 See AOM 1215, no foliation, letters of 5, 10 and 21 August 1696 and 3 August 1701.

176 AOM 265, f. 92v. Colongues, a brigadier in the French corps of engineers, was received into the Order as a knight of grace.

177 See AOM 1561, ff. 319, 726, 739, 857, 870 – letters of 11 September 1705, 18 March 1708, 3 July 1708, 20 March 1710, 28 July 1710; AOM 1216, ff. 319, 579, 691 – letters of 11 September 1705, 18 May 1708, 13 June 1710.

178 AOM 265, f. 199v. (13 March 1708).

179 AOM 1469, no foliation, letters of 23 March and 6 April 1708.

180 AOM 1320, no foliation, letter of 14 April 1708; AOM 1469, letter of 30 April 1708.

181 AOM 6554, f. 214; AOM 6551, f. 74.

remained in the island to supervise the work until July when his services were urgently required by the pope who, having supported the French in the War of the Spanish Succession, was faced with an invasion of his territory by the Hapsburg forces.[182] Although Hecker's return was promised once the emergency facing the Papal States was over, he did not, in fact, ever revisit Malta, and it is not possible to attribute any specific defence work to his exertions.

The grand master had not, however, abandoned his search for a French engineer although it was not until 1713 that he finally secured the services of François Bachelieu, a native of Lyons. But Bachelieu was not, strictly speaking, employed by the French crown. He had been in Sicily for several years supporting the cause of Philip V, the French Bourbon claimant to the Sicilian throne. When in July 1713, as part of the aftermath of the international congress of Utrecht, Philip ceded Sicily to Savoy, and the Bourbons withdrew, Bachelieu offered his talents to the Order. The grand master, perhaps doubting his credentials, offered him employment only as second engineer, which he accepted.[183] The fact, however, was that the Order now had no chief engineer under whom Bachelieu was to work, so that the quest continued for a suitable Frenchman to fill the position.

IV. Valletta and Floriana in the Eighteenth Century

A fresh alert in the closing months of 1714 added a new note of urgency to the search for a fully competent engineer; news reached Malta of a huge Turkish fleet assembling for an attack on the island.[184] Although the threat soon receded, and the general citation summoning the knights to the convent, which had been issued in January 1715, was revoked the following June,[185] on the passing of the immediate danger the Order did not sink back into its accustomed somewhat lethargic attitude towards the fortifications in time

---

182 AOM 1320, letters of 12 July and 1 September 1708; AOM 1469, letters of 30 June, 27 July and 6 August 1708.

183 AOM 1561, f. 1147 (9 September 1713). In the early years of the century Bachelieu was employed by the Spanish Bourbon rulers of Sicily and is known to have worked on the defences of Palermo. He left Sicily when the Bourbons were ousted in accordance with the terms of the Peace of Utrecht but had returned by 1720 to serve as second engineer (Giuffrè, p. 57; F. Meli, 'Degli architetti del senato di Palermo nel secolo XVII e XVIII', *Archivio storico siciliano*, (1939), 352; H. Capel et al. *Los Ingenieros militares en España siglo XVIII: repertorio biográfico e inventario de su labor científico y espacial*, (Barcelona, 1983), p. 56.)

184 Cavaliero, p. 112.

185 AOM 266, ff. 126 (5 January) and 167 (19 June).

of peace. A body of French engineers visited the island and over the succeeding years their ideas were put into effect and exercised a decisive influence over the development of the fortifications of Malta and the sister islands.

When rumours of the Turkish preparations reached Malta in 1714, the fortifications were still in an unfinished state. Despite the exhortations of successive engineers, Floriana remained incomplete; work on the Sta. Margherita lines had ceased when the construction of Cottonera commenced in 1670 and the latter project had been virtually abandoned on the death of its instigator, Grand Master Nicholas Cotoner, in 1680. The commissioners of fortification and war instructed to inspect the fortifications in September 1714 recommended that the covert-way and glacis of Floriana should be finished and that work on Sta. Margherita should recommence.[186] The council issued a decree to this effect and decided to press the viceroy of Sicily to release two engineers to assist in the task. Nothing came of this request[187] and the knights continued their preparations with the resources at hand. The commissioners produced a further report in December in which they again urged that work should be carried out on Floriana, Sta. Margherita and around the coasts in order to prevent an invasion.[188] However, they believed it imperative that an experienced engineer supervise these works and advised awaiting the arrival of such an expert who was expected any day from Italy. The following month, no engineer having materialized, the knights made further provisions to protect the islands. To divert available resources to the fortifications all other building was forbidden and permission was even given for work on the defences to be carried out on feast days; a general citation was issued summoning knights to the defence of the convent;[189] knights were delegated to supervise the construction work; and civil law suits against persons engaged in defence work were suspended.[190] The council even went so far (despite the absence of an expert from overseas) as to decide to implement the recommendations for the defence of the coasts made

186 AOM 6552, f. 1 (18 September 1714). Report and decree registered in the *Liber Conciliorum Status* on 20 September (AOM 266, f. 114).

187 AOM 61, f. 66 (letter from receiver in Turin, dated 14 November); copy at AOM 266, f. 122v.

188 AOM 266, f. 125v.; 6552, f. 4 (19 December 1714).

189 AOM 266, f. 126 (5 January 1715); AOM 6552, f. 10.

190 AOM 266, f. 134 (28 January 1715).

by the knights D'Arginy and Fontet and the little-esteemed second engineer Bachelieu.[191]

The long-awaited engineers arrived in February, not from Italy, but from France, the grand master never having abandoned his attempt to secure the services of a member of the prestigious French engineer corps.[192] The group was led by René Jacques de Tigné with Charles François de Mondion as second-in-command, and also included the engineers Delafon, Grillot de Predelys, D'Artus and Maigret.[193] Some weeks later the French presence on the island was augmented by the arrival of Philippe de Vendôme, the grand prior of France.[194] Among his entourage was Jean Charles de Folard, a man experienced in military matters, but who, by his arrogant manner, offended the official party of engineers led by Tigné.[195]

A difference of opinion soon arose as to the most effective method of fortifying the island: whether the Order should direct its main effort towards the completion of those fortresses under construction, or whether it would be better to fortify the coastline so as to prevent

---

191 AOM 266, f. 129v.; AOM 6552, f. 6v. (10 January 1715).

192 AOM 1217, ff. 425, 439, 467, 485, 511 (21, 27 November 1713; 3, 19 January, 23 February 1714); AOM 1562, f. 1245 (28 October 1714).

193 In 1715 Le Pelletier, the French minister of fortifications, described Tigné as one of the king's most experienced engineers with twenty-six years service. In 1720 he was appointed director of fortifications in Charlemont and in 1723 he was transferred to a similar position in La Rochelle where he remained until his death in 1730 (M. Augoyat, *Aperçu historique sur les fortifications, les ingénieurs et sur le Corps du Génie en France*, 3 vols. (Paris, 1860-4), I, 447, II, 44 and 56; A. Blanchard, *Les Ingénieurs du 'roy' de Louis XIV à Louis XV: étude du Corps des Fortifications* (Montpellier, 1979), pp. 160 and 340). Several of these engineers eventually occupied high positions in the French corps of engineers. In 1739 Delafon and Grillot de Predelys became directors of fortifications, the former of Dunkirk and the latter of Burgundy (Augoyat, II, 183-4). Victor-Hyacinthe d'Artus (1690-1751) served widely in Germany, Spain, the Low Countries, Italy and America. In 1747 he was appointed director of fortifications in Bordeaux and Blaye and in 1748 was promoted to the rank of field marshal (*DBF*, III, 1222).

194 Vendôme, born in 1655, was a great-grandson of Henri IV. He had made his military début at the siege of Crete under the command of his uncle the Duke of Beaufort, and subsequently served in Germany, the Low Countries, Spain and Italy, achieving the rank of lieutenant-general. He retired to Rome for five years in disgrace after disobeying orders at the battle of Cassono (August 1705), but returned to France, restored to favour, in 1710.

195 Folard's military career commenced in 1688 when he served as a sub-lieutenant in the Regiment of Berri. He became aide-de-camp to Louis Joseph, Duke of Vendôme, who later transferred him to his brother Philippe. Folard gives his own account of his sojourn in Malta in his *Histoire de Polybe nouvellement traduite du Grec par Dom Vincent Thuillier... avec un commentaire ou un corps de science militaire... par M. de Folard, Chevalier de l'Ordre Militaire de Saint Louis, Mestre de Camp d'Infanterie*, 6 vols. (Paris, 1727-30), I, 163-4. He admitted that he was not an engineer by profession and departed in disgust when Tigné's proposals were preferred to his.

the enemy gaining a foothold on the island. Tigné and his followers favoured the former course and recommended that the fortifications of Floriana and Sta. Margherita be completed while, at the same time, work on the coastal defences be continued. However, as this was probably too ambitious a programme to be carried out at one time, the half-built fortifications which were vulnerable to attack by the elements should be, Tigné felt, perfected first, and only then should the Order direct its energies to defending the shoreline. Vendôme and Folard, on the other hand, could see little wisdom in adding to the proliferation of forts around the harbour when the islands' coastline offered such an excellent natural barrier to an enemy. Those few places where a landing was possible could be protected by redoubts and entrenchments and the whole island defended by a far smaller body of troops than would be necessary if all the completed and half-built forts had to be garrisoned. As Floriana required, however, only the finishing touches to make it perfect, they were prepared to allow this work to continue.

The congregation of fortification and war met on 4 June to consider the conflicting views put to it, but being unable to decide on either course of action, came to a compromise solution.[196] The council in turn reacted unfavourably to Vendôme's actual proposals for the coastal fortifications,[197] as did Tigné and his engineers,[198] but Vendôme's position and background were such that it would have been impolitic to reject his views out of hand; besides, his opinion commanded support among a section of the Order. The council therefore compromised by accepting Vendôme's scheme without instructing that work elsewhere should cease. This was made possible, in part, by the prior's offer to advance an interest-free loan of 40,000 scudi repayable in three years, thus removing any problem caused by the lack of immediate funds. Once the scheme had been sanctioned Vendôme made a donation of 4,000 scudi which proved a stimulus to other knights to contribute, albeit on a rather less generous scale.[199] The engineer Maigret was put in charge of the project and Tigné confined his attention to the major forts surrounding the harbours.[200]

---

196 AOM 6552, f. 35; AOM 6556, f. 27. This is the only surviving report that bears the signatures of Delafon, Grillot de Predelys and D'Artus.

197 Read to the council on 6 June (AOM 266, f. 163v.; AOM 6552, f. 37v.; AOM 6556, f. 11).

198 AOM 6556, f. 19.

199 AOM 266, f. 163v. (6 June 1715).

200 AOM 266, f. 166v. (17 June 1715). Philippe Maigret, when he visited Malta in 1716, was an ordinary engineer of the French king. He remained in the island supervising the coastal

In July 1715 Tigné was instructed by the congregation of war to draw up a report on the fortifications.[201] He was to make a general plan and to decide once and for all what was necessary to bring them to perfection. After two months Tigné presented his report.[202] Although he would have preferred three rather than four bastions he commended the bastions of the Valletta front as the fullest and best built of all the completed works; nevertheless he did find the parapets and the low orillion batteries in a neglected state and obstructed by rubbish. The gardens, trees and houses which had encroached on the platforms and parapets would, he argued, have to be removed. He criticized also the system of communication between the main enceinte and the outworks, on the grounds that the counterguards were linked by means of bridges which could easily be destroyed by bombardment. He therefore recommended that communication should be via sally ports and caponiers in the ditch, a route which could be protected by flanking fire from the orillions. The section of the Valletta front with which Tigné found greatest fault was the covert-way; this was too narrow, its parapet too low, and it lacked traverses or places of arms. In short, it did not conform to the established rules of fortification. Moreover the glacis needed rebuilding so that its slope was more uniform, especially at the extremities where the steep incline afforded the enemy cover. Tigné suggested that the main gate of Valletta should be defended by a lunette, although he realized that even then it could be bombarded from the heights of Corradino and the Isoletto. To remedy this he suggested that an alternative means of communication be provided at each flank of the front which would pass under the covert-way and glacis and along the lateral walls of Floriana.

In discussing the Floriana front Tigné repeated the common criticism that the centre was over-protected while the flanks were too weak. The bastion on the left was incomplete, but even if finished according to plan, could still be bombarded in the rear from

defences until August 1716 (AOM 1562, f. 1464). He later rose to be engineer-in-chief, and a chevalier of the Order of St. Louis. He wrote the *Traité de la sûreté et conservation des états par le moyen des forteresses* (Paris, 1725) which became the standard work on the strategic importance of forts used by the École de Mézières. Folard held Maigret in high regard describing him as one of the most able engineers in Europe (*Histoire de Polybe*, V, 123).

201 AOM 6552, f. 39; RML MS. 1301, p. 54.

202 Royal Malta Library, Valletta, Manuscript Collection (hereafter referred to as RML MS.) 1219, f. 159; RML MS. 1301, p. 57; AOM 6560, no foliation.

Corradino hill. He, therefore, proposed a retrenchment. The perpetual problem of the Capuchin convent would thus have to be faced as its presence prevented the completion of the left face of the bastion. The right flank of the front was no better, as the salient angle of the bastion was too acute and defended by a small flank which could accommodate only two cannon. It suffered from the same defect as the left bastion – it could be bombarded from neighbouring heights. For this Tigné prescribed a similar remedy, a retrenchment to prevent attack from the rear. Other faults of the front Tigné ascribed not to design faults but to errors in execution. He listed various alterations of a minor nature which he believed would improve the enceinte: he wished to construct caponiers to connect the ravelins to the main defence; in the fausse-braye he proposed the erection of traverses, sally ports, the realignment of parapets and the resiting of the main gate (the Porte des Bombes) in a reentrant angle with a small lunette to cover it. Although he considered the horn and crownworks too small to be of much value, these were so far advanced that there was now no alternative but to complete them. The covert-way and glacis of the Floriana front were unfinished, so that naturally they would have to be perfected before the enceinte could be considered complete. Finally Tigné supported the proposals of Floriani and Valperga that houses be built within the enceinte. He advocated a limited number of buildings, sited at least a hundred canes from the covert-way of Valletta. Clearly Tigné found Floriana in a reasonably complete state. He did not suggest any major alterations, realizing that work had in any case progressed too far to allow such, but he did advise that the scheme (which by then had taken the appearance of an interminable undertaking) be finally perfected, so that the Order could devote its attention to other sections of the fortifications. In putting forward his proposals for the other harbour forts, Tigné outlined in his report a comprehensive system for the defence of the harbour area based on the works already in existence or under construction.

The commissioners of fortification and war recommended that the council should act upon Tigné's report, and the procurators of the common treasury were instructed to enquire into how the 50,000 scudi per annum, the estimated cost of these proposals, could be raised.[203] In the past, the commissioners averred, needless

---

203 AOM 266, f. 174v.; RML MS. 1219, f. 185; RML MS. 1301, p. 111.

expenditure and changes of plan had resulted from an over-abundance of conflicting advice from numerous engineers. To prevent such a recurrence in the future they suggested that Tigné's plan be adopted as the definitive masterplan for the defence of the harbour area. They expressed their utter confidence in Tigné as an engineer, and, since he was compelled to return to France, they requested that his colleague Mondion remain to supervise the work until he could revisit the island. The French minister of fortification, Le Pelletier, was advised of the decision to retain Mondion, and Tigné departed for France shortly afterwards, leaving behind him exact plans of the work to be executed.[204] During the summer of 1715 Tigné himself had been in contact with Le Pelletier sending to the minister for approval his scheme for the protection of the harbours;[205] in advising the man who was, in effect, his patron and employer, of his proposals, Tigné was merely conforming to current practice and was not showing any disloyalty towards the knights. In the following winter he submitted copies of his project to the chief engineers of France and proudly attached their certificates of approval to a letter which he wrote to the congregation of war in April 1716.[206]

Tigné's letter was primarily concerned with the grand master's request that he return to Malta. Unfortunately, from the Order's point of view, his services were required by the Duke of Orléans, who was acting as regent for the young Louis XV.[207] Mesmes, the Order's ambassador in Paris, doubted whether Tigné had any urgent business to detain him in France and claimed that the engineer himself was most anxious to obey the grand master's summons. That he was prevented from doing so, was, believed Mesmes, the outcome of an

---

204 AOM 1562, f. 1357; AOM 6560; RML MS. 1301, p. 119.

205 RML MS. 1301, pp. 80 and 81 (letters of Le Pelletier, dated 19 June and 29 July), p. 141 (letter of Marshal de Villars, president of the council of war, dated 22 September).

206 RML MS. 1301, pp. 129 (Tigné's letter of 1 April), 133 (15 February 1716; certificate of Antoine le Prestre de Vauban, nephew of Sébastien; he was appointed lieutenant-general in 1714 and in 1728, when he certified his approval of B. Forest de Bélidor's *La Science des ingénieurs dans la conduite des travaux de fortification et d'architecture civile* (Paris, 1729), he was serving as director general of fortification in Artois), 136 (24 February; Charles Guy de Valory, lieutenant-general and director of fortifications in Flanders; he occupied the same position in 1728 when he also commended Bélidor's work), 138 (8 March; Jean Baptiste Favart director of the fortifications in Pays d'Autun, Ile de Ré, Ile de Oléron, Poitou, Blaye, Medoc, etc.).

207 AOM 1562, f. 1418 (letter of grand master, dated 6 February 1716); RML MS. 1301, p. 129 (Tigné's letter of 1 April); AOM 1218, f. 517 (letter of Order's ambassador in Paris, dated 29 March).

intrigue whereby Vendôme sought to protect his protegé Maigret and further the project to fortify the coasts of Malta and Gozo. Finally in June, through the good offices of Dasfeld, the then French minister of fortifications, Tigné obtained leave of absence on condition that he return to France the following February (1717); Maigret, on the other hand, was instructed to return to France forthwith.[208]

Tigné reached Malta in early September 1716 and by the 15th of that month had produced a new report on the state of the fortifications.[209] Floriana, he announced, was indeed nearing completion, and what little remained to be finished could be carried out by two masons working on the left branch of the hornwork and on the construction of some traverses in the ditch. So far, however, no action had been taken to resite the main gate or to construct the retrenchments on the two flanks of Floriana. He therefore recommended that the former work should now be taken in hand but that the latter be left for consideration at a later date.[210] Tigné's report continued with detailed comments on Cottonera, a paragraph on fort Ricasoli, but made no mention of Valletta. At first sight it might appear that by the autumn of 1716 the fortifications of Valletta and Floriana were in order; however, attached to the report of 15 September was an estimate of the cost of proposed works, among which works in Valletta and Floriana, of both an urgent and non-urgent nature, are listed. In the first category Tigné estimated that 9,300 scudi would have to be spent in improvements to the covert-way, glacis, parapets, banquettes, sally ports, caponiers, communications and orillion batteries of Valletta. Non-urgent work – the construction of bombproof magazines, the establishment of parapets and banquettes around the ramparts, the building of caponiers and traverses to link the counterguards to the covert-way, and setting in order the interiors of the counterguards – would consume a further 4,000 scudi. In Floriana provision was made for expenditure of 13,300 scudi on the following urgent works: the construction of the main gate, lunette and bombproof powder magazines, and the modification and completion of the centre bastion of the front, traverses and caponiers in the main ditch, the crownwork, hornwork, parapets and banquette

208 RML MS. 1301, pp. 146 (letter of Orléans to the grand master, 19 June 1716) and 147 (letter of Dasfeld to the grand master, ? 23 June 1716); AOM 1562, f. 1464 (letter of grand master to Dasfeld, 14 August 1716).

209 RML MS. 1301, p. 153; AOM 6560.

210 In 1738 the non-construction of these works was ascribed to their high cost.

Plate 8 Lunette, Floriana.

of the front. A total of 24,000 scudi would be required for less pressing work, namely, the retrenchments behind the two demi-bastions of the front, communications along the lateral walls and additional bombproof magazines. Thus, Valletta and Floriana together were assigned 22,600 scudi out of a total allocation for urgent work of 146,950 scudi and 28,000 of the 102,800 scudi assigned to secondary works, or, in other words, over a fifth of all the proposed expenditure was to be on fortifications which, judging by the report of 15 September, were supposed to be virtually perfect. Since the estimate of proposed expenses is not actually dated it is possible that, despite its position immediately after the 1716 report, its calculations refer to the work proposed in September 1715 in addition to that of the later year. In fact, these figures demonstrate no more than the obvious: the upkeep of the fortifications was a never-ending task, and it was never possible to stand back and declare a work perfect or beyond improvement. Changing theories of strategy, new ideas about the function and design of fortifications, together with the constant need to repair and maintain existing buildings ensured that the defences were a constant drain on the resources of the Order even when no grandiose new scheme was under construction.

The grand master was particularly anxious that Tigné supervise the execution of his proposals for as long as possible, and to this end he requested that his leave of absence be prolonged beyond the original deadline of February 1717. A short extension until May was allowed, and in June the grand master was reporting that he had permitted Tigné to depart as there was no longer a project on which to employ him.[211] Tigné was at the time regarded as the originator, designer and mastermind of the defence plan for the island. The more mundane task of supervising the day-to-day work on the fortifications could, however, be safely entrusted to Mondion. Although it was only after 1720 that Mondion was officially appointed the Order's resident engineer, he was acting in this capacity, apart from a year's interlude in 1720, from September 1715 onwards. Between September 1715 and October 1719 Mondion was granted repeated extensions of his leave of absence by the French authorities,[212] but in the autumn of 1719 they finally insisted that he leave Malta for France.[213] The knights were reluctant to let Mondion sever his ties with Malta; he was admitted to the Order as a knight of grace and the grand master resolved to request that he be allowed to return to serve as resident engineer on a permanent basis.[214] The grand master's wish was granted and Mondion was employed by the Order as its engineer from January 1721 until his death in December 1733.[215]

Before his departure in 1719 Mondion submitted to the congregation of war a memorandum in which he outlined the state of the fortifications.[216] He recalled that in 1715 the engineers had decided

---

211 28. AOM 1562, ff. 1497, 1519, 1532, 1534, 1538 (letters of the grand master dated 29 November 1716, 4 April, 3 June, 10 June 1717); AOM 1218, ff. 775, 811 (letters of the ambassador in Paris dated 19 February, 15 May 1717); AOM 267, f. 10 (congregation of fortification and war reports that Tigné is about to leave Malta, 23 May 1717).

212 AOM 1562 (letters of grand master dated 25 September 1715, 29 November 1716, 4 April, 3 June, 10 June, 30 September 1717, 19 August 1718, 27 May 1719); AOM 1218, ff. 775, 811, 891, 925 (letters of the ambassador dated 19 February, 15 May, 29 October, 15 December 1717).

213 AOM 1562 (letters of the grand master dated 7 and 8 October 1719).

214 On 30 August 1718 he was allowed to wear the cross of the Order (AOM 522, f. 162); on 3 October 1719 (AOM 1562) the grand master claimed that he had been admitted to the Order, but Vertot (IV, 143, third pagination) records that he was made a knight of grace in 1723.

215 AOM 1563, ff. 14, 38, 49, 112, 123, 147, 200 (letters of the grand master dated 20 January, 14 March, 2 April, 8 June, 22 June, 5 July, 30 October 1720).

216 AOM 1011, f. 22 (September 1719).

upon three principal objectives: to construct the covert-way, glacis and communications of the Floriana front in preference to those of Valletta; to put the Birgu front in order in preference to those of Sta. Margherita and Cottonera since it was already far more advanced, and it would be so costly to complete the other two works; lastly, to finish and improve Ricasoli. In 1719 he could report that the Floriana front was finished except for some alterations to the course of the aqueduct, and he, therefore, now proposed that the Order's main effort should be concentrated on Birgu. There is no reason to doubt that by the standards of the day, Floriana was then complete. Work was carried out in both Valletta and Floriana in the later eighteenth century but no attempt was made at wholesale reform or redesign of the fortifications to bring them into line with modern standards. Such work as was performed was of a minor nature: repairs and maintenance,[217] modifications aimed at greater convenience and specific measures taken to face an emergency. St. Elmo underwent two major reconstructions in the course of the century, both aimed at providing improved accommodation for the garrison. Between 1727 and 1730 the courtyard of the fort was enlarged into a square surrounded by barrack rooms capable of housing the two hundred soldiers of the grand master's guard. For the spiritual well-being of the soldiers a new chapel was also constructed.[218] The accommodation of the fort was further extended in 1762 when a range of barracks, now referred to as lower St. Elmo, designed by the knight René Jacques de Tigné who was then acting as engineer, was added.[219]

The threat of attack by the Moslem powers was particularly acute on three occasions in the eighteenth century, 1722-3, 1731-3 and 1761. In March 1722 word reached Malta that a combined Algerian and Turkish fleet was heading for the island.[220] Steps were immediately taken to meet the enemy, including work in Valletta and Floriana. Although the Order maintained its state of preparedness throughout the summer, no attack materialized.[221] Five Algerian

---

217 Year-by-year summaries of these minor works, drawn up by the engineers, are to be found in Clerkenwell, MS. O 1, item 20 (Mondion, 1722-32) and item 21 (Marandon, 1732-62).

218 Clerkenwell, MS. O 1, item 20.

219 AOM 1015, p. 37 (October 1762 – construction ordered) and p. 95 (18 September 1771 – doors and windows ordered to be made).

220 Cavaliero, p. 114.

221 The various preparations are recorded in AOM 267 ff. 113v. (26 January 1722), 124 (8 May), 130 (22 June), 137 (28 July), 147 (25 September), 171 (2, December), 186v. (1 February 1723); AOM 1011, ff. 11 (2 December 1722), 35-9 (25 June 1722), 43-4 (8 July 1722); Clerkenwell, MS. O 1, items 5 (25 June 1722), 6 (8 July), 7 (26 January 1722), 8 (1 and 14 October 1722), 9 (21 March 1723).

ships appeared off Malta in June but their commander confined his warlike attentions to a letter ordering the grand master to release all his slaves and to firing a salvo at Valletta. Alarming rumours of a fleet fifty strong arming to assault the island continued to emanate from Constantinople but, although formal truce negotiations with the Turks came to nothing, after 1723 the Order effectively confined its naval activities to the western Mediterranean. It therefore no longer came into conflict with the Porte as such, although the struggle against the Barbary Regencies, fanned by the actions of the corsairs, both infidel and Christian, persisted throughout the century.

Early in 1731 the knights' intelligence service again reported the arming of a formidable Turkish fleet. The general strategy of the Order was by then inclining toward a policy of forestalling any siege attempt on the enemy's part by denying him a foothold on the island and opposing any landing on the beaches and in the open countryside. Accordingly, Mondion was instructed to ensure that the coastal batteries and retrenchments were in readiness, but no specific mention was made of Valletta or Floriana.[222] This alarm, in common with so many others, came to nothing. The threat in 1761, however, was of an altogether more serious nature; the knights, albeit involuntarily, became involved in an action which the Turks regarded as provocative. The Christian slave crew of a galley belonging to the Pasha of Rhodes revolted, captured the ship and sailed it into Malta in October 1760. The Order could hardly refuse the Christians sanctuary and the Turks were bound to take revenge, so that the knights prepared their defences against the coming onslaught.[223] A commission appointed to review the situation advised that, in order to overhaul the fortifications of the towns and the countryside, the knights should secure the services of a company of engineers. As the Order in the late eighteenth century was very much within the orbit of French influence,[224] it naturally turned to that country in its search. In April the ambassador in Paris reported that a company of four engineers headed by Lieutenant-Colonel Pontleroy had been engaged. In addition, François Charles de Bourlamaque, a brigadier in the French armies,

---

222 Clerkenwell, MS. O 1, items 11 (23 April 1731-concerned with signalling procedure, the towers and the militia) and 20.

223 Commission appointed to prepare the defences 14 February 1761 (AOM 271, f. 165v.); AOM 6558, f. 1; Clerkenwell, MS. O 1, item 21; its report is found at AOM 271, f. 166 (19 February).

224 See J. Godechot, 'La France et Malte au XVIIIe siècle' in *Revue historique*, CCVI (1951), 67-79.

had volunteered his services as commander of the French engineers.[225] The company arrived in Malta on 5 July 1761, too late to carry out any effective measures should the Turks attack that summer. In August the Order decided that the danger, for that year at least, had passed and revoked the citation summoning knights to the island.[226] The engineers, however, did not abandon their mission. In October and November they produced a whole series of reports covering all aspects of defence.[227] Bourlamaque first drew up a general survey report on the defences of Malta.[228] After enumerating the various advantages possessed by the island, both natural and man-made, Bourlamaque proceeded to demonstrate that in the condition in which it then was, it could not in fact withstand a powerful attack for any length of time. Assuming that the enemy army would be three times as numerous as the defenders, the invaders would not find it difficult to land and then overrun the island, forcing the defenders to retreat into the fortresses. For all its commanding situation and its powerful front and flanks, the interior of Valletta was not well protected, mainly because there were no bombproof magazines or cisterns and the garrison had no secure shelter. Although Cottonera had been built to afford protection to the people of the countryside, it could not be held for more than a few days. Even when completed, Bourlamaque believed it would fall sooner or later, and once Sta. Margherita, Birgu and Senglea were lost too, a mob of 40,000 persons, some quite useless militarily, would have to withdraw into Valletta itself.

---

225 AOM 6558, f. 15v. (17 April 1761). The Count Bourlamaque was of Italian origin. He entered the regiment of infantry of the Dauphine in 1739 and between 1742 and 1744 was active in Flanders and the Rhineland. In 1756 he served under Montcalm in Canada and on his return to France in 1759 was created commander of the Order of St. Louis. The year after his visit to Malta, 1762, he was appointed a field marshal and governor of Guadeloupe where he died the following year. (*DBF*, VI, 1515). Pontleroy served in the late 1750s in Canada where he was the engineer-in-chief of the colony. He was appointed director of fortifications in Dauphiné and Provence in 1777 (Augoyat, II, 505 and 595). The other engineers in the party were Desandroüins, who had also worked in Canada, Fournier and De Cuire (Augoyat, II, 503-05 and 639).

226 AOM 271, ff. 168v. (19 February, citation issued), 198 (27 August, revoked).

227 AOM 6555 and AOM 6519, 'Memoire général sur l'isle de Malte'; AOM 6557, f. 62 and AOM 6558, f. 70 (18 October 1761), 'Memoire sur les fortifications des villes de Malte'; AOM 6557, f. 1 and AOM 6558, f. 37v. 'Memoire sur le fort Chambray'; AOM 6557, f. 27 and AOM 6558, f. 53 'Memoire sur la deffense de l'isle de Gozo'; AOM 6557, f. 120 and AOM 6558, f. 100 (24 October 1761) 'Memoire sur la deffense des isles de Malte et du Goze'; AOM 6557, f. 189 and AOM 6558, f. 134 (15 November 1761) 'Memoire sur l'artillerie'; AOM 6557, f. 62 and AOM 6558, f. 86v., criticism of the report of 18 October by Marandon (14 November) with replies by Pontleroy (18 November).

228 AOM 6519 and 6555.

Bourlamaque listed the four commonest arguments on which eighteenth-century confidence in the security of Malta was based. In the first place, there was the alleged difficulty in landing and the large number of fortresses; secondly Malta had withstood the siege of 1565 although then less heavily fortified; thirdly, the Turkish military machine had weakened through a long period of inactivity; lastly, the Christian princes would not allow Malta to fall. Bourlamaque did not, however, believe that any of these were sound. The first point he dealt with in a long memorandum on the defence of the coasts. The second argument no longer held good since the whole military climate of Europe had changed; in 1565 Malta was virtually a school for war, the nobility of Europe was military-minded and the people accustomed to wars such as those of Charles V and Francis I. Although the Turks had not fought for twenty-two years, a religious war would, Bourlamaque believed, stir them into action, and they could always obtain officers from Europe. After nineteen years' peace in 1737 the Turks were able to defeat the experienced troops of the emperor, and Bourlamaque doubted whether the Christian princes could be relied upon to send aid; after all, they had allowed Rhodes to fall in 1522.

Bourlamaque urged the Order to make the best possible use of the natural advantages possessed by the islands. Those shores where a landing was possible should be fortified to prevent such an occurrence, thereby averting any possibility of siege or devastation of the island. Should the enemy succeed in landing it was essential that the fortresses should be impregnable; Corradino should be fortified and Sta. Margherita completed; Città Vecchia and the Gozo Castello should be demolished, and fort Chambray in Gozo should be finished. Although the cost would be considerable, this would be far outweighed by the risk of defeat if such measures were neglected. Since the yearly sum assigned to the fortifications was relatively meagre, it was essential that it be spent intelligently; he therefore recommended the employment of well-known and experienced engineers for the tracing and construction of the fortifications.

Bourlamaque and his followers were firmly committed to a strategy of defending the coast against an enemy landing. On the fortifications of Valletta and Floriana they reiterated the criticisms put forward by Tigné in 1715.[229] They considered the parapets, flanks and communications of the former weak, but, on the whole, they found

229 RML MS. 1219, f. 159; RML MS. 1301, p. 57.

the Valletta defences to be good although suffering from certain faults common to all the fortification: insufficient bombproof cisterns and casemates, parapets which were too low and narrow, parapets and terrapleins constructed of masonry whereas earth was a more suitable material since it eliminated dangers from ricochet and splinters. The engineers had general praise also for Floriana, but complained that Tigné's proposed improvements such as the retrenchment in the Capuchin bastion and the removal of the convent, had not been executed. They believed that the ravelins could be strengthened by the addition of redoubts in their interiors, defensive constructions which gained in popularity in the course of the century thanks to the championship of Montalembert, and realized that the fausse-braye was overlooked by the ravelins and tenailles but in its turn commanded the covert-way, crown and hornworks. These last two might appear small but could, the French engineers reckoned, accommodate sufficient men for their defence, their principal defect being the large area of dead ground remaining in the deep valley directly in front of the crownwork; even this defect, however, could be corrected quite quickly should the fortresses come under siege.

There is little evidence to suggest that the recommendations put forward in 1761 had any direct effect on the fortifications of Sciberras. The modest suggestions made by Bourlamaque and his men for improvements to Valletta and Floriana came under attack from the resident engineer Marandon,[230] and Pontleroy felt duty bound to refute these criticisms.[231] It is, however, unlikely that the opposition of Marandon impeded the execution of the proposals. In the normal course of events he would have been entrusted with their supervision, but in March 1762 he resigned after thirty-five years' service and returned to his native Turin.[232] Although some new bombproof shelters were provided,[233] these appear to have been the only concrete outcome of all the reports produced in 1761.

230 Francesco Marandon, a native of Turin, arrived in Malta in January 1727 to take up the post of second engineer. On Mondion's death in December 1733 he became resident engineer at the salary of fifty scudi per month. He paid a four-month visit to Sicily in September 1734 and was present at the siege of fort Gonzaga and the blockade of Messina, and in 1748 he visited Agrigento at the request of the viceroy. He was highly critical of the French engineers' recommendations in 1761 but never had to assume responsibility for their implementation because he left the island in March 1762 with a pension of thirty scudi a month.

231 AOM 6557, f. 62; AOM 6558, f. 86v.

232 AOM 1020, f. 572. (3 March 1762).

233 AOM 271, ff. 253 and 258 (23 June and 14 December 1763).

A survey of the fortifications carried out about 1789 made it clear that many of the proposals of 1715 and 1761 still remained to be implemented.[234] In addition many of the existing works had deteriorated seriously; the stone *franka*, which was the principal building material on the island, required constant attention if it were not to disintegrate through the action of the weather, or the careless treatment by the Maltese who were continually encroaching on the fortifications in their search for living space. Undoubtedly this neglect of the fortifications had arisen partly because of the precarious financial state of the Order. The final blow came with the confiscation of the French estates in 1792, but already attempts had been made to limit expenditure on the fortifications, as on other items.[235] The surrender of Valletta and Floriana, the very heart of the Order, practically without a shot being fired, on the first occasion on which they were to come under serious attack cannot be blamed on the design or the condition of the fortifications. Certainly shortage of money was one of the factors which led to the surrender, but the conquest of the islands by Napoleon in 1798 was far more than a military defeat; it signalled the final collapse of the Order itself which no fortress, however strong, perfect or up-to-date, could have prevented.[236]

---

[234] AOM 1054.
[235] See chapter 11.
[236] See chapter 12.

Chapter 5

The Fortification of the Harbour

I. The Sta. Margherita Lines

The decision taken in March 1566 to construct a fortified city on Sciberras and thence transfer the convent, left unresolved the problem of the settlements on the south-eastern shore of Grand Harbour. The vulnerability of these to bombardment from nearby heights had long been recognized and it was generally agreed that the existing defences could not be adapted to eliminate this danger. Yet the Order could not abandon these fortresses, as it was essential that the naval installations be retained in the sheltered creeks under their walls. Immediately after the siege the Order could do no more than rebuild the shattered defences to their former design, but by the 1630s a scheme to improve the defences of Birgu and Senglea could be contemplated as a practical alternative to the fortifications proposed by Floriani. Their restricted sites precluded drastic redesigning of the old enceintes, which were instead enclosed within a new ring of fortifications encompassing the threatening heights of Sta. Margherita hill.

Enclosed within the Sta. Margherita lines were fort St. Angelo and the cities of Birgu and Senglea. St. Angelo dated back to the ninth century and had been the first home of the grand masters in Malta. The knights had strengthened it in various ways before the siege, deepening the ditches, enlarging the bastions and adding the Homedes cavalier in 1541 and the La Valette water-level battery in 1558. Birgu, a huddle of sailors' houses when the knights arrived, had become the headquarters of an aristocratic military order and had been fortified as befitted its new role. The new town of Senglea had been founded by the Grand Master de la Sengle to relieve the over-crowding in Birgu. Its exposed eastern flank was defended by bastioned ramparts and the land front by fort St. Michael. All three fortresses had suffered severe damage in the siege of 1565; so much so that it was reckoned that it would cost as much to repair them as to build a new city on Sciberras, and there were even suggestions that the settlements should be razed to concentrate the knights' military resources.[1] All the experts recognized that their position made these fortifications inherently weak, but in the autumn of 1565 the Order had to have a fortified stronghold if it were to remain in the island, so the former headquarters were rebuilt to accommodate the convent for a few more years. However, Grand Master del Monte transferred to the half-completed new city at the earliest opportunity to forestall any opposition from those knights who remained unconvinced that a move was necessary.[2] By 1582 no reluctant knights remained, officially at least, in Birgu or Senglea and Giovanni Battista Leone, a member of a papal delegation to the island, described the former as consisting of 1,500 dwellings, almost all occupied by Maltese and sailors, and the latter of 500 dwellings occupied by 'persons of lower condition'.[3] Laparelli was particularly pessimistic as to the ability of the reconstructed Birgu and Senglea to withstand any kind of assault, and thought it therefore essential that if they did fall their captor could not turn them to his advantage.[4] Fort St. Angelo was an altogether more formidable obstacle whose capture would cost the enemy dear, and in the schemes advocating the withdrawal of the headquarters to Sicily the garrison left in the island would have been stationed in that fort and in St. Elmo and Città Vecchia.[5] At least one expert, however, recommended that St. Angelo should be razed along with Birgu and Senglea.[6]

---

1 For opinions on the state of Birgu, Senglea and St. Angelo see: Ascanio della Cornia (Bosio, III, 709); Sancho de Londono, 1 October 1566 (*Col. doc. inéditos*, XXIX, 538); Laparelli, 3 January 1566 (Cod. Lap. f. 6), 5 January 1566 (AOM 430 f. 268v.), 30 January 1566 (Cod. Lap. f. 13), 1 February 1566 (AOM 430, f. 272); Duke of Alba (*Col. doc. inéditos*, XXX, 121); Count of Vicari (*Col. doc. inéditos*, XXX, 128); Gabrio Serbelloni, 17 March 1566 (*Col. doc. inéditos*, XXX, 205); 24 August 1574 (Vat. Lat. 7776, f. 39); Leone, 1582 (ASV Fondo Pio 246, f. 260); Bosio, III, 728, 33, 38, 39.

2 Bosio, III, 829.

3 ASV Fondo Pio 246, f. 260

4 Cod. Lap. ff. 44 (21 October 1566) and 52v. (22 September 1567).

5 On the plans to withdraw see chapter 4 i.

6 Author of the report of 24 August 1574 (Vat. Lat. 7776, f. 39).

Although the towns of Birgu and Senglea sprang quickly back to life after the siege, their fortifications had been repaired hurriedly and none too solidly. While they could repel an attempt at scaling, they could not withstand bombardment.[7] But the Order concentrated its energies on the construction of Valletta, and despite the decision to rebuild them, in 1568 the walls of Birgu and Senglea were described as still very ruined.[8] Once the enceinte of the new city was completed, however, some attention was given to the other strongholds, and Girolamo Cassar claimed in 1581 that he had been responsible for putting Birgu and fort St. Michael into good shape.[9] Whether or not this claim was justified it is impossible to know; the records of the Order remain silent on the subject of the fortifications of Birgu and Senglea for over fifty years, by which time the defences had had ample opportunity to fall into ruin and disrepair.

Rumours reached Malta in 1633 of a Turkish fleet arming for an attack on the island. The fortifications of Valletta, Birgu and Senglea were inspected and it was thought expedient to restore their walls and, where possible, perfect their design. This work, it was calculated, would cost 33,000 scudi altogether, but there is no indication as to how the money was to be divided between the three fortresses.[10] Whatever repairs and improvements were made in 1633, by 1635, when an assault was once again feared, further measures were advised.[11] The terrapleins of some of the Senglea platforms were to be enlarged; the parapets were to be raised, especially those facing Corradino Hill; the gate giving onto Corradino was to be closed and the ditch outside the Bormla gate widened. These works in Senglea it was estimated would cost 6,000 scudi. In fort St. Michael the parapets demanded attention; the same was true of the Birgu front and elsewhere on the enceinte. The parapets were normally the first part of the walls to show signs of wear since they were open to depredations by the civilian population, so that restoration of the parapets was a routine preparation when an attack was anticipated. Thus it was suggested that the debris be cleared from the post of Castile, Birgu and a retrenchment constructed in the

---

7 Cod. Lap. f. 6.

8 Urb. Lat. 833, f. 197 (1568).

9 AOM 439, f. 270v. (18 May 1581).

10 AOM 110, f. 247 (7 June 1633); AOM 111, f. 14 (7 November); Dal Pozzo, I, 810.

11 16 February 1635 a commission appointed to examine defences (AOM 256, f. 126); its report, 4 March (AOM 256, f. 128v. and AOM 6553, ff. 19 and 37).

Plate 9 Fort Ricasoli, St. Angelo and Senglea.

rear. The knights also planned to add a much-needed covert-way to Birgu, financed by the proceeds of a customs levy.[12] The picture of the Senglea and Birgu fortifications which emerges from the inspection of March 1635 is that they were in reasonable repair, but that the knights were still disposed to tinker with their design in a desperate attempt to remedy their intrinsic weakness.

Although work went ahead on the repairs to Birgu and Senglea,[13] before the end of the year the Order was considering a proposal to remove these fortresses from the first line of attack by enclosing them and the heights of Sta. Margherita in a ring of new fortifications. Floriani, while recommending a new front at the Capuchin convent to strengthen the defences of Valletta, the heart of the island, also contemplated the fortification, at some future date, of Sta. Margherita hill to protect the harbour and Bormla.[14] At the council meeting of 10 December Floriani's opponents concentrated their attack on the time and money which would be

12 AOM 256, f. 129 (5 March 1635). For further details of finance see chapter 11.

13 AOM 256, ff. 129v. (11 March) and 131 (15 March 1635). In November Floriani described them as better fortified than at the time of the siege (AOM 6554, f. 25).

14 AOM 6554, f. 21 (17 October 1635).

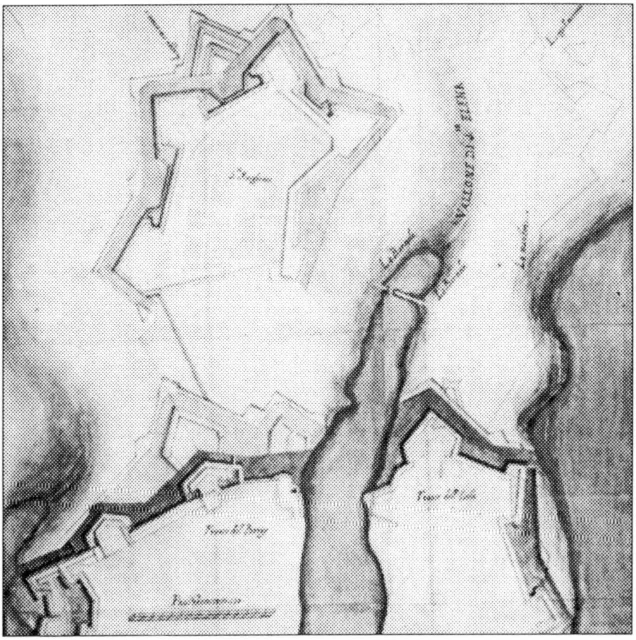

Plate 10 Plan of Sta. Margherita, Birgu and Senglea fortifications.

required to execute the new enceinte on Sciberras. They did not question that the Valletta fortifications should be modernized but held that Floriani's grandiose scheme was unnecessary and would, by consuming all available resources, preclude any attempt at the defence of the harbour, the vital lifeline in time of siege.[15] The provision of more modest improvements to Valletta which would permit some protection of the port to be undertaken was favoured by many of the knights.[16] Floriani himself, on the defensive against any proposal to sacrifice his new enceinte in favour of fortifying Sta. Margherita, played down the danger to be expected from that quarter and denounced schemes to defend the harbour as far more expensive than his original plans.[17] The council was not convinced

---

15 Borg, p. 33.

16 Chigi, R I 25, f. 303 (Imbroll, 1636); Borg, p. 200 (8 April 1636); the proposals were also criticized in a report sent from Messina signed only N.N., Chigi R I 25, f. 344 (30 June 1638).

17 Chigi, R I 25, f. 329 (29 September 1636); Chigi, A III 57, f. 51 (10 January 1637).

that once Floriana was completed an enemy would not deign to attack Birgu and Senglea and in December 1636 decreed that a breakwater be built to protect a large part of the harbour, to afford shelter to the vessels, to allow relief to be received when under siege, and to strengthen the two towns by linking their defence.[18] Indeed, the growing doubts as to the wisdom of pursuing Floriani's scheme led in 1638 to the dispatch of Vertoa armed with plans and reports to seek the advice of foreign military experts. Among those consulted, Bolognino, Garay, Lecamus and Grassi recommended some form of fortification on Sta. Margherita hill.[19] But before Vertoa could return to Malta bearing these reports, the Order's vacillations had been stilled by the arrival in the island of the engineer Firenzuola.

On 26 November 1638 Firenzuola presented recommendations regarding the fortifications to the council.[20] He drew attention to the undoubted weakness of Birgu and Senglea; for if they should fall, as they probably would in a few days, the defenders could be succoured only with the greatest difficulty. If, however, Sta. Margherita hill were fortified the port would be protected, relief ships could enter, Birgu and Senglea would be strengthened, the enemy forces would be very extended if they attempted to outflank the new fortifications and the people from the countryside could shelter within its walls. However, the fortification of these heights posed two problems. Firstly, if the Sta. Margherita lines fell to the attacker he might turn them against Birgu and Senglea. Firenzuola solved this difficulty by siting the main defences at a fair distance from the old works, and by ensuring that those sections which linked up with Birgu and Senglea were to be well mined. Moreover, he designed an open fort which could be attacked in the rear from Birgu, Senglea and Valletta. Secondly, there was the problem of the expense. This Firenzuola believed to be of little consequence in comparison with the urgent need for such a fort. Besides, he reckoned it would cost no more than 60,000 or 70,000 scudi. This was indeed a modest sum compared with the 200,000 to 300,000 scudi which critics calculated as the cost of Floriana, or even Floriani's own estimate of 125,000 scudi; however, as engineers' estimates of the costs of their own schemes were notoriously unreliable, too much weight should not be

---

18 AOM 256, f. 160v. (24 December 1636).

19 Chigi, Q III 69, ff. 31, 35, 39v. and 43.

20 AOM 6554, f. 47. The plan at Barb. Lat. 9905/7 probably shows Firenzuola's design. I do not know why Marconi (p. 385) attributes this to Floriani.

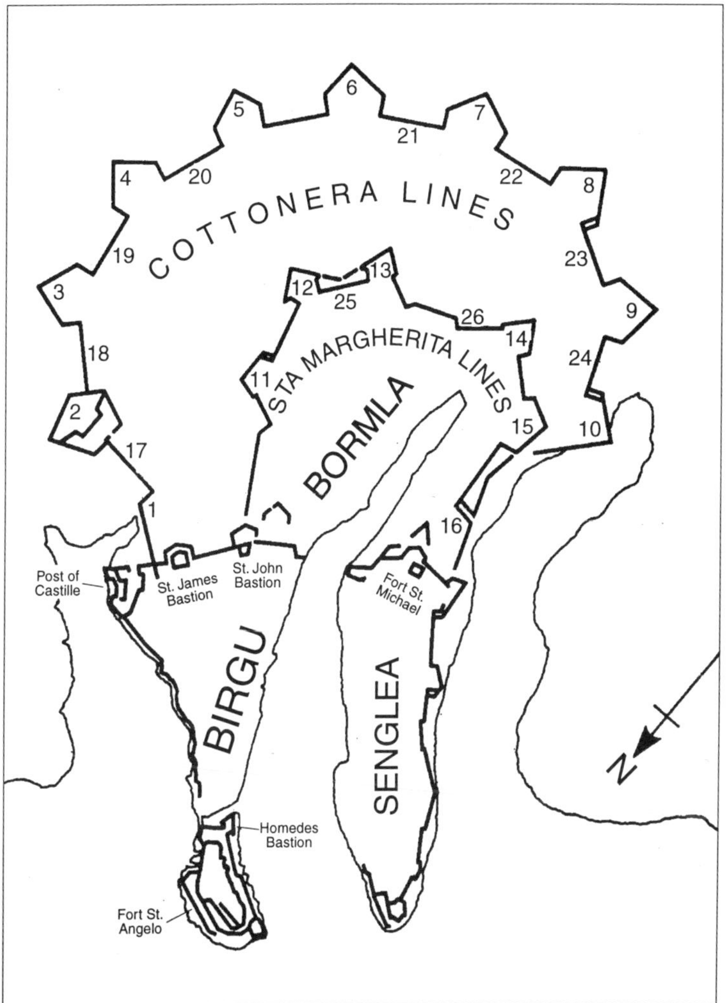

Bastions

1 St. Lawrence
2 Salvatore
3 St. Louis
4 St. James
5 Notre Dame
6 St. Clement
7 St. Nicholas
8 St. John
9 St. Paul
10 Valperga
11 Firenzuola
12 Sta Margherita
13 St. Helen
14 St John Almoner
15 St. Francis
16 St Raphael

Gates

17 Salvatore
18 St Louis
19 St. James
20 Notre Dame
21 St. Clement
22 Polverista
23 St. John
24 St. Paul
25 Verdala
26 St. Helen

Fig. 4. Birgu, Senglea, Sta. Margherita and Cottonera.

given to Firenzuola's figures. The true cost of the fortifications, Firenzuola maintained, lay not in the initial building but in the perpetual expense of a garrison. The open fort design minimized this, removing as it did the necessity of providing a garrison except when an assault was anticipated. Taking a long-term view, once the Sta. Margherita fortifications were completed and the harbour protected, the island would be in a constant state of readiness whenever an enemy chose to attack. Thus the existing pattern of hurried and expensive emergency preparations on each alarm would become a thing of the past. He reckoned that the makeshift measures in which the Order had hitherto indulged cost 200,000 scudi each time the Turk armed himself. Turning to the fortifications on Sciberras, Firenzuola found no fault with the design or execution of the Floriana lines, but believed them to be superfluous since the Valletta front occupied the best site on the peninsula. Thus he recommended the addition of three ravelins to the latter but gave overall priority to the building of the Sta. Margherita lines, suggesting that work on all other projects should cease until they were defendable.

The council approved Firenzuola's report on 26 November but appointed a commission to examine the proposals more thoroughly. After this had been done the council once again determined to execute Firenzuola's designs, and to take advantage of his presence ordered that the works be outlined immediately in earth. The foundation stone was therefore laid as early as 30 December. The decision to proceed with Sta. Margherita and cease work on Floriana was, however, apparently controversial because it was confirmed yet again on 9 December and on 12 January 1639.[21] Firenzuola's plans received their fair share of criticism, but, as was so often the case, construction was well under way before any constructive criticism from experts abroad could reach the island. Details of the schemes were sent to the Christian princes and in particular to the Spanish king and his Sicilian viceroy, but this was a mere formality and no pretence was made of awaiting their opinions before embarking upon the execution of the project.[22] Philip IV of Spain handed the plans over to Claudio Riccardo for appraisal, but it was not until October 1639 that he produced his comment on them.[23]

---

21 AOM 256, ff. 185 (26 November 1638), 186 (2 December), 186v. (9 December); AOM 112, f. 117v. (30 December); AOM 257, f. 4 (12 January 1639).

22 AOM 256, f. 185 (26 November 1638); Borg, p. 58.

23 AOM 6554, f. 59; Borg, p. 58.

The general criticism levelled by Riccardo at Sta. Margherita was similar to that encountered by Floriana: that the construction would take too long and cost too much and that to provide a garrison was beyond the Order's resources. But every major project undertaken by the knights from the building of Valletta onwards had been open to this criticism and the knights were by now singularly unimpressed by such arguments. Their overriding interest was the security of their island base and the survival of their Order. Even in the most unfavourable circumstances they contrived to build fortifications, always optimistic that the work would eventually be completed. Riccardo recommended that Birgu and Senglea be protected by two forts rather than by a ring of fortifications. This advice was conveyed to the Order in a letter from the king which reached Malta in December 1639, by which time work on the Sta. Margherita lines had been under way for a full year.[24]

The criticisms voiced by the Bailiff Estampes de Valençay, when building had already been in progress for five months, that the project would demand too much time and money, likewise passed unheeded.[25] The Marquis of St. Angelo, who visited Malta in the spring of the following year, also believed that Firenzuola's project was unnecessarily ambitious.[26] He would have retained the portion in front of Birgu, the building of which he described as 'well-advanced', linking it to the Birgu front by simple walls. He recommended the strengthening of Birgu and Senglea, the former by the addition of two ravelins to the front and the retrenching of the post of Castile, the latter by remodelling the front and raising some of the walls. Other criticisms of Firenzuola's lines emphasized much the same complaints as Riccardo and St. Angelo and put forward similar solutions. One author suggested restricting the defences to a five-bastioned fort on Sta. Margherita hill which would require an ordinary guard of 700 men as opposed to the 1,800 of the more ambitious scheme. The fortifications of Senglea were, this writer believed, near perfect; so that they required no new fort to add to their security.[27] Domenico

---

24 Letter dated 25 November 1639 (AOM 6554, f. 61); registered in the *Liber Conciliorum Status*, 26 December 1639 (AOM 257, f. 40); decrees that work should continue on the Sta. Margherita lines, dated 30 March and 14 September 1639 (AOM 257, ff. 10v. and 36v.).

25 AOM 257, f. 14 (16 May 1639).

26 AOM 6554, f. 31 (1 April 1640); plan (see plate 10) Chigi, N III 77, f. 146 and Barb. Lat. 9905/6; Dal Pozzo, II, 45-6; detailed instructions for work given in AOM 6554, f. 35 (12 April 1640).

27 AOM 6554, f. 55.

Plate 11 Post of Castille, Birgu.

Guazzo, who was in Malta during the emergency of 1645, also advocated a single fort, but wished to site it nearer the old fronts of Birgu and Senglea rather than on the heights of Sta. Margherita.[28] Giovanni Bendinelli Pallavicino suggested shortening the Sta. Margherita lines so that they protected the harbour at Bormla which could remain open to friendly ships.[29] His proposals for improvements to the post of Castile imply that the Marquis of St. Angelo's proposed retrenchment had not been executed. The Senglea front, Pallavicino argued, could be covered even from the truncated Sta. Margherita lines and for further protection a water-filled ditch joining Galley and French creeks could be cut. Of the other engineers present in the island in 1645 Pagan supported the fortification of the two hills, Sta. Margherita and the hill in front of Senglea, which could, he believed, be manned by the garrisons of Birgu and Senglea.[30] The Sta. Margherita lines were also commended by an author who submitted his report anonymously to the Vice-Chancellor Bueno;[31] he

28 AOM 6554, f. 53. Domenico Guazzo was sent by the grand duke of Tuscany in 1645 to assist in the fortification of the island.
29 AOM 6554, f. 75 (8 July 1645).
30 AOM 6554, f. 84.
31 AOM 6554, f. 70.

advised the Order to execute Firenzuola's design in preference to Floriani's; the latter's, he maintained, was the most useless, defective and costly of all the fortification schemes, while Clerville advocated improvements to Senglea and Birgu, particularly to the post of Castile which he regarded as the weakest point in the defences, but expressed no opinion on the merit of the Sta. Margherita lines.[32]

The Order was indeed inundated with conflicting advice and it is difficult to discover which, if any, it acted upon. In February 1645 the council decreed that the report of the commissioners of fortification should be executed but this report referred only to the old fortifications;[33] they recommended improvements to the ditch, covert-way and glacis of Senglea which would entail the demolition of houses in Bormla. In Birgu the parapets needed attention, as did the covert-way. It appears from further council decrees that these modifications were carried out.[34] On 31 May the congregation decided to 'follow the advice of the engineers', probably Arpajon and Pallavicino, regarding the fortifications at Valletta, Birgu, Senglea and Floriana.[35] The 'new' bastion at the post of Castile, probably the hornwork, and the 'modern' mezzaluna outside the front of Birgu mentioned in a report of 1665 may owe their origin to this decree; they certainly date from the decade 1636-46 but without more information it is impossible to know precisely when they were commenced or whose design was adopted.[36] The completion of Floriana took priority over the other work and the congregation was soon transferring workers from Senglea to Floriana.[37] Indeed, despite the strain on their resources the knights were not prepared to abandon either the Floriani or the Firenzuola scheme, although in 1645 they did approve modifications to both projects. It appears that the congregation decided to implement the proposal of Pallavicino to restrict the Sta. Margherita lines and the new trace was outlined by means of trenches, but in the event the completion of even this less ambitious scheme was beyond the Order's capabilities.[38]

---

32 AOM 6554, f. 92.

33 AOM 257, f. 198v. (21 February); copy of report at AOM 6553, f. 51v.

34 AOM 257, f. 204 (27 February and 2 March); AOM 6553, ff. 28, 28v., 29 and 63v. (27 February, 2 March, 7 March and 15 June).

35 AOM 6553, f. 62v.

36 AOM 6554, f. 111 (4 May 1665); Blondel, writing in 1681, claimed that the large high tenaille behind the post of Castile was built in 1645 (PRO WO 55, 1555/1, p. 177).

37 AOM 6553, f. 63v. (11 June 1645).

38 AOM 6553, f. 61v. (6 July 1645); Blondel in 1681 comments on these trenches (PRO WO 55, 1555/1, p. 230).

The original estimate of the cost of the Sta. Margherita lines, as designed by Firenzuola, was 70,000 scudi, which appears unduly modest.[39] However, acting upon this figure the Order arranged to borrow 60,000 scudi, thus raising the problem of repayment.[40] An authorization permitting the grand master to receive a hundred minors into the Order would bring in only 5,000 scudi,[41] and by the spring of 1639 difficulties were already being encountered so that work progressed only subject to the availability of money.[42] In May a further 122,000 scudi were borrowed, thus extending the debt with no firmer prospects of repayment.[43] Not unnaturally this expensive project had its critics among the members of the Order, one of whom, the Bailiff Valençay, calculated in May 1639 that 100,000 scudi was needed to complete and perfect it.[44] In fact, after an initial burst of enthusiasm work on the Sta. Margherita lines ground to a halt. The Marquis of St. Angelo found them half-built in 1640 and Pallavicino described them in much the same state in 1645. By the following year it had become abundantly clear that the effort to complete both Floriana and Sta. Margherita was producing an intolerable drain on the Order's resources and that the treasury was exhausted.[45] The Sta. Margherita lines therefore remained in a very imperfect state, with only the Sta. Margherita bastion more or less complete and the Firenzuola and St. Helen bastions half-built, until the early eighteenth century when the Order gathered its strength for a final attempt to perfect these memorials to its lack of purpose and of money.

II. The Cottonera Lines, St. Angelo, Birgu and Senglea

The Order's abandonment of the Sta. Margherita lines in the latter half of the seventeenth century should not be taken as an indication that it had lost interest in the defence of the harbour, Birgu and Senglea. Work practically ceased on Sta. Margherita in the fifteen years after 1645 but these were years of some financial stringency, and the knights were lulled into a false sense of security by the

39 Borg, p. 59.
40 AOM 256, f. 186v. (8 December 1638) and AOM 1417 (20 December 1638).
41 AOM 256, f. 186v. (9 December).
42 AOM 257, f. 10v. (30 March 1639).
43 AOM 257, ff. 13v. and 14v. (16 and 19 May 1639).
44 AOM 257, f. 14 (16 May 1639).
45 AOM 258, f. 67 (9 August 1646).

Turkish assault on Candia. Although any attack on a Christian power was to be deprecated, no assault on Malta was likely while the Turk was engaged elsewhere. Once Candia fell in 1669, however, and an attack on Malta became a distinct possibility, the knights did turn their attention to the need to fortify the harbour and summoned Antonio Maurizio Valperga to survey the islands' defences and advise on improvements.

Contemporary rumour has it that the scheme which Valperga first outlined for the defence of the harbour, a modification of the Firenzuola lines, was rejected by Grand Master Nicholas Cotoner on the grounds that it was insufficiently large to act as a memorial to his grand mastership. The trace approved by the council on 2 April 1670 consisted of eight bastions and two demi-bastions encircling Sta. Margherita hill and linking up with the fronts of Birgu and Senglea; beyond the main enceinte were eight mezzalunas, a ditch, covert-way and glacis. Further protection for the port was to be afforded by a fort constructed on Orsi point at the harbour entrance.[46] It was indeed a grand project the designer of which had three aims: to occupy the heights from which the enemy might batter Birgu, Senglea and Bormla; to protect the harbour; and to afford shelter to the people of the countryside in time of siege.[47]

The money to pay for these new works had to be raised and there was some months' delay while this was set in hand. The commissioners of fortification were instructed to examine ways of finding money and on 13 May they produced a report outlining five possible sources.[48] Firstly they recommended that every effort should be made to extract the money owing from the French king for the island of St. Christopher which he had purchased from the Order; secondly, a permit should be obtained from the same king to fell and sell timber from the French estates; all outstanding debts should be collected; authority should be sought from the pope to impose a levy of 100,000 scudi on the non-moveable goods of the island; and abuses of the postal system costing the treasury some 8,000 scudi a year should be prevented by the appointment of a postmaster. The grand master undertook to support the building effort with 100 scudi a month of his own money and the use of his personal slaves in the construction work.[49] The common

46 AOM 261, f. 161v.

47 Dal Pozzo, II, 388; the actual report presented by Valperga on 2 April does not appear to have survived.

48 AOM 261, ff. 162 (8 April 1670) and 164v. (13 May); Dal Pozzo, II, 390.

49 AOM 261, 162 (8 April); Dal Pozzo, II, 391.

treasury was instructed to pay out 8,000 scudi a month as from 1 June 1670 towards the cost of the new fortifications on Sta. Margherita hill and Orsi point.[50] In addition the French king permitted the sale of wood up to the value of 300,000 livres,[51] and the pope responded favourably to a request for help. He allowed the conversion of a tax on eatables, sanctioned in 1645 but never levied, into a levy on non-moveable goods whereby 100,000 scudi could be raised.[52] The Order argued that this later levy was a fairer basis of taxation since it distributed the burden equitably between rich and poor but the proposed change ran into opposition led by the clergy and a customs duty was imposed to raise the sum.[53] The imposition of new taxes on the islanders was hardly a speedy way of raising money. But the military situation required prompt action and the allocation of 8,000 scudi a month from the treasury was considered sufficient, with the prospect of further revenue being raised in the future, to commence construction. The knights moved cautiously at first sanctioning only the building of one bastion as a specimen and model for the others.[54] Nearly three months later the official stone-laying ceremony took place at the bastion of St. Nicholas[55] and work continued throughout the lifetime of Nicholas Cotoner.

Valperga's scheme was not well received abroad. It undoubtedly placed a strain on the Order's resources, and whatever may have been the grand master's part in insisting on a grandiose project, it was the engineer who had to bear the criticism. The necessity of fortifying the harbour was not questioned, but the manner in which Valperga chose to do this was. Gaspare Beretta, a Milanese engineer of some repute who had served the Hapsburgs in Italy, Spain and Burgundy, attacked the design of the bastions, curtains, mezzalunas, ditches and covert-way; but, not having examined the terrain, he did not comment on the wisdom of occupying the site in question.[56] Beretta considered the curtains and bastions to be too

---

50 AOM 261, f. 166 (10 June 1670).

51 AOM 261, f. 177 (25 May 1671).

52 AOM 261, ff. 166 (31 May 1670), 173v. (23 January 1671); Pauli, II, 362 (brief dated 22 November 1670); Dal Pozzo, II, 390.

53 AOM 261, f. 170v. (18 September 1670); Mifsud, 'Papi', p. 425.

54 AOM 261, f. 166 (10 June 1670); a recent margin note in the volume claims that this bastion, presumably the Valperga bastion, was demolished in 1900 to make way for a large dockside crane.

55 AOM 261, f. 169v. (28 August 1670); Dal Pozzo, II, 389.

56 AOM 6402, f. 296 (4 December 1670, Milan) and other copies at AOM 1011, f. 27 and AOM 6554, f. 136. Gaspare Beretta (1624-1703) undertook commissions for the rulers of Mantua, Savoy and Genoa, and became chief engineer of the state of Milan (*DBI*, IX, 48-51).

small, and recommended curtains of at least one hundred paces, about four hundred feet, and bastion faces of sixty paces, although even this was less than was being recommended by some French engineers at the time. He also argued that if the same area were encircled with only six bastions the enceinte would be greatly improved. Because the bastions were crowded together it was impossible to construct mezzalunas, and the enemy might easily turn Valperga's mezzalunas to their advantage. Beretta also disapproved of ditches running parallel to the faces of the bastions. But, above all, he doubted whether any site would permit the execution of the completely regular trace which Valperga had designed; it was always advisable to adapt the fortifications to the terrain deriving what benefit one could rather than laying out a geometrically regular trace. A few months later, in April 1671, Beretta once again expressed his opinion on Valperga's fortifications, when commenting on the report of Valperga's proposals which the Order's Vice-Chancellor Manoel Arias had presented to the grand master.[57] He acknowledged the need to protect the port, but again cautioned against a design in which the mezzalunas could easily be turned against the main enceinte, an enceinte in any case too restricted for the number of bastions which it included.

Like Beretta, Count Verneda, the chief engineer of the Venetian Republic, felt that the enceinte should be stretched out. He favoured retaining the original number of bastions but wished to expand the line to enclose Salvatore point and the fort on Orsi point, for the fort designed by Valperga was not, he believed, capable of prolonged resistance.[58] An enceinte of 1,130 canes (about 2,500 yards) extending from the Valperga demi-bastion to the sea could be sustained by the same number of bastions as Valperga's lines, eight full and two demi-bastions. The longer enceinte, enclosing far more ground, represented, however, a more profitable use of resources. Verneda found fault not only with Valperga's general conception but also with the details of his scheme: he criticized the cavaliers sited on the bastions, the ditches running parallel to the bastion faces and the outworks. If anything French opinion was even more firmly opposed to Valperga's

---

57 AOM 6402, f. 304; AOM 6551, f. 52; AOM 6554, f. 143; the first two copies claim that the remarks were made by Beretta on 1 April 1671; if this is indeed the case he refers to himself in the third person, but even if the remarks were not actually written by Beretta, the author was recounting Beretta's opinions.

58 AOM 6551, f. 55v.(30 July 1671); the plan in the Royal Malta Library which accompanied this report is wrongly dated 1761. Verneda had served for twenty-nine months as engineer and superintendent of artillery and fortification in Candia.

project. Louis XIV objected to it *in toto* as far beyond the resources of the Order either to construct or to defend.[59] The Order's resident engineer, the Frenchman Blondel, writing in 1681, voiced the same objections as the earlier critics:[60] Valperga was trying to impose a regular enceinte on irregular terrain; his design followed the Dutch school which, as Beretta had also pointed out, was rapidly becoming outdated; the parts, such as the bastions, were too small, and, consequently, the line of defence was too short. Blondel favoured Verneda's proposition that a far larger area be enclosed by eight bastions fortified in the manner of Vauban. But by 1681 Cottonera had been under construction for ten years and there was no question of changing the design.

Before he departed in October 1670 Valperga had drawn up a report in which he recommended various adjustments to adapt the fortifications to the terrain, leaving the details to Blondel.[61] Blondel was abroad throughout 1670 and probably did not return until well into the following year, by which time work was in full swing.[62] Even after his departure Valperga naturally retained an interest in the project which was to stand as evidence of his skill, and a full ten years later wrote from Turin urging that the mezzalunas be constructed according to his design.[63] Building had continued throughout the decade but with the death of Nicholas Cotoner in 1680 the scheme lost its great champion who had seen the fortifications as a memorial to perpetuate his name. In those ten years the whole enceinte had been laid out and revetted almost up to the cordon, and even to the parapets in some places.[64] Nearly everywhere a third of the terrapleining and half of the ditch had been completed. As any major alterations such as those suggested by Verneda were clearly impossible, Blondel merely suggested improvements: the re-siting of the cavaliers which in the original design encumbered the bastions, the provision of low flanks, the widening and realignment of the ditches, the extension of the terrapleins to provide space for retrenchments, adjustments to the heights of the various parts, and the addition of

---

59 W. Porter, *The History of the Fortress of Malta* (Malta, 1858), p. 153.

60 PRO WO 55, 1555/1, p. 183. Blondel had been abroad on sick leave in 1670 and obviously resented having to implement a scheme on which his advice had not been asked. He shared with his brother François a very low opinion of Valperga's merits as an engineer.

61 AOM 6554, f. 119 (15 October 1670); AOM 6551, f. 45.

62 The earliest records of payments being made to contractors engaged in Cottonera cover the period 22 December 1670 to 17 May 1671 (AOM 1011, f. 9).

63 AOM 6551, f. 60 (10 October 1680).

64 Details taken from Blondel's report of 1681 (PRO WO 55, 1555/1, p. 204).

two large mezzalunas in front of St. John's and St. Louis's bastions to impede the approach of the enemy. Grunenberg, also reporting in 1681, was not satisfied with the mutual flanking support which the bastions offered each other and suggested additional improvements.[65] When it became possible to construct the mezzalunas, he recommended that the knights should commence with those near the bastion of St. Louis.

Valperga in 1680 had described the fortifications as almost complete except for the mezzalunas whose construction he urged.[66] But the mezzalunas were never built. By 1680 Cottonera had consumed an immense sum of money, sufficient indeed to have completed the Sta. Margherita lines. Carafa, Cotoner's successor as grand master, ordered that work should cease, and the expert whom he summoned to review the fortifications, Grunenberg, directed the Order's attention and resources elsewhere, to St. Elmo, Floriana, Ricasoli and St. Angelo, so that the main enceinte of Cottonera remained incomplete until well into the eighteenth century and the outworks were never constructed.

Grunenberg is perhaps best remembered for his additions to fort St. Angelo. These were indeed memorable since they altered the whole outline of the fort giving it the distinctive profile which it retains to this day. The decision taken in 1638 to fortify Sta. Margherita hill undoubtedly relieved the pressure on the defences of St. Angelo, Birgu and Senglea. The existing fortifications were not neglected as can be seen from references to work carried out in them,[67] but no serious attempt was made to modernize them; they were, instead, superseded as the first line of defence. St. Angelo, however, still had an important part to play in the defence of Grand Harbour. In recognition of this fact the council in 1658 ordered the common treasury to allocate 10,000 scudi to be used in the restoration of the fort.[68] This was hardly a large sum compared with the 8,000 scudi a month which the treasury was to spend on Cottonera, and one may wonder at the extent of the repairs when it is realized that the estimated cost of rebuilding the wall adjacent to the gate of Birgu was 12,000 scudi.[69] Although the restoration of St. Angelo was intended to improve its defence, by the standards of the late seventeenth century

---

65 AOM 6554, f. 167 (14 March 1681).
66 AOM 6551, f. 60.
67 See above, chapter 5 i.
68 AOM 260, f. 38 (18 June 1658).
69 AOM 261, ff. 166 (10 June 1670) and 22 (5 May 1665).

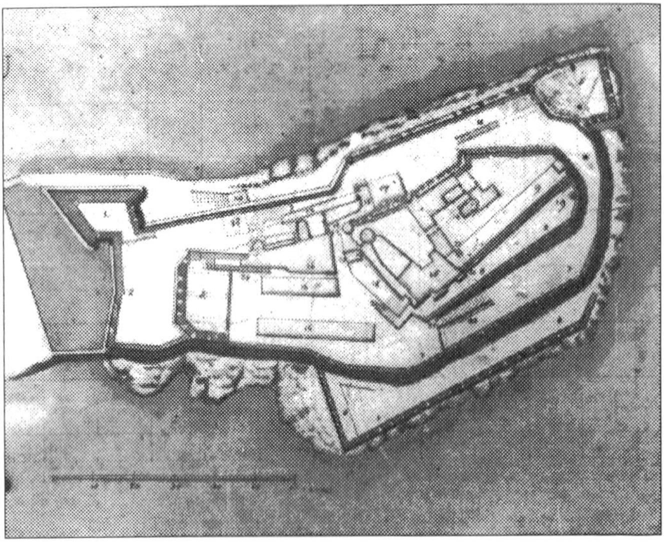

Plate 12 Plan of fort St. Angelo, eighteenth-century (RML Map A1).

it remained a weak work. Blondel described it as surrounded by high irregular scarped walls in need of repair,[70] and the low-level La Valette battery was also in need of attention. The land front was protected by a high revetted tenaille in front of which was a water-filled ditch separating the fort from Birgu. Blondel believed that the rocks at the foot of the castle should be occupied by a strong wall six to eight feet thick to prevent a lodgement by an enemy. Valperga had also recognized the threat posed by these rocks and those around St. Elmo, Birgu, Senglea and Ricasoli, but no action had been taken to deny an enemy access. These rocks attracted the attention of Grunenberg and on his second visit to Malta in the spring of 1687 he drew up a scheme for the protection of the harbour entrance,[71] in which he suggested that the rocks around St. Angelo, Senglea point, Ricasoli and St. Elmo be levelled into a form of fausse-braye, which would act as water-level batteries. Around St. Angelo the rocky shore was, he thought, sufficiently wide to build a further three batteries, one above the other,[72] while at Senglea point it would be possible to

70 PRO WO 55, 1555/1, p. 173 (1681).

71 AOM 262, f. 289 (26 February 1687); AOM 6554, f. 187; Dal Pozzo, II, 632.

72 The water-level battery of St. Angelo was frequently damaged by the sea; after its destruction by a *gregale* or storm in 1851 it was not rebuilt (Porter, p. 160).

Plate 13 Fort St. Angelo from Valletta.

construct both a water-level and a higher battery, and around St. Elmo a new enceinte of three bastions. However, the Order felt unable to undertake the work at St. Angelo as well as the St. Elmo enceinte, and the latter project was considered the more urgent. Finding that building at St. Angelo had not commenced when he made his third visit in the winter of 1689-90, Grunenberg offered to finance the construction of three batteries from his own pocket, as well as a water-level battery at Senglea.[73] The knights accepted his generous offer and building seems to have commenced immediately.[74] Grunenberg did not linger to supervise the execution of these works, nor did he return to the island to inspect their progress. It would appear that, as was the case with the St. Elmo enceinte, once the decision to build was taken the project was swiftly carried out, and by the time of the next general examination of the islands' defensive system in 1715 the relevant additions had been made to St. Angelo.

---

73 AOM 263, f. 62v. (17 December 1689) and AOM 6554, ff. 205 and 209; AOM 263, f. 65v. (23 February 1690) and AOM 6554, f. 207.

74 See AOM 1016, *passim*, for references to work in St. Angelo and Senglea.

The circumstances in which the fortifications of Birgu and Senglea had been rebuilt after the siege to their original design at a time when the Order's main effort was directed elsewhere, and their increasing age, ensured that during the seventeenth century their upkeep became a growing burden. The Maltese building stone had a long life but only if well maintained and cared for, and, with the construction of Valletta, Floriana and then Sta. Margherita, Birgu and Senglea did not have first call on the knights' meagre funds. Birgu was found to be in serious need of repair in 1654 and again in 1665;[75] on the first occasion a wall had collapsed, and on the second, the wall adjacent to the harbour gate was threatening to do so. In the latter case the estimated cost for making good the damage was 12,000 scudi. The general state of the defences of Birgu and Senglea as revealed by the report of May 1665 was hardly encouraging. The walls of Birgu along Kalkara creek and the land front needed attention. The modern mezzaluna outside the front was one cane below its intended height and its ditch and counterscarp had barely been begun. Senglea point which provided protection for St. Angelo was in a state of near collapse; the walls of Senglea opposite Corradino along French creek required revetting afresh although they could be patched up; the front also demanded repair, especially the bastion which guarded the harbour and the mole beneath. However, the restoration of the wall between the two gates of Birgu, the Marina and upper gates, was singled out as the most urgent task, and funds were made available. Within two years the Order was also able to undertake improvements to the Corradino flank of Senglea, but, as was so often the case, this had to be abandoned before completion.[76]

Although he recognized the weakness of the Senglea fortifications, Valperga preferred to enclose them in an outer ring of defences rather than undertake any substantial work in the old fortifications, so that eleven years later Blondel painted a depressing picture of the Senglea defences.[77] The land front was a hundred years out-of-date and in bad repair. The shoulder of the centre bastion had collapsed into the ditch a short while before and the only outwork was a little ditchless ravelin built in the time of De Paule

---

75 AOM 259, f. 100v. (30 September 1654) and AOM 261, f. 22 (5 May 1665).
76 AOM 739, f. 39v. (9 May 1667).
77 PRO WO 55, 1555/1, p. 165.

(1623-36). Alterations had been made to the bastion on the right wing of the front in 1645 but these had never been completed and the bastion was nine feet below its intended height. Rock had to be cut down to water level to the right of the bastion, in front of the tenaille adjoining the bastion, and all along the French creek flank of the town. A large part of the stonework of that flank had been renewed in 1667 but it was necessary to finish the task as the masonry near the point had deteriorated very badly and was near to collapse. The bastion in the centre of the French creek flank, designed to protect the town from bombardment from Corradino, would, in Blondel's view, have to be perfected, although he pointed out that as yet the builders were still some distance short of the cordon. The other flank, opposite Birgu, was without any fortifications. In the past, strategists had relied on the two towns to protect each other, but this was not good enough for Blondel. He advocated four platforms, jutting out as far as possible, even to the extent of being in the sea.

Blondel also proposed to fortify the Galley creek flank of Birgu. Its other flank, along Kalkara creek, was in a reasonable state, the breaches having been repaired a few years earlier; but even here work had not been completed and part of the parapet would have to be restored. The post of Castile had been repaired in haste and in the course of time had become totally dilapidated. The breaches would have to be repaired and the whole revetted afresh with more batter than that possessed by the old walls. Despite earlier reports and resolutions by the council the bastion on the right wing of the land front, and the Marina gate situated in the bastion's right face, were very ruined. Blondel proposed a new bastion, the salient angle of which would project some sixty feet further than that of the old, and at least thirty feet into the sea. A large part of its right face would have foundations under water and its right flank would defend the arsenal and the shore line. The Marina gate would in addition have to be re-sited in the left flank of the new bastion.

It was not until the 1690s, however, that the knights implemented any of Blondel's recommendations apart from his suggestion that the rocky shore be fashioned into a fausse-braye. This measure was advocated by Grunenberg in his report of 26 February 1687 and in December 1689 he offered to finance the construction of such a battery at Senglea point.[78] In the early 1690s a considerable

[78] AOM 6554, ff. 187, 205 and 209.

volume of repair work was carried out in both Birgu and Senglea,[79] and in June 1695 the question of repairs to the Marina gate of Birgu came up once again.[80] Blondel had pointed out its sorry state on numerous occasions and eventually on 4 July 1695 persuaded the congregation of fortification to visit the site and decide on an appropriate course of action. In consequence he was instructed to compile a report which was presented to the council on 14 July.[81] He proposed that a medium-sized demi-bastion be built in front of the old walls so that it would flank the main gate of Birgu. Within the demi-bastion he suggested the construction of magazines to give much-needed accommodation for galley stores. The exposed faces of the demi-bastion were to be protected against the elements by a facing of hard stone, mortar and pozzolana. He recalled an earlier proposal to restore the gate during the grand mastership of Nicholas Cotoner, probably in 1665, and lamented that nothing had been done while costs were constantly rising. The total cost of the work which he now recommended would be 4,500 scudi not including the cost of the foundations. The council sanctioned Blondel's design, and on the 28 July he marked out the site of the foundations and saw to it that building material was prepared.[82] There is no actual record of the work being carried out but we must assume that it was, for at the next general review of the fortifications in 1715 the Marina gate was no longer singled out for particular criticism. But the fortifications of Birgu were still old and intrinsically weak and in constant need of care and attention. In the hiatus which appears to have followed Blondel's death, when no resident engineer was appointed, the Birgu fortifications suffered heavily, so that by 1714 all Blondel's good work had been undone and the walls were again in a parlous state.

III. Sta. Margherita and Cottonera in the Eighteenth Century

During the early years of the eighteenth century the fortifications in general appear to have been somewhat neglected, and except for brief periods in 1703 and 1708 the Order was without an engineer. The knights were unhappy about this state of affairs, but these

79 AOM 1016, *passim*.
80 AOM 1016, pp. 351, 361, 363-76.
81 AOM 1016, pp. 367 and 370; AOM 6551, ff. 71v. and 72v.
82 AOM 1016, p. 374; AOM 6551, f. 73v.

were relatively peaceful years and there were no regular reports from Constantinople of alarming preparations which might presage an attack. Although maintenance work on the fortifications continued, without the stimulus provided by fear of an assault, the Order's provisions for defence were inadequate. Fortunately no major developments were proposed between 1700 and 1714 but even the existing fortifications suffered when no engineer could plead their needs, and no emergency force the knights to acknowledge their importance.

In September 1714 the commissioners of fortification reported that the fortifications of Sta. Margherita were unfinished, those of Birgu almost destroyed and those of Cottonera incapable of completion in the near future.[83] As a compromise solution they suggested that Sta. Margherita should be rendered defendable since it would cover Birgu, Senglea and Bormla, and protect the interior of the Cottonera lines. The commissioners' advice was accepted and work on Sta. Margherita commenced without delay.[84] When Tigné arrived in Malta in the spring of 1715 he was faced with a collection of unfinished fortresses, Floriana, Sta. Margherita, Cottonera and Ricasoli. Despite his reluctance to allow works to remain half-built and exposed to the elements, he soon decided that, for the time being at least, any thought of completing Cottonera, on which the enormous sum of 1,400,000 scudi had already been expended, would have to be abandoned. However, since the most northerly demi-bastion, St. Lawrence, covered both Birgu and the Salvatore hill he recommended that it be converted into a detached fort.[85] The modifications could be completed in two months with little expense and when the lines were perfected the fort could revert to its original function as one of the demi-bastions in the enceinte. The Cottonera lines, however, found a champion in Philippe de Vendôme, the prior of France.

The fate of the Cottonera lines was one of the points at issue in the controversy which raged during the summer of 1715 between the Vendôme faction and the group of engineers led by Tigné.[86] Once the fortification of the coasts and Floriana was complete, Vendôme believed nothing to be more urgent than the perfection of Cottonera. The ditch, counterscarp and parapets should be constructed immediately, and when the funds were available the mezzalunas and

---

83 AOM 266, f. 114 (20 September); AOM 6552, f. 1.

84 AOM 6552, ff. 1v. (24 September), 2v. (11 October) – permission sought to demolish the chapel of Sta. Margherita in order to proceed with the fortifications – and 4 (19 December).

85 AOM 266, f. 145 (1 March 1715); AOM 6552, f. 13v.

86 See chapter 4 iv for further discussion of the controversy.

covert-way could also be built.[87] Maigret, the French engineer appointed to execute Vendôme's scheme for the defence of the coast, also preferred the Cottonera to the Sta. Margherita lines.[88] The former he believed were inherently stronger, would provide shelter for the Maltese, and give a better return on the capital invested. Maigret's attack on Tigné was, however, construed as a criticism of the congregation of fortification and its conduct of the defences since 1714, and the Order's second engineer Bachelieu took upon himself the task of disabusing those readers of Maigret's report of any misconceptions which he had managed to instil in them.[89] Although Maigret had claimed to be expressing the views of Vendôme this was refuted by Bachelieu who insisted that before his departure Vendôme had approved Tigné's projects.

Tigné never suggested abandoning or demolishing Cottonera but believed the Sta. Margherita scheme more appropriate to the Order's resources. Should it ever become possible to complete Cottonera he was prepared to support this provided Sta. Margherita were not neglected.[90] He admitted that even in its present state Cottonera would act as an outer defence for the Sta. Margherita lines, but in his report of September 1715 he advocated the construction of a counterscarp, ditch and detailed variations to the parapets. He gave no such detailed instructions for Sta. Margherita. The glacis and parts of the ramparts had, he realized, to be completed, but his chief concern was the provision of strong lines of communication between Sta. Margherita and Birgu and Senglea. If all went according to plan these last two fortresses should be secure within an outer ring of defences, so Tigné made only modest suggestions for their improvement. He would occupy all the shore of the Corradino flank of Senglea by a tenaille or faussebraye and complete the covert-way around the mezzaluna on the land front. In Birgu he was seriously concerned only about the post of Castile which lay outside the protection of the Cottonera enceinte. Its parapets and banquettes had to be in good repair to repulse the first shock of an enemy attack. For further security he recommended the construction of a retrenchment which could flank the ditch of the left face of the St. James bastion of the Birgu land front.

---

87 AOM 6552, f. 39v.; RML MS. 1301, p. 121.
88 AOM 6552, f. 40v.; RML MS. 290; Clerkenwell, MS. 0 1, item 1.
89 AOM 6552, f. 50v.
90 See Tigné's report of 25 September 1715, R.M.L. MS. 1301, p. 77.

Plate 14 Salvatore Bastion, Sta. Margherita, from Birgu.

On his return visit to Malta a year later Tigné found that some progress had been made under the direction of Mondion.[91] Work was under way on the retrenchment at the post of Castile, and on the parapets, flanks and covert-way of Cottonera. But it appears that the Order was unwilling because of its financial state to commence the lines of communication between Birgu, Senglea and Sta. Margherita. Although the communication with Birgu was a relatively simple affair estimated to cost only 5,000 scudi, that with Senglea, because of the difficult terrain, would cost 60,000 scudi. The other works in Sta. Margherita which Tigné listed as being urgent were the building of the interior ramparts, some underground passages and the completion of the covert-way and glacis in front of the three centre bastions. These would cost 11,000 scudi and less pressing work on the covert-way and glacis 5,000 scudi. For the Cottonera lines he outlined a less costly programme, postponing, for the time being, any thought of constructing the mezzalunas. For urgent work he allocated 13,500 scudi: comprising 6,000 scudi to finish the parapets, 6,000 to build three magazines, 1,000 for a road to allow troop movements

91 RML MS. 1301, p. 153 (15 September 1716).

along the foot of the ramparts and 500 to construct a tenaille in front of the gate of Notre Dame della Grazia (Żabbar gate). The programme of non-urgent work was more extensive and was to cost a total of 34,000 scudi. Three powder magazines in the gorges of bastions would come to 9,000 scudi, 10,000 would be needed to construct a counterscarp and 15,000 to level the ditch. In Senglea only the modest expenditure of 6,700 scudi was necessary, of which 5,000 would go to finish a retrenchment along the shore and 1,000 to vault the low flanks of the little bastion on the Corradino flank. Just under 25,000 scudi was to be spent on work in Birgu, virtually all of which was classified as urgent. The major expenditure, 10,000 scudi, was for the repair of the land front, the covert-way from the Marina gate to the communication with Sta. Margherita would consume 5,000 scudi, retrenchments in the Salvatore bastion of Cottonera 4,000 and the post of Castile about 3,000. In 1716, therefore, the two great schemes commenced in the seventeenth century to protect the harbour, Sta. Margherita and Cottonera, required over 128,000 scudi to bring them into a defendable state, more than half the total outlay on fortifications recommended by Tigné But one of the knights' objects in summoning Tigné to inspect the defences had been the hope that he would produce a final solution to the problems arising from the conflicting advice of former engineers and the resultant half-finished fortifications. Tigné's recommendations were therefore accepted by the Order and his plans became the basis for all subsequent developments. It would appear that his advice did impel the knights towards the completion of Sta. Margherita, Cottonera (in a modified form without the mezzalunas) and Floriana.

The enormity of the task which lay before the Order in 1715 can be gauged by the comments made by Mondion after four years later, in 1719.[92] During these years the Order had more or less completed the fortifications of Floriana. In 1717 the Turkish preoccupation with affairs in Hungary promised to be prolonged, so that the knights were encouraged to undertake a fairly lengthy project: the construction of the parapets of Cottonera. They reckoned at least three years would be needed to complete this task, but the very next year, in an attempt to economize, the project was temporarily abandoned. By 1719 the left flank of the Birgu front was in a good state of defence but the Order would derive no benefit from this while the right flank

92 AOM 1011, f. 22v.

remained in so deplorable a condition. Mondion recommended that now Floriana was complete, the Order should concentrate its efforts on the perfection of Birgu, which could be achieved in two years at a cost of 25,000 scudi. Birgu could then withstand a siege for three or four months, whereas Cottonera even with its parapets would delay the enemy for a mere fortnight. Mondion fully intended to complete both Cottonera and Sta. Margherita when circumstances permitted it. When workers could be transferred from Birgu to Cottonera his first priority was to retrench the Salvatore bastion to afford additional protection to Birgu, after which work could then proceed on the Cottonera parapets. In the Sta. Margherita lines he thought it advisable to construct the bastion of St. John the Almoner in such a way that it could be converted into a redoubt at the approach of the enemy if the Sta. Margherita lines were not yet completed.

Tigné's masterplan for the defence of the harbour area, the Order's resolution to finish for once and all the half-built fortifications, and the devoted labour of Mondion ensured that the building work maintained its momentum for a number of years, and in 1722 further spirit was injected into the effort by rumours of a Turkish fleet arming to attack Malta.[93] In consequence, the commissioners of fortification and war were in January 1722 optimistic that by June the defences would be in a reasonable condition, especially if the number of workmen was increased.[94] Birgu, Ricasoli and Cottonera would probably be defendable by June; only Sta. Margherita would remain incomplete and in an emergency some benefit could possibly be derived even from this fort by using it as a retrenchment behind Cottonera. And indeed in June the congregation found it necessary to order only minor amendments to the fortifications of Cottonera, Birgu, Ricasoli and Senglea.[95] The following month, however, the congregation was looking beyond the immediate needs of the emergency and approved a schedule laying out the estimated costs for perfecting various fortifications.[96] From this it emerges that Birgu remained far from complete and that the congregation planned to spend over 18,000 scudi there: 7,000 on the curtain of the right flank, 5,000 at the post of Castile, 3,600 in the construction of magazines, 2,200 to complete the small lunette on the right flank of the front and 1,000 for the glacis in front of this work.

---

93 AOM 267, f. 113v. (16 January 1722).

94 AOM 267, f. 113v. (26 January 1722); Clerkenwell, MS. O 1, item 7.

95 Clerkenwell, MS. O 1, item 5 (25 June 1722) and AOM 1011, f. 38.

96 AOM 1011, f. 43 (8 July 1722).

The total for Cottonera was a more modest 7,600 scudi of which 3,500 was to be employed in building the platforms in the flanks of the bastions and 3,000 in finishing the Salvatore bastion as a small fort. The only work listed in Sta. Margherita was the construction, at a cost of 4,000 scudi, of the bastion of St. John the Almoner as a redoubt which would cover Senglea and the harbour. In December of that year the commissioners of fortification recommended that work should continue along the same lines but they limited expenditure to 2,000 scudi a week.[97] Birgu remained incomplete, especially the right flank of the land front and the post of Castile. The finishing of the retrenchments in the Salvatore bastion and in the St. Raphael bastion were considered urgent tasks. Moreover they advised that an effort be made to perfect Sta. Margherita, and emphasized that, besides the bastion of St. John the Almoner which would defend the right side of the St. Helen valley, another was needed to the left which would link these new fortifications to that part of the Sta. Margherita lines built in the seventeenth century. In addition, beyond St. John's bastion the Sta. Margherita enceinte would have to be joined to those of Cottonera and Senglea. Despite rising costs the knights felt obliged to complete all the works under construction, but decided that no new work was to be commenced unless it could be finished by the following April, before the campaigning season. In the event, by April 1723 the immediate danger of an assault was deemed to have passed. But, although the general citation had been revoked, the council had particularly ordered no slackening of the effort to perfect the fortifications.[98]

By the end of the 1720s the major improvements to Birgu were complete.[99] The alterations to the left of the land front and the mezzaluna covering the main gate were reported finished in 1725; the curtain between the bastions of St. James and St. John was rebuilt in 1727 and by 1728 the whole front was declared renovated.[100] Thereafter the work in Birgu was confined to routine repairs and

---

97 AOM 267, f. 171 (2 December 1722); AOM 1011, f. 11.

98 AOM 267, f. 186v. (1 February 1723).

99 Details taken from Clerkenwell, MS. O 1, item 20.

100 The dates inscribed on the main entrance to Birgu, 1722 on the mezzaluna, 1723 on the gate into St. John's bastion and 1727 on the innermost gate, might suggest that the mezzaluna was completed earlier than Mondion claimed. However I would tend to treat inscriptions with care; they certainly do not indicate when the construction of any particular work commenced, nor even probably when it was finished. They are possibly reliable only as to the date of the inscription itself.

making good damage caused by the elements. The French engineers who visited Malta in 1761 reported favourably on the fortifications of Birgu. They recommended only that the covert-way and glacis should be perfected, and suggested that the weakest section, to the left of the front, might be protected by a tenaille in the ditch.[101] However, these recommendations shared the fate of so many of the proposals made by Bourlamaque and his followers: no action was taken.[102] By the end of the eighteenth century, therefore, the knights believed that the fortifications of Birgu, considering the nature of the site, could not be improved. The various alterations advocated by Tigné had been executed and the land front virtually rebuilt. But the satisfaction with the state of Birgu owed a great deal to its changed role in the overall defence strategy. The addition of two further enceintes, Sta. Margherita and Cottonera, had removed Birgu from the front line of attack and allowed it to act as a citadel. The occupation by these new lines of defence of the heights surrounding Birgu also removed at least some of the danger to the old fortress.[103]

Fort St. Angelo and Senglea also benefited from the cover provided by Sta. Margherita and Cottonera. St. Angelo continued in its dual role as protector of the port and final stronghold for the complex of fortifications on the south-eastern shore of Grand Harbour. It had been greatly strengthened in its former role by the addition of the Grunenberg batteries and no further improvements against external attack were believed to be necessary or possible, although some alterations were made after the abortive slaves' revolt of 1749.[104] Bourlamaque advised only that the fort should be well maintained. However, it appears that in 1761 it was in a poor state of repair,[105] so that the Bailiff de Tigné took in hand its renovation making extensive

---

101 AOM 6557, f. 62 and AOM 6558, f. 70 (18 October 1761).

102 See AOM 1054 (1789).

103 Corradino hill dominated the settlements of Birgu, Senglea and Bormla (see figure 2); there had been various proposals to fortify the heights: Valperga, 1670 (PRO WO 55, 1555/1, p. 239), Verneda, 1671 (AOM 6551, f. 57), Blondel, 1681 (PRO WO 55, 1555/1, pp. 239 and 254), Tigné, 1715 (RML MS. 1301, p. 104), Vendôme, 1715 (RML MS. 1301, p. 124), Maigret, 1715 (AOM 6552, f. 48), Bourlamaque and Pontleroy, 1761 (AOM 6558, ff. 81 and 84), anonymous author, 1789 (AOM 1054, p. 35). However a fort was never constructed there, only a powder magazine in 1756 on Ras Ħanżir.

104 Clerkenwell, MS. O 1, item 21; these alterations included the walling up of a gate and window in the Homedes bastion. Although there is no further record of any modification of this bastion, it bears, among other escutcheons and dates, the arms of Pinto (1741-73) and the date 1769, the significance of which must remain a matter for conjecture. For the slaves' revolt, see chapter 1.

105 AOM 6557, f. 62; AOM 6558, f. 70 (18 October 1761).

use of *żonqor* which would weather better than the common building stone, and work was finished by 1790.[106] At the end of the eighteenth century, therefore, St. Angelo was in good condition, the fort which withstood the siege of 1565 having been strengthened over the intervening years but particularly in the seventeenth century.

Senglea, because it was to be defended by the Sta. Margherita and Cottonera lines, had not featured prominently in Tigné's defence scheme, and this may account for its apparent neglect in the eighteenth century.[107] The reports in 1761 likewise paid little attention to the fortress beyond mentioning that the front required a covert-way the utility of which would itself be greatly enhanced if the crownwork designed by Tigné could be added.[108] In the closing years of the century, however, perhaps because of earlier neglect, the Senglea fortifications appear more frequently in the engineers' reports. In 1762 repair work was in progress at Senglea point.[109] And in the early 1780s urgent work, which necessitated a special allocation of 7,000 scudi, was being carried out on one of the town's bastions then threatening to collapse.[110] But in 1789 the fortifications were again reported to be in very bad condition and their repair was deemed to be second in importance only to that of Valletta and Floriana.[111] Thus in the last decade of the Order's sojourn in Malta Senglea was competing for the dwindling sum still available for the upkeep of the fortifications and it is probable that in 1798 its defences were not in first class condition.

In the course of the eighteenth century, therefore, Cottonera and Sta. Margherita were completed, after a fashion; the encircling ramparts of each fortification were closed, and a would-be attacker was now faced with an unbroken bastioned line. But the outworks were never built and the vast extent of the Order's fortifications ensured that the funds available for their maintenance were barely adequate. Despite continuing work on Sta. Margherita and Cottonera between 1723 and 1761,[112] in the latter year the French engineers reported that they were far from perfect. Bourlamaque estimated that Cottonera

106 AOM 1054, p. 17.
107 Clerkenwell, MS. O 1, item 21.
108 AOM 6557, f. 62; AOM 6558, f. 70 (18 October 1761).
109 AOM 1015, p. 35 (23 July 1762).
110 AOM 6571, f. 124; Royal Malta Library, Valletta, Treasury collection of manuscripts (hereafter referred to as RML Tres.), A 105.
111 AOM 1054, p. 31.
112 See Clerkenwell, MS. O 1, items 20 and 21. In 1734 we find Marandon consulting Antonio de Montaigut, the director of the fortifications in Sicily, about problems which had arisen over alterations to the Cottonera bastions. For details of Montaigut's career see Capel, p. 335.

could only be held for a few days, and even when completed would fall sooner rather than later.[113] The knights' first task was still, he argued, the carrying out of the recommendations made by Tigné over forty years earlier,[114] after which it would be advisable to link the bastions of Notre Dame and St. Clement to the Sta. Margherita lines so that a hornwork was formed, and to construct a large mezzaluna, with redoubt, tenaille, caponier, covert-way and ditch in front of the two bastions. The hornwork would protect Sta. Margherita from assault if an attacker broke through the Cottonera lines. Bourlamaque condemned the bastions of St. John, St. Paul and Valperga as being particularly weak and advised that they should be mined for quick destruction should they fall to the enemy. The Salvatore bastion which could be turned against Birgu should also be mined. Indeed, the engineers were also on the whole very surprised at the poor state of Sta. Margherita. Tigné's designs had, it seems, not been followed faithfully, so that the fortifications were not as well adapted to the terrain as they might have been. They therefore urged the implementation of those parts of his plans, such as the mezzalunas, on which no action had yet been taken.

The French engineers in 1761 were hardly more successful than Tigné in ensuring that their wishes were carried out. In 1789 the enceintes of Sta. Margherita and Cottonera were still incomplete, parapets were unfinished, the ramparts were not terraced throughout, and the occupation by the Maltese of those terrapleins that had been constructed caused their deterioration.[115] The ditch of Cottonera was merely outlined and no counterscarp, glacis or other advanced work had been built. In Sta. Margherita the ditch in front of the St. Helen bastion was scarcely even outlined and elsewhere the ditch was of uneven depth and littered with stones and debris while the covert-way and glacis already constructed were in a bad state, often because the earth had been carried off by earth-hungry civilians. Once the repairs to Valletta, Floriana and Birgu were finished the knights were urged in an anonymous engineer's report to complete first Sta. Margherita and then Cottonera according to Tigné's plans; and afterwards they could consider the construction of the hornwork in front of Sta. Margherita suggested by Bourlamaque and his engineers.

---

113 AOM 6519 and 6555.
114 AOM 6557, f. 62; AOM 6558, f. 70.
115 AOM 1054, p. 13.

At the end of the century it is clear therefore that Sta. Margherita and Cottonera were competing for the Order's fast diminishing resources not only for maintenance work but also for funds to allow the completion of Tigné's plans. It is however, not possible to cite a date on which these fortifications were completed; in some respects they were never finished. Although by the mid-century each presented an unbroken line of bastions and curtains, in eighteenth-century eyes they were imperfect and little more than retrenchments, so long as they lacked outworks, however large and impressive the bastions. Sta. Margherita and Cottonera are therefore perhaps the most dramatic evidence that the Order had sorely over-reached its resources in a compulsive desire to secure its stronghold. Work on both forts dragged on interminably even after Tigné had limited the knights' immediate objectives and postponed indefinitely the execution of Valperga's full scheme. The Order struggled on throughout the eighteenth century to complete the works, but, although finished after a fashion, these never revealed themselves in the full glory conceived by their designers.

IV. FORT RICASOLI

The promontories which intersect the Grand Harbour and Marsamxett appear, at first sight at least, to be ideal positions from which to defend the ports. Having fortified Sciberras, Birgu and Senglea the knights therefore turned their attention to the other peninsulas, Rinella or Gallows point, the Isoletto (actually an island, but only just) and Sta. Maria or Dragut point. By occupying these the Order could provide invaluable flanking support to the main fortifications, and, perhaps more importantly, deny the enemy access to favourable attacking positions.

During the siege of 1565 a battery had been established by the Turks on Rinella point at the entrance to the Grand Harbour opposite St. Elmo and this had played a significant part in the downfall of that fort. However, once Sciberras had been occupied by a strong fortress, namely Valletta, the damage or inconvenience which might be caused by an enemy battery at Rinella was greatly reduced; indeed the very establishment there of hostile artillery within range of the Valletta guns would now be almost impossible. The earliest fortification constructed on Rinella, therefore, was designed to protect the Order not so much from external assault, as from the enemy within. The council decreed in 1602 that a water-level battery be built to prevent escaping slaves from slipping out unnoticed and unchallenged, but there are doubts as to whether or not the order was obeyed.[116] The detection of fleeing slaves was also the primary purpose of the tower built on Rinella point in 1629 at the expense of the knight Alessandro Orsi.[117] Only in the late 1630s were suggestions made that Rinella point might play a more positive role in the defence of the harbour and its fortresses. Two of the engineers consulted by Vertoa, Bolognino and Garay, believed that the whole of the Rinella peninsula should be occupied by fortifications so that an attacker could not establish himself there and hinder the entry of a relief force, and the Marquis of St. Angelo in his report of 1 April 1640 also recommended that a fort be built to remove any threat of enemy bombardment from that quarter.[118] The construction of the fort, however, came well down his list of priorities, which probably accounts for the delay in executing his design. Four years later no action had been taken, although the Order still intended to carry out St. Angelo's recommendations. In fact the knights were considering more drastic action than that proposed by the Marquis and instructed the commissioners of fortification to examine the proposal that the name and garrison of fort St. Angelo be transferred to the new fortress on Rinella point.[119] No trace remains of their report and the matter was never raised again in the council. In 1644, therefore, the knights although committed to construct a fortress on Rinella point had taken no practical steps to implement their intention. They were urged to execute the Marquis's design by two of the engineers who visited Malta the following year, Pallavicino and Pagan,[120] but no action was taken until nearly thirty years later.

---

116 AOM 100, f. 248 (9 August 1602); AOM 296, f. 146v.

117 AOM 109, f. 164v. (15 January 1629); although officially named S. Petrino the tower was generally known as the Orsi tower. It was destroyed by a storm in 1821. It seems to have been constructed on the same model as the other square watch towers of the island. At its base was a semicircular battery which may date from 1602, or may, on the other hand, have been built at the same time as the tower. The 1629 council minute implies that the earlier decrees had not been implemented.

118 Chigi, Q III 69, ff. 31 (4 November 1638) and 35 (16 November 1638); AOM 6554, f. 31 (1 April 1640). There is a drawing of Rinella dated Malta 1647 which purports to show the project of the Marquis. It shows the Orsi tower and semicircular battery incorporated into the proposed new *enceinte*. This occupied about half the present area of Ricasoli and had a land front of two bastions, a ditch and ravelin beyond.

119 AOM 257, f. 165 (7 May 1644).

120 AOM 6554, ff. 75 (8 July 1645) and 85; the same course was advocated by the author of the report presented by Vice-Chancellor Bueno (AOM 6554, f. 70).

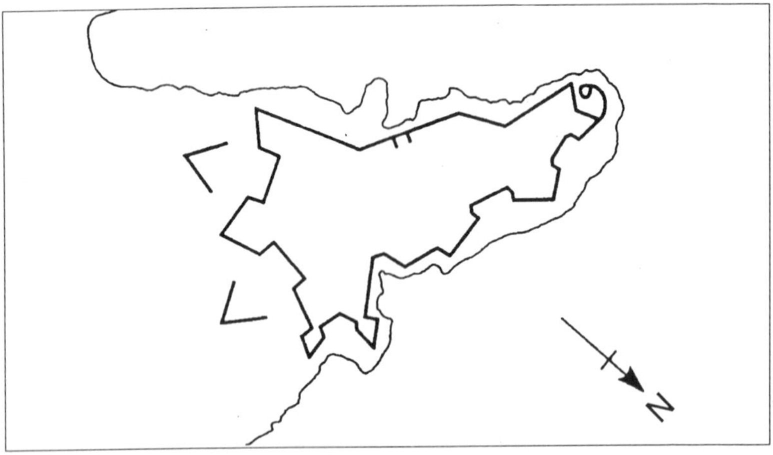

Fig. 5. Fort Ricasoli

Valperga in his scheme of 1670 to protect the harbours included a fort on Rinella point. He designed a land front consisting of a centre bastion, two demi-bastions, a fausse-braye, two ravelins, a ditch, covert-way and glacis; and around the sea shore curtain walls and platforms.[121] On this occasion the scheme progressed beyond the planning stage, and construction commenced in June 1670. This was made possible by the provision of funds by the common treasury which assigned 8,000 scudi a month to the fortifications of Cottonera and Rinella point and the generosity of Commander Giovanni Francesco Ricasoli.[122] This knight gave 20,000 scudi to assist the Order in its ambitious defence programme and the council decided to use the money to finance a fort on Orsi point and to name it Ricasoli in his honour. Even at the outset the council would of course have been aware that this sum would come nowhere near to covering the cost of the fort. In 1693 when it was nearing completion estimates suggest that it had already cost over 100,000 scudi.[123] However, Ricasoli's gift was gratefully received and work began immediately, and in July provision was made that the Maltese labouring there on feast days should receive

121 Dal Pozzo, II, 388; the present fort is basically Valperga's design; there is no evidence to support Porter's claim (p. 157) that Valperga adopted St. Angelo's design.

122 AOM 261, f. 166 (10 and 15 June 1670).

123 AOM 264, f. 21 (2 November 1693).

two loaves per day.[124] When the time came for Valperga's departure in October work had progressed far enough for him to consider in detail the alignment and heights of various parts of the fort.[125]

The Rinella point fort was not, however, excluded from the criticisms of Valperga's defence project, but whereas Cottonera was thought too large and grandiose, Ricasoli was criticized for being too small and cramped, a complaint voiced by Verneda and repeated more vociferously by Blondel.[126] The latter described the fort as a mere crownwork, its land front too short, and, as a result, all its parts too small and restricted. Besides, the sea walls had been set back from the shore, leaving rocks on which an attacker could establish himself. Blondel had modified the sea walls to remove much dead ground and he also proposed adding low outworks to occupy some of the rocks. But improvements to Ricasoli came well down his list of priorities. Grunenberg writing in the same year of 1681 also described Ricasoli as a crownwork.[127] He suggested extending the fausse-braye so as to cover the dead ground to the left of the land front, and recommended alterations to the right flank of the land front to prevent enfilading from Salvatore hill, and the addition of a water-level battery at Orsi point. Apart from this last suggestion, which he repeated in his report of 26 February 1687, his recommendations do not appear to have been carried out.

By the mid-1680s the fortifications were well under way and the buildings within the fort were being constructed. In September 1686 the council sanctioned the building of a governor's house and in 1696 work started on a chapel which was dedicated two years later. The final touches, the provision of artillery, the affixing of the coats of arms of the Order, and of Nicholas Cotoner and Ricasoli, and the appointment of a governor were carried out in the winter of 1697-8.[128] The fort was manned, the garrison being provided for out of the so-called Cottonera Foundation set up for that purpose in 1674 by Nicholas Cotoner.[129]

Although the fort was garrisoned, armed and performing its part in the defence of the harbour, it was by no means perfect and remained

---

124 AOM 261, f. 167 (17 July).

125 AOM 6554, f. 129 (15 October 1670).

126 AOM 6551, f. 55v. (30 July 1671); PRO WO 55, 1555/1, p. 231.

127 AOM 6554, ff. 176 (15 March 1681) and 187 (26 February 1687).

128 AOM 262, f. 279v. (18 September 1686); AOM 264, ff. 97 (31 March 1696) and 166v. (15 May 1698); AOM 1016, pp. 425 (28 September 1697) and 426 (16 January 1698); until damaged by bombing there was an inscription above the gate recording the fort's completion in 1698.

129 AOM 262, f. 30v. (12 June 1674).

open to criticism. The land front was a particular target for complaints. Tigné believed that the bastions of the front should have been larger so that they could offer a more effective defence.[130] As it was no longer possible to remedy this defect, he attempted to adapt the existing works as best he could, and recommended the addition of traverses to the land front, and improvements to the covert-way, ditch and glacis. Inside the fort, Tigné found it necessary to repair the parapets, banquettes and embrasures. As it would, however, still remain weak, even if all his suggested repairs and improvements were executed, he proposed that a retrenchment, consisting of a tenaille and mezzaluna, be built within the enceinte which would effectively divide the fort in two, and offer a second line of defence. In addition as the fort had an essential part to play in the defence of the harbour, he also wished to add a large circular battery at Orsi point.

Vendôme, likewise, ascribed great importance to the protection of the port, but in contrast to Tigné thought the Sta. Margherita lines of marginal value, while maintaining that fort Ricasoli was vital to the Order's safety because of its importance in controlling the entry of relief forces.[131] However, the fort itself, he agreed, was weak and would fall in fifteen days. He suggested therefore that it could be strengthened if isolated from the mainland by a sea-filled ditch, although he was not prepared to insist on this as a matter of high priority. In his turn Maigret admitted that thus isolating the fort would make it unassailable, but he ruled out the scheme as too costly and time-consuming.[132] He recommended instead the extension of the covert-way and fausse-braye up to the sea shore.

On his return visit in 1716 Tigné found that little had been done to improve Ricasoli.[133] He listed the work on the covert-way and outworks as urgent, and estimated the cost at 3750 scudi. The repair of parapets and banquettes he also thought pressing, but this would cost a mere 200 scudi. The major undertakings, such as the large internal retrenchment costing 6,000 scudi and the large circular battery at Orsi point costing 1,000 scudi, he was prepared to postpone until the knights were better able to afford such expenditure. And the financial state of the Order being as it was in the eighteenth century, postponed could (and in this case did) mean cancellation. Although

130 RML MS. 1301, p. 57 (25 September 1715).
131 RML MS. 1301, p. 121.
132 AOM 6552, f. 40v.
133 RML MS. 1301, p. 153 (15 September 1716).

the completion of the Ricasoli covert-way had come third on Tigné's list of priorities after Floriana and Birgu, work had by 1719 still not commenced.[134] The feeling was that because it could be perfected in four or five months there would be time enough to carry out this work should the Turks show any signs of aggression. Thus when such signs reached Malta in 1722 the knights immediately attended to the covert-way and glacis, but found that only a modest investment if 3,400 scudi was necessary to complete them.[135] By the following December, however, the workmen were already being employed in general repairs making good the damage caused to the fort by time and the elements.[136] The long northern flank of the fort suffered greatly from its exposure to the sea and in 1752 it was decided to face it with more durable stone at the expense of the Cottonera Foundation.[137]

The French engineers who reported in 1761 had little to add to Tigné's observations;[138] the revetments and parapets required repair, the covert-way should be protected from enfilade and the interior retrenchment and circular battery should be built. Marandon, the Order's resident engineer, proposed that the fausse-braye be removed and the bastions of the land front somewhat enlarged.[139] This was rejected, however, by the Frenchman Pontleroy on the ground of excessive cost and because there was little to be gained from such an alteration, for although Blondel and Tigné had criticized the fort on account of its smallness, to be significant, any increase in size would have to be far greater than that proposed by Marandon. Needless to say the opinions of the visiting Frenchmen prevailed over those of the resident engineer and no major improvements were undertaken.

By the latter half of the century the fort, because of its exposed position and earlier neglect, was in a very bad state of repair, and a full-scale programme of renovation and maintenance had to be undertaken. By 1789, under the direction of the Bailiff de Tigné the repairs to the sea flank were complete, a small tenaille had been added to the left flank of the land front, and work had begun on improving and repairing the covert-way,[140] but because the Cottonera Foundation

134 AOM 1011, f. 22v. (September 1719).

135 Clerkenwell, MS. O 1, item 5 (25 June 1722) and item 20; AOM 1011, f. 38 (25 June 1722), f. 43 (8 July 1722) and f. 45 (3 July 1722).

136 AOM 267, f. 171 (2 December 1722).

137 Clerkenwell, MS. O 1, item 21; this work commenced in August 1753 and continued throughout 1754.

138 AOM 6557, f. 62 and AOM 6558, f. 70 (18 October 1761).

139 AOM 6557, f. 94 and AOM 6558, f. 86v. (14 November 1761).

140 AOM 1054, p. 18.

which was financing the project was exhausted, work had ceased. However, Tigné had managed to obtain modest additional funds and in May 1788 work had recommenced, although the money available would allow no more than the repair of the mezzalunas on the land front. But even in what were obviously difficult times, the knights were prepared to consider improvements to the fortifications. The engineers in 1761 had condemned the widespread use of stone parapets in Malta as dangerous and in 1788 the congregation decreed that in repairing Ricasoli earth parapets supported by masonry were to be installed.[141] Thus, in the closing years of the eighteenth century fort Ricasoli was accounting for a fair proportion of the Order's expenditure on fortifications, although this was to some extent being supplied from special funds.[142] The repairs were in fact being financed by the Cottonera Foundation which drew its income from property rents, and by the *nuovo imposto*, a customs due. But even these sources were not inexhaustible, so that gradually and inexorably work on Ricasoli, as on the other forts, slowed down and eventually came to a halt.[143]

V. Fort Manoel

The danger posed to Valletta by the Isoletto in the Marsamxett had long been recognized. Sixteenth-century authorities such as Campi and Leone had pointed out that the Valletta front, especially the bastion of St. Michael, could be enfiladed by batteries established on the island.[144] Although at least one design for a fort on the island was submitted to the Order shortly after the construction of Valletta,[145] no action was taken. The Floriana fortifications were likewise threatened from this quarter.[146] Even the knights' decision in 1643 to acquire the island from the canons of the cathedral was not taken for strategic reasons, but because the Isoletto, or Bishop's isle, had been used from time to time as a quarantine station and the Order

---

141 AOM 1015, p. 331 (11 December 1788).

142 See AOM 1015, p. 323 (29 April 1788), p. 436 (8 August 1795) and p. 562 (25 February 1797). See AOM 1013 for payments to workmen carrying out repairs to Ricasoli between May 1788 and August 1795, and AOM 6408, ff. 108-117v. for the cost of magazines, April 1792 to February 1794.

143 See AOM 1015, p. 436 (8 August 1795) – work on outworks suspended until May 1796.

144 Vat. Lat. 7776, f. 39 (1574); ASV Miscellanea, Arm. II, 88, f. 393 (*c.* 1570); Chigi, Q III 69, f. 20 (Campi, 17 July 1577); ASV Fondo Pio 246, f. 260 (Leone, 1582).

145 ASV Miscellanea, Arm. II, 88, f. 393; this account has been published by R. Vella Bonavita in 'A sixteenth-century proposal for a fort on "Manoel" island', *Melita Historica*, VI (1973), 141.

146 Chigi, Q III 69, ff. 25 (Baracca, 23 November 1638), 31 (Bolognino, 4 November 1638).

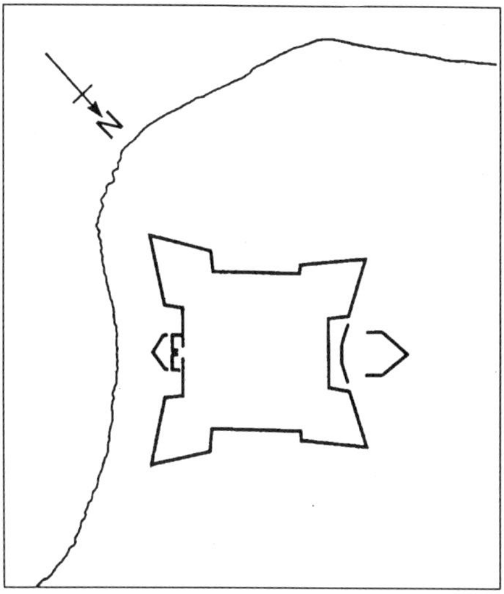

Fig. 6. Fort Manoel

wished to establish a permanent lazaretto on the site.[147] The first fortification on the island, a tower, was built at the instance of the commissioners of health not to protect the flank of Valletta but to house guards to ensure that the quarantine regulations were being observed.[148]

It was only in the late seventeenth century that the Order seriously contemplated fortifying the Isoletto. A small fort of irregular hexagonal design, which was to act as an outwork of Valletta, featured in Valperga's scheme for the defence of the harbours, but because of the Order's commitment to the Cottonera lines, it was never constructed.[149] Although Valperga's was more than a mere watch tower, it was criticized by both Verneda and Blondel as being too small.[150] Grunenberg therefore designed a larger fort with an exterior polygon of a hundred canes, a fausse-braye and covert-way, but it was not among

147 Dal Pozzo, II, 76; p. Cassar, *Medical History of Malta* (London, 1964/5), pp. 166-71, and 298-300.

148 AOM 260, f. 85 (9 September 1660).

149 AOM 6554, f. 119 (15 October 1670); the plan reproduced by Vella Bonavita (p. 147) probably shows Valperga's design.

150 AOM 6551, f. 55v. (Verneda, 1671) with plan, wrongly dated 1761, which shows a larger bastioned fort with two demi-bastions and a ravelin on the land front; PRO WO 55, 1555/1, p. 241.

Plate 15 Fort Manoel from Valletta.

those projects of his which were ever executed.[151] With the increasing range and effectiveness of artillery it became more than ever essential that an attacker be denied access to the Isoletto. Nonetheless its fortification remained well down the list of priorities drawn up by Tigné in 1716. On his visit the previous year Tigné had designed a little squarish fort, with a bastion at each corner and a front of some hundred canes facing Valletta;[152] he estimated that it would cost 25,000 scudi but classified the work as non-urgent and to be postponed until the Order's financial state became more favourable.[153] Maigret, on the other hand, believed a more modest construction, a casemated redoubt with covert-way costing a mere 2,600 scudi, would suffice.[154] He too thought this work could be delayed and placed it last on his list of priorities. Mondion, however, argued strongly that a fort should be built on the Isoletto without undue delay,[155] for the Marsamxett flank of Valletta and Floriana remained (once the other fortifications had been completed) the weakest spot in the harbours'

151 AOM 6554, f. 193 (26 February 1687).
152 RML MS. 1301, p. 105 (25 September 1715).
153 RML MS. 1301, p. 165 (15 September 1716).
154 AOM 6552, f. 49v.
155 RML MS. 1301, p. 181; this was probably written in the early 1720s (Clerkenwell, MS. O 1, item 20).

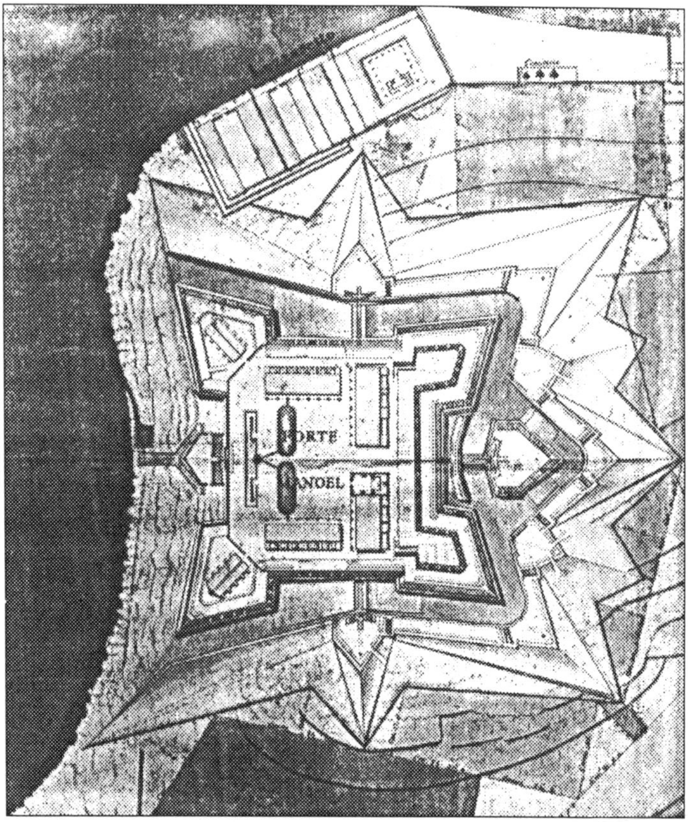

Plate 16 Plan of fort Manoel, eighteenth-century (RML Cabreo of Grand Master de Vilhena).

defences. Of three possible sites for a fort, Dragut point, Ta' Xbiex point or the Isoletto, Mondion preferred the last, although its restricted site limited the design to the small square fort designed by Tigné. The decision to fortify the Isoletto was finally taken in 1723 and the first stone laid with due ceremony on 14 September.[156] As resident engineer Mondion supervised the project; he described the fort as having four bastions, and a mezzaluna facing the mainland to the north-west, surrounded by ditches, a covert-way with places of arms, and, in the centre of the fort, a large piazza, the two landward bastions being

---

[156] AOM 267, f. 223v.

Plate 17 Fort Manoel, Valletta and fort Ricasoli.

reinforced by cavaliers linked by an internal curtain. This inner work dominated the whole Isoletto and the neighbouring hills.[157] Underneath the platform of the cavaliers and curtain was bombproof accommodation for more than 500 soldiers. No upsurge in the Order's financial fortunes making possible the fort's construction had actually taken place in 1723 but, as was so often the case, the generosity of an individual transformed the wish to build into the action. Grand Master Manoel de Vilhena had offered to pay for the fort and to establish a fund of 6,000 scudi to provide for its garrison and maintenance. In acknowledgement of his benefaction the fort was named Manoel.[158] Once the project was under way progress was swift; by 1732 work had reached an advanced state and the mines under the glacis were being excavated. At one stage, however, early in 1728 it had looked as though work might be halted by a dispute between the engineer and the contractors.[159] The latter claimed that a further 29,000 scudi were required

157 Clerkenwell, MS. O 1, item 20.
158 Clerkenwell, MS. O 1, item 20; AOM 267, f. 242 (31 August 1724); RML Tres. A 23 gives details of the Manoel foundation.
159 Clerkenwell, MS. O 1, item 15 (26 January 1728).

to complete the project; Mondion declared this demand excessive, and the two sides settled on 25,000 scudi. This was to be paid according to the work performed, but at the rate of no less than 300 scudi a week. To accelerate the work-rate, 1,000 scudi would be held back until construction was completed. By the beginning of 1728 the main ramparts appear to have been built and within the fort attention was concentrated on the erection of buildings such as the chapel, chaplain's house, governor's residence, barracks and magazines. Outside the ramparts the mezzaluna, ditch and covert-way were under construction.

The design of fort Manoel encountered no criticism. Indeed, it was considered a strong, well-built little fortress. Bourlamaque described it as a 'model of fortification' and complete in all its parts.[160] He recommended measures to render it more secure: the demolition of the houses and barns on the Isoletto, the removal of all earth which might afford an attacker cover, and the construction of a redoubt to obstruct access from the mainland. Although none of his recommendations were carried out, the fort was maintained in a good state of repair,[161] possibly because its maintenance was provided for out of a separate fund, the Manoel Foundation which had an annual income of over 10,000 scudi in the 1780s.[162] The condition of the fort, however, had no influence on the events of June 1798, for its garrison under the Bailiffs Gurgao and La Tour St. Quentin shared in the general collapse and surrendered without a shot being fired.

VI. FORT TIGNÉ

After the siege of 1565 the knights were left in no doubt as to the damage which could be inflicted by enemy batteries stationed on Sta. Maria point at the entrance to the Marsamxett. Indeed, the headland had been renamed Dragut point in memory of the corsair who established the batteries on that site and later died there. At the time of the siege Sciberras was occupied only by the small fort St. Elmo, but even with the fortification of the whole peninsula, Dragut point represented a threat to Valletta and Floriana, for it was sufficiently elevated to allow the enemy guns to bombard and damage Valletta. This weak link in the defences of the city was mentioned by

---

160 AOM 6557, f. 62; AOM 6558, f. 70 (18 October 1761).
161 AOM 1054, p. 20.
162 W. H. Thornton, *Memoir on the Finances of the Order* (Malta, 1836), p. 16.

various engineers from the sixteenth century[163] but it was not until the closing decade of the eighteenth century that the Order occupied the site with a fort. By the early years of the century the knights were, however, already considering actual designs for a fort on Dragut point. Maigret advocated a large casemated redoubt enveloped by a covert-way which he estimated would cost 2,600 scudi.[164] Tigné proposed a work on much the same scale which he described as a large battery closed at the gorge costing 3,000 scudi.[165] But Tigné classified this as non-urgent, and Mondion, although he recognized the importance of fortifying Dragut point, realizing that the Order's resources were not equal to the construction of two forts on the Marsamxett flank, preferred to build the one on the Isoletto, which, he believed, would afford more general protection than that on Dragut point.[166] The French engineers who visited the island in 1761 found that a battery had been built in 1757 at Qala Żembi close to Dragut point, but as this alone could not have prevented an enemy from occupying the latter site, the engineers again recommended that a good fort be built at Dragut.[167]

Finally in 1792 the knights decided to build on Dragut point itself, and the congregation of war ordered that a redoubt be constructed.[168] This consisted of four wings at right angles to each other and a round tower towards Valletta surrounded by a ditch and well mined throughout, and was designed by the Order's engineer Tousard. The Bailiff Tigné gave 1,000 scudi towards its cost and the work was named fort Tigné in his honour, although a larger sum, 6,000 scudi, was donated by Grand Master Rohan.[169] In two years the fort was in a state fit to receive artillery.[170] Although Tigné was a very small fort by Maltese standards, it alone of all the harbour defences put up a brave, if futile, resistance to the French invaders in 1798.

---

163 For instance, Campi (Chigi, Q III 69, f. 20, 1577). Verneda (AOM 6551, f. 55v. 1671); his plan shows a fort about the size of Ricasoli with a land front of three bastions with outworks. Blondel (PRO WO 55, 1555/1, p. 241, 1681). Grunenberg (AOM 6554, f. 187, 1687).

164 AOM 6552, f. 40v. (1715).

165 RML MS. 1301, p. 169 (1716).

166 RML MS. 1301, p. 181.

167 AOM 6557, f. 62 (1761) and AOM 6558, f. 70.

168 AOM 1015, pp. 389 (11 December 1792) and 394 (28 January 1793).

169 AOM 1015, pp. 412 (12 April 1793) and 413 (24 April); medals were struck in commemoration dated 1793. Tousard, a serving brother in the Order, who arrived in Malta 1789, had trained in the French engineers' corps. After Napoleon's conquest of the islands, he joined the victorious army and served in Egypt, Russia and Austria (Blanchard, p. 233; Miège, III, 36).

170 AOM 1015, p. 430 (23 February 1795).

Chapter 6

Città Vecchia

When the knights took possession of Malta in 1530 the island's capital was the inland city of Notabile or Mdina, later, after the building of Valletta, known as the Città Vecchia. Its fortifications were obsolete and crumbling and many of its buildings had been abandoned. But the overriding reason for the Order's not establishing its convent there lay in the town's situation. The seafaring knights needed a harbour-city as their headquarters, and therefore set about fortifying Birgu. However, despite its neglected and depressing state in 1530, the rejection of the capital city did not lead to its complete collapse, although at times it looked as though it would have to be abandoned.

Militarily the Città Vecchia presented the knights with a problem. It had only a minor place in the order's defence strategy, which concentrated on the protection of the heartland of the island, the harbour area. Although Città Vecchia could have its uses as a refuge for the islanders or as an isolated redoubt from which to launch raiding parties against an invader, as an inland fort it suffered from an irremediable weakness – the difficulty of supply in time of siege. In the early years the knights had few resources to spare for the improvement or repair of a fort the defensive potential of which was doubtful. Later, as the harbour defences became more complex and comprehensive, the strategic value of Città Vecchia and the wisdom of its continuance as a fortress were seriously questioned. In the eighteenth century, however, the city secured a role in the Order's changing defence strategy, and was recognized as a useful outpost from which troops could be deployed to oppose a hostile army in the

Plate 18 Città Vecchia showing the St. Mary's, St. Peter's, and Redin bastions.

open countryside. The establishment of the knights in Birgu, and afterwards in Valletta, undoubtedly accelerated the decline in the vitality of the old capital. The Order itself in the late sixteenth century attempted to halt its depopulation by exempting all the inhabitants from militia service, but this concession had no apparent effect.[1] However, the Università survived from Aragonese days, and, as a result, the city enjoyed a measure of self-government. Although the Università retained certain rights, powers and duties, the ultimate control of the city, as of the rest of the island, belonged to the Order in the person of the grand master, who was sovereign of the island. In matters such as defence, the demarcation between the Order and the Università was bound to be a delicate problem. The Università claimed to retain its pre-1530 privileges and duties which included the oversight of island defences, but defence was too important a duty for the knights to abdicate even part of the responsibility to a body over which they did not have absolute control. In practice, the Università maintained the walls of the Città Vecchia and some of the coastal towers, but the Order intervened even in these areas when it considered the overall defence of the island to be involved.

The Città Vecchia itself was situated on rising ground in the centre of the island overlooking a countryside which sloped gradually

---

1 Blouet, p. 117.

down to the harbours. When the knights arrived they found a fortress unadapted to the needs of modern warfare. Its outline was then an irregular quadrilateral which followed the contours of the rocky promontory on which it was sited. The walls were high and more or less vertical, without outworks, unsuited either to resist artillery bombardment or themselves deploy modern artillery. Within the enceinte guarding the entrance stood the Mastra tower, later altered and known as the tower of the Standard.[2] The knights attempted to strengthen these defences but in the years before the siege were neither willing nor able to undertake any drastic reform, so that work seems to have been restricted to sorely needed repairs.[3] The fortifications did not suffer any damage in 1565, and from the massive building and reconstruction programme carried out in the wake of the siege, Città Vecchia emerged untouched. That is not to say that the knights were happy about the defences of the city, but that, given the state in which they found themselves, the improvement of Città Vecchia could hardly be considered an urgent task. Laparelli visited the city early in January 1566 and drew up plans for work to be carried out there for which he estimated that 1,000 workmen would be required.[4] However, he did not consider that the fortress could ever be made secure since it could so easily be dominated and bombarded from neighbouring heights.[5] Between the Cathedral and St. Paul's bastions, on the eastern flank, the hillside rose directly from the edge of the ditch, and further round on the southern flank the hill was divided from the city by a large natural ditch. The fortress lacked any flanking defence; an attacker could approach right under the walls, the ditch could only be defended from above, the bastions could not cover each other with flanking fire and a low earth bastion was collapsing into the ditch and damaging the wall in the process. Laparelli therefore recommended the deepening of the ditch between the Cathedral and St. Paul's bastions to allow these to provide mutual cover, while the rest of the

---

2 See Mifsud, 'La milizia', p. 69.

3 E.g. A. Mifsud, 'Un cenno al 1565 nel 1915', *Archivum Melitense*, II (1915), 229; Mifsud, 'Papi', p. 414; Bosio (III, 110, 140 and 325) says Piccino and Prato visited Città Vecchia in 1532 and 1552 respectively to carry out repairs. The curtain under the cathedral was renovated under Homedes and it is possible that the bastions of St. Peter and St. Paul were added by Prato. Indeed the latter bastion is also known as the Homedes bastion. Hughes suggests ('Defence of Malta', p. 9) that these two bastions were added by Piccino but there is insufficient evidence to make a definite attribution. In 1564 a tax was imposed to repair the walls of the city (RML MS. 438, f. 53).

4 Cod. Lap. f. 9 (13 January 1566); Bosio, III, 727.

5 The following description is taken from Cod. Lap f. 13 (30 January 1566).

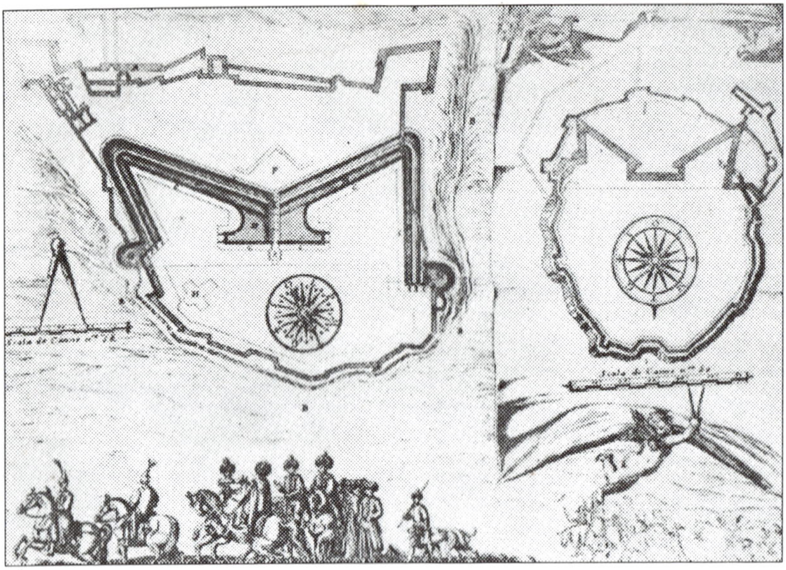

Plate 19 Engraving by Matteo Perez d'Aleccio showing the proposed alterations to Città Vecchia and the Castello (plate xvi).

enceinte should be given spacious terrapleins and parapets of earth. In two months with 1,000 workmen and twenty-five master masons Laparelli estimated that the city could be in a defendable state.

But there is no evidence that Laparelli's recommendations were carried out. Indeed, the indications are to the contrary. In 1568 the city was described as being weak and surrounded by old walls;[6] and later in the century some engineers took the view that it would be better to abandon the fortifications and reduce the settlement to village status.[7] Despite attempts to maintain the defences, such as the levying of taxes, the provision of money by the knights, and the involvement of the Order's engineer Cassar, by the early seventeenth century the fortifications were in a sorry state and the city itself

6 Urb. Lat. 833, f. 215v.

7 ASV Miscellanea, Arm. II, 88, f. 393 (1570s); Vat. Lat 7776, f. 39 (1574); Leone's description of the city as being surrounded by modern walls must be discounted: he was a courtier not a practising engineer – ASV Fondo Pio 246, f. 260 (1582). There also seems to have been a proposal shown in an engraving by M. Perez d'Aleccio (*I Veri ritratti della guerra e dell'assedio dati alla isola di Malta dall'armata turchesa l'anno MDLXV* (Rome, 1582), plate XVI) to shorten the enceinte of the city but it is not possible to attribute this scheme to any particular engineer. It does not appear to be in Laparelli's style.

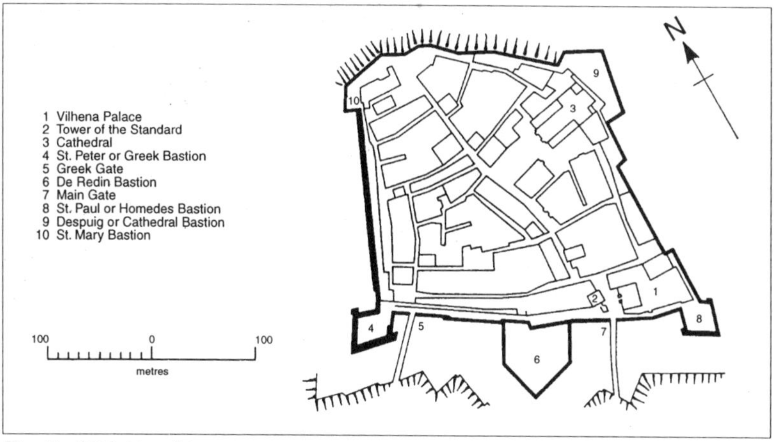

Fig. 7. Città Vecchia

was described as an uninhabited ruin.[8] It was hardly surprising, therefore, that a proposal to abandon the city attracted support. At first the council resisted this movement, repairing the walls and ordering that no inhabitant desert the city,[9] but with the building of Sta. Margherita which would serve as a more secure retreat for the rural population, the proposition became more attractive. The Marquis of St. Angelo advocated such a course on the grounds that it was unlikely that the Order would have sufficient soldiers to defend Città Vecchia adequately.[10] In February 1645 the congregation of fortification visited the city and various knights reported on its condition.[11] All agreed that it was very weak; that the defences lacked effective ditches, flanks and parapets; that the houses of its suburb Rabat would give the enemy excellent shelter and that the Order would be hard pressed to provide a garrison. The renowned French engineer, Count Pagan, expressed the same opinion: the place might be defended if it were encircled by seven or eight bastions, but the

---

8 RML MS. 438, f. 58 (1569); Mifsud, 'Papi', p. 419 (1614); AOM 460, f. 332 (1621); AOM 464, f. 326 (1628); AOM 439, f. 270v. (Cassar, 18 May 1581); Blouet, p. 117.

9 AOM 6553, ff. 19 and 19v. (5 and 11 March 1635).

10 AOM 6554, ff. 42 and 287 (8 April 1640).

11 Flaminio Balbiano, 22 February (AOM 6551, f. 83v. and AOM 6554, f. 245); Bernardo de Noronha, 3 February (AOM 6551, f. 84 and AOM 6554, f. 246); De la Romière, 3 February (AOM 6551, f. 84 and AOM 6554, f. 247).

cost and the men required to guard it (5,000 to 6,000) rendered such a scheme impracticable.[12] The council therefore decided to abandon all hope of defending Città Vecchia from attack and resolved to evacuate the inhabitants.[13] An order on 22 March 1645 to withdraw the bronze artillery caused a near riot as islanders armed with sticks and agricultural implements marched upon Valletta itself. The tumult was only quelled by the intervention of Bishop Balaguer upon which the Order performed a *volte face* and resolved to do what it could to improve the defences of the old capital. To encourage repopulation – only one in five houses was still inhabited – debtors prepared to move there were promised legal immunity. At the same time the Università repaired the walls and more modern cannons were provided. But while the Città Vecchia may thus have been reprieved as a refuge, it remained inherently weak and cramped from a military point of view. Henceforth the Order was committed to the city's survival.[14]

The Order, however, seems to have been fighting a losing battle in its effort to maintain the old city in a reasonable state of defence. The friable nature of the rock and the increasing age of the original walls made its task no easier. In 1658 the bastions of St. Peter and St. Paul and one of the curtains were threatening to collapse. The grand master of the day, De Redin, offered to carry out repairs and also construct an exterior work between the two bastions.[15] He was prepared to meet the whole cost himself and set aside 4,000 scudi so that work could commence. Blondel, who arrived in the island the following spring, appears to have supervised the work. He designed a flat bastion with ditch and counterscarp to be added to the front and proposed to improve the flanking defence elsewhere in the enceinte.[16] However, the scheme made no headway, perhaps because of the death of De Redin in February 1660. Only the foundations and lower courses of the bastion, to be known as the De Redin bastion, were built, to which were then added (without Blondel's knowledge) a cordon, parapet and sentry-box a mere six feet above ground level. The culprit responsible for this distortion of the design was Tarascone, the knight appointed to supervise the work in the absence of the

---

12 AOM 6554, f. 84 (1645).
13 AOM. 257, ff 209v. (22 March 1645) and 220v. (9 May 1645).
14 Dal Pozzo, II, 101; Blouet, p. 117.
15 AOM 260, f. 44 (7 October 1658).
16 PRO WO 55, 1555/1, p. 243.

resident engineer.[17] Antonio Maurizio Valperga for his part supported the retention of Città Vecchia as a fortress, but his own grandiose Cottonera scheme ensured that other fortifications were starved of funds, so that even his limited objectives were not achieved. He accepted that the Città Vecchia could not be made impregnable, but believed it could play an important delaying and diversionary role. He therefore proposed restricting the enceinte to its present size, so that if it were to fall, the enemy would not be in possession of an unassailable stronghold. However, in 1681, despite Valperga's opposition to any abandonment of the city, the defences remained incomplete, while the De Redin bastion had been ridiculously distorted by Tarascone.

A severe earthquake on 11 January 1693 badly shook the Città Vecchia, destroying houses, the Norman cathedral and damaging the walls. The Università, fearing lest its resources would be insufficient to carry out permanent repairs, appealed to the knights for assistance in rebuilding.[18] Blondel, the Order's engineer, was dispatched to the city to inspect the damage. His report of 14 March makes it clear that the major damage was to the north-east quarter of the enceinte from St. Mary's bastion around to the cathedral; that the foundations of the enceinte had been badly shaken; and that it would cost 700 or 800 scudi to make good, in addition to the 200 scudi which had been allocated some months earlier to repair the St. Mary bastion.[19] Elsewhere the parapets had suffered both internally and externally. Blondel estimated, surely optimistically, that the expenditure of this 1,000 scudi would not only restore the city but guarantee well-maintained defences for a number of years to come. The rebuilding of the cathedral, however, also necessitated some alterations to the adjoining fortifications,[20] although these were not considered to be prejudicial to the defences because the new works would encroach no more than the neighbouring houses had already done. In December 1694 the repairs to the bastion of St. Mary were eventually completed at the expense of the Università.[21] Two years

---

17 AOM 1016, p. 348.

18 AOM 1016, p. 157 (21 February 1693).

19 AOM 1016, p. 157.

20 AOM 1016, p. 165 (March 1693).

21 AOM 1016, p. 348 (19 December 1694); but the Order's master of works had measured the work executed in that post and had calculated the payment owing to the workmen (AOM 1016, pp. 319 and 326, 30 August 1694).

Plate 20 Plan of the Città Vecchia, early eighteenth-century (RML Map N5).

later, however, the restoration of the city still claimed the attention of the commissioners of war, and further visits to Città Vecchia followed in 1698 and 1700.[22] On this last occasion the commissioners reported that some portions of the walls were actually ruined and others nearly so.[23] The bridge leading to the main gate was in a parlous state since the stonework of the supporting arches had been eroded, and, to the great detriment of the defences, some 160 feet of the ramparts north of St. Paul's bastion had been appropriated by the Muscat family to enlarge their house. The Muscats had introduced unauthorized windows into the enceinte, occupied an area used to

22 AOM 1016, pp. 412 (2 December 1696), 426 (23 February 1698) and 471 (24 October and 3 November 1700).

23 AOM 265, f. 26 (8 November 1700) and AOM 1016, p. 471 (7 November 1700).

assemble the militia and obstructed access to the walls. The commissioners ordered the rebuilding of the walls and of the bridge and an enquiry into the Muscat case, which was settled in 1701 on the basis of the *status quo*.[24] In addition part of the foundations of the enceinte to the north-east opposite the casa Manduca was in such bad condition that the congregation of fortification recommended rebuilding it fourteen feet within the old line of the defences. For this twenty-eight square canes of property had to be purchased and the owners compensated at the rate of two scudi six tari per square cane.[25] There is evidence that the congregation was vetting measurements and payments made to workmen until April 1702, but thereafter the Order's records are silent on the fortifications of Città Vecchia until 1715.[26]

When Tigné visited the island in that year he found the fortifications of the city had changed little since the sixteenth century.[27] True the De Redin bastion had been added, but it was too low to be of any use. The rest of that 180 cane front, the only part of the enceinte not protected by a natural escarpment, was defended only by the two small bastions of St. Peter and St. Paul. Despite earlier recommendations the defences did not provide mutual protection; the ditches had been obstructed by debris during the rebuilding of the cathedral and would have to be deepened and opened out so that the bastions could cover each other with flanking fire. Along the southern front facing Rabat, Tigné urged the construction of a covert-way terminating in two demi-counterguards under the bastions of St. Peter and St. Paul, but this work was never in fact carried out.

The grand master Manoel de Vilhena (1722-36), renowned for his interest in the Maltese people, their language and customs, attempted to revitalize the old city. During his magistracy a large part of the town and fortifications was rebuilt. Within a month of his election, to meet the threatened Turkish attack, trenches were ordered to be cut under the city walls, to be paid for by the Università.[28] Between 1723 and 1728 work was continually in progress remaking the greater part of the enceinte and renovating all the parapets;[29] the badly situated

---

24 AOM 1016, p. 480 (19 and 24 May 1701).

25 AOM 1016, p. 481 (7 May 1701).

26 AOM 1016, p. 507 (7 May 1702).

27 RML MS. 1301, p. 57 (25 September 1715).

28 AOM 1011, f. 45 (3 July 1722); payments for the cutting of trenches are recorded in RML Univ. 95, 'Spese per le fortificazioni di questa Città Notabile, 24 luglio 1722 – 28 agosto 1723' and RML Univ. 96, 'Spesa giornale della fabrica, 4 settembre 1723 – 30 ottobre 1728'.

29 Details are taken from Clerkenwell, MS. O 1, item 20.

gates were changed, the main gate bearing the date 1724 being moved some forty feet to the west of its former site; the ditch was deepened, the counterscarp remade, and a good covert-way added terminating in two batteries on the model suggested by Tigné. After all this work Mondion described the city as fit to sustain a siege. Within ten years, however, part of the enceinte was threatening to collapse and Marandon was sent to investigate.[30] A stretch of the northern rampart about 180 feet long had to be rebuilt and strengthened. Rain-water had permeated the poorly built wall which, lacking any scarp to act as a buttress, had collapsed under its own weight. The repairs to this part of the enceinte were eventually finished in 1739,[31] and the congregation then authorized the building of the bastion under the cathedral, a project which had been proposed many years earlier.[32] On 5 June 1739 work commenced on the cathedral bastion, later known as the Despuig bastion after the grand master of the time, but building halted at the onset of winter because construction costs rose in the rainy season. Work on excavating the lower courses of the bastion recommenced on 2 May 1740, and continued into the late 1740s.[33] Simultaneously from 1745 to 1750 St. Paul's bastion was also being renovated.[34]

The adoption in the eighteenth century of a defence strategy based on opposing the enemy on the beaches and in the countryside allowed the city a niche in the overall defence scheme whereas before its position had been very much that of an outpost. In the 1720s and early years of the next decade two entrenchments, the Falca and Naxxar lines, were constructed close to the city along a natural fault as part of a network designed to hinder any invader landing in the north of the island.[35] Città Vecchia was included in the defence preparations of February 1761 when rumors of a Turkish attack were rife,[36] but the French experts summoned to advise on the islands' fortifications had a poor opinion of the city. It could not receive sea-borne supplies, so could not withstand a siege, and, having fallen, could serve the enemy

---

30 Clerkenwell, MS. O 1, item 21 (1736).

31 RML Univ. 97, 'Spese per le fortificazioni, 1738-9' contains payments for the rebuilding of the bastion Ta' Bakkar which was on the northern flank.

32 Clerkenwell, MS. O 1, item 21; Marandon claimed that it was already projected in 1715 but it does not appear in Tigné's reports.

33 RML Univ. 98, 'Spese per le fortificazioni, 1745-48' contains payments for the finishing touches to this bastion in 1748.

34 Clerkenwell, MS. O 1, item 21.

35 AOM 1011, f. 45 (3 July 1722) and Clerkenwell, MS. O 1, item 8 (1722) – the Naxxar trenches; Clerkenwell, MS. O 1, item 20 (1731) – the Falca trenches.

36 Clerkenwell, MS. O 1, item 21.

Plate 21 Città Vecchia, main gate.

as a strong point. Therefore they recommended that the walls be razed.[37] This advice was, however, never acted upon and the city survived to surrender to the French in June 1798 after the inhabitants had been guaranteed their religion, liberty and property. It was in Città Vecchia, nevertheless, less than three months later, that the insurrection against the French broke out when an attempt was made to dispose of convent property.

37 AOM 6555; AOM 6557, f. 62 and AOM 6558, f. 70 (18 October 1761).

Chapter 7

Coastal Defences

While Malta was under Aragonese rule the responsibility for the defence of the coasts rested with the Università. The ability of that institution to perform this duty effectively may, however, be questioned. The paucity of settlements around the coast and the virtual abandonment of the northern part of the island do not suggest secure shores.[1] The Università maintained a coastal guard, some watchtowers and a mounted militia, but such a force was no match for the swift-raiding corsairs.[2] The inhabitants found their best protection in flight or in their fortress-like farmhouses built around a courtyard and practically windowless to the exterior, and even in the construction of private tower houses. The building of towers and other defences by individuals and the Università continued during the rule of the Order, but was of decreasing importance as the knights extended their influence and control over fortifications outside the immediate harbour area.

In the sixteenth century the Order confined its attention to the harbour, Città Vecchia and the Castello of Gozo. Until 1566 the knights were not fully committed to the island as a permanent base and were unwilling to undertake any but essential building works; after that year the construction of Valletta was consuming all their energy and funds. However, even after the Order was established in its new fortified stronghold of Valletta, the danger of corsair raids or

---

1 Blouet, p. 93.

2 A. Mifsud, 'La milizia e le torri antiche di Malta' in *Archivum Melitense*, IV (1920), 55-100, *passim*.

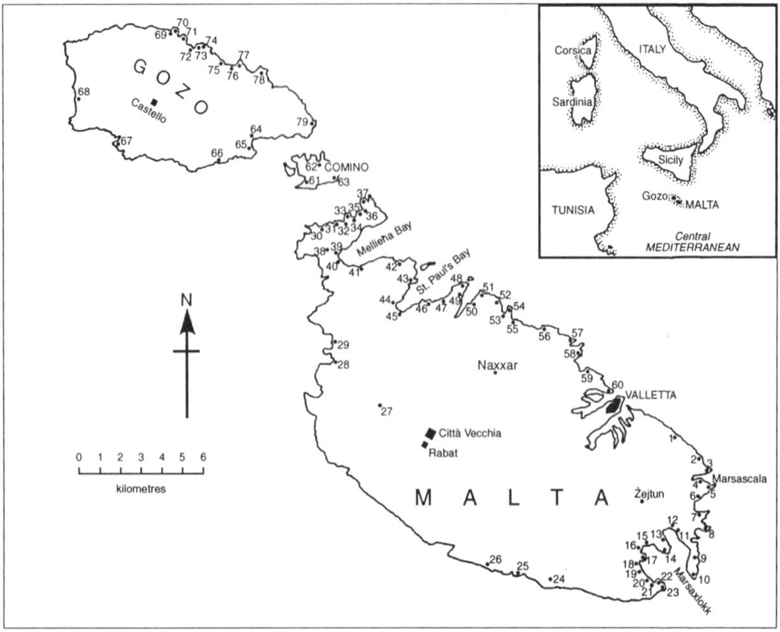

Coastal Defences

Malta

1 Sta. Maria della Grazia Tower (demolished)
2 Triq il-Wiesgħa Tower with Entrenchment to Fort Ricasoli
3 Żonqor Tower (demolished)
4 Marsascala Redoubt and Entrenchment
5 Fort St. Thomas and Battery
6 Maħsel Redoubt
7 Ducluseaux Battery
8 Xrob il-Għaġin Tower and Entrenchment (demolished)
9 Tombrell Battery
10 Delimara Tower and Battery (demolished)
11 Ta' Wilġa Battery
12 Del Fango Redoubt and Entrenchment
13 Vendôme Redoubt, Marsaxlokk
14 Fort St. Lucian
15 Ferretti Battery
16 St. George's Redoubt
17 Pinto Battery
18 Spinola Redoubt
19 Birżebbuġa Entrenchment
20 Elminiech Battery
21 Fresnoy Battery
22 Balbani Battery
23 Bengħisa Tower and Entrenchments (demolished)
24 Wardija Tower
25 Wied iż-Żurrieq Tower
26 Ħamrija Tower
27 Nadur Tower
28 Lippija Tower
29 Għajn Tuffieħa Tower
30 Wied Mosa Battery
31 Tal-Bir Redoubt
32 Eskalar Redoubt
33 Vendôme Battery
34 Armier Redoubt
35 Louvier Entrenchment
36 Louvier Redoubt
37 L-Aħrax Tower
38 St. Agatha Tower
39 Kassisu Battery
40 Mellieħa Redoubt (demolished)
41 Rasus Redoubt
42 Għajn Ħadid Tower

43 Mistra Redoubt
44 Arrias Redoubt
45 Vendôme Redoubt
46 St. Paul's Bay Tower and Battery
47 Buġibba Battery
48 Qawra Tower and Battery
49 Perellos Redoubt, Salina
50 Ximenes Redoubt, Salina
51 Għallis Tower
52 Għallis Battery (demolished)
53 Vendôme Battery (demolished)
54 St. Mark's Tower and Battery
55 Baħar iċ-Ċagħaq Redoubt
56 Madliena Tower
57 St. George's Tower
58 Spinola Entrenchment
59 St. Julian's Tower and Battery
60 Fort Tigné

Comino
61 Comino Tower
62 St. Mary's Redoubt
63 St. Mary's Battery

Gozo
64 Garzes Tower (demolished)
65 Fort Chambray
66 Mġarr ix-Xini Tower
67 Xlendi Tower
68 Qawra/Dwejra Tower
69 Xwieni Redoubt (demolished)
70 Il-Qolla l-Bajda Battery
71 Il-Qolla s-Safra Battery (demolished)
72 Marsalforn Redoubt (demolished)
73 St. Paul's Battery and Redoubt (demolished)
(71–73: Entrenchment)
74 Marsalforn Tower (demolished)
75 Xagħra Battery (demolished)
76 Vendôme Battery
77 Nadur Battery (demolished)
(75–77: Entrenchment)
78 San Blas Tower
79 St Anthony Battery

Fig. 8 The Coastal Defences of Malta and Gozo

of a Turkish landing remained. In the early years of the seventeenth century, thanks to the generosity of the grand masters Garzes and Wignacourt, several of the more accessible bays were defended by means of towers. Garzes made provision in his will for the construction of a tower in Gozo to protect the channel, and Wignacourt financed the building of towers at St. Paul's bay (1609), Marsaxlokk, St. Lucian's tower (1610), St. Thomas's bay (1614), Comino (1618) and at Blata il-Bajda the tower of Sta. Maria delle Grazie (1620).[3] The Wignacourt towers were built to the same general pattern, and were probably designed by Vittorio Cassar. They were square forts with scarped curtain walls, and, at each corner, a vertical tower projecting slightly from the scarped wall. Those at Marsaxlokk, St. Thomas's bay and Comino were similar in size, and cost, fully armed and equipped, respectively 11,745, 13,450 and 18,628 scudi, whereas the other two were smaller, Sta. Maria costing a mere 4,948 and St.

3 AOM 101, f. 191 (14 October 1605); AOM 103, ff 103 (6 November 1609), 146v. (1 July 1610); AOM 105, f. 76 (11 July 1614); AOM 106, ff. 124v. (11 October 1618) and 209 (21 April 1620).

Plate 22 Wignacourt tower, St. Paul's Bay.

Paul's 6,748 scudi.[4] St. Lucian's tower soon proved its worth by fighting off an attempted Turkish landing in July 1614 but the Turkish fleet continued round the coast and proceeded to disembark at St. Thomas's bay, which prompted Wignacourt to propose the erection of a tower at the latter site.[5] Perhaps somewhat belatedly, since the Turks had by then passed on, the grandmaster was authorized on 9 July to post up to thirty foreign soldiers at St. Lucian and St. Paul's bay.[6] The towers were normally under the command of a master bombardier who received an annual salary of seventy-four scudi, or twenty-four

4 AOM 6385, f. 192; the 55,000 scudi spent on the fortresses amounted to only one-eighth of Wignacourt's benefactions to the Order and island. The largest single item provided out of his gift was an aqueduct to carry water to Valletta which cost 114,868 scudi.

5 AOM 105, f. 71v. (6 July 1614).

6 AOM 6553, f. 8.

scudi above the rate for an ordinary bombardier. In addition he was provided with oil to light the room in which eight local men kept watch without pay.[7] In 1631 the normal complement of the towers was established as two bombardiers in addition to the commander, but in an emergency the Order was prepared to augment the garrison. In May 1645 two hundred foreign soldiers were sent to St. Thomas and St. Lucian and one hundred to Sta. Maria delle Grazie. The knights, however, clearly thought it possible to defend the northern towers with fewer soldiers: Garzes with twenty-five men, Comino with thirty and St. Paul's with twenty.[8]

This apparent discrepancy in the size of garrisons may perhaps be explained by the difference of function between the various forts. While a force of 100 or 300 men might be expected to sally forth and oppose a raiding party, twenty to thirty men could hardly do more than indulge in an odd skirmish or two. The task of these smaller garrisons lay therefore in the defence of the fort rather than in opposing an invader in the field. The Order did not have the manpower to post troops at every prospective landing place, and in the mid-seventeenth century, recognizing its limitations, embarked on a programme to build less substantial coastal forts to act as watchtowers rather than garrisoned outposts. A number of such towers were erected during the rule of Grand Master Lascaris (1636-57), and, apart from St. Agatha's tower on the ridge beyond Mellieħa, all followed a remarkably similar pattern.[9] They were about thirty feet square in plan, two or three storeys tall with the lower masonry scarped and all topped by a flat roof protected by a parapet. Lascaris does not appear to have financed these forts himself. Indeed St. Agatha's, the largest of the towers, was built at the expense of the Università, although the council ordered the provision of artillery.[10] The chain of watch-towers was

---

7 AOM 6397, f. 387.

8 AOM 110, f. 88v. (6 May 1631); these bombardiers were local men having Maltese names such as Grima, Caruana, Calleja, Zammit, Muscat, Grech and Gatt; AOM 6553, ff. 35 (24 May 1645) and 62v. (31 May 1645).

9 I have identified the following Lascaris watch towers some of which carry inscribed dates: St. George's (1637), Qawra, St. Agatha or the Red tower or Wied Musa (1649), Għajn Tuffieħa (1637), Lippija or Ġnejna (1637), Nadur, and Wied iż-Żurrieq or Xutu. Although one should always be wary of inscribed dates these do tally with other information and the dating of a simple, quickly built structure like a tower is altogether less complex than that of alterations and additions to a larger work.

10 The tower was completed by November 1648 (AOM 258, f. 154v.) and in April 1649 the council ordered the provision of artillery similar to that found in the other coastal towers (AOM 258 f. 174v.). St. Agatha was not situated on the coast but on the ridge overlooking the Gozo channel. In design it was similar to the Wignacourt towers having four corner turrets.

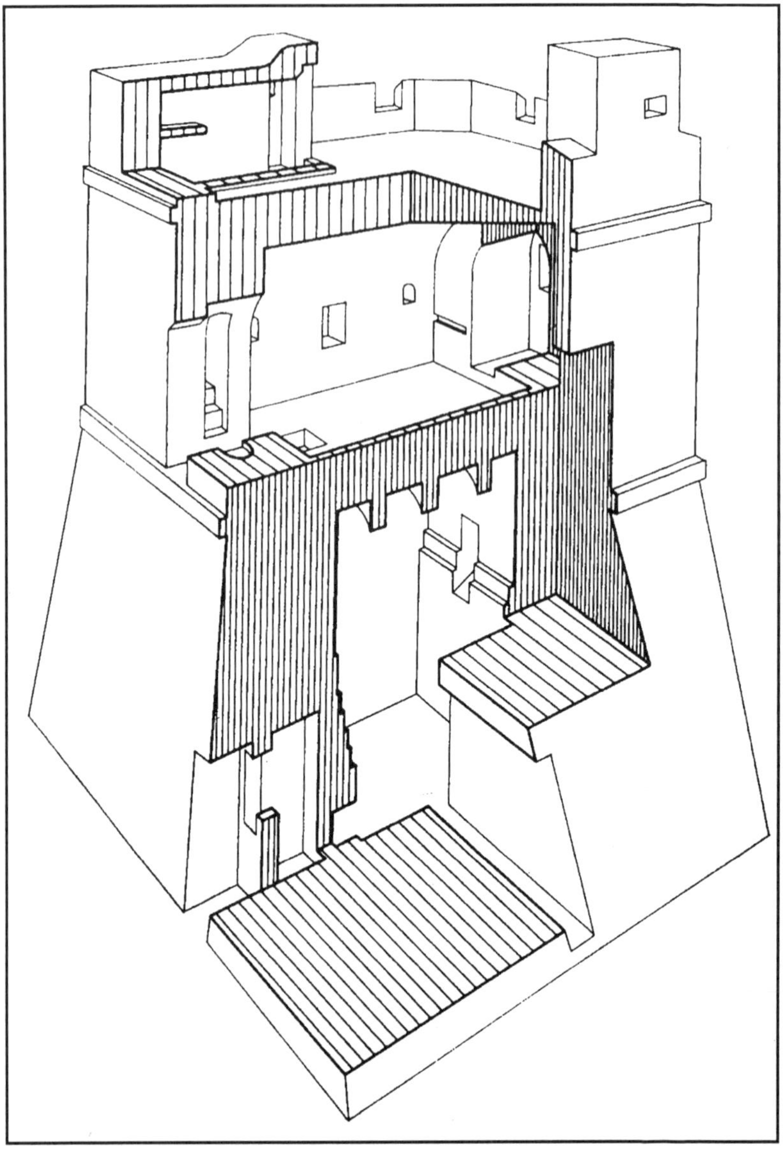

Fig. 9. Maltese coastal watch-tower

augmented by Grand Master de Redin (1657-60), who in March 1658 offered to build at his own expense a further twelve or fourteen.[11] He considered that the system whereby the peasants manned sixty look-out posts by night after a day's toil in the fields to be unsatisfactory. He proposed therefore to establish permanent guards to be paid by the Università, each tower to support one bombardier paid thirty scudi a year and three others at an annual salary of twenty-four scudi, rates much inferior to those offered by Wignacourt many years earlier. Building seems to have proceeded at a fast pace, so that in May, within two months of De Redin's original proposal, a tower at Mellieħa was ready to be armed, by November a further five were at this stage, and a total of thirteen towers was completed, at a cost of 6,428 scudi, by July 1659.[12]

However, De Redin died in February 1660 and enthusiasm for the coastal defences appears to have waned. In July 1681 they were described as being in a deplorable state and the Università was instructed to bear the cost of repairs.[13] During the remainder of the century and in the early years of the next the knights showed little interest in the coastal defences. Blondel, who was undoubtedly conscientious and kept a careful record of his work, did not concern himself with these fortifications. After his death the Order was without a permanent engineer and in these circumstances it was hardly surprising that the coastal towers, which were not primarily the responsibility of the Order, were neglected, so that when an inspection was made in the autumn of 1714 their poor condition was evidence of this lack of interest. On the 28 September 1714 the two commissioners of fortification, Arginy and Fontet, resolved to visit the coasts of Marsaxlokk and Marsascala; they later extended their inspection to cover the whole coastline and presented their full report on 10 January 1715.[14] They recommended that those beaches where a large army might disembark should be protected by batteries and entrenchments.

---

11 AOM 260, f. 31v. (30 March 1658).

12 AOM 260, f. 37 (14 May 1658); AOM 120, f. 213v. (20 November); AOM 260, f. 63 (6 July 1659); the towers are identified as follows: (i) Selmun or Għajn Ħadid (1658), ruined; (2) Għallis (1658); (3) St. Mark; (4) Madliena (1658); (5) St. Julian (1658); (6) L-Aħrax, L-Abjad or Despinasse (1658); (7) Bengħisa (1659), demolished; (8) Xrob il-Għaġin, demolished; (9) ? ta' Triq il-Wiesgħa – on the coast below fort Leonardo, ruined; (10) Delimara (1659), demolished; (11) Żonqor, demolished; (12) Ħamrija (1659); (13) Wardija (1659).

13 AOM 646, f. 95 (5 July 1681).

14 AOM 6556, f. 2 (28 September); they submitted a report on Marsaxlokk and Marsascala by 28 December (AOM 6552, ff. 3v. and 27); the report of 10 January is to be found at AOM 266, f. 129v., AOM 6552, f. 6v. and AOM 6556, f. 3.

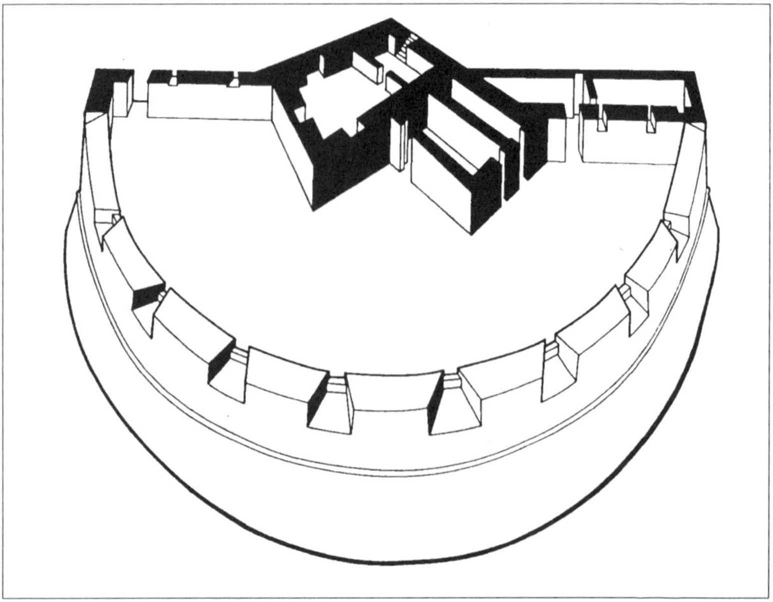

Fig. 10 St. Mary's battery, Comino

In the island of Malta they named the bays of Marsaxlokk, St. Thomas, Marsascala, St. Julian, Madliena, Salina, St. Paul, Mellieħa and the shore of the Gozo channel as likely landing spots and drew up a plan showing the location of the proposed batteries: Marsaxlokk and Gozo being the most vulnerable, work commenced on these shores.[15] In the half year between October 1714 and April 1715 a total of 8,067 scudi was spent in the defence of the coasts.[16] The Bailiff Zondadari contributed 3,000 scudi towards the work at Marsaxlokk and St. Thomas's bay and the *cassa della fortificazione* paid out a further 1486 scudi under contracts to craftsmen. Commander Mongontier supported the work to the tune of 2,455 scudi divided between the batteries of St. Julian's tower (166 scudi), St. Mark's (307), Kassisu (423), Mistra (133), Pwales (103), and five batteries overlooking the Gozo channel (1,323); another 875 scudi went towards two batteries at Mġarr in Gozo and one on Comino, and a further sum of 249 scudi for sundry expenses made up the total.

15 AOM 6552, f. 23 (10 January 1715); the people of the countryside who would benefit most from these defences were ordered to assist in their construction.

16 AOM 6556, f. 9.

A scheme to defend the coasts was, therefore, well under way before the arrival of any of the foreign experts in the spring of 1715. In the event Philippe de Vendôme and his protégés Folard and Maigret espoused the cause of coastal defence in preference to Tigné's advocacy of the harbour fortifications. At a congregation of war meeting of 4 June the pros and cons of the two schemes were discussed, but no conclusion was reached.[17] Vendôme bombarded the Order with reports explaining, expounding and pleading for his project.[18] The knights were evidently in something of a quandary as to which of their distinguished experts' advice to follow. In the end they compromised and agreed to carry out the plans of both men. Vendôme's offer to advance a loan of 40,000 scudi which he estimated to be the cost of his scheme, and to reimburse any expenditure over that amount probably swayed the council towards the approval of works beyond their immediate means.[19] Vendôme's project obviously enjoyed support among members of the Order and eight knights were prepared to back their approval with money. The record of their generosity survives in the batteries named in their honour.[20] The scheme for the defence of the coast was comprehensive. Vendôme planned to strengthen existing works by additional batteries, and to protect accessible points around the shores by the erection of batteries, redoubts and retrenchments.[21] The active, vigorous support of Vendôme was undoubtedly crucial in deciding the fate of the coastal fortifications. Although there was no shortage of defence works competing for funds, and although the knights were by no means fully convinced of the necessity to defend

---

17 AOM 6552, f. 35; AOM 6556, f. 27.

18 AOM 6552, ff. 37v. (copy at AOM 6556, f. 11) and 39v. (copy at R.M.L. MS. 1301, p. 121); AOM 6556, ff. 79, 91 and 93. Folard (*Histoire de Polybe*, I, 163) claimed that he suggested the scheme of coastal defence to Vendôme but Folard's account is hardly impartial. Generally contemporaries gave Vendôme the credit for the project (see AOM 1011, f. 18, 1716).

19 AOM 266, f. 163v. (6 June 1715); Maigret was appointed engineer in charge of the coastal defences.

20 AOM 266, f. 164. Figuella donated 200 Spanish doppie for one at Birżebbuġa; Balbiani 2,000 onzie for one at Kalafrana, now ruined; Ferretti 1,000 scudi for one at St. George's bay at Birżebbuġa; Pinto 1,000 scudi for one at Birżebbuġa; Spinola 1,000 scudi for one at Pretty Bay at Birżebbuġa, now destroyed; Vaini 1,000 scudi for one at (?) St. George's, Birżebbuġa or at (?) Tumbrell near Peter's Pool; Zondadari 1,000 scudi for one at Ta' Wilġa at Marsaxlokk; Fresnoy 1,000 scudi for one at Kalafrana. Several batteries were named after Vendôme: (i) east of Marfa; (2) near Tal-Qrajten point, Marsaxlokk; (3) at south-east corner of St. Paul's bay known as Ta' Dellia, now almost completely demolished; (4) Fedeau on the north coast of Mellieħa bay; (5) at the foot of St. Mark's bay, now demolished. In 1758 and 1774 the Spanish doppia was quoted as equivalent to eight Maltese scudi.

21 AOM 6556, f. 79.

the shoreline, they preferred to allow Vendôme full rein rather than risk offending him or causing dissension in their own ranks. The scale of the work undertaken in 1715 and 1716 is revealed by the records of the payments made to workmen.[22] The fortifications of Marsaxlokk and Marsascala consumed 15,466 scudi, those from St. Julian's bay along the north-east and north coasts to Marfa, 20,794 scudi and Gozo and Comino a further 1,499 scudi.[23] The more the Order invested in batteries and redoubts intended to prevent the enemy setting foot on the island, the more essential it became to ensure that no weak link remained in the chain which would allow the invader to out-flank the whole system. Thus, by adopting the project advanced by Vendôme, the Order embarked upon a task without end. In theory the coastal defences were open to infinite augmentation and strengthening: in practice, the perfection of the system was limited by the resources of the Order.

In the eighteenth century, therefore, the coastal works feature regularly as a component in the defensive system of the island. When the alarm was raised in 1722 the batteries and redoubts had to be prepared, armed and garrisoned;[24] but already the fatal flaw in the grandiose scheme had become clear: the Order did not have the troops to man the system, and the works to the north of the great fault had therefore to be abandoned.[25] As a result, should an invasion take place in the north of the island, the defenders would attempt to hold the line of the natural entrenchment running from Madliena past Naxxar to Mtarfa ridge. Troops would defend the three possible routes through the high ground, Falca gap, Naxxar where entrenchments had been

---

22 AOM 6543, p. 1.

23 The works in Malta listed as under construction in this period at Marsaxlokk and Marsascala are: Kalafrana/Fresnoy redoubt; Elminiech/Figuella battery; Birżebbuġa/ Spinola redoubt; Gżira/ Pinto battery; St. George's redoubt; Qajjenza/Ferretti battery; St. Lucian's battery; Qrajten/ Vendôme redoubt; Del Fango redoubt; ta' Wilġa/St. James's battery; Riħana/tal-Franċiż/Duclu-seaux battery; Maħsel battery; St. Thomas's tower battery; Marsascala redoubt. The works listed as under construction from St. Julian's northwards are: St. Julian's tower battery; St. George's redoubt; Madliena redoubt; St. Mark's point battery; St. Mark's bay/Vendôme redoubt; Għallis battery; Salina east/Ximenes redoubt; Salina west/Perellos redoubt; Qawra battery; Buġibba battery; St. Paul's tower battery; Ta' Dellia/Vendôme battery; Xemxija/Arrias battery; ir-Rasus/ Vestrem battery; Mellieħa redoubt; Kassisu/ Fedeau/ Vendôme battery; L-Aħrax battery; Louvier redoubt; Armier/Barriera redoubt; Vendôme battery; Ħossiliet/ Eskalar redoubt; Tal-Bir/Wied Musa redoubt; Wied Musa battery. I have retained the designation 'battery' or 'redoubt' as given in AOM 6543 although this may not be an accurate description of the present-day structures.

24 Clerkenwell, MS. O 1, item 20.

25 AOM 267, f. 124v. (8 May 1722); AOM 1011, f. 38 (25 June 1722); Clerkenwell MS. O 1, item 5.

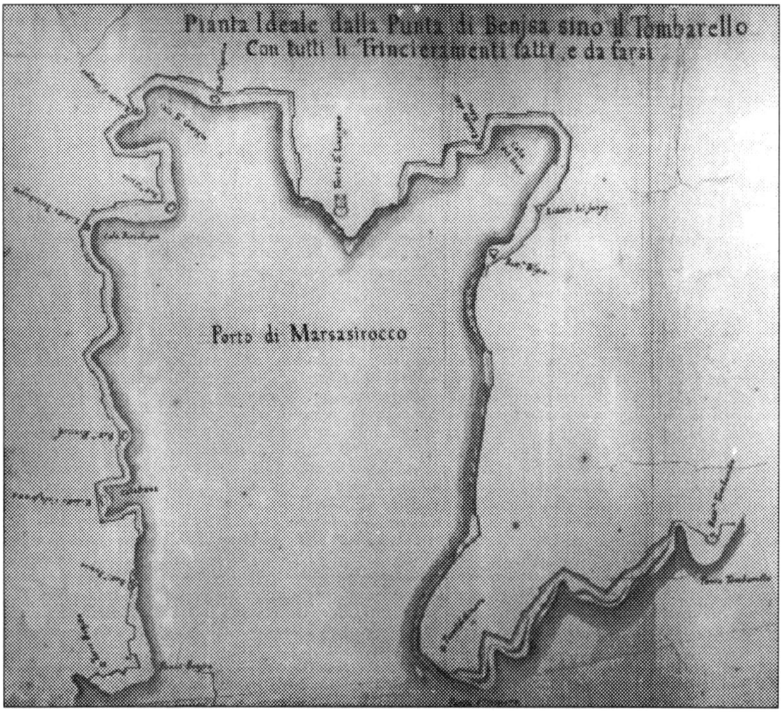

Plate 23 Coastal defences of Marsaxlokk, 1761 (RML Map B2).

recently constructed, and a coastal passage near the Madliena, tower. The need for additional troops was but one burden which the maritime defences placed on the resources of the Order. These scattered works, by their very nature exposed to salt air and sea spray, had to be regularly repaired. Despite these difficulties, however, the Order attempted to maintain them as best it could. Marandon attended conscientiously to his duties and detailed the various repairs and improvements required for the coastal defences.[26] He appears indeed to have been responsible for developing a novel form of coastal defence, the fougasse, a form of stone mortar excavated out of solid rock. On 28 September 1740 Marandon fired his first experimental fougasse and was so pleased with the results that the following year he excavated a network of fougasses at vulnerable points around the coasts

26 Clerkenwell, MS. O 1, item 21.

of the island.[27] Pontleroy, who visited Malta in 1761, also conducted experiments with fougasses and declared them well-suited to the defence of the coastline.[28]

The French engineers under Bourlamaque fully endorsed the strategy of opposing the enemy on the beaches; in fact, they took the knights to task for failing to defend all accessible shores.[29] Believing that an invader would require calm waters to moor his ships and sheltered shores on which to disembark his troops, the knights had concentrated the fortifications in the bays of the island. Bourlamaque argued that during the calm summer months an enemy could as easily land on one of the many approachable headlands. He, therefore, recommended the scarping of the coastline where it was not by nature precipitous, and the construction of entrenchments and some thirty additional batteries and redoubts.[30] Vendôme had included entrenchments at Birżebbuġa, Madliena, St. Mark's bay, Salina and the Gozo channel as part of his master-plan for the island. It was only in the 1720s, however, that construction of these began. On 21 March 1723 the congregation optimistically ordered entrenchments along the coasts from Ricasoli to Marsaxlokk and between Dragut point and St. Mark's bay,[31] while inland trenches were to be constructed at Torre Falca and at Naxxar to bar the advance southwards of an invader.[32] Under Marandon's direction entrenchments were cut at Bengħisa, Marsaxlokk and at Xrob il-Għaġin,[33] but in 1761 the network of entrenchments still fell far short of what Vendôme had envisaged. Bourlamaque thereupon drew up an ambitious scheme whereby the island would be completely encircled, every accessible beach protected either by an entrenchment, or by the cutting of the rock to form an artificial escarpment.[34]

---

27 Clerkenwell, MS. O 1, item 21; in 1715 the council had ordered sixty stone mortars to be cut but no action seems to have been taken until 1740; AOM 6552, f. 38 and AOM 6556, f. 187 list proposed fougasses.

28 AOM 6557, f. 94 and AOM 6558, f. 86v. In 1770 there were said to be about fifty fougasses in Malta (Brydone, II, 1).

29 AOM 6557, f. 120 and AOM 6558, f. 100 (24 October 1761).

30 Other reports drawn up about this time also advocated the additional defence of the coast: RML MS. 140, ff. 142 'Osservatione sopra i littorali di ponente dell'isola di Malta... 1761' by Masini Valperga, 153 'Vantaggi de' fossi e trincieri incavate nel rocco', Borro, 1762, 188 'Reflessioni circa la difesa delle marine di Malta', 1761, Bailiff Antoine de Blacas d'Aups. An engineer De Blacas is listed among French engineers in 1760. (Augoyat, II, 516).

31 Clerkenwell, MS. O 1, items 8 (1722) and 9 (1723).

32 Clerkenwell, MS. O 1, item 21; work had begun on those at Naxxar by 1722 (AOM 1011, f. 45).

33 Clerkenwell, MS. O 1, item 21.

34 AOM 6557, f. 120 and 6558, f. 100; RML maps B2, C6, F24, F25, M1, M2, M34, M35, M38, M42, P1, P2, P3, R11, R12, R16, R20.

The knights responded to his suggestions as best they could; they accepted the strategy underlying his plans, but were limited in their execution by restricted resources. But however bleak the outlook, the Order never allowed itself to be deflected from the construction of any fortification which it deemed essential to the safety of itself and the island. In course of the next decade entrenchments therefore took shape around the coasts of the island at Marsaxlokk, Marsascala, on the coast south of Ricasoli and at St. Julian's.[35]

In the closing years of the knights' rule the maritime defences appear to have been surprisingly well maintained. Indeed, such funds as were available seem to have been channelled towards these works.[36] Nor were the knights content only to repair existing structures; in January 1793 the congregation sanctioned the construction of a battery on Delimara point, of a redoubt on Dragut point and the strengthening of fort St. Lucian by the excavation of a ditch.[37] Fort Tigné on Dragut point was completed by February 1795, and the improvements to St. Lucian by June 1795 when the fort was renamed fort Rohan to commemorate the grand master's care and concern not only for that fort but for the whole system of coastal defences.[38] Perhaps the grand master's personal interest in these works explains their freedom from neglect despite the difficulties facing the Order during the final decade of the century. When put to the test in June 1798 the strategy to which the knights had committed themselves in the course of the eighteenth century failed. Despite advice to withdraw all his forces into the ring of harbour forts, Hompesch insisted on the defence of the whole island, thereby spreading his resources too thinly. The coastal fortifications proved no obstacle to Napoleon's troops; the regiments and militia offered no significant opposition in the open countryside, or at the Falca or Naxxar entrenchments; the signalling towers may have conveyed news of the assault to Valletta, but such was the turmoil within the city and the Order that Grand Master Hompesch was

---

35 AOM 6543, item 11; AOM 6546 (St. Julians, 1767-70); AOM 1015, p. 28 (scarp the coast from Qala Żembi to St. Julian's, 25 March 1762).

36 See the reports on the condition of batteries and their artillery, AOM 1015, p. 72 (4 September 1769), AOM 6543, item 15 (1770), AOM 1015, pp. 289 (27 November 1783), 349 (17 December 1791), 357 (5 November 1792), 386 (3 December 1792), 389 (16 December 1792), 393 (28 January 1793). The costs of maintaining the guards in the towers and batteries feature in the treasury accounts of the Administrazione di guerra 1779-97 (RML Tres. A 105).

37 AOM 1015, pp. 389 (16 December 1792), 392 (28 January 1793).

38 AOM 1015, p. 434 (2 June 1795); De Rohan was grand master from 1775 to 1797.

unable to take any effective action. The loyalty of the knights themselves was in question; the Order was collapsing from within rather than from external assault. However, the decision to man the coastal defences was not in itself disastrous, for even if all the troops had been concentrated in the harbour forts it is doubtful whether a more heroic resistance would have ensued.

Chapter 8

Gozo

I. The Castello

The Castello of Gozo posed much the same problems of defence as the Città Vecchia. It was an old fort, not easily adaptable to the needs of modern warfare, standing on a rocky hill in the centre of the island, and providing a citadel into which the Gozitans could retire when raiding corsairs approached. But often the raiders descended swiftly before the inhabitants could flee to safety; and even if they managed to reach the Castello, their days of safety were numbered, for the fortress was land-locked and unlikely to receive any reinforcement or reprovisioning in the face of a determined siege. Gozo therefore suffered far more severely than its larger sister from the depredations of the corsairs, and many Gozitans were taken captive or killed. But the island was too fertile to be abandoned; people wished to inhabit and cultivate it and the Order felt obliged to offer them some hope of protection.

The commission sent to inspect Malta and Gozo in 1524 reported that the Castello was badly fortified and of little importance. Although Gozo was undoubtedly weak, if the Order were to occupy Malta it would have to accept the burden of defending Gozo which might otherwise prove a convenient base from which an attack on Malta itself might be mounted. Even before the arrival of the main body of knights, work had begun on the restoration of the fortifications, and De l'Isle Adam lost no time in providing for the defence of Gozo, visiting the Castello and ordering the provision of artillery, munitions, victuals and an infantry company.[1] In these early years the knights were content, *faute de mieux*, to repair the fortress and made no attempt at modernization by equipping the walls to withstand artillery bombardment. The irregular trace of the enceinte therefore continued to follow the contours of its hilltop site unadorned by such modern innovations as bastions.[2] Indeed, it appeared to many knights to be beyond any improvement, and as early as 1551 suggestions, which were to recur during the succeeding centuries, were made that the castle be razed to the ground and the inhabitants transported to safety in Sicily. This advice was not heeded and in the course of the disastrous corsair raid of July 1551 the Castello was reduced to ruins. By 1565 it had been rebuilt, but no concessions had been made to contemporary theories of fortification; the Castello had been resurrected as a mediaeval citadel and, without bastions, the walls were not covered by flanking fire, nor were there satisfactory artillery emplacements.[3] As the scale of the impending Turkish attack in 1565 became apparent, it was again suggested that the Castello, together with the Città Vecchia, should be demolished, but this proposal was defeated and it was in the event manned by a garrison of eighty soldiers.[4] In the light of this it was doubly fortunate that the Turks chose not to attack Gozo. Instead of capturing the weak fortresses in their rear, Città Vecchia and the Castello, the Turks bypassed them in an attempt to conquer the nerve-centre of the Order.

Although Laparelli visited Gozo, and may have drawn up a plan to modernize the castle, this work could hardly compete for a share of the limited resources with the prestigious and essential task of constructing a secure headquarters.[5] Until the final years of the century the knights had therefore to be content to keep the existing structure in as good repair as possible.[6] Disquiet about the Castello of Gozo grew

---

1 Bosio, III, 85.

2 See Perez d'Aleccio, plate 19.

3 See Perez d'Aleccio, plate 19.

4 Pius IV had granted a tenth on all the ecclesiastical goods of Gozo in 1564; the proceeds were to be used to prepare defences against corsair raiders and even against the Turks (AOM. 430, f. 240; Pauli, II, 213).

5 The plan published by Perez d'Aleccio may have been one drawn by Laparelli for plate XV (Valletta) is based on his design. Laparelli visited Gozo on 8 September 1567 (Bosio, III, 802); however, the design does not seem to be in his style. On the other hand, the Count of Vicari felt unable to comment on the defences of Gozo as he had not visited the island (*Col. doc. ineditos*, XXX, 128, 1566).

6 In 1579 it was described as undefendable (document published by P. Collura in 'La difesa militare di Malta nella seconda metà del secolo XVI' in *Archivio storico di Malta*, XI (1940), 177).

Plate 24 Gozo Castello from the north.

over the years and by the 1590s the Order was determined to seek a solution to the problem of the defence of the smaller island. It tried to enlist the support of Philip II in the hope that he might supply both money and an engineer.[7] Philip responded by releasing 40,000 scudi which had accumulated during a vacancy in the priory of Leon, but died before any other action could be taken.[8] Finally in 1599 the Order secured the services of the Anconan engineer, Giovanni Rinaldini, who had studied the art of fortification under Germanico Savorgnano.[9]

In 1583, when a raid by the galleys of Bizerta was feared, a papal brief was obtained authorizing the collection of 5000 scudi over five years for use in the Castello, by means of a customs levy on eatables (AOM 441, f. 259, 23 August 1583). The testimonial for Gerolamo Cassar, dated 18 May 1581, mentions his work in the Castello (AOM 439, f. 270v.).

7 Dal Pozzo, I, 370; AOM 449, f. 251v. (27 May 1595); AOM 451, f. 268v. (7 November 1598).

8 Dal Pozzo, I, 404.

9 Rinaldini served with the Spanish armies in Flanders and Burgundy before being entrusted with the fortification of Otranto by the viceroy of Naples. After 1595 he fought for the Catholic league in the French wars but with the Treaty of Vervins in 1598 transferred to the employ of Henri IV. He stayed several months in Malta and then returned to Italy. In 1601 he was living in Rome as the agent of the Spanish crown and pursuing his career as a public and private architect. He died in 1620. (C. Promis, 'Gl'ingegneri militari della Marca d'Ancona che operano e scrissero dall'anno MDL all'anno MDCL'in *Miscellanea di storia italiana*, VI (Turin, 1865), 308.)

Rinaldini subjected the defences of Gozo to a critical reappraisal in an attempt to find a permanent solution to the island's problems. He first considered objectively the best possible site for the island's citadel.[10] The Castello had little to recommend it beyond its central position which enabled all Gozitans to reach the dubious safety of its walls when a corsair raider approached. The walls themselves were weak, ruined, unflanked and without the terrapleins essential in an era of gunpowder artillery. The rock on which the citadel stood was soft, riddled with caves, and provided ideal material for an attacker to mine. To the north-west, the Castello was dominated by the heights of Gelmus which were less than a quarter of a mile distant; to the south-east lay its suburb Rabat which would provide excellent cover for an assault. To fortify the Castello according to modern standards, to construct parapets and terrapleins and to strengthen the walls, it would be necessary to encroach on the already restricted internal area of the fort and to demolish the existing houses. The Castello might as a result and at great cost, be made secure, but could then no longer fulfil its primary function as a refuge for the island's inhabitants. Nor would an alternative method of strengthening the castle by the construction of outworks to provide flanking protection be any more satisfactory, for these would be unduly expensive, and in any case the site was unsuitable and the Order had neither the men nor the artillery necessary to defend them. Similarly, fortifying Rabat, either in part or whole, offered no solution to the problem of protecting the Gozitans and their beasts. It would be an expensive undertaking and, because Rabat itself was donated by Gelmus, worthless. To fortify Gelmus was out of the question as the Order would then be committed to three forts, the Castello, Rabat and Gelmus. All in all, Rinaldini had to advise against fortifying the Castello. He considered three other possible sites for the citadel. Mġarr, although it had advantages – it would deny shelter and fresh water to an enemy fleet – he dismissed because it was overlooked by high ground at Għajnsielem which it was impracticable to enclose within the enceinte. Moreover the rock at Mġarr was friable and the material excavated from the ditch would be unsuitable for building. Rinaldini, however, suggested that a tower should be constructed to defend the bay and to prevent corsairs from watering there. The two other sites were at Marsalforn on the heights between that bay and Ramla bay. There was little to chose between

[10] AOM 6554, f. 253; copy at AOM 6551, f. 85.

the two, which were separated by a valley called delli Giardini or Wied il-Pergla. Both were surrounded on three sides by precipitous cliffs where a small parapet would suffice for protection, while the landward flank, some two hundred canes long, could be defended by a front of one bastion and two demi-bastions. The more northerly hill dominated Marsalforn bay and could protect Ramla; the southerly overlooked Ramla, and, although a part of Marsalforn was hidden, its entrance could still be observed. Rinaldini at first favoured the Ramla site because the ground appeared easy to work; however, further investigation showed that he was mistaken and he therefore transferred his preference to the hill overlooking Marsalforn. In his second report Rinaldini examined in detail the design of such a fort and the difficulties likely to be encountered in its construction.[11] For 80,000 scudi he estimated that a strong fort could be constructed. While he was still prepared to discuss modifications to the Castello, these would be inordinately expensive and never wholly satisfactory. The prime threat to the security of the Castello was Gelmus hill; the enceinte on that quarter could however be strengthened by the addition of a projecting shoulder with a terraplein of eight canes depth; a similar work could be constructed on the other side of the fort to give protection from another possible point of attack, the post of St. Francis; while the main gateway could be covered by the construction of a mezzaluna. Elsewhere he suggested that the existing walls should be terrapleined, that all debris be removed from the outside circumference, that the ditch be deepened and widened, and that all stone walls and other potentially useful material be removed from the grasp of a would-be attacker. The houses within the enceinte were to be restored to receive the inhabitants of Rabat, some forty families in all. Rabat itself and a partially-built wall – the fruits of a scheme to enclose the suburb – should, he suggested, be demolished.

Despite Rinaldini's condemnation of the Castello and his strong recommendation that a fort be built at Marsalforn, the knights rejected his advice and decided to fortify the old Castello.[12] They were prepared to demolish Rabat, giving the owners a fair price for their houses, but in the event nothing came of this suggestion. Unfortunately Rinaldini's plans have not survived, so that it is difficult to ascribe to him responsibility for any particular part of the present fort; all we

11 AOM 6554, f. 267; copy at AOM 6551, f. 88v.

12 Dal Pozzo, I, 426; AOM 100, ff. 122 (22, September 1599), 123v. (13 October), 128 (20 November).

know for certain is that work commenced towards the end of 1599 and was still in progress in July 1601.[13] A small part of Rinaldini's original concept for the defence of the island was, however, salvaged thanks to the provision in the will of Grand Master Garzes for a tower overlooking Mġarr and, probably in the reign of Alof de Wignacourt, a tower was constructed at Marsalforn.[14] The council asserted that once the modifications were complete the Castello would be defendable, an opinion not, however, shared by the engineers who inspected the island's defences in later years. Almost without exception they advised abandoning the Castello in favour of a new fortress at Marsalforn. The Marquis of St. Angelo, who visited the island in March 1640, agreed with Rinaldini that Marsalforn should be fortified, but did not believe the time yet appropriate, on the grounds of cost and the great inconvenience it would cause the Gozitans.[15] The Castello could serve quite well as a refuge, although he admitted that it was somewhat small for the population, the surplus of which could, he suggested, be shipped to safety in Malta. The alternative was to surround Rabat with a simple wall at a cost of ten or twelve thousand scudi. The Castello was probably still in a reasonable state of repair having been attended to at the time of the general alarm in 1635.[16] St. Angelo, moreover, thought it unlikely that an attacker bent on conquering Malta would waste time and men storming the Castello merely to capture the inmates. By 1643, however, the Order felt itself in a position to proceed with the fortification of Marsalforn.[17] But although the building of a new fort was sanctioned, the proposal to demolish the Castello gave rise to controversy. A commission of knights who visited the fortress in May 1643 assumed that it would remain standing and reported on work, mainly repairs, essential to ensure its safety.[18] In June the grand master visited the island to see the situation for himself and confirmed that the new fort be built. Contracts for the work were drawn up, papal permission obtained for the project to be financed by a levy on wheat grown in the island, and the

---

13 AOM 100, f. 193v. (9 July 1601).

14 AOM 100, f. 212 (17 December 1601); AOM 101, f. 191 (14 October 1605). The Marsalforn tower is mentioned in the following: AOM 100, f. 88v. (6 May 1631); AOM 257, f. 211v. (5 April 1645); AOM 116, f. 71 (20 December 1647); AOM 260, f. 143 (15 December 1662) and AOM 6551, f. 103v. (1681).

15 AOM 6554, f. 42 (report dated 8 April 1640); copies at AOM 6554, f. 287 and AOM 6551, f. 94v. (dated 9 April).

16 AOM 256, f. 129v. (11 March 1635).

17 AOM 257, f. 136v. (15 May 1643).

18 AOM 257, f. 138 (27 May 1643).

Marquis of St. Angelo set to revising his original design.[19] But the Gozitans intervened before anything could be done. They protested that they were too poor to pay the tax, and that the disruption caused by the transfer of their homes to Marsalforn, many miles from their fields, would be too great.[20] As the prospect of financing the fort by a levy on the island itself vanished, the Order decided its own resources were unequal to the task and the project was abandoned for the time being.

The emergency of 1645 brought a fresh inflow of engineers to the islands and the criticism of the Castello was renewed. Arpajon and Pallavicino recommended the evacuation of the old fortress as soon as the Turkish fleet appeared off Gozo, leaving only a garrison with supplies for two weeks, although as a longer-term project they supported the scheme to fortify Marsalforn.[21] Members of the Order sent to inspect the Castello were of much the same opinion, and, encouraged by the volley of advice, the council again determined to abandon the Castello on the approach of a powerful hostile armada.[22] Pallavicino's advice was heeded and the Castello mined ready for destruction should the fleet appear.[23] Thus, although the Order was prepared to demolish the fortress which was agreed to be undefendable, the actual deed was delayed and the inhabitants of the Castello and its suburb won a reprieve until hostile ships actually appeared over the horizon. The construction of a fortress at Marsalforn remained, however, the knights' long-term objective to be realized when resources permitted.

Before long the project was revived. In July 1654 Grand Master Lascaris commissioned yet another report on the state of the Castello, possible remedies, and likely sources of funds, but from it he learnt nothing new.[24] The opinions expressed by Rinaldini and the Marquis

---

19 AOM 6402, f. 146v. (contracts, 22 October 1643); AOM 470, f. 266 (papal permission, 11 September 1643); AOM 6551, f. 94v. and AOM 6554, f. 289 (Marquis of St. Angelo, 5 April 1644).

20 AOM 257, f. 165 (7 May 1644).

21 AOM 6554, ff. 299 (16 June 1645), 301, and 303.

22 AOM 6554, f. 291 (anonymous), f. 293 (De Redin, and De la Vallière) and f. 297 (De la Romière); copies at AOM 6551, ff. 95, 95v. and 96. The anonymous writer who transmitted his opinions via Vice-Chancellor Bueno objected to the scheme to fortify Marsalforn as wasteful of resources. If the Order wished to protect the Gozitans from the odd corsair raid then the Castello was undoubtedly the best site; if an attack appeared to be more serious, the Gozitans should be withdrawn to Malta (AOM 6554, f. 70).

23 RML MS. 742, pp. 431 (15 June 1645) and 433 (1 July 1645); AOM 6553, f. 64v. (1 July).

24 AOM 6402, f. 152 (7 July 1654); copy at AOM 6554. f. 283; the report is anonymous and there is no indication as to its authorship.

of St. Angelo were well known to all and endorsed by this later author, who concluded that the Order had only to decide whether to adopt St. Angelo's design or that of Buonamici for the fort at Marsalforn. Probably the best method of financing the project would be to invoke the papal brief sanctioning a levy on wheat, and, to solve any short-term liquidity problems, to issue copper money to be redeemed as the levy was collected. On this occasion the Gozitans did not display their accustomed hostility to the scheme. Perhaps recognizing the inadequacies of the Castello they requested that a new spacious fortress be built at Marsalforn.[25] The commission of knights appointed to examine the petition reported that the Castello, besides being weak, without flanking defences and easily mined, could accommodate only 1,000 persons out of an island population of 9,000.[26] The advantages of a fort at Marsalforn were more indisputable than ever, for it provided a strong defensive position, an abundance of water, good air and the possibility of relief by sea. St. Angelo had already produced an unimpeachable design, so that rather than starting from scratch with a new engineer imported from abroad, the council decided to construct the fort to the Marquis's original plans.[27] By the following May, Buonamici had traced the outline of the fortress and calculated the work involved and the approximate cost, namely 30,000 scudi.[28] To raise this a papal brief was procured sanctioning a levy of three scudi per salmata of land for three years.[29] But for some reason or other, perhaps lack of ready money, work came to a halt, and the fortress at Marsalforn remained no more than an outline.

Antonio Maurizio Valperga's ideas for the defence of Malta elicited little sympathy from his fellow engineers. His scheme for Gozo likewise encountered criticism. Almost alone of the engineers who examined the island, he opposed the fortification of Marsalforn, preferring to protect Rabat.[30] Although he conceded that the Marsalforn site could be strongly fortified, he claimed that it would be a costly business especially if the spring at the foot of the hill were to be enclosed. Such expense, he argued, would place too heavy a burden on the poor

---

25 AOM 259, f. 171 (30 May 1656).
26 AOM 259, f. 172 (9 June 1656).
27 AOM 259, f. 174 (21 June 1656).
28 AOM 6551, f. 105v. and AOM 6554, f. 309 (9 May 1657).
29 Dal Pozzo, II, 271; Mifsud, 'Papi', p. 424.
30 He visited Gozo on 20 April 1670 (AOM 261, f. 163); His report is dated 13 May (AOM 261, f. 163v.; AOM 6551, f. 99; AOM 6554, f. 311 and a plan of the project is inserted loose into this volume; Dal Pozzo, II, 389).

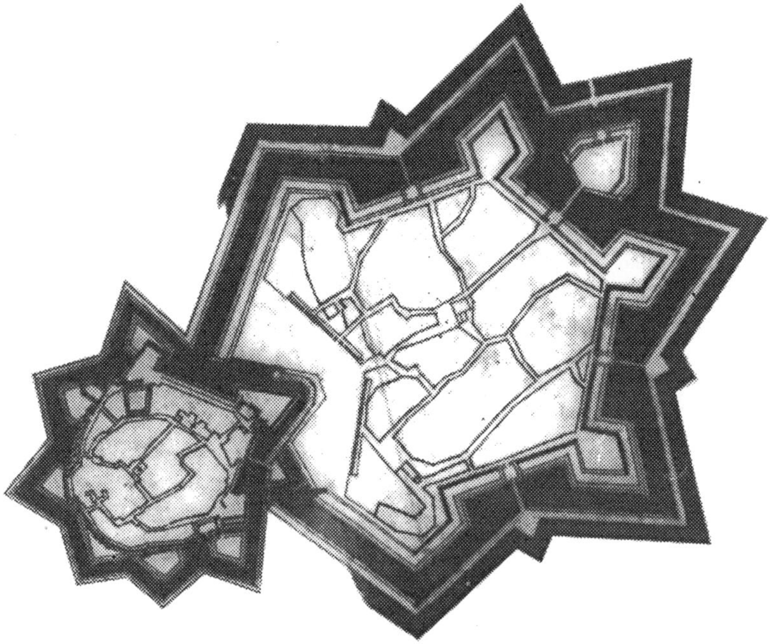

Plate 25 Plan of Valperga's proposal to enclose Rabat, Gozo, with a bastioned enceinte, 1670 (AOM 6554).

islanders, who, moreover, would be deprived of their conveniently situated central refuge. Valperga dismissed as minimal any damage which might be inflicted on the Castello or Rabat from neighbouring heights. He proposed to enclose the suburb by a wall linked to the Castello which would itself remain as a final retreat. The knights decided to follow Valperga's advice, but because of their commitment to the construction of Cottonera, the actual implementation of the scheme to fortify Rabat had to be postponed. Although Blondel strongly supported the Marsalforn project, he was given no opportunity to put his ideas into practice,[31] and in the closing decades of the seventeenth century the scheme to fortify Marsalforn no longer featured among the Order's immediate plans. As a result Blondel was called to concentrate his energies on the repair and maintenance of the Castello.[32]

---

31 PRO WO 55, 1555/1, pp. 245 and 255.

32 The Marsalforn scheme remained a long-term objective and was mentioned by the commissioners of fortification in 1701 (AOM 265, f. 39).

The repairs to the Castello in the 1690s are well documented but lack of evidence for the earlier years does not of itself imply that the castle was neglected. The knights, through the common treasury, the *cassa della fortificazione* and the proceeds of the *neuba*, were financing its upkeep. During his early years with the Order, in 1661 to be precise, Blondel was sent to Gozo to rebuild a part of the enceinte situated on steep rock to the north and north-west, and later in the mid-1670s rock to the north and north-east which was crumbling away was strengthened.[33] In 1681 the counterscarp and the mezzaluna guarding the gate were found to be faulty.[34] By 1692 the mezzaluna had been repaired together with St. John's cavalier and some of the adjoining enceinte.[35] Whether or not the counterscarp had been attended to in 1681, in 1692 it was in a parlous state and although Blondel urged its immediate repair on the 'stitch in time' principle, a dispute arose as to whether the Università or the Order was responsible for its repair, and this ensured that nothing was actually done.[36] In 1695 the counterscarp was still in an unsatisfactory state, so that, despite the continuing dispute over payment the congregation advanced 200 scudi from the *cassa della fortificazione* to allow the work to proceed; a year later, however, large parts of the counterscarp were still awaiting renewal.[37]

Although Gozo suffered from the earthquake which shook the islands in 1693, Blondel was careful not to exaggerate the damage caused to the fortifications.[38] He had observed a finger-wide crack in one of the Castello bastions on his very first trip to Gozo and suspected that it dated back to the sixteenth century. The ruinous condition of the houses was the result of neglect rather than the earthquake, and he suggested that their owners should be made responsible for their renovation within a specified time. The counterscarp needed no earthquake to render it ruinous, for, notwithstanding Blondel's strenuous efforts, it had not been satisfactorily repaired. Untold damage was being done by the roots of weeds, especially those of a grass named Sanda or Kali, which were allowed to grow over the parapets of the

---

33 AOM 1016, p. 114.

34 AOM 6551, f. 103 (17 May 1681).

35 AOM 1016, p. 114.

36 AOM 1016, pp. 75 (17 August 1692), 85 (31 August), 89 (14 September), 109 (2 October), 111 (19 October), 114 (23 October), 125 (14 December 1692).

37 AOM 1016, pp. 351 (5 June 1695), 355 (15 June), 357 (18 June), 358 (23 June 1695), 404 (11 August 1696).

38 AOM 1016, p. 195 (20 June 1693).

Castello and the mezzaluna despite Blondel's warnings of the harm they could do. This grass also caught the attention of a commission inspecting the Castello three years later.[39] It had to be dug out, and to prevent regrowth, the crevices and cracks filled with mortar and sand. The commissioners also recommended the reconstruction of parapets at St. Martin's and St. John's cavaliers and at the ravelin outside St. John's bastion. On this occasion the congregation acted upon the recommendations, the work being put out to contract and completed within a year.[40] So it was that when the commissioners of fortification and war visited Gozo in May 1701 they found the defences of the Castello in a reasonable state except for the ravelin under St. John's cavalier, where the parapets and walls were in need of attention, and the glacis which was not protecting the covert-way correctly.[41] The houses were, however, in a sad state, and to supervise their reconstruction and the construction of powder magazines in St. Martin's cavalier, the commissioners suggested that an engineer skilled in military and civil architecture be summoned from abroad. Somewhat belatedly the Frenchman Claude de Colongues arrived in March 1703 in answer to their requests for assistance. Colongues criticized the old-fashioned design of the Castello and its general decrepitude.[42] He rejected the solutions offered by Arpajon and Valperga to these problems – namely the mining of the Castello or the enclosing of Rabat by a wall. The population had, it seems, in any case multiplied so rapidly in years of relative peace that the castle could no longer realistically be regarded as a refuge for all the islanders; he therefore opposed the reconstruction of the houses which would only encourage vast numbers of non-combatants to clutter the Castello and impede its defence; he preferred to transform it instead into a purely military establishment. Colongues had doubts as to the wisdom of defending Rabat on the grounds that its very fortifications might attract an enemy who would otherwise have ignored it. However, out of Christian charity to protect the islanders, he proposed that two lines of trenches be constructed from the Castello to the suburb which would allow the latter to be defended in an emergency. But before any of his proposals could be implemented, Colongues departed for France, where he died

---

39 AOM 1016, p. 404 (11 August 1696); AOM 264, f. 108 (3 September 1696).

40 AOM 1016, pp. 416 (26 June 1697) and 417 (final measurement of repairs).

41 AOM 265, f. 39 (18 May 1701); AOM 6552, f. 30v.

42 He submitted two reports: AOM 6554, ff. 317 and 323 with copies at AOM 6552, ff. 101 and 102v.

when on the point of returning to Malta. His idea to enclose Rabat by trenches was revived a few years later when a Turkish attack appeared imminent, and the work was then supervised by the Order's engineer, a German, Johan Person, from Mainz.[43] Although the Turks descended on Gozo in 1708, the raid was an insignificant affair and neither the Castello nor the new trenches were put to the test.

The great review of the fortifications prompted by the general alarm which swept the islands in 1714 and 1715 included the inspection of the defences of Gozo as well as those of the larger sister island, and the disagreements and disputes between the supporters of Tigné and those of Vendôme also had their repercussions in Gozo. Tigné favoured enclosing Rabat by a bastioned enceinte, whereas Vendôme recommended the protection of the coastline.[44] Although some coastal works were built in the eighteenth century, Rabat was never enclosed; nor was the scheme to construct an alternative fortress at Marsalforn revived. However, with the increasing emphasis as the century progressed on coastal defence, the small, inland Castello became even more obsolete. Thus although the knights attempted to maintain the Castello in a fair state of repair, they were fully aware that they were throwing good money after bad.[45] In 1722 the commissioners of fortification therefore reappraised the whole question of the defence of Gozo.[46] They outlined three possible strategies: to fortify the coasts so that a landing would be impossible, or, at best, costly; to increase the defence of Rabat; to fortify another site so that an attacker would have two strongholds to besiege. The first proposal was dismissed as too costly; the second also, to be effective, would cost an inordinate sum; the third was recommended but with the proviso that the new fort be established at Mġarr rather than Marsalforn. Mġarr was the only secure harbour in the island, and through it passed all the traffic between Malta and Gozo. A fortified town at Mġarr would, it was hoped, act as a catalyst to revive the flagging commerce of the island and even attract new settlers. The site had a ready supply of water, and, although it consisted of difficult, uneven terrain, was neither dominated nor flanked from the neighbouring countryside. The proposed fort could

---

43 AOM 265, f. 214v. (19 July 1708); AOM 6552, f. 34; AOM 513, f. 118 (8 October 1709) – passport for Person leaving the island after two years' service. He had been employed as second engineer although the Order does not appear to have had a chief engineer at that time.

44 RML MS. 1301, p. 108; AOM 6556, f. 79.

45 Repairs noted in Clerkenwell, MS. O 1, item 20 (1722 and 1723), item 21 (1740, 1745, 1754 and 1755); AOM 1011, f. 98 (November 1732-May 1734); AOM 267, f. 137 (28 July 1722); AOM 1015, p. 56 (27 June 1766).

46 AOM 267, f. 147 (25 September 1722).

be relieved by sea and would help in the defence of the Gozo channel. In addition, the whole harbour of Mġarr and the Garzes tower would be covered by outworks from the fort to be built on the high ground to the west of the harbour. The council approved this project, and the pope, from whom aid was awaited, was informed of the scheme; no move was, however, made to commence construction.[47] In 1724 the implementation of the scheme was formally postponed until fort Manoel, then consuming all the Order's energies, should be completed.[48] However, even after its completion, no start was made on the fort at Mġarr, and, but for the generosity of one knight, Jacques Chambray, it seems likely that the project would never have progressed beyond the planning stage.

In 1749 Chambray offered to finance the construction of a fort designed many years earlier by Tigné, on the heights of Ras it-Tafal overlooking Mġarr harbour.[49] Marandon was therefore dispatched to Gozo immediately to examine the site, and make all preparations necessary before work could commence.[50] However, the knights then appear to have had second thoughts about the fort. Possibly fearing lest the design, drawn up over thirty years earlier, was outdated, they decided instead to seek expert advice abroad, from Spain, France and Italy.[51] Such an effort to obtain the most informed opinion in Europe

---

47 AOM 267, f. 150 (25 September 1722).

48 AOM 267, f. 234v. (5 June 1724).

49 Clerkenwell, MS. O 1, item 21 (15 September 1749), item 24; AOM 1012, f. 67; the records say that the fort was to be constructed to the design of Tigné but no report or plan by him for such a fort has come to light; indeed, Tigné's only surviving comments on Gozo recommend the encirclement of Rabat by a bastioned enceinte (RML MS. 1301, p. 106).

50 Clerkenwell, MS. O 1, item 22 is Marandon's notebook concerned with the building of Ras it-Tafal fort. The earliest dated entry is October 1749; by December he had valued the houses which would have to be purchased to make way for the fort (Clerkenwell, MS. O 1, item 24). Between October 1749 and October 1751 13,413 scudi were paid out to workmen (Clerkenwell, MS. O 1, item 21).

51 AOM 1012, f. 42; by September the Order had received opinions from the Duke of Belleisle, and from Palmieri, Zermano and Bertola. Charles-Louis Auguste Fouquet de Belleisle was born in 1684. He fought widely in the later campaigns of Louis XIV and served in the Rhineland, Bavaria and Italy in the 1730s and 1740s, attaining the rank of field marshal in 1743. He was admitted to the Académie Française in 1753 and in 1758 was a secretary of state in the department of war. He died in 1761. (*DBF*, V, 1336 and Blanchard, 'Les ingénieurs', p. 182). Marquis Giuseppe Palmieri (1720-93) was a well-known Neapolitan soldier, minister and writer, the author of *Riflessioni critiche sull'arte della guerra* (Naples, 1761), *Nuova dizionario istorico* (Naples, 1791-4). Juan Martin Zermeno or Cermeño, served the Spanish crown. He was present at the siege of Gibraltar in 1727, and in 1749 was appointed commandant general of the corps of engineers in Spain. He became president of the Academy of Barcelona, and, put forward proposals for the fortification of that city in 1750 and of Cadiz in 1770. (Capel, pp. 309-10). Giuseppe Francesco Ignazio Bertola (1676-1755) was employed by the rulers of Piedmont against the French. He rose to the rank of first military architect and general of infantry. (*DBI*, IX, p. 564).

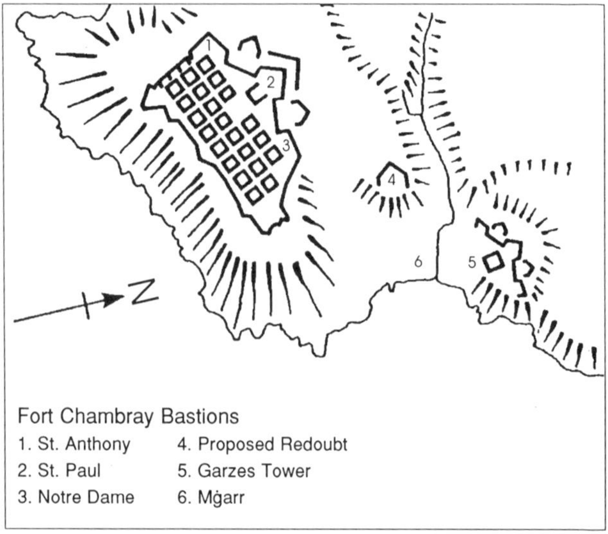

Fig. 11. Fort Chambray, Gozo

brought its own problems, for the foreign engineers were far from unanimous in their suggestions for the improvement of fort Chambray, and the Order had to make the best it could of conflicting advice.[52] The fort was eventually constructed with its major defences to the north, the only quarter from which it was easily accessible, by means of a front consisting of three bastions, two ravelins, a counterguard, ditch and covert-way. On the other sides the cliffs formed an excellent natural defence, especially on the southern flank, and the enceinte was therefore made less powerful in these parts, the south-western and south-eastern bastions being far less important than those on the. northern front Although Marandon was in charge of building work, he left the day-to-day control in the hands of an overseer on site with whom he communicated regularly by letter.[53] In 1755 the northern front had reached the level of the cordon, and within two years, despite a decision to cut back expenditure, the ravelins were almost complete and work was under way on the south-western curtain.[54] The following year, 1758, the chapel in the fort was dedicated to the Madonna della Grazia, indicating that the fortifications were sufficiently advanced

52 AOM 1012, ff. 29 (21 August 1753), 33 (27 July 1753), 41 (October 1753).
53 AOM 1012, ff. 230-248v. – series of letters, 1752-3.
54 Clerkenwell, MS. O 1, item 21.

Plate 26 Fort Chambray with Mġarr, Gozo.

to allow a diversion of effort to non-military construction.[55] And by 1760 the congregation was able to turn its attention to attracting settlers to Chambray which had been designed as a fortified city rather than as a purely military establishment.[56]

All the advice from abroad and all the care lavished by Marandon could not, however, remedy one fundamental weakness: the friable nature of the rock along the eastern flank. This defect had been recognized while the project was in the planning stage but had not been considered sufficiently serious to halt the scheme. This proved a serious error of judgement and a source of later criticism. Although Bourlamaque and his company of engineers approved the concept of the fort, the design of the northern front and the manner in which it had been built,[57] they regarded the western and eastern flanks of the work as weak, for both were threatened from nearby hills, the former by Busuttil height, and the latter from the site of Garzes tower. To reduce any danger to the fort should these walls be breached, Bourlamaque recommended the construction of interior retrenchments, and that the right flank be further strengthened by the erection of a redoubt indicated in earlier plans on a small plateau between Chambray and

55 AOM 271, f. 90v. (6 August 1758).

56 AOM 1015, pp. 6 (21 January 1760) and 10 (9 October 1760), contract for the excavation of cisterns.

57 AOM 6557, f. 1 (28 July 1761); AOM 6558, f. 37v.; Clerkenwell, MS. O 1, item 25.

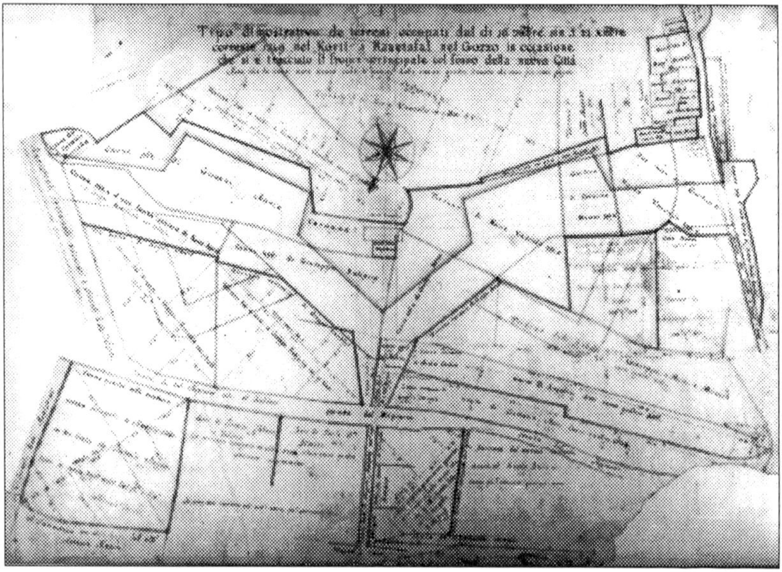

Plate 27 Plan of land appropriated in building fort Chambray with Mġarr, Gozo, (RML Map G24).

Garzes tower. He recommended that the tower itself should be surrounded by ditches, and that additional magazines and casemates be provided within the fort itself. However, the construction of such interior works, and in particular the retrenchments, would diminish the size of the fort which could then no longer perform one of the tasks for which it had originally been designed – the protection of the Gozitans. The islanders would as a result have to shelter on the ground between the fort and the sea, although Bourlamaque did at least intend to enclose this area and provide communications with the fort. Despite Marandon's criticisms, Bourlamaque's report was accepted by the council. However, the present fort Chambray displays no evidence that the proposed modifications were ever implemented.[58]

In the years that followed the fort deteriorated; by 1789 it could be described as in ruin, its sorry condition being ascribed in part to the terrain and partly to masonry which was of inadequate thickness.[59]

---

58 Criticisms and Pontleroy's replies on Bourlamaque's behalf are found as follows: AOM 6557, f. 11; AOM 6558, f. 43; Clerkenwell, MS. O 1, item 26.

59 AOM 1054, pp. 20 and 36.

Its restoration involving major reconstruction was a task not to be undertaken lightly given the Order's precarious financial state. The repairs undertaken in 1795 and 1796 were therefore of a minor nature, being merely an attempt to salvage some benefit from the existing works.[60] As it happened, a new town never became established within the walls of Chambray; perhaps by the 1750s the dangers of a corsair attack had diminished so drastically that the benefits of a secure refuge were outweighed by the inconvenience of moving house. Surprisingly, the edifice did see action as a fort and was one of the few fortresses to put up a spirited, if short, resistance to the troops of Napoleon.

II. The coastal defences of Gozo and Comino

Prior to the arrival of the knights the coasts of Gozo, like those of Malta, had been guarded by a local militia whose task was to alert the island should a hostile fleet appear.[61] Opposition to raiders tended to be passive; the islanders, with their beasts, withdrew to the relative safety of the Castello, and the coasts were left undefended. Although the system of lookout posts was well established, until the coming of the knights the militia enjoyed no support from coastal fortifications.[62] The weakness of the defences was already recognized early in the fifteenth century when Alfonso of Aragon gave the Università permission to erect a tower on Comino and allowed a tax to be levied to offset the cost. The tower was not, however, built in 1418, but two hundred years later by Grand Master Alof de Wignacourt. Early in their sojourn on the islands the knights investigated the possibility of defending the Gozo channel by building a tower on Comino. The engineer Piccino was sent to examine the island but was recalled, before anything could be done, to work on the more urgent task of designing a fort on the tip of Sciberras.[63]

The first tower built to protect the channel was not, however, sited on Comino but on Gozo. Rinaldini in 1599 had recommended that one be built at Mġarr and Grand Master Garzes, who died in 1601, made

60 AOM 1015, pp. 428 (5 November 1794), 432 (26 March 1795), 436 (8 August 1795), 440 (14 September 1795), 470 (12 April 1796), 493 (26 April 1796) and 536 (17 September 1796).

61 E. R. Leopardi, 'The island of Gozo, 1432-53' in *Melita Historica*, IV (1964), 70. Very few documents relating to Gozo in the Middle Ages have survived. Many may well have perished in the devastating corsair raid of 1551. The earliest volume in the archives of the Università of Gozo is dated 1560-2.

62 No fortification in Gozo, except the Castello, can definitely be said to predate the arrival of the Order.

63 Bosio, III, 128 (1533).

provision in his will for the financing of such a work. Four years after his death, the tower, dedicated to St. Martin, was built.[64] Perhaps the workmanship, or even the design (said to be an imitation of the tower at cape Passero in Sicily) was not of the highest quality, for twelve years later it was already in need of repair.[65] The tower at Mġarr did not, however, diminish the necessity for a similar structure on Comino. Indeed, two such works would be complementary, together protecting the channel all the more efficiently. Grand Master de Wignacourt certainly subscribed to this reasoning when, in 1618, he financed the construction of St. Mary's tower on Comino.[66] This was similar in design to St. Lucian's and St. Thomas's towers, all three probably sharing the same designer, Vittorio Cassar. St. Mary's was, however, the most expensive of the five towers erected by Wignacourt, costing, fully armed and provisioned, no less than 18,628 scudi.

The coast of Gozo, like that of its larger sister, was in many places defended naturally by steep cliffs and inhospitable rocks. The bays where an invader might disembark with ease were few in number, and in the course of the seventeenth century watchtowers were erected to give warning of an approaching fleet, and to discourage the casual raider. Two such forts, built and wholly maintained by the knights, were already in existence in 1631, namely Garzes and one at Marsalforn.[67] Two more were added during the reign of Lascaris at Xlendi in 1650 and at Qawra/Dwejra in 1652; under De Redin one was constructed at Mġarr ix-Xini in 1661, and in 1667 under Nicholas Cotoner another was built, the Torre Nuova to the east of San Blas bay.[68] Although the Università paid for the construction of these last four and was responsible for their upkeep and the wages of any professional soldiers employed, it was the Order which supplied the artillery.[69] Both the Università and the Order appear, however, to have

---

64 Dal Pozzo, I, 439; AOM 100, ff. 175 (11 February 1601), 212 (17 December 1601); AOM 101, f. 191 (14 October 1605); Dal Pozzo, I, 492; Garzes tower was demolished in the nineteenth century.

65 AOM 106, f. 62v. (7 November 1617).

66 Dal Pozzo, I, 637; AOM 106, f. 124v. (11 October 1618); AOM 6385, f. 192 (28 September 1621) – copy of Wignacourt's will.

67 AOM 110, f. 88v. (6 May 1631); the origin of this latter tower is something of a mystery; there is no record among the Order's papers of its construction.

68 AOM 258, f. 222 (29 June 1650) and AOM 259, f. 53v. (22 October 1652); AOM 260, f. 103 (14 June 1661); Mifsud, 'La milizia', p. 97; AOM 6551, f. 104 is a description, with measurements, by Blondel of the tower to be built at Mġarr x-Xini. These towers were similar in design to their contemporaries in Malta, square, normally two storied, with battered lower courses.

69 See AOM 645, p. 91 (3 March 1670).

been somewhat remiss in their maintenance of the towers. On inspection in 1681 only Garzes needed no repairs;[70] of the other towers, Mġarr ix-Xini requiring only a new bridge was in the best state; Marsalforn was threatening to collapse; the stonework of Torre Nuova, Xlendi and St. Mary's on Comino, had been badly eroded by the salt air. By the early 1690s Blondel had repaired Marsalforn and it remained in reasonable condition throughout the decade,[71] although no amount of care and attention could remedy one serious fault: the tower had been sited on a cliff of friable rock which was crumbling away. In 1701 the commissioners of fortification repeated a suggestion made twenty years earlier by Vauvilliers: that the tower should be abandoned and a new one built on the plateau between Marsalforn and Ramla bays.[72] Although the council ordered a model to be made of the new fortress no further steps were taken until after 1715 when the artillery from the old tower was transferred to St. Paul's battery and, presumably, Marsalforn was abandoned.[73] The earthquake of 1693 had, it seems, been blamed for the destruction of some of the towers, although on examination Blondel found that normal wear and tear together with less than adequate maintenance were alone responsible for their condition.[74] Although the governor of Gozo expressed concern about the state of the fortifications in 1696, the commission of inspection appointed by the congregation found little at fault in the Order's towers at Marsalforn and Garzes.[75]

The coastal defences were the subject of a thorough review by the engineers summoned to Malta in 1715. Even before the arrival of the foreign engineers, two knights, D'Arginy and Fontet, had inspected the coast and presented a plan for its defence to the council.[76] They proposed to construct batteries at Mġarr, Ramla, Marsalforn and Qolla l-Bajda, and in consequence work began immediately on those at Mġarr and the Qolla is-Safra area of Marsalforn, with the help of a donation from the Bailiff Gironda.[77] Vendôme's advocacy of a defensive strategy

---

70 AOM 6551, f. 103v. (17 May 1681) – report of examination by Vauvilliers.

71 AOM 1016, pp. 199 (20 June 1693) and 404 (11 August 1696); AOM 264, f. 108 (3 September 1696).

72 AOM 265, f. 39 (18 May 1701).

73 Mifsud, 'La milizia', p. 96.

74 AOM 1016, p. 199 (20 June 1693).

75 AOM 1016, pp. 400 (19 June 1696) and 404 (11 August 1696).

76 AOM 6552, ff. 6v. and 23 (10 January 1715).

77 AOM 6556, f. 9. The cost of work in the two batteries up to 30 April 1715 was 875 scudi. The latter was also known as the Sta. Maria or Gironda battery.

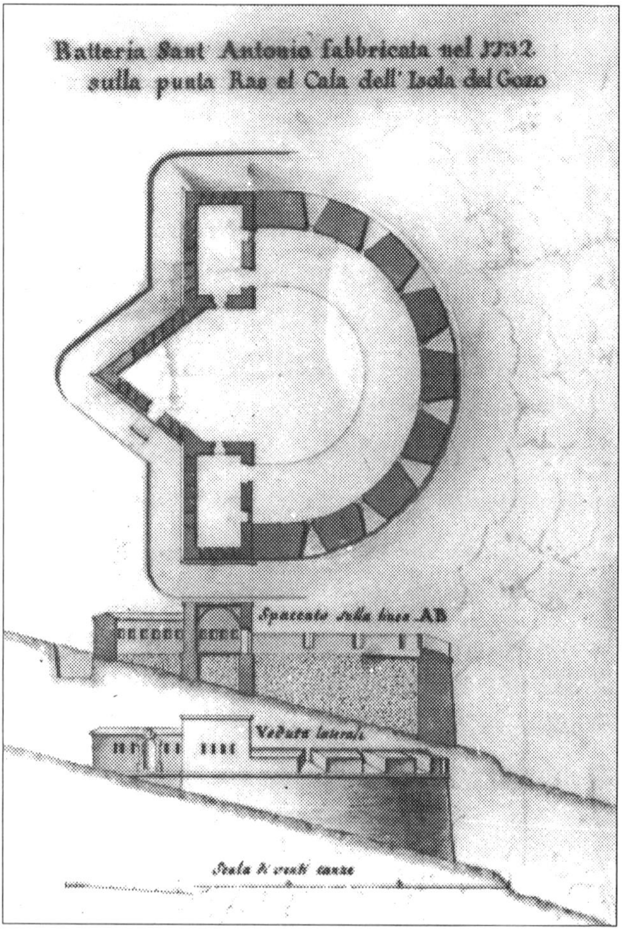

Plate 28 Plan of St. Anthony's battery, Gozo, 1732 (RML Map G11).

based on a system of coastal defences led, however, to a more ambitious scheme for the protection of Gozo's shoreline. Around the vulnerable bays he recommended the construction of a complete chain of fortifications: on the north coast a redoubt at Nagħaġ il-Baħar, a battery on the point of Qolla l-Bajda, retrenchments in the bay of Qolla l-Bajda, a ditch around the Sta. Maria battery, a redoubt at the foot of Marsalforn bay, a battery at St. Paul's chapel at Marsalforn, a battery to the left of Ramla bay, a redoubt in the centre of that bay,

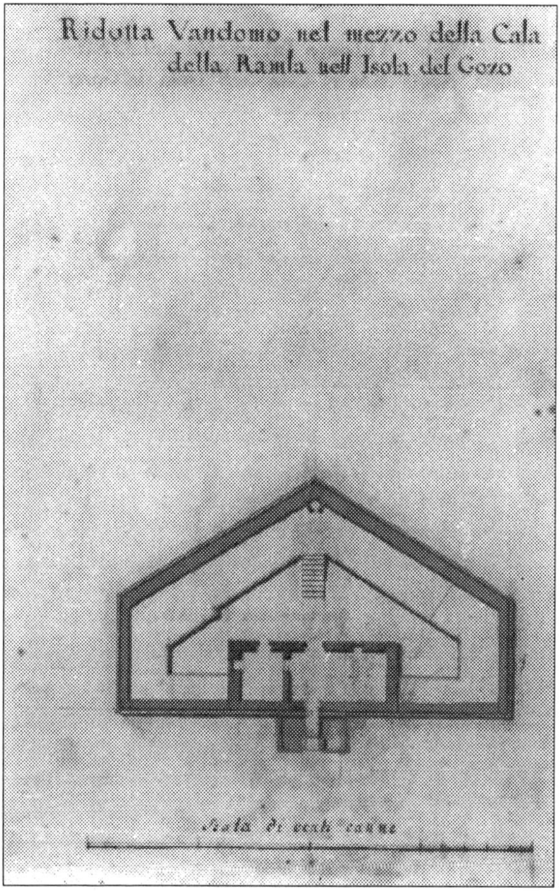

Plate 29 Plan of Vendôme redoubt, Gozo, 1732 (RML Map G11).

and a battery to the right.[78] On Comino he wished to build a battery on the south-east corner, and a redoubt at St. Mary's bay. His advice bore fruit and in the years 1715 and 1716 4,281 scudi were spent in fortifying the north coast of Gozo, and another 1,018 in constructing the battery on Comino.[79] Some of these works were ready for action in 1722

---

78 AOM 6556, f. 79.

79 AOM 6543, pp. 43-51; the following works are listed in Gozo: Xwieni redoubt (now destroyed), Qolla l-Bajda battery, Gironda/Qolla is-Safra/Sta. Maria battery (now destroyed), Marsalforn redoubt (now destroyed), St. Paul's redoubt, Xagħra/Sciarra/left battery Ramla (now destroyed),

when the council ordered that they be armed in preparation for the expected attack.[80] Trenches had been excavated at Qolla l-Bajda, Marsalforn and Ramla, but they were very weak and in the 1720s the Order worked at their improvement.[81] To impede still further an enemy landing, underwater obstructions were built,[82] and in the 1730s the chain of defence was further strengthened by the construction of the redoubt at Ramla and of St. Anthony's battery at Ras il-Qala overlooking Comino.[83]

But salt water and salt air soon took their toll of the coastal defences; in 1738 all the works on the north coast were in need of repair, especially the Sta. Maria battery.[84] Various repairs were undertaken and when alarm swept through the islands in 1761 the fortifications were found to be in good condition.[85] The foreign engineers who inspected the fortifications in 1761 found little to criticise in the batteries and redoubt of Gozo, but felt that the system was too restricted and recommended additions at places they believed vulnerable:[86] a battery between Chambray and Mġarr ix-Xini, a redoubt at Qbajjar bay, artillery emplacements under Marsalforn tower and on the cliffs overlooking Ramla bay, a redoubt to the right of Daħlet Qorrot bay, four or five batteries along the coastline to Ras il-Qala, batteries on the coastline opposite Comino, and entrenchments at all accessible places along the shore. To man these works and maintain an adequate reserve, it was reckoned that 6,050 men would be required. It was, however, quite inconceivable that so many men would ever be assigned

---

Ramla/Vendôme redoubt, Nadur/right battery Ramla (now destroyed). AOM 6543, item 18 contains measurements of coastal defences made by Maigret in 1716.

80 AOM 267, ff. 124v. (8 May 1722) and 137 (28 July 1722) – the council minute orders that the fort and battery of Comino and the batteries of Mġarr, Ramla, Marsalforn and the two smaller ones to the west be armed. Mondion (Clerkenwell, MS. O 1, item 20) claimed that the battery in the middle of Ramla bay was built in 1731, but 840 scudi is recorded as being spent on this work in 1715 and 1716 (AOM 6543, p. 50).

81 AOM 6552, f. 7; AOM 6556, f. 79; AOM 267, ff. 147 and 150 (25 September 1722).

82 Clerkenwell, MS. O 1, item 20.

83 Clerkenwell, MS. O 1, item 20 states that St. Anthony's battery was commenced in 1731. The battery itself bears an inscribed date, 1732, and Agius de Soldanis (RML MS. 140) dates it 1734. AOM 1011, f. 98 records the expenditure at Ras il-Qala, Ramla and Marsalforn between November 1732 and May 1734.

84 Clerkenwell, MS. O 1, item 21.

85 See Clerkenwell, MS. O 1, item 21 (1743, 1750 and 1756); AOM 1012, f. 18 (20 August 1749) – when the works listed included a battery at Għajn Barrani between Marsalforn and Ramla, a battery to the left of Marsalforn (not the Sta. Maria battery) and two batteries to the left of Ramla bay. AOM 271, f. 175 (11 March 1761).

86 AOM 6557, f. 27; AOM 6558, f. 53 (24 October 1761, 'Mémoire sur la deffense de l'isle du Goze').

to the defence of Gozo. Indeed only 2,300 men on Gozo, including clerics, were capable of bearing arms and it was unlikely that the Order would dispatch more than a small detachment of regular troops to the island. The French engineers recognized the problem of manning the fortifications but could offer no solution save for the age-old one of shipping non-combatants to Malta, and leaving the 2,300 to defend the coasts as best they could, and retreating if necessary into Chambray where they would be secure, and from whence, if besieged to the point of surrender, they could withdraw to Malta. It is therefore hardly surprising that the Order hesitated to implement a scheme which however sound strategically, might well have been no more than a costly white elephant. Although the Order accepted the engineers' reports, none of the recommendations appears to have been acted upon. And for the remainder of the century the knights repaired and maintained the existing fortifications of Gozo but without adding to their number.[87] However, the manning of even a modest system of coastal defences was beyond their resources, and without sufficient soldiers the best equipped and maintained fortifications were powerless to resist. Thus, despite coming under heavy fire as they landed at Ramla bay, Napoleon's troops soon overran the island and neither the Castello nor Chambray defied the enemy for more than a few hours.

87 AOM 1015, pp. 72 (4 September 1769), 289 (27 November 1783), 322 (7 April 1788), 349 (17 December 1791), 354 (5 November 1792), 424 (10 May 1794), 427 (5 November 1794); AOM 274, f. 136 (7 July 1788); AOM 6571, f. 124; RML Tres. A 105 (1788-94).

Part III

The Social and Administrative Context

Chapter 9

The Administration of the Fortifications

The design, construction and maintenance of the fortifications undoubtedly consumed a large share of the Order's resources and energies, for these represented not only a major investment in financial terms but also symbolized the military nature of the Order, and its position, fast diminishing in significance, as the bastion of Christendom against the infidel. The administration of the fortifications reflects both the importance attached to military affairs and the growth of more formalized bureaucracy in the eighteenth century.

Although supreme legislative authority was vested in the chapter general, within the government of the Order the day-to-day administration was performed by the council. It was therefore this body which concerned itself with the routine maintenance and modification of the fortifications, and also with the initiation of new projects. Major works were authorized by council decrees recorded in the *Libri Conciliorum* before 1623, but after the establishment in that year of separate registers for all but the more formal matters of state, they are more usually, though not invariably, to be found in the *Libri Conciliorum Status*. The council decrees tend to record only the final decision of that body and do not necessarily reveal the bitter and lengthy arguments which may have taken place. The personal accounts of the participants, particularly their correspondence, can supply the missing details. For instance, the proposal to build Floriana, sanctioned by decree on 10 December 1635, gave rise to considerable bad feeling.[1] When the council decided by thirty-five votes to fourteen to accept Floriani's design, the Bailiff Signorino Gattinara resigned from his position as one of the commissioners in charge of the new fortifications.[2] Later when Gattinara was a contender for the magistracy, Floriani declared publicly that he would no longer serve an Order headed by Gattinara.[3] Thus in dealing with the fortifications as in other matters, the Order was liable to disruption by factional disputes.

Since the council decrees themselves do not afford much elucidation as to how a decision was reached, or how it was implemented, it is necessary to look elsewhere. The council operated a system of delegation whereby commissioners were appointed to perform specific tasks, including those concerned with defence. At first these commissioners appear to have been set up on an *ad hoc* basis to deal with a particular aspect of the fortifications. Thus in 1552 three commissioners were appointed to consider the defences of Birgu and the construction of forts, while a further two were to draw up a list of all men available for construction work.[4] Knights seem to have been commissioned in a similar *ad hoc* manner to examine the fortifications of Gozo in the closing years of the sixteenth century, and those of the harbour area in 1633.[5] Shortly after this latter date, however, there are references to a body of a more permanent nature. Commissioners of fortification were appointed for an indeterminate period of office with general oversight of all the defence works, and by the mid-seventeenth century effectively constituted a permanent sub-committee of the council. The constant threat from the Turks in the decade after 1635, and the resultant high level of military activity may have been responsible for this extension and institutionalization of the role of the commissioners.

Thereafter it soon became the custom for the council to nominate four commissioners and the importance attached to this committee is indicated by the fact that knights serving on it were invariably grand crosses, senior dignitaries of the Order. As a rule each of the four nations was represented, so that in 1700 we find an Italian – Tancredi prior of Messina, a Frenchman – Bayers bailiff of the Morea, a Spaniard – Tavora bailiff of Leza, and Guttenberg the lieutenant bailiff – a

1 AOM 111, f. 176v.
2 Barb. Lat. 6697, ff. 73 and 74v.; Borg, p. 33.
3 Borg, p. 35.
4 AOM 88, ff. 106v. (8 January 1552) and 107v. (23 January 1552).
5 AOM 100, f. 122 (22 September 1599); AOM 110, f. 247 (7 June 1633).

German, and fifteen years later Bailiff Spinola, Saint Viance prior of Auvergne, Ribas prior of Catalonia, and Count Königsegg lieutenant bailiff. Königsegg appears again in 1722, now as prior of Hungary, together with the Bailiffs Visconti, De la Salle and Almeida, while the commissioners in 1753 were the prior of Dacia Baron Capell, and the Bailiffs Tommasi, Chambray and De Sousa.[6] It was these four grand crosses who formed the core of the body known as the congregation of fortification which appears in the records of the Order from 1645 onwards.[7] The composition of the congregation varied from time to time, but displayed a tendency, common to most of the Order's institutions, to become larger and more complex in the course of the eighteenth century, a development which in this instance can in part be explained by an expansion of the function of the congregation. After 1660 the commissioners of fortification were also the commissioners of war, positions which had formerly been held by a different set of four knights.[8] This had the effect of combing two previously separate congregations into the congregation of fortification and war which now had oversight of everything concerned with the defence of the island: fortifications, munitions, artillery, firearms, troops, militia and even the provision of fresh water in the fortresses.

It was however still possible for the four commissioners to sit merely as the congregation of fortification when dealing with business of an appropriate nature. In the late seventeenth century they were joined by the resident engineer, the commissioner of posts, and a secretary to constitute the congregation of fortification.[9] Although the chapter general of 1776 laid down the composition of a much enlarged congregation of fortification and war,[10] in practice it was the four commissioners, assisted when necessary by the engineer or the chief of artillery, who were responsible for the day-to-day administration of the fortifications.[11] There was, however, additional provision made that in times of special need, when an attack appeared imminent and

---

6 AOM 1016, p. 471 and AOM 265, f. 26 (1700); AOM 6552, f. 39 (1715); AOM 267, ff. 147-50 and 171 (1722); AOM 1012, f. 29 (1753).

7 The earliest reference is to a meeting held on 6 July 1645 (AOM 6553, f. 61v. and RML MS. 742, f. 410).

8 AOM 121, f. 98 (8 May 1660).

9 AOM 1016, p. 2.

10 The members were to be the marshal of the Order, or his lieutenant, the four commissioners, the seneschal commanding the militia, the engineer-in-chief, the commissioner of fortification, the commander of artillery, the colonel and quartermaster of the Malta regiment, the colonel of the Cacciatori and a judge advocate (F. Ryan, *The House of the Temple* (London, 1930), p. 106).

11 AOM 1015, *passim*.

there was increased military activity, as was the case in 1647, 1670 and 1761, the council could appoint four additional commissioners to assist in expediting the work in hand.[12]

The commissioners of fortification met, usually twice a week, in a room in the chancery. The proceedings of the meetings were carefully recorded and filed away under lock and key at the chancery in the *camera delle consultationi dello stato e della guerra.*[13] The various reports made by engineers and commissioners were also retained. Access to these papers was restricted, but it is clear that engineers were able to consult the plans, designs and recommendations of their predecessors, for they often refer back to previous projects and on occasion mention the fact that these papers were deposited in the chancery.[14] In addition, engineers would often display models of their proposed amendments to the fortifications and these too were deposited in the chancery.[15] The congregation also kept careful weekly records of the money paid out to various workmen in the registers *de' mandati*. In the mid-seventeenth century a new accounting procedure was introduced whereby the commissioners were required to submit a record of their accounts to the council every six months, thereby ensuring that the council retained ultimate control over expenditure.[16] A considerable amount of the commissioners' time was taken up in examining petitions from Maltese requesting planning permission to carry out building work in the vicinity of the fortifications or tenancy of a building controlled by the congregation, and in approving the sums paid to various craftsmen. The congregation also had to administer certain properties, the income of which was employed in the maintenance of the fortifications.[17]

---

12 AOM 258, f. 78 (4 April 1647); AOM 124, f. 25v. (7 July 1670); AOM 271, f. 165v. (14 February 1671).

13 AOM 1016, p. 1; this volume is a copy made from the original notebooks. The records of the congregation which have survived all appear to be copies except perhaps AOM 1015. On the other hand many original engineers' reports have survived.

14 AOM 6560; Clerkenwell, MS. O 1, item 21.

15 Only those models made by Grunenberg survive. They are now displayed in the Palace Armoury, Valletta. The making of models was common practice and Bosio mentions those made by Genga (III, 398) and Lanci (III, 456).

16 AOM 120, f. 153 (2 May 1658). It would appear that some reform of the financial system was being attempted because several other commissions were also to render six-monthly accounts. In fact the accounts of the fortifications did not appear regularly but as follows: 14 October 1658 (AOM 120, f. 205v.); 10 June 1661 (AOM 121, f. 191v.); 17 January 1663 (AOM 260, f. 143); 23 January 1664 (AOM 260, f. 178); 23 June 1664 (AOM 261, f. 2); 18 March 1665 (*ibid.*, f. 18); 11 September 1665 (*ibid.*, f. 29v.); 10 March 1668 (*ibid.*, f. 97).

17 AOM 1016 (1690-1705) and AOM 1015 (1759-98) give the best overall picture of the congregation's work. Volumes AOM 1017-23 contain the petitions to the congregation (1714-98). The

Although the commissioners themselves rarely came into contact with the craftsmen, by the eighteenth century there was a well defined chain of command comprising the engineer, the ordinary commissioner of fortification, the commissioner of works and the foreman.[18] The member of the congregation most directly in control of the fortifications was the resident engineer of the Order. Until the end of the seventeenth century this post was combined with that of architect, so that all building, military and civil, was the responsibility of one man. The combination of the duties of architect and military engineer was common practice in Europe at that time.[19] It was only in the course of the seventeenth century that the branches of architecture, civil and military, developed into distinct, if often still linked, professions.[20] As the century wore on, however, those employed in military projects came increasingly from a soldiering background, familiar with principles of gunnery, and knowledgeable about tactics, as well as practised in the skills of surveying, draughting, estimating costs and actually constructing both permanent and field fortifications.[21] The career structure in the engineering corps was more open than that found in cavalry or even infantry regiments. Social status was less important, although never without advantages, and the growth of corps of engineers which took place not only in France but also, for instance, in the Netherlands under Menno van Coehoorn and Sweden under Erik Dahlberg, ensured regular channels of promotion.[22] Indeed meritorious service could itself be the key to advance up the social ladder, as can be seen in the cases of these engineers, both visiting and resident, who were admitted, in various degrees, to the Order. Similar examples of such elevation by rulers can be found elsewhere in Europe.[23]

---

collection of manuscripts formerly preserved in the government treasury (RML Tres.) includes volumes which deal with the administration of the properties of the congregation. See *Bulletin of the* [*Maltese*] *Institute of Historical Research, List of Volumes and other Documents of the Order of St John of Jerusalem and of the Municipal Institutions Known as the Università Preserved in the Government Treasury*, II (Malta, 1932) which lists these treasury volumes.

18. The descriptions of the functions of these various officials are taken from AOM 6397, f. 98 and AOM 1012, ff. 165 and 187.

19. S. Pepper and N. Adams, *Firearms and Fortifications: Military Architecture and Siege Warfare in Sixteenth-Century Siena* (Chicago, 1986), p. 174; Duffy, *Siege Warfare*, pp. 40-2 and 257. The Order appears to have employed only one architect whose interests lay primarily in the civil sphere, Romano Carapecchia, active between 1688 and 1738, and even he designed military gates (J. Tonna and D. De Lucca, *Romano Carapecchia: Studies in Maltese Architecture*, I (Malta, 1975)).

20. Hoppen, 'Military engineers', pp. 414, 420-24 and 428.

21. J.R. Hale, 'The military education of the officer class in early modern Europe', in *Cultural Aspects of the Italian Renaissance*, ed. C.H. Clough (Manchester, 1976), pp. 440-41.

22. Duffy, *Siege Warfare*, pp. 248-9.

23. See appendices ii and iv.

The admission to different ranks within the Order reflects, in large measure, the esteem in which the engineers were held, as also, whether or not they were of noble birth. The standing of the resident engineers clearly emerges as lower than that of the visiting experts. This fits the general pattern of the knights' attitudes towards the two categories of military men. The visiting experts were fêted, deferred to, and often loaded with gifts on departure. Only they were thought capable of the vision or expertise required to devise large-scale, innovative schemes of defence. The knights' admiration of the talent of these distinguished visitors was somewhat tempered by their high opinion of their own abilities. While not doubting the inadequacies of the resident engineer in this respect they themselves (or many of them) were confident that their own upbringing and military experience equipped them to pass judgements on the merits of various schemes. Thus, although he was a permanent member of the congregation of fortification and always well-trained and experienced, in practice the freedom of the resident to initiate large new defensive systems was limited by the Order's tradition of calling in acknowledged experts whenever any extensive project was in the air.

These visiting engineers were not strictly employed by the Order. They were normally on loan from one of the princes of Europe and received no salary from the Order although they could expect their travelling and living expenses to be met. Often they were presented with a gift on their departure. Laparelli, however, although a papal engineer does seem to have been paid by the knights. He claimed to have received 800 scudi a year while in their employ but his visit was somewhat longer than was usual for a foreign expert.[24] Instead of the customary few weeks or months Laparelli was in Malta from January 1566 to April 1568 and again for a year from late 1568. He was, in effect, performing many of the tasks of a resident engineer, supervising the detailed execution of his plans.

In the normal course of events once the initial design had been traced out on the site the expert departed entrusting the implementation of his project to the resident engineer, often leaving detailed written instructions for this purpose.[25] Thus the engineer Buonamici executed the designs of Floriani, Firenzuola, the Marquis of St. Angelo, Count Pagan and Clerville; and later in the century Blondel worked

---

24 Cod. Lap. f. 140.

25 For instance, Laparelli's instructions to Cassar (Cod. Lap. f. 70) and those of Floriani to Buonamici (AOM 111, f. 258 and Chigi, R I 25, f. 329v.).

under Valperga and Grunenberg. Should the resident be in any doubt as to the intention of the expert he could always consult the reports and plans preserved in the chancery, or if the problem remained unresolved, could write for clarification of the expert's intentions.[26] Indeed, several engineers revisited the islands to monitor progress, most noteably Grunenberg who made three separate voyages and Tigné who returned in 1716, and also in 1723.[27]

It would appear that the Order was a good employer able to inspire long and devoted service from its resident engineers. The Cassars, father and son, gave over forty years' service; Buonamici, who came in 1635 intending to stay only a few months, finally departed in 1659; Blondel was employed for almost forty years, Mondion for twenty-eight and Marandon for thirty-five years. In the sixteenth century at least, the salary of twenty-five scudi a month paid to the engineer compared not unfavourably with the three hundred ducats per annum received by the resident engineer in Sicily.[28] Over the years the salary rose, reaching thirty scudi a month in the seventeenth century and fifty scudi a month in the eighteenth century until it was halved as one of the economy measures in 1795.[29] It was not unusual for the salary to be continued after retirement, or departure from the island. Evangelista Menga, for example, was entitled to receive three hundred scudi a year whether or not he was in Malta, or in the Order's service.[30] Over a century and a half later Charles François de Mondion was likewise able to draw his salary whether or not he might be forced to leave the island, while after thirty-five years' employment Francesco Marandon was awarded a pension of thirty gold scudi a month.[31]

Any major works proposed by the resident engineer had to be approved by the congregation, and all minor ones by the ordinary commissioner of fortification. This latter official, who acted the role of watch-dog over the engineer and the fortifications ensuring that the interests of the Order were well served, was a fully-professed knight

---

26 For instance, a letter of the Marquis of St. Angelo dated Florence 1644 (AOM 6551, f. 94v.), one from Valperga dated Turin 1680 (*ibid.*, f. 60), and one from Grunenberg from Sicily in 1682 (AOM 6554, f. 185).

27 D. De Lucca, 'French military engineers in Malta during the 17th and 18th centuries', *Melita Historica*, VIII (1980), p. 32.

28 AOM 431, f. 267 (1567); Ferramolino, p. 4, gives 300 ducats as the Sicilian engineer's salary in 1546.

29 AOM 116, f. 263 (1649); AOM 260, f. 60v. (1659); RML MS. 186, II, 177 (1670); AOM 269, f. 26v. (1734); AOM 1015, p. 455 (1795).

30 AOM 431, f. 267 (1567).

31 AOM 268, f. 52v. (1726); AOM 565, f. 206 (1762) and AOM 1020, f. 572.

of justice, in contrast to the engineer who did not have to be a member of the Order at all, although some engineers such as Blondel and Mondion were admitted as knights of grace, or as confraters, as in the case of Girolamo Cassar.

Once his plans were accepted the engineer was expected not to alter them without permission. He was ultimately responsible for the execution of his designs, and was to be present when the outline of the new work was measured and traced out on the ground, when the first stones were cut, and until the angles were built up to two or three courses of masonry so that he could ensure that the walls would have the correct scarp. Once work was under way he had to make regular inspections of the quality of the workmanship and its trueness to the original design. Another important duty was that of putting the building work out to contract. The craftsmen employed in the fortifications worked on a contractual basis, each master undertaking to complete a specified section of the defences at an agreed price per square or cubed cane.[32] The engineer had to see that the contracts were in order and that the master craftsmen knew exactly what was required of them. If problems cropped up in the course of the work he was expected to solve them. The contracts themselves were drawn up by a notary and, as a rule, were strictly enforced. The masters could even be expected to provide a ten-year guarantee against bad workmanship.[33] As payment depended upon canes completed, regular weekly measurements were made of the work of each master.[34] When a section of work was finished the engineer had to check that the final measurements and payments were correct, for it could be found that workmen had been overpaid, in which case they were expected to repay the difference to the common treasury.[35]

The interests of the treasury were further safeguarded by the commissioner of works who was in charge of the building stores and had to supply materials such as lime, sand, pozzolana, wood, the necessary tools and the means of transport.[36] It was laid down by the chapters general that the commissioner had to give an account of his

---

32 The treasury registers of contracts contain copies of the contracts (AOM 737-74, 1620-1794).

33 Clerkenwell, MS. O 1, item 15 (26 January 1728), item 21 (1742).

34 These measurements can be found: AOM 6554, f. 15 (1636); AOM 1016, *passim* (1690-1705); AOM 6545 (1714-15); AOM 1011, f. 98 (1732-4); Clerkenwell, MS. O 1, item 22 (1750s); AOM 1012, *passim* (mid-eighteenth century); AOM 6546, *passim* (1767-70); AOM 692-9 (1781-96); RML Tres. A 105 (1779-97).

35 AOM 116, f. 262v. (16 September 1649).

36 The day-book recording the issue of materials for use in the fortifications for the years 1764-77 has survived – AOM 1918.

administration to the treasury every six months.[37] It seems that the Order was troubled by the misappropriation of building materials, so much so that in 1776 very elaborate regulations were drawn up to ensure that everything could be accounted for.[38] Until the late seventeenth century the commissioner of works also maintained a general oversight of all building works including fortifications, but as the functions of the civil and military architect became more specialized, an ordinary commissioner of fortification (merely a knight rather than a grand cross) was appointed to assist the engineer.[39] The commissioner of works, and later the ordinary commissioner, scrutinized the contracts with master craftsmen and the final measurement of work. They were expected to exercise constant vigilance over building progress, to see that no workers were idling, and no supplies being misused. Merely the visiting of sites in passing, or at a fixed time each day was not considered adequate, and inspections had instead to be thorough and at random.

The post of ordinary commissioner of fortification was, therefore, both onerous and responsible. It was also one which required some tact, for the commissioner, who was a layman in matters of military architecture, was expected to co-operate and consult with the professional engineer. Blondel made no secret of his opinion of the architectural ability of Vauvilliers, a knight who had been in charge of building while he was absent abroad,[40] but Blondel was perhaps unusually critical and had, for example, an equally low opinion of the work of the well-known engineer Antonio Maurizio Valperga.[41] Marandon, on the other hand, welcomed the assistance of the ordinary commissioner and complained of overwork when he was left to deal with the fortifications single-handed.[42] Any rift which might occur between the engineer and the commissioner would place the foreman of the works (*capomastro dell'opere*) in a difficult position. He had to execute the orders of both men, and also attend to the general day-to-day supervision of the work and workmen. Any problems which were encountered in carrying out the designs had to be reported to the engineer,

---

37 AOM 291, f. 51v. (1583).

38 AOM 644, f. 40 (24 December 1656); AOM 1016, p. 327 (26 September 1694); AOM 1012, f. 165 (mid-eighteenth century); AOM 309, f. 92 (chapter general regulations).

39 AOM 1016, p. 327 (26 September 1694).

40 AOM 1016, p. 6. Vauvilliers had been commissioner of posts, one of whose duties was to act as under-commissioner of fortification (AOM 1016, p. 326).

41 PRO WO 55, 1555/1, p. 106.

42 Clerkenwell, MS. O 1, item 21.

yet all the work had to be open to inspection by the commissioner who was acting in the interests of the Order as a whole. The foreman had to be present when the workers were paid so that there would be no confusion about their contracts or as to how much work they had done. Naturally, all the large building sites had a foreman, himself a Maltese craftsman.[43] As the engineer could not visit all the sites every day, he depended on such foremen, whom he furnished with a small plan and profile of the work, to carry out his intentions. The close relationship between these two officials is shown by a series of letters between Marandon and the foreman in charge of the fort at Ras it-Tafal in Gozo.[44] Below the foreman came the masters, each of whom had his company of workers for which he was responsible. The actual supply of labourers, Maltese or slaves, was the duty of the commissioner of works. The participation of the Maltese in the provision of the fortifications was not, however, confined to the supply of craftsmen and labourers.

Although the Maltese had assumed that the Order would take over the full burden of defending the islands, this did not prove to be the case. The division of responsibilities always proved to be a somewhat grey area and the Universitàs retained many of their pre-1530 powers and duties. Although the Order took control of all planning and design of fortifications, the Universitàs were expected to maintain the Città Vecchia and the Castello in Gozo, and certain towers, and to pay for such alterations as the Order deemed necessary.[45] However if the overall integrity of the islands was at stake, the knights tended to intervene even in these areas.[46] In theory, whoever had paid for the original construction remained liable to maintain it in good condition, but disputes often arose as to who should pay for any particular work.[47] The Universitàs had, however, no real control over the defences which they were obliged to repair, and the Order probably allowed them a place in the administration of the fortifications simply because they then shouldered some of the heavy burden of protecting the islands.

---

43 For instance, Muscat, 1646 (AOM 471, f. 270); Valletta, 1753 (AOM 1012, f. 195); Bonici, 1762 (AOM 566, f. 170v.). See also D. De Lucca, 'The Maltese "perit" in history', *Melita Historica*, VI (1975), 431-6.

44 AOM 1012, ff. 230-48v. (1752-5).

45 RML Univ. 95-8, 'Spese per le fortificazioni di questa Città Notabile' (1722-8 and 1738-48).

46 E.g. the Wignacourt and de Redin towers and Grand Master de Vilhena's work on Città Vecchia and in Gozo in the 1690s.

47 RML MS. 186, II, 172; AOM 1016, p. 348 (19 December 1694). In 1670 there was an investigation about the towers in Gozo (AOM 645, f. 91) and in 1692 about the Castello of Gozo (AOM 1016, pp. 114-15 and 125).

Chapter 10

The Maltese Involvement

The engineer who was summoned to Malta to design fortifications encountered certain problems which were peculiar to the island. The very fact that it was a small island, not over-endowed with natural resources, seventy miles from the mainland, raised difficulties of supply and made it imperative that, wherever practical, local materials should be used. Moreover, the designer, who was normally an engineer on loan from a friendly ruler, was often in the island for a relatively short time in which he had to assess the requirements of the Order, the terrain, the available resources, present a scheme to be approved by the council and supervise the initial building stage; thereafter he entrusted the work to the Order's resident engineer, who might or might not be sympathetic to the design. Apart from the haste necessary because of the engineer's impending departure, speed was frequently essential because the knights were often goaded into undertaking long-contemplated improvements only by the rumours of an imminent Turkish attack.

On arrival in Malta the visiting engineer lost little time before inspecting the site and submitting plans to the council; Laparelli's first report is dated five days after his arrival.[1] The initial reports by the engineers tended to be assessments of the defence requirements and outline proposals rather than detailed plans. Normally the written report was supplemented by plans, and even by models in stone or wax,[2] which may very well have shown the precise measurements

---

1 AOM 430, f. 267 (arrived 29 December 1565); Cod. Lap. f. 6 (report, 3 January 1566).

2 Models are mentioned as accompanying reports in 1558 (Genga, Bosio, III, 698), in 1562 (Lanci, Cod. Lap. f. 21), 1632 (AOM 256, f. 108), 1635 (Floriani, Barb. Lat. 6697, f. 71 and

and disposition of the fortifications. There are no surviving sixteenth- or seventeenth-century plans of the Maltese fortifications which can be regarded as detailed blueprints for schemes. Even the extant plans drawn up by Laparelli in 1566 appear to be concerned with the street-plan of Valletta and not with the design of the fortifications.[3] If working plans ever existed for this period they may have been destroyed to prevent their use by enemy agents, although this is rather unlikely as provision was made for preserving all reports and plans in the chancery. On the other hand, plans tended to be bulkier and less easily stored than written reports and may easily have been lost or destroyed over the centuries. The greater abundance of material surviving from the eighteenth century would seem to support this contention. Indeed, in the eighteenth century the engineer Marandon made frequent working drawings and measurements, but even these were for his own use rather than proposals to be submitted to the council.[4]

Whether or not it had received precise details of the proposed scheme, the council was prepared to make a decision as to the type of fortifications to be erected and their position. Once approval had been obtained the engineer traced out the design on the site by means of rubble walls and shallow ditches,[5] and it was probably at this stage that the exact outline of the enceinte adapted to the terrain was revealed. It was considered important that, if possible, the visiting engineer who had designed the works should undertake this task which may again point to the fact that all the specifications had not been put down on paper. On the departure of the visiting expert the Order's engineer took charge of construction, and, in theory at least, carried out the designer's intentions, sometimes helped by written instructions.[6] When a trusted assistant was taking over, as was the case when Floriani handed over to Buonamici, few problems should have arisen,[7] but when the resident engineer disagreed with the proposals (and Blondel for example forcefully denounced Valperga's schemes)[8] it may be wondered

---

AOM 6554, f. 25), 1681 (Grunenberg, AOM 262, f. 128v.). Only those by Grunenberg survive; V. Scamozzi in *Dell'Idea dell'architettura universale* (Venice, 1615), p. 203, recommends making a model so that people can see exactly what is to be done.

3 In the library of the Countess Laparelli Pitti in Cortona.

4 Marandon's notebook on the building of fort Chambray (Clerkenwell, MS. O 1, item 22).

5 Cod. Lap. f. 22 (1562); Bosio, III, 741 (1566); Barb. Lat. 6697, f. 76 (1636); AOM 112, f. 177v. and Dal Pozzo, II, 30 (1638); PRO WO 55, 1555/1, p. 106 (1670); AOM 1012, f. 67 (1749). See C. Duffy, *Fire and Stone: The Science of Fortress Warfare, 1660-1860* (Newton Abbot and London, 1975), pp. 33-42.

6 For example, Laparelli's instructions to Cassar (Cod. Lap. f. 70).

7 AOM 111, f. 258 (1 October 1636).

8 PRO WO 55, 1555/1, p. 106.

whether the work was ever faithfully executed. The resident engineer was naturally expected to make minor modifications to suit local conditions and materials as work progressed, and if he felt uneasy about any decision, could always consult the original designer by letter or ask to have him recalled to Malta.

The engineers were ready to acknowledge the skill of native masons in working the local stone. Whenever possible, Maltese craftsmen were employed in building works although at times pressure of work necessitated the importation of foreign labour. The method by which the knights financed construction ensured that money was forthcoming only in an emergency. Consequently the engineers were frequently racing to complete programmes before the opening of the campaigning season. Practically the only way in which the rate of building could be increased was by enlarging the workforce. In Malta itself there was a limited amount of labour available, but with a growing population the pool of possible workers increased. It appears that the acute shortage of labourers experienced in the sixteenth century had passed by the middle of the next century, for during this time the population had grown from about 20,000 in 1530 to about 50,000 in 1650.[9]

The scarcity of labour was such that in 1552 when forts St. Elmo and St. Michael were being constructed, workmen had to be imported from Sicily.[10] The need to use foreign labour on this occasion may be explained in part by the death of many Maltese in the famine which followed the bad harvest of 1550.[11] The siege in 1565 accounted for another fall in population, both through death and emigration to Sicily, at the very time when an ambitious building programme was being undertaken. There was indeed such a dearth of workmen in the autumn of 1565 that the clearing of the debris of St. Elmo could proceed only slowly, although the Order's claim that there were only 1,000 fit men on the island was probably an exaggeration made in the hope of raising more aid from abroad.[12] Attempts were made to hire Sicilians but, not surprisingly, these were unwilling to cross to Malta where the defences were in ruins and the Turkish armada was expected to renew its attack.[13] Even the threats and promises of the Count of Modica backed by the authority of the viceroy did not persuade a single workman to come to Malta until several months after the

9 For estimates of the population see Blouet, pp. 89-92.
10 Bosio, III, 323.
11 Blouet, p. 90.
12 AOM 430, ff. 267 and 268v.; Bosio, III, 710.
13 Bosio, III, 715.

siege.[14] Sicilians were further discouraged by the fact that of the many Maltese who had fled to Sicily, few if any had chosen to return to their own island.[15] This lack of labour was one of the reasons given for the delay in starting work on the new city.

Eventually it was decided to begin with those labourers who were available.[16] Gradually more workmen arrived in the islands during the summer of 1566, especially after the harvest was in and as the Turkish threat grew more remote. Moreover the word soon spread that the workers were paid and fed well and regularly.[17] The Maltese who had fled were particularly encouraged to return as their knowledge of the local building materials and methods was invaluable.[18] Despite this influx Laparelli was faced with a constant labour shortage, so that in August 1566 he even undertook to hire 500 workmen himself.[19] In a further attempt to alleviate the shortage the Order obtained a papal brief permitting work on the fortifications to take place on feast days,[20] and as late as 1575 members of the Order were not allowed to employ a building worker without a licence from the commissioner of works.[21]

The workmen employed in building Valletta received wages and rations; normally they were paid each Sunday according to how much work they had done, but, in order to entice men from abroad, Laparelli contracted to pay the the men whom he engaged a basic monthly salary in addition to a payment for each day they actually worked.[22] Although many of the Maltese did receive wages, the obligation to perform labour service in the fortifications survived. This, however, amounted to only four days a year and was clearly insufficient for the Order's purpose. It would appear, therefore, that if the Order was exacting such unpaid labour from the Maltese, it was also employing further forced labour for which it may actually have been paying, and local inhabitants were used in this way in 1552, 1645, 1651 and 1715.[23] In 1645 they were ordered to give service far in excess of what was

---

14 AOM 430, f. 268v.; Bosio, III, 716.
15 AOM 430, f. 267.
16 Bosio, III, 741.
17 Bosio, III, 750 (May), 771 (June), and 778.
18 Bosio, III, 778.
19 Cod. Lap. f. 42.
20 AOM 431, f. 279 (19 August 1566).
21 AOM 94, f. 70v.
22 Cod. Lap. f. 42.
23 AOM 88, f. 107v. and Bosio, III, 323 (1552); AOM 257, f. 197 (1645); AOM 258, f. 237 (1651); AOM 266, f. 129v. (1715).

customary, to work in the fortifications for one day a week, for which they would be rewarded with two loaves a day.[24] It would seem, however, that this amount of compulsory service was exceptional as its enforcement necessitated the enactment of a council decree. Apart from the building of Valletta, when, if Bosio is to be believed, everybody toiled willingly, such forced labour was highly unpopular. Even in 1601 when rumours of a Turkish attack were rife, men had to be 'persuaded' to work on the defences of Gozo and boatmen forbidden from carrying Gozitans or foreign labourers from the island.[25] The workers at fort Chambray in 1754 were so disobedient that a troop of soldiers (a sergeant, two corporals and twelve men) had to be sent to keep order.[26] This was usually maintained by threatening those absent without permission with six months' labour in the public works if they did not perform their obligatory service.[27] One could, however, escape the customary four days' work a year on payment of a tax, the *neuba*, and it was probably also possible for the well-to-do to pay a substitute to perform the other forced labour. But the mass of the Maltese had no option but to set to work in the fortifications when required by the Order. Indeed, even gangs of children were employed in clearing ditches at Senglea in 1692 and Birgu in 1723.[28] On the other hand, it seems that the knights were prepared to initiate building projects which would provide employment and relief for needy islanders. In 1742, for instance, Gozitans who had suffered from two bad harvests were employed in the building of a mole at Marsalforn.[29]

The slaves of the islands were another group of labourers on whom the Order could call if the need arose. The Order's galleys required between two and three hundred rowers each and the majority of these would have been slaves. If the work was sufficiently urgent the Order was prepared to put the galley crews to work in the fortifications even in the summer months when this would result in a restriction on naval activities.[30] In 1632, 1,284 slaves were employed in the

---

24 AOM 257, f. 197 and AOM 258, f. 7 (1645); AOM 116, f. 6v. (1647).
25 Mallia-Milanes, 'Vittorio Cassar', p. 257.
26 AOM 1012, f. 15.
27 AOM 1012, f. 102 (1754-5).
28 AOM 1016, p. 126 (1692); Clerkenewell, MS. O 1, item 9 (1723).
29 Clerkenwell, MS. O 1, item 21.
30 AOM 423, ff. 208 (December 1551), 216v. and 217v. (April 1552); AOM 88, f. 121 (January 1552); AOM 431, f. 266 (January 1567); AOM 432, f. 231 (April 1568); AOM 99, f. 120v. (December 1596); AOM 258, ff. 7 and 24v. (May and June 1645) and f. 237 (February 1651); AOM 266, f. 207 (March 1716).

six galleys[31] but besides the galley slaves the Order had other slaves owned by the common treasury who were regularly employed in public works including the fortifications.[32] In exceptional circumstances the personal and house slaves of the knights and Maltese were also ordered to labour in the fortifications,[33] and despite the fact that slaves were less easily procurable in the eighteenth than in earlier centuries, Napoleon found a slave population of 2,000 when he captured the island.[34] Nor indeed were soldiers of the Order considered to be above such work where they could labour alongside a motely collection of beggars, vagrants, convicts and other down-and-outs.[35]

In the years after 1600 the Order seems to have been able to muster a sufficient workforce on the islands themselves and there was no further need to import men. It is not possible, however, to calculate with any accuracy the actual number of men employed on the various fortifications. It is generally accepted that the large labour force at work on Valletta enabled the fortifications to be built in a relatively short time. The question is, how large a labour force? Bosio claims that 8,000 persons, skilled and unskilled, were normally working on the new city, but this is double the number which Laparelli assumed to be at his disposal,[36] and indeed the only occasion on which Laparelli mentioned the figure of 8,000 was when he dismissed a particular scheme because such numbers were not available.[37] Further evidence that contemporaries believed 4,000 to be the maximum number of persons employed on Valletta is found in a brief of 1587 granting the secretary of the building works his salary for life,[38] which makes it clear that he had then been secretary for twenty-four years during which time there had, on occasion, been 4,000 persons working on the new city. This was probably the largest number ever engaged on a single project. Floriani, for example, envisaged that 2,000, or at most 3,000, men might be employed to execute his proposals made in November 1635.[39]

---

31 Earle, p. 169.

32 AOM 288, f. 29 (1555).

33 AOM 115, ff. 7v.-8 (January 1645); AOM 258, f. 7 (May 1645); AOM 116, f. 24 (June 1647); AOM 266, f. 143v. (February 1715); Clerkenwell, MS. O. 1, item 8 (1722).

34 Cavaliero, p. 80.

35 AOM 105, f. 42 (1614); AOM 468, f. 154v. (1636); AOM 258, f. 7 (1645); AOM 738, f. 17v. (1646).

36 Bosio, III, 781; Cod. Lap. ff. 47 (1567) and 49.

37 Cod. Lap. f. 14 (30 January 1566).

38 AOM 443, f. 98 (1587).

39 AOM 6554, f. 25.

With the smaller total the front of Floriana could be in a state of defence by the following May or June, with 3,000 the flanks as well as the front would be ready. Judging, however, from the progress of Floriana, its designer grossly overestimated either the amount of work each man could do, or, more likely, the number of men the Order was prepared or able to make available.

There is no evidence that skilled craftsmen were expected to give their services free, for careful contracts of employment were invariably drawn up between them and the Order. The forced labour, Maltese and slave, was used to do the heavy unskilled work – to dig ditches, level terrapleins and clear glacis. Although unskilled they were essential members of the workforce, for the craftsmen found that they were unable to fulfil their contracts if too few labourers were at their disposal, and the Order bore the responsibility of supplying the gangs of unskilled workers. The Order's slaves could be assigned to work under a particular contractor, and in these circumstances the Order, to which the slave was a capital asset, had to ensure that the contractor did not overwork or ill-treat the slaves in his desire to make a profit.[40]

Public projects, and particularly the fortifications, afforded regular employment for building workers from the resident engineer down to the labourers. It was, however in the civil sphere that Maltese architects were able to pursue successful careers. Men who served the Order as masters of works, such as Tommaso Dingli (1591-1666), Giovanni Barbara (1660-1730), Francesco Zerafa (died 1758), Giuseppe Bonnici (1707-79), Domenico Cachia (1710-79) and Michele Cachia (1760-1839), spent much of their time designing churches, palaces and houses, in effect translating European ideas into a characteristically Maltese style. While on the one hand, therefore, the military construction programme provided continuing employment for the building workers of the island, on the other hand, the administrative structures of the Order set out a career path for large numbers of local craftsmen and designers.

For the population generally, however, the fortifications could not be said to have had so positive an impact. Many were displaced by the compulsory purchase of land required for defence works. Although they received compensation, either in land or cash, some, perhaps many, resented the consequent disruption to their lives.[41] As the years went

---

40 Clerkenwell, MS. O. 1, item 15 (January 1728).

41 AOM 113, f. 113v. (1641); AOM 114, ff. 59 (1643) and 222v. (1644); AOM 482, f. 280v. (1670); AOM 489, f. 288v. (1682); AOM 1016, p. 471 (1701); AOM 1015, *passim* (mid-eighteenth century); C. Galea Scannura, 'The building of the Cottonera fortifications: A Maltese protest against taxation', *Hyphen*, III (1982), p. 196.

on the Order became more generous in its assessment of the losses incurred but nevertheless disputes inevitably arose from which the main beneficiaries were lawyers.[42] On occasion people and their possessions had to be cleared from the area surrounding fortifications so the defenders might enjoy an uninterrupted line of fire, and this could cause complaints and difficulties.[43] In peacetime the regulations governing the erection of buildings near fortifications tended to be relaxed with the result that the Maltese moved into convenient archways and corners and set up house. This was especially true of Valletta where a rising population produced increasing pressure on living space. The congregation of fortification attempted to keep control of the situation by issuing licences permitting such occupation, but such was demand that regulation proved an uphill task.[44]

But the building of the fortifications impinged not only on the lives of town dwellers. By tradition the Maltese had long been obliged to perform militia duties. These duties had never been popular and the advent of the knights only served to place the islands firmly in the front line of the confrontation between Christian and Moslem. Although the Universitàs remained responsible for the provision of the militia, the Order itself supervised its development and control, dividing Malta into eight districts – Żejtun, Bir Miftuħ/Gudja, Żurrieq, Qormi, Birkirkara, Naxxar, Siġġiewi and Żebbuġ – each under the command of a knight chosen by the grand master.[45] This knight (the captain of militia) resided in the village and in addition to his strictly military duties, gradually took on a political role as well. The rule of some of the captains (and their concubines) was oppressive, especially because being the local source of the Order's patronage, they possessed considerable power. Indeed so unpopular did one captain of Żurrieq, Pietro de Rovere, become that he was murdered in 1560. However others integrated rather better into their local community – among them Commander Giovanni Alenton who was an expert on the antiquities and village customs of Birkirkara.[46]

---

42 e.g. The case of Domenico Bonnici discussed by Galea Scannura, p. 195.

43 AOM 257, f. 204 (1645); AOM 6553, f. 59 (1645); AOM 6552, 2v. (1714); AOM 1015, f. 16 (1761).

44 Petitions requesting permission to occupy such land can be found in the volumes AOM 1016-1025; descriptions of the state of the fortifications are given in Mallia-Milanes, 'Vittorio Cassar', pp. 257 and 268 (1603) and AOM 1016, p. 48 (1701), AOM 6547, ff. 75-90 (1716) and AOM 1054, p. 4 (1789).

45 Mifsud, 'Cenno', pp. 237-9; A. Bonnici, 'Due secoli di storia politico-religiosa di Malta nel Fondo Berberini Latino della Biblioteca Vaticana', *Melita Historica*, IV (1967), p. 235.

46 G. Wettinger, 'Early Maltese popular attitudes to the government of the Order of St. John', *Melita Historica*, VI (1974), pp. 268-9; L. Butler, 'The Maltese poeple and the Order of St. John

The captains had the authority to grant villagers exemptions from the unpopular guard duties on payment of three scudi.[47] So convenient a source of income did this prove, that the number of exemptions granted came to undermine the efficiency of the coastal defence system. In 1647 the captains were awarded salaries simply in order to curb their eagerness in selling exemptions.[48] Guard duties remained an unwelcome chore, and the severe penalties for defaulters suggest that neglect and bad time-keeping were far from uncommon.[49] In an attempt to put the militia on a more regular and efficient basis, rolls were kept of those liable to serve, proper training was instituted and even noncombatants (boys aged from twelve to sixteen) were expected to follow the regiments with baskets, hoes and picks.[50] In an attempt to improve standards plans were made in 1658 to raise a militia regiment no less than 4,000 men strong but nothing significant was achieved by these measures.

By the eighteenth century the very extent of the fortifications brought into sharp focus the ever-present problem of manning. Engineers produced estimated garrisons far beyond anything the Order could reasonably hope to supply, whether from its own ranks, through conscription of locals, by employment of mercenaries, or any combination of these possibilities. In the early years of the century Mondion suggested that the harbour forts alone needed 8,000 men for normal guard duties. At more or less their full extent in 1761 the fortifications were reckoned to require 20,000 infantry with an appropriate complement of artillery.[51]

For many years the Order hankered after a regiment of regular foreign troops and in 1776 used the pretext of the priests' revolt in the previous year to undertake the recruitment of such a force.[52] It was

---

in the sixteenth century', *Annales de l'Ordre Souverain Militaire de Malte*, XXIV (1966), p. 96; Mifsud, 'La milizia ', pp. 88-9; AOM 90. f. 120 (1560).

47 Wettinger, 'Popular attitudes', p. 267.

48 Mifsud, 'La milizia', p. 55; in 1630 375 men were exempted from coastal duties and 2,150 from the mounted guard.

49 Mifsud, 'La milizia', p. 89.

50 On militia rolls see G. Wettinger, 'Lost villages and hamlets of Malta' in Luttrell, *Medieval Malta*, pp. 184-9; G. Wettinger, 'The militia lists of 1419-20'. *Melita Historica*, V (1969), 80-106; S. Fiorini, 'Status Animarum I: a unique source for the 17th and 18th century Maltese demography', *Melita Historica*, VIII (1983), 325-44. Various regulations can be found in the Order's archives for example, AOM 260, f. 31v. (1658); AOM 265, f. 205 (1708); AOM 266, f. 14 (1710); AOM 6547, ff. 109-111 (1715); AOM 269, ff. 112v.-127v. (1738); AOM 271, ff. 92v.-95v. (1758) and 136v.-145 (1760); Mifsud, 'La milizia', pp. 91-2.

51 AOM 6547, f. 1 (1715); AOM 6558, f. 84v. (1761).

52 AOM 309, ff. 103v.-104 (1776).

not a success. The recruits proved to be the dregs of European society – deserters, beggars, and other riff-raff – who terrorized the countryside. Discipline was restored only after the worst troublemakers had been weeded out and thereafter Maltese soldiers were allowed to enlist, something which altered the whole nature of the enterprise. Maltese men were, in fact, eager to join because the regiment offered steady employment and even career opportunities for their children who could be apprenticed to such tradesmen who were attached to the barracks.[53] Thus certain sections of the population benefited in a very direct way from the massive enterprise to fortify the islands. However no one was untouched by the undertaking, and the most pervasive manner in which the building of the fortifications impinged on the lives of the majority of the Maltese was in the tax demands made to finance the projects. This aspect of the inhabitants' contribution is discussed in Chapter 11. The islands themselves made one outstanding contribution to the fortifications – the building stone, the one material of which there was an abundant local supply.

The islands are composed almost entirely of limestone, one stratum of which, globigerina limestone, traditionally provided the principal building material, known as *franka*.[54] This limestone occurs in a deep bed of soft, easily quarried rock which hardens on exposure to the air. It was, and still is, quarried by means of wedges and dressed with a broad axe.[55] Although specialized quarries existed, where, as around the harbour area, the underlying rock was globigerina limestone, the ramparts were frequently constructed from the stone excavated from the ditches. On occasion, however, a layer of stone unsuitable for building would be encountered and then supplies would have to be brought from further afield.[56] In many places the contours of the site enabled the fortifications to be carved out of solid rock, so that only the upper courses of the bastions and curtains and the parapets needed to be constructed of masonry blocks, while elsewhere the masonry is often merely facing the natural rock which forms the mass

---

53 Ryan, pp. 106-109; AOM 273, ff. 169-70v. (1778) and 192-4v (1779).

54 Details of the geological structure of the islands and the suitability of stone for building can be found in J. Murray, 'The Maltese islands with special reference to their geological structure' in *Scottish Geographical Magazine*, VI (1890), at pp. 459-75.

55 Bosio, III, 788; he also mentions experiments with explosives to enable ditches to be excavated more quickly.

56 For instance: building regulations for Valletta specified that all building material was to be obtained from one area, the manderaggio. (AOM 92, f. 141) This was to be excavated to below sea level so as to form a galley-pen but work ceased when a layer of unsuitable stone was reached (Dal Pozzo, I, 67).

of the bastions and ramparts.[57] The provision of mines and countermines, so essential to the defence system, presented no problem in Malta; the rock underlying most of the fortifications was easily excavated and large chambers and passages could be formed without need of wooden supports.[58] Provided the protective skin which develops on exposure to the atmosphere is not damaged, *franka* weathers reasonably well and proved a satisfactory building stone for the greater part of the fortifications. Where it is exposed, however, to the sirocco (the humid, grit-laden wind from north Africa) or to sea-spray, *franka* decomposes rapidly. From the late seventeenth century a more resistant local material, lower coralline limestone, known in Malta as *żonqor*, was used in those situations exposed to salt-spray.[59] The stonework also suffered at the hands of the Maltese whose practices of lighting fires, keeping goats and planting trees on the ramparts helped the stone to deteriorate more swiftly than would otherwise have been the case. The Order itself was not blameless; if maintenance was neglected and plants were allowed to seed themselves in the fortifications their roots soon split the masonry.[60]

Besides building stone the islands were also able to supply the ingredients for the mortar to bind the masonry. Although it was claimed, by Floriani among others, that earth was an adequate binding agent,[61] the normal practice in Malta was to use a mortar composed of sand, lime and water. Some sand was available from quarries, but when there was a heavy demand, as occurred during the building of Valletta, this source was supplemented by sea sand taken from the tops of the beaches where it was hoped that most of the salt would have been washed away by rains.[62] Although lime could be obtained by burning the local stone,[63] the imported product was often of better quality. In particular, the local lime, unless well soaked, tended to produce a friable mortar,[64] although this tendency could be obviated by the addition of pozzolana, a volcanic earth of calcinated clay brought in from Italy, which imparted hydraulic qualities to Maltese lime.[65]

---

57 This can be observed in the bastions of Valletta.

58 AOM 6551, f. 57v.

59 See AOM 1016, *passim* and Clerkenwell, MS. O 1, item 21.

60 AOM 1054, p. 5.

61 Chigi, R I 25, f. 336v. In the nineteenth century an earth and water mortar was still used for common building and for backing revetment walls (see Jones, p. 201).

62 Cod. Lap. f. 20v.

63 Murray, p. 463; Jones, p. 200.

64 Cod. Lap. f. 20v.; AOM 1016, p. 286.

65 Murray, p. 454.

Architects and engineers in Malta had, however, to contend with a dearth of two important materials, earth and timber. Although lack of the former might present no great problems to the civilian architect, it impeded the military engineer. Earth is an excellent shock-absorber, so that its use was advocated in the building of parapets and terrapleins in order to deaden the impact of missiles, diminish the possibility of ricochet and avoid injury to defenders from splinters of stone. In an island already unable to feed its population, the scant covering of earth had, however, to be reserved for agriculture, and, despite the laments of engineers, the parapets and terrapleins of the fortifications were almost invariably of stone.[66] The islands themselves also produced very little timber, and all the better construction wood, such as olive or chestnut, had to be imported. As a result a method of floor and roof construction was evolved, which, by employing stone arches and slabs, avoided the use of wooden supporting beams.[67] Although wood was used in the building of the fortifications, and the precious supplies were carefully guarded and accounted for, the prevalent scarcity did not lead to significant modifications in the design and construction of the defences. A vaulted stone roof was in any case stronger and less vulnerable than a wooden one, more likely to be bombproof and totally fire-resistant. The lack of wood and earth could, however, have been a serious handicap when the knights were under attack, for it was customary to throw up temporary defences and retrenchments composed of timber, earth, fascines and gabions, but, fortunately, after 1565, there was no major assault on the island.

The climate far more than a particular lack of certain local supplies influenced the building of the fortifications in Malta. It was clearly inadvisable to build during the intense heat of summer, and impracticable during the heavy winter rains. Laparelli, for example, calculated that at least two months between October and April were lost because of bad weather.[68] The torrential rain which marks the onset of winter could do untold damage to half-completed works.[69] It was, therefore, essential that all projects should be rainproof by October, a necessity which heavily influenced the building schedule. On the other hand, any work carried out at the height of summer was unlikely to prove durable; the heat dried out the mortar too quickly

---

66 AOM 6557, f. 62 (1761); AOM 1054, p. 37 (1789).

67 For details of house construction in Malta see the article by Jones; and J. Quentin Hughes, *The Building of Malta* (London, 1956), pp. 195-9.

68 Cod. Lap. f. 50v.

69 AOM 266, f. 169v. (1715); AOM 267, f. 171 (1722); Clerkenwell, MS. O 1, item 21 (1739).

so that it crumbled into a powder and was useless.[70] For this reason Laparelli advised against building at all during June, July and August,[71] while even at other times all supplies of lime were to be kept moist[72] and, to ensure that the mortar dried slowly, the walls were to be constantly bathed with water.[73] In those months when actual construction was not possible stone could, however, be cut and other materials stockpiled so that work could start immediately the weather was favourable.[74]

The knights were fortunate in having to hand an ample supply of easily-worked stone well suited to the construction of fortifications. Indeed, they could scarcely have contemplated a defensive system on so grand a scale had the principal building material had to be imported. The local stone imparts to the ramparts their characteristic warm yellow colouring; as they rise from their foundations of natural rock they appear to grow out of the rock itself; the large blocks of masonry, the ditches hewn from the rock and the walls rising from the sea, give an impression of overwhelming size. Yet these fortifications, although instantly recognizable as Maltese, do follow the common European pattern. Less timber and less earth than average may have been used in their construction and they undoubtedly stand as monuments to the expertise of the native masons. They are adapted to the local situation, but their design follows the principles current in contemporary Europe and their relationship to their continental cousins is clearly recognizable.

70 Cod. Lap. ff. 46, 47 and 71v.; AOM 1016, p. 286.
71 Cod. Lap. f. 47.
72 Cod. Lap. f. 46v.
73 Cod. Lap. f. 46; AOM 1016, p. 286.
74 Cod. Lap. f. 45.

Chapter 11

The Financing of the Fortifications

The financing of the fortifications cannot be considered in isolation but must be seen in the context of the Order's overall financial situation. Our present knowledge of the financial affairs of the Order during its sojourn in Malta is not, however, such that it is possible to give authoritative answers to many of the more obvious questions as to the source from which funds were raised, how they were allocated to different works, the total cost of any defence scheme, or what proportion of income in any particular year was devoted to the building of fortifications.[1] Indeed, even to calculate the annual income of the Order presents some difficulties.

In common with that of most early modern states the Order's income was divided into two categories: ordinary and extraordinary. The ordinary revenues, known as responsions, were those drawn each year from the estates and properties owned by the Order in Europe. Throughout the Maltese period the commanderies (as the estates were called) were expected to remit to Malta a third of their annual income, and assessments of resources were made from time to time to ensure that the responsions reflected the true value of the commanderies in question. Unfortunately these reassessments were few and far between, and took place only in 1533, 1583 and 1776, so that at times the money due bears little relationship to ability to pay.[2]

---

1 For further consideration of the Order's general financial position see: A. Hoppen, 'The finances of the Order of St. John of Jerusalem in the sixteenth and seventeenth centuries', in *European Studies Review*, III (1973), 103-19; and for the eighteenth century, Thornton.

2 AOM 286, f. 39 (reassessment ordered, 1533); AOM 297, ff. 40-50v. (new assessment, 1533); AOM 291, ff. 67-74 (new assessment, 1583); AOM 309, ff. 233-273 (new assessment, 1776).

Commanderies were also frequently in arrears in the payment of their responsions. At times this could be the result of circumstances beyond the control of the commander (the knight administering the estate), as, for example, when the European princes were at war and the Order's properties as a result devastated and the system of revenue collection disrupted. France in the late sixteenth century, Flanders, Spain and Germany in the early seventeenth, all reported arrears on account of wars.[3] Less excusable were losses accountable to inefficiency or maladministration on the part of officials of the Order.[4] In addition the treasury in Malta had to contend with the problems of fluctuating exchange rates for the various currencies in which the responsions were paid. In particular, because the *livre tournois* was exchanged at a rate fixed in the late sixteenth century, and no allowance made for its relative devaluation against the Maltese scudo in the course of the seventeenth century, by 1700 the actual sums received in Malta from the French properties were less in practice than on paper.[5]

The figures put forward as the Order's income from ordinary revenues tended to be based on the money due from the commanderies rather than on a statement of the actual money received, a fact which must constantly be borne in mind throughout any discussion of the Order's financial position. The basic responsions following the assessment of 1533 amounted to about 64,000 scudi a year,[6] although from 1574 onwards a further 40,000 scudi was raised from the commanderies on the basis of the existing assessment.[7] The original responsions and the imposition of 40,000 scudi continued to be levied on this assessment even after 1583, the year in which a new valuation was ordered which formed the basis of a further imposition of 50,000 scudi on the commanderies. Until about 1600 the two impositions were listed under extraordinary revenue, but their permanent nature was soon acknowledged and thereafter they were combined with the old responsions (of about 64,000 scudi) and all three together were referred to simply as the 'responsions'. Thus, although the responsions appear to rise from 60,000 scudi in 1587 to over 167,000 in the 1630s, the major part of the increase can be explained by this change in accounting

3 AOM 435, f. 268 (France, 1574); AOM 442, f. 239v. (France, 1586); RML MS. 742, p. 445 (Flanders, 1645); A.S.V. Particolare, T. 15, f. 367 (Spain and Germany, 1645).

4 See, for instance, Dal Pozzo, I, 98, 389, 721, II, 542.

5 Hoppen, 'Finances of the Order', pp. 106-7; RML MS. 186, II, 40-1.

6 AOM 424, f. 228 (1554); Urb. Lat. 826, f. 238v. (1567); Urb. Lat. 833, f. 182v. (1568).

7 AOM 290, f. 30 (chapter general, 1574).

procedure.[8] A true increase came only in 1776 when the chapter general authorized a tax of 500,000 per annum on the European properties, and decreed that the amounts raised by responsions and impositions established prior to this date were to be included in this sum.[9]

However, it is generally agreed that the income of the Order at the end of the eighteenth century averaged 1,315,296 a year, or more than double the revenue from ordinary sources,[10] the difference between this and the earlier figures mentioned being made up by the extraordinary income. In times of special need or emergency the chapter general, or the council acting on its behalf, had the power to impose additional levies, normally of three years' duration, on the commanderies to supplement the responsions.[11] Other sources of extraordinary income were more regular, although unpredictable in the amount they might produce in any given year. Some revenue depended upon the number of knights who had died in the previous accounting year (which ran from 1 May to 30 April), for on the death of a commander the treasury in Malta received the entire net revenues of his commandery from the date of death until the following 30 April. This payment was termed the mortuary. In addition the treasury claimed a vacancy payment which amounted to the revenues of the following year. Another source was the *spoglio*, that is the property of a knight which reverted to the treasury on his death. Variable sums were also derived from entry fees, called passage dues, from the naval activities of the knights through the sale of booty and slaves, and from gifts made to the Order from time to time.

Responsions, impositions on the Order's property in Europe, mortuary and vacancy fees, *spoglios*, passage money, the spoils of war and gifts were, therefore, the major sources of revenue open to the common treasury in Malta. Unfortunately the treasury records which survive in the Archives of the Order do not supply the answer to the question, 'What was the annual income of the knights?' Although in the late

---

8 A. Donna d'Oldenico, *Redditi e spese dell'Ordine Militare Gerosolimitano di Malta nel 1587* (Ciriè, 1964), p. 25; Chigi, R I 25, f. 340 (1630s).

9 AOM 309, f. 76.

10 AOM 274, *passim* (1783-95); *Bilanci decennale de Comun Tesoro* (Malta, 1789) – various copies of this printed statement survive in the Archives of the Order, for instance, AOM 881 and 6406. It is reproduced by L. de Boisgelin in *Ancient and Modern Malta*, 2 vols. (London, 1805) I, 296-326; this statement is also the source of many of Thornton's figures.

11 A tax of 30,000 scudi per annum was authorized in 1558 to be used for defences (AOM 288, f. 65v.); it was unusual in that it continued for nearly twenty years; more normal were the 12,000 scudi per annum raised for three years in 1633 (AOM 111, f. 15v.), a total of 122,000 over three years in 1645 (AOM 257, f. 197v.) and 12,000 per annum for three years in 1652 (AOM 259, f. 36v.).

eighteenth century, in accordance with a council decree of February 1762 the treasury presented annual statements of income and expenditure to the council,[12] for the earlier period the evidence is of a very fragmentary nature and consists mainly of balance sheets occasionally drawn up in an attempt to assess the financial condition of the Order. As might be expected in a time of inflation, these reveal a steady rise in total income, ordinary and extraordinary, from 127,000 scudi in 1568, to 243,000 at the end of the century, reaching 296,000 in 1630.[13] For the following hundred years no figures for total income, whatever their limitations, are available, and all that can be said is that the overall upward trend, in so far as it can be seen in the physical manifestations of expenditure, seems to have continued. The first of the regular statements of income which appear in the council minutes was prepared as part of an investigation into the state of the treasury ordered in 1762. It recorded an income of 1,921,642 scudi, but thereafter the entries show a dramatic fall to 1,073,920 scudi in 1767 and a gradual decline to 832,049 in 1771.[14] The figure for 1762 may represent the peak level of the Order's income, or it may itself show a decline from previous levels which remain unknown to us. However, the knights viewed their financial position with concern, and the chapter general of 1776 ordered a reform of the treasury which took place under the Secretary of the Treasury Bosredon. He introduced a new accounting system, checked wastage, and allowed public scrutiny of the accounts by means of printed balance sheets. About this time the French financier, Necker, had already achieved a European reputation for his advocacy of the importance of increased public information regarding national accounts, and himself published the French *compte rendu* in 1781. A growing pressure for similar revelations elsewhere resulted, and the French knight Bosredon may have been influenced by Necker's example.[15] Bosredon's good stewardship may also have been responsible for the temporary increase in the Order's income which took place between 1779 and 1788 when it averaged 1,364,174 scudi per annum. The danger, however, remained that actual receipts might

---

12 AOM 271, f. 214v. (11 February 1762); statements appear in AOM 272, *passim*; 273, *passim*; and 274, *passim*.

13 Urb. Lat. 833, f. 183v. (1568); Clerkenwell, MS. P 4, 'Catalogo e stima delli priorati baliaggi e commende di tutta la Religione Hierosolimitana fatto l'anno 1583', pp. 38-40 (1594); Barb. Lat. 5036, f. 13v. (1630).

14 AOM 272, ff. 15v. (7 February 1765), 88v. (1767), 249 (1771).

15 For the financial reforms in France at this time see: J. F. Bosher, *French Finances, 1770-1795* (Cambridge, 1970), especially pp. 139-40.

be somewhat lower because of non-payment, something which occurred on an unprecedented scale in 1792 when the Estates General confiscated the Order's French property. The devastating effect of this measure can be appreciated when it is realized that France alone had contributed to the common treasury almost as much as Spain, Portugal, Italy and Germany together.[16] The greatly reduced income, 839,975 scudi, for the year ending 30 April 1796 clearly reflects this loss and despite economy measures the accounts showed a deficit after 1792.[17]

Under normal circumstances the Order was usually able to remain solvent with the gradual increase in income keeping pace with steadily rising costs brought about partly, at least, by inflation. The income of 208,000 scudi in 1587 allowed a small surplus over the current expenditure of 201,393 scudi.[18] The same was true over forty years later in 1630 when the income was 296,116 and expenditure 278,833 scudi,[19] and at the end of the eighteenth century Bosredon could show an average annual surplus between 1779 and 1788. However, as soon as the Order became involved in extraordinary expenditure it found itself in financial difficulties, and it was not surprisingly the military rather than the hospitaller activities of the Order which led to excess spending. Whenever Turkish invasion scares occurred, the defences were hurriedly put in order, and munitions, victuals and men were procured. Thus two constant reasons put forward for the unhealthy state of the treasury were 'preparations for war', and 'the cost of the campaign' (whether military or naval).[20]

The normal expenditure of the Order, as set out in the sixteenth and seventeenth centuries, made no provision, however, for exceptional military expenses. A large sum was regularly allotted to the upkeep of the galleys and this was always the largest single normal item of expenditure.[21] No account, however, was taken of the cost of supplying new galleys, despite the fact that these vessels, even if no accident befell them,

---

16 AOM 6406, no foliation. In the 1780s France contributed 580,406 scudi per annum, the rest of Europe 648,390 while 48,875 scudi came from special funds (Thornton, p. 14).

17 Thornton, p. 26; for the economy measures see AOM 274, *passim*.

18 Donna d'Oldenico, pp. 25 and 27.

19 Barb. Lat. 5036, ff. 13v. and 14v.

20 For instance, a Turkish threat in 1562 (AOM 429, f. 254); the loss of three galleys in 1570 (AOM 93, f. 19).

21 The cost of the upkeep of the galleys was as follows: 1568, 45,000 scudi at the rate of 9,000 per galley (Urb. Lat. 833, ff. 188r. and v.); 1630, 135,000 scudi at 25,000 for the capitana and 22,000 for each of the other five galleys (Barb. Lat. 5036, f. 14); 1640, 123,000 scudi at 23,000 for the capitana and 20,000 for the others (RML MS. 698, p. 212); 1663, 143,000 scudi at the same rate as 1640 (AOM 6397, f. 226). This rate was laid down in 1637 (Dal Pozzo, II, 17).

had a life limited to seven or eight years.[22] In a similar fashion, the accounts of the sixteenth and seventeenth centuries contain no provision for the large-scale programme of building and fortification then being undertaken. Although fortifications or building works are mentioned in all the accounts, often the expenses noted are only those associated with administration: the salaries of the commissioner of works, his deputy and secretary and the provision of food for the cart-horses.[23] The references to fortifications clearly do not tell the whole story. For example, the accounts of the 1560s do not include any information on the amount spent in building Valletta, although they do record that over 16,000 scudi had been spent annually on building works in Birgu, St. Elmo and St. Michael in the years before the construction of Valletta.[24] In the 1630s the modest provision for the fortifications amounted in one year to 5,200 scudi despite the fact that these were years when rumours of an impending Turkish attack were rife.[25] The account for 1663 states specifically that in addition to 7,222, scudi allotted to 'works', 2,760 scudi were spent on 'new fortifications', but again these are administrative costs and bear little relationship to the total cost of the new fortifications.[26] The 2,760 scudi comprised the engineer's salary at thirty scudi a month, and payments to the master builders at the rate of 200 scudi a month.

It is obvious that the amounts which the treasury contributed to the fortifications, as shown by the sixteenth- and seventeenth-century balance sheets, were insufficient to support any large-scale building. In fact, the fortifications were financed out of a separate fund, the *cassa della fortificazione*, to which the treasury contributed regularly, but which had other additional sources of income as well. Thus the congregation of fortification and war itself controlled property, land and buildings in Malta, the revenues of which were used to defray the day-to-day cost of the fortifications.[27] Funds were established for specific purposes: the Cottonera Foundation supported the garrison in fort Ricasoli, while the Manoel Foundation performed a similar service for fort Manoel. At the end of the eighteenth century these funds were producing an average of over 10,000 scudi each per annum,[28]

---

22 Blouet, p. 128; Earle, p. 105.
23 RML MS. 698, p. 231 (469 scudi), AOM 6397, f. 228 (7,222 scudi).
24 Urb. Lat. 826, f. 236; Urb. Lat. 833, f. 187; ASV Misc. Arm. II, no. 81, f. 265v.
25 Barb. Lat. 5036, f. 14.
26 AOM 6397, ff. 228-9.
27 See RML Tres. A. 106, 110, 111 and 113 for its income from property in the eighteenth century.
28 Thornton, p. 16.

although the non-specialist Congregation of War Foundation, set up for general purposes in 1721, was then producing only 1,000 scudi a year.[29] The bulk of the money being spent in the fortifications, however, was derived by the *cassa* from sources beyond its immediate control. The *cassa* kept detailed accounts of income and expenditure which were examined by the council, but no trace survives of the account books in the Archives except for those of the Order's last years in Malta.[30] It is possible, therefore, only to make general observations as to the funds available to the *cassa*, and the way in which they were spent.

There were three basic sources from which the Order could derive money: firstly it could hope to receive donations from foreign princes and the papacy; secondly it could draw on its own resources, the property owned by the Order or its members; finally it could tax the Maltese and the Maltese islands. Although the Order kept the princes of Europe constantly and zealously informed of its precarious financial state, the only, and much quoted, occasion on which these responded on a grand scale to an appeal for assistance towards the expenses of fortification was in 1565 when the Order appealed for funds to rebuild the defences damaged in the siege and to build Valletta. In answer to the pleas of the Hospitaller envoys, Pius IV gave 15,000 scudi, Philip II promised 30,000 scudi, Sebastian of Portugal 30,000 *cruzados*, and Charles IX 140,000 *livres tournois*. Even these sums were hardly princely, and the Order was in any case then faced with the task of ensuring that this money was in fact paid.[31] However, the knights liked to look back to the support they received in the years following the siege as an example of how Europe would rally round in an emergency, but undoubtedly deluded themselves if they believed that the European princes would supply large sums of money in further times of need. In fact, it was the Order itself and the Maltese who provided the vast sums which were constantly being eaten up by the fortifications.

29 Thornton, p. 16; for the setting up of the fund see AOM 267, f. 69v. (27 January 1720) and AOM 140, f. 362 (15 July 1721).

30 2 May 1658, commissioners of fortifications were ordered to submit their accounts to the council every six months (AOM 120, f. 153). RML Tres. A 105, 'Administrazione di Guerra, 1779-97', contains detailed weekly accounts of the money being spent in the fortifications; it probably reflects the new accounting procedures introduced after the chapter general of 1776.

31 There is evidence of the French money being collected gradually: 35,000 *livres* by 1567 (AOM 431, f. 266v.), a further 20,000 *livres* by 1570 (AOM 433, f. 252v.). The Portuguese money had been paid to the Order's officials by August 1566 (AOM 431, f. 248v.).

Many individual members of the Order were exceedingly wealthy, for, although all took a vow of poverty, personal wealth reverted to the treasury only on death. There are thus various examples of knights donating sums of money to be spent on the construction of the fortifications, and if the amounts were sufficiently large a work would be named after the generous donor. Thus, Alessandro Orsi offered to build at his own expense a tower at the entrance to the Grand Harbour,[32] which was later replaced by a fort named after Giovanni Francesco Ricasoli who had supplied 20,000 scudi towards its construction.[33] The heavy expenditure at that time also inspired Juan Galdiano to offer to pay for the crownwork proposed by the engineer Valperga, while Jacques de Lussan Carboneau donated 10,000 scudi, a sum however insufficient to merit commemoration.[34] This tradition continued and in the eighteenth century the wealthy Jacques de Chambray defrayed part of the costs of building a fort in Gozo.[35] Fort Tigné was named after Bailiff René Jacques de Tigné who gave the initial 1,000 scudi towards the building expenses, although a far larger sum, 6,000 scudi, was contributed by the Bailiff Hompesch.[36] Many smaller gifts by knights were recorded, especially in a time of emergency as, for instance, after the siege of 1565.[37] A special appeal was launched in 1715 to which several knights responded with sums ranging from 3,000 to 1,000 scudi but by far the largest contribution was 200,000 from Grand Master Perellos.[38] The most remarkable gift from an individual came from a man who was not a fully-professed knight, but a knight of devotion; in 1689 the engineer Grunenberg, realizing that the Order could not afford the three batteries which he proposed should be added to fort St. Angelo, offered to execute them at his own expense.[39]

It became fashionable for grand masters to perpetuate their memory by erecting a suitably impressive fort. Apart from any personal fortune, grand masters enjoyed revenues as sovereign of the Maltese, and also a pension from the common treasury, so that they were able from time to time to contribute to the financing of the fortifications.[40]

---

32 AOM 109, f. 164v. (15 January 1629).

33 AOM 261, f. 166 (15 January 1670); Dal Pozzo (II, 390) says that he gave 30,000 scudi plus all his income of 3,000 scudi per annum, reserving only enough for his keep.

34 AOM 261, f. 176v. (14 May 1671).

35 AOM 270, f. 202 (23 June 1752.); Clerkenwell, MS. O 1, item 21.

36 AOM 1015, pp. 412 (12 April 1793) and 413 (24 April 1793).

37 A list of the knights who contributed is found at AOM 289, f. 20.

38 AOM 266, ff. 130v., 133 and 164.

39 AOM 263, ff. 62v. (17 December 1689) and 65 (23 February 1690).

40 The income of the grand master in 1568 was calculated as being approximately 30,000 scudi (Urb. Lat. 833, f. 167); in the 1790s it was 234,897 scudi (Thornton, p. 28).

Grand Master Garzes in his will made money available for the building of the tower which bore his name.[41] His successor, Alof de Wignacourt, on a rather grander scale, built at his own expense the towers known as St. Paul's, St. Lucian's, St. Thomas's, Sta. Maria delle Grazie and St. Mary's, Comino, and bequeathed them to the Order together with a small income for maintenance.[42] The forts had cost Wignacourt about 40,000 scudi from the magisterial revenues.[43] The Grand Masters Lascaris and De Redin later in the seventeenth century also built coastal towers from their own resources.[44] Although these do indeed seem to have been built at no cost to the common treasury, the same cannot be said of the Cottonera lines inspired by Nicholas Cotoner. Cotoner did supply 100 scudi a month towards the building costs, but this could cover only a fraction of the expenses, as can be seen in the fact that in the same year the Order assigned 1,000 scudi a month to the construction works in Floriana and a further 8,000 a month to be divided between forts Sta. Margherita and Ricasoli.[45] Cotoner's donation compares badly with the 2,000 scudi a year, admittedly limited to three years' duration, which Lascaris had contributed to the fortifications almost thirty years previously.[46] In contrast to the Cottonera lines, fort Manoel was actually financed by Manoel de Vilhena who also set up a fund to provide for its garrison.[47] This was the last major fort financed by the generosity of a grand master, for the decision to give St. Lucian the name of fort Rohan in honour of the ruling grand master was in recognition not of a large monetary donation but rather of his general interest in the provision of coastal defences.[48]

Leaving aside the wealth of any individual member, the Order as a body had vast capital assets in its European estates, but could encounter problems in trying to mobilize these resources. The properties did, however, provide excellent securities against which loans could be raised. In the years immediately after the siege envoys were frequently dispatched with instructions to seek loans,[49] but there is no

---

41 AOM 101, f. 191 (14 October 1605).

42 AOM 103, ff. 103 (6 November 1609), and 146v. (1 July 1610); AOM 105, f. 72v. (11 July 1614); AOM 106, ff. 62v. (7 November 1617), and 124v. (11 October 1618); AOM 107, ff. I14v. (22 September 1622), and 199 (23 May 1623).

43 AOM 107, f. 199.

44 Mifsud, 'La milizia', p. 79; AOM 261, f. 31v. (30 March 1658).

45 AOM 261, ff. 162 (8 April 1670), and 166 (10 June 1670).

46 AOM 257, ff. 95v. (8 November 1641), and 102v. (8 January 1642).

47 AOM 267, f. 242 (31 August 1724).

48 AOM 1015, p. 434 (2 June 1795).

49 AOM 431, ff. 241v. (6 May 1566), 208 (16 December 1566), 209v. and 210 (4 Januray 1567), 211 (23 June 1567), 232 and 233 (17 October 1567), 225v. and 223v. (20 October 1567; Cod.

way of knowing how much money reached Malta from these sources. When building was again undertaken on a grand scale in the 1630s the Order employed this same method of raising money,[50] and the war scare of 1715 also produced similar measures, although again there is no evidence as to how effective they were.[51] As an exceptional step, because it depleted capital resources, the Order was prepared to sell some of the wood which it owned in France, and 300,000 *livres tournois* were realized in this way in 1671 just at the time when the knights felt particularly threatened after the fall of Crete to the Turks, and had in addition embarked on an ambitious building programme.[52]

The one European power which consistently supported the Order in its struggle to finance its building works was the papacy. Apart from a donation of 20,000 scudi, during the building of Valletta Pius V actually supplied 5,000 scudi a month for six or seven months until the need to assist Charles IX in his fight against Huguenots diverted papal funds to France.[53] Pius V also assigned to the Order the proceeds, up to a sum of 30,000 scudi, from a tithe on the Kingdom of Naples.[54] Moreover, the popes lent their moral support, urging the princes and others to come to the Order's aid, and issuing a variety of briefs enabling the knights to use their European properties as securities against loans and permitting them to levy special taxes on both the Order's possessions and those of the Maltese.

In addition to being elected head of the Order, the grand master was sovereign of the Maltese islands. As such he inherited the right to taxes which had been imposed by the former Aragonese rulers.[55] The tax most directly concerned with the fortifications was the *neuba*. This had originally arisen out of an obligation on the part of the

---

Lap. f. 55v., a copy of the report carried by the envoys), 215v. (24 October 1567), 217 (12 December 1567); AOM 432, ff. 237v. (7 September 1568), 256 (27 June 1569), 210v. (17 December 1569).

50 AOM 256, ff. 129 (5 March 1635), 186v. (8 December 1638); AOM 257, ff. 13v. (16 May 1639), 49v. (12 April 1640); AOM 737, ff. 94 (23 May 1639), 95v. (4 August 1639), 99 (9 May 1640), 106 (18 May 1641), 107 (26 July 1641).

51 AOM 266, ff. 116v. (28 September 1714) and 153v. (26 March 1715); AOM 519, f. 199 (26 March 1715).

52 AOM 261, f. 177; money had also been raised in this way in 1562 (AOM 429, f. 210) and 1571 (Dal Pozzo, I, 7).

53 ASV Arm. XLII, 26, ff. 118-19 (brief appointing papal commissioner to pay money, July 1566); Bosio, III, 807.

54 Bosio, III, 831; AOM 92, ff. 169 and 183; Pauli, I, 236; AOM 93, f. 19; AOM 433, f. 260; Dal Pozzo, I, 7.

55 H. Bresc, 'The "Secrezia" and the royal patrimony in Malta: 1240-1450', in *Medieval Malta: Studies on Malta Before the Knights*, ed. A. T. Luttrell (London, 1975), pp. 126-62, contains interesting information on the finances of mediaeval Malta.

Maltese to perform labour service in the fortifications, which in the passage of time became open to commutation on payment of a levy. The exact amount of service owed, and the rate of the levy or *neuba* became matters of dispute, so much so, that estimates of the value of the tax in 1673 ranged from 1,200 scudi per annum by the grand master, who calculated that four days were owed a year at one taro a day, to 6,000 scudi by the Maltese, who considered its demands more onerous.[56] Indeed, the Maltese appear to have had grounds for their complaints against the level of taxation which they were forced to bear. As with the forced labour, which could be avoided if one could pay a substitute, the taxation fell particularly heavily on the peasants and labourers.

The Maltese protested not only at the level of taxation but also at the infringement of their ancient rights and liberties. However, individual action could prove dangerous as was discovered by Matteo Callus, a Maltese doctor who wrote a letter of complaint to the Spanish king objecting to the grand master's appropriation of the revenues of the Università. His judicial strangulation in 1560 discouraged further protest by individuals.[57] But the cause of the Maltese was assisted by the church, which as an institution not dependent on the Order and able to call on support outside the islands, was sometimes prepared to take a comparatively firm stand over its rights.

An attempt in 1636 to raise a levy of 5,000 scudi on the revenues of the clergy, which together with the much larger sum of 50,000 scudi from the laity, was to help finance the latest project – the Floriana lines – led to trouble which the Order alleged had been orchestrated by the parish priests. The clergy led by the cathedral chapter and bishop made a formal complaint by way of a memorandum sent to Rome setting out their grievances. This memorandum was undoubtedly in the nature of a national protest rather than an attempt merely to protect the revenues of churchmen.[58] The clergy claimed that the fortifications were not essential to the defence of the island, that the Order itself was divided as to their worth, and that the knights owned sufficient property and already imposed sufficient taxes on the Maltese

---

56 Mifsud, 'Papi', pp. 405-6. The actual monetary value of the *neuba* to the Order was just over 1,000 scudi a year in 1660 (AOM 121, f. 191v.).

57 Mifsud, 'Papi', p. 420; Wettinger, 'Popular attitudes', pp. 266-7; Cassar, *Medical History of Malta*, pp. 17-19. Callus's true Christian name was Giuseppe but it is as Matteo that he is celebrated as a national hero.

58 For details of the uprising see Borg, pp. 51-4.

to be able to finance the business. Moreover, the Order, with an annual income of some 2,000,000 scudi, had decided to spend only 36,000 scudi on the fortifications, whereas the islanders whose annual income was barely 160,000 scudi were being asked to pay 55,000 scudi. To make matters even worse the Order had excluded its own property in Malta and that of its members from the proposed tax. Finally the document declared that unless costs were shared in a more equitable manner the Maltese would not contribute a single scudo towards the new fortifications. The protest met with little response in Rome. The pope, Urban VIII, formerly Maffeo Barberini, supported the Order's project, having lent his own engineer Floriani to draw up the plans. Furthermore, the papal representative in Malta, the Inquisitor Fabio Chigi, who was in constant contact with Francesco Barberini the cardinal nephew, also supported the scheme. Chigi acted as mediator when Grand Master Lascaris, who had delayed collection of the tax, perhaps anticipating trouble, finally decided to implement the briefs in 1637. The tax collectors met with opposition and it began to look as if all the casals or villages of the islands would rise in revolt.

The uprising began in September 1637 in Żejtun, the first village where collection was attempted. The leaders hoped to assemble the people of Malta at Marsa and to march on Valletta with a crucifix or statue of a saint at their head. There were suggestions that they might be armed. Despite the initial lead given by the clergy in opposing the tax, the parish priest of Żejtun was not unnaturally alarmed at these warlike preparations and informed the bishop who sent him to Chigi, who, in turn, ordered him to go to the grand master. Meanwhile Chigi tried to persuade the representatives of the people of Żejtun to pay the tax, although they continued to maintain that the island was exempted by royal, presumably Aragonese, concessions from such taxation. However, negotiations had to be broken off when the representatives found that their fellow country men regarded them as traitors because of their dealings with Chigi. The grand master imprisoned the lay leaders of the revolt, and although he suspected that some local priests were behind the uprising, acting on Chigi's advice, he never denounced them as agitators.[59] Chigi indeed seems to have been able to exercise some influence over the priests and the prospect of a united uprising of the casals receded. Resistance to the tax, however, remained fierce and although some money was collected it was far short of the 50,000

59 Borg, p. 304 (letter dated 19 September 1637).

scudi anticipated. Since Chigi regarded the 5,000 scudi from the clergy as a subsidy tied to the amount forthcoming from the laity he made no attempt to force payment from the clergy. The immediate object of the revolt had been secured; in effect this particular tax was not collected and the brief authorizing it was later exchanged for one sanctioning an imposition of 50,000 scudi on eatables. Although the brief authorizing the imposition on consumable goods was granted in 1640, it was not implemented until 1643. But again the yield was low so the basis of taxation was changed to non-moveable goods and eventually in 1653, it was related to crops harvested in the islands.[60] Apart from the specific grievance of the new tax there is evidence that the casals were also objecting to the oppressive and autocratic rule of the Order in general.

Popular resentment on the matter continued to simmer away, waiting to boil over at the next provocation, which was to occur in 1670 when Grand Master Nicholas Cotoner embarked on the grandiose scheme which bears his name. The Order proceeded as before, this time seeking to commute a papal brief sanctioning a tax on consumable goods.[61] Various churchmen, anxious to protect certain exemptions from taxation which they enjoyed, appealed to Rome seeking to establish their position, but they received an unsympathetic response. The discontent became more widespread when 150 priests from the countryside invaded the Inquisitor's Palace on 2 July 1672 protesting against the erosion of their ancient privileges enshrined in the awards of Charles V. Such actions by the clergy did not pass unnoticed by the population at large. Indeed the Order began to fear that a general revolt might well break out.[62]

After much negotiation a compromise was reached which preserved the dignity of the Order, the inquisitor and the bishop. Once these authorities had secured their own positions pressure to accede to the demands was applied to the clergy and others claiming similar exemptions. However, general opposition to the tax still continued and the pope, Clement X, began to take soundings as to whether a tax on consumable goods might be more acceptable. By early 1673 the grand master and council had concluded that the islands could only be pacified by such a course and on 1 July 1673 a papal brief was issued substituting a tax on consumables for that on non-moveables. This took

---

60 Mifsud, 'Papi', pp. 421-5.

61 AOM 261, ff. 166 (31 May 1670), 173v. (22 November 1670) and 194v.; for details of the troubles see Galea Scannura, 185-96.

62 Galea Scannura, p. 189.

the form of a customs duty levied on brandy, tobacco, playing cards, leather, soap and coffee, which became known as the *nuovo imposto*.

There had long been a tradition of levying customs dues and general taxes on food to finance the building of fortifications stretching back to at least the fifteenth century,[63] and the Università continued to impose such taxes to raise money to meet the costs of the fortifications for which it remained responsible after 1530. It also approved the duties imposed by the Order, and exercised a general oversight of the farming out of their collection.[64] Even in this sphere, however, the Order pursued interventionist policies. In 1636 the Order assumed from the Università the responsibility for collecting the wine tax (first imposed in 1419) so as to finance work on Comino and repairs to Città Vecchia.[65] The Università was allocated a fixed sum of 625 scudi per annum, while the Order granted the right of collection to the highest bidder, and profited as the contract price rose, reaching 25,000 scudi by 1793.[66]

Originally the *nouvo imposto* of 1673 was to operate only until 100,000 scudi had been raised but soon it became a permanent tax and its continuation a major grievance amidst the early-eighteenth-century protests against heavy taxation in general.[67] It was claimed that by 1711 the treasury had collected a total of more than 225,000 scudi from this tax even though Grand Master Perellos was then requesting papal authority to levy yet another 100,000 scudi. Opposition was again expressed by the clergy. At a chapter general of all ecclesiastics held in September 1713 all but two of the delegates objected to the new tax. Despite the intervention of the bishop who argued that the people should be relieved of some of their tax burdens because of their courageous service to the Order, the pope supported the grand master. Clement XI further extended the briefs of his predecessors and authorized a further 100,000 scudi for repairs and for the construction of new works.[68] Moreover he forbade the calling of another chapter general thereby depriving the islanders of a forum for the expression of discontent. By this action the pope stifled the protests of the clergy and through them of the people in general. Appeals to Rome

---

63 Mifsud, 'Papi', pp. 407, 408 and 414.
64 Mifsud, 'Papi', p. 423; RML MS. 672, f. 1.
65 J. Debono, 'The wine trade of Malta in the eighteenth century', *Melita Historica*, IX (1984), 90; Wettinger, 'Popular attitudes', p. 264.
66 Debono, p. 91: Wettinger, 'Popular attitudes', p. 267.
67 Mifsud, 'Papi', pp. 427-8.
68 Mifsud, 'Papi', p. 428.

had become fruitless and the papacy no longer seemed prepared to act as a protector of the Maltese. The Order in turn simply ceased to bother about obtaining briefs authorizing taxation (except in the case of the rather special crusading brief obtained in 1670 in order to raise 3,000 scudi to support two coastguards). The eighteenth century can therefore be said to have witnessed a growth in the autocratic power of the grand master at the very time when the influence of the papacy in the church as a whole was in decline.

In the disputes over taxation a recurring theme was the vexed question of copper coinage. Such money had been minted during the building of Valletta to supply immediate needs while income from abroad was being mobilized.[69] Subsequent grand masters made further issues of both a fiduciary and fractional nature. While the latter had some beneficial role in assisting commercial transactions, copper money was generally disliked and regarded with suspicion. However, in the seventeenth century Grand Master Lascaris attempted to solve his financial problems (caused largely by ambitious building projects) by flooding the market with fiduciary coins.[70] By 1643 a 250,000 scudi of new fiduciary two- and four-tari pieces had been minted in addition to the 60,000 scudi already in circulation at the time of Lascaris's election.[71] Such a large influx of copper money distorted the economy and caused gold and silver to disappear almost completely; merchants complained that the local currency had become so discredited abroad that their foreign trade was now devastated.[72]

The Order acknowledged the seriousness of the situation but fuelled discontent by failing to apply to their assigned purpose taxes specifically levied to extinguish the copper coinage. Some of the 55,000 scudi sanctioned in 1646 had, for example, been reserved for this purpose but the yield had proved so low that nothing was actually achieved.[73] January 1645 saw the first serious attempt at recall but before this could get fully under way large-scale building work resumed in response to rumours of an imminent Turkish attack.[74] Once this

---

69 Bosio, III, 748; J. C. Sammut, 'The coinage of the Order of St. John in Malta', Thirteenth Council of Europe art exhibition, *The Order of St. John in Malta*, (Malta, 1970), pp. 47-61.

70 M. Sant, 'Minting and attempted recalling of fiduciary copper coinage in Malta', *Melita Historica*, VI (1972), 60-80.

71 Sant, pp. 63-6.

72 Mifsud, 'Papi', p. 422; RML MS. 438 (1670).

73 AOM 111, f. 243 (1636).

74 Sant, pp. 69-72.

threat had receded redemption went forward in fits and starts with progress being largely dictated by the financial state of the Università which was responsible for recalling coins worth 97,000 scudi. The Order even devised a scheme designed to benefit the islanders, by which the Università undertook to import wine and wheat from Sicily and assign twenty-five per cent of the profits to the task of redemption. At the same time a third of the profits which the Order derived from its own imports of wheat were to be likewise applied. The plan, however, proved only partially successful. After various adjustments the Order and the Università had managed to recall 21,970 and 30,874 scudi respectively by the beginning of 1662 leaving no less than 211,273 still in circulation – well above the 60,000 deemed necessary to oil the wheels of internal retail trade. Both the Maltese and the knights themselves continued to be plagued by the ill-effects of too much copper coinage. Although natural wear and tear led to a gradual decline in the amount in circulation about 200,000 scudi (fiduciary and fractional) was still in being when the Order's copper money was finally withdrawn in 1827. Even if the fortifications had never been the sole cause for the issue of such coins, they had undoubtedly played an important part and had certainly hindered the implementation of programmes for recall. The manner in which building schemes were undertaken – in response to threats, at short notice, with little regard to the Order's financial resources – undoubtedly meant that large sums had often to be raised very quickly indeed so that the issue of copper coinage was always a tempting short-term expedient, however damaging it may have been to the economy as a whole.

The nature of the sources on which the Order could draw to finance its building programme having been indicated, the question remains, 'How much was being spent on the fortifications?' Although there is no simple or complete answer to this question, it is possible to make some general observations which may illustrate the problems involved in determining costs, as well as give some indication of the extent of the Order's financial commitment to the casting of itself and its island home in the role of the bastion of Christianity against Islam.

There is no doubt that within limits the Order attempted to keep a close control on the costs of the fortifications. All the skilled workers were engaged on a contractual basis at an agreed price per cane which varied according to the complexity of the work undertaken. Exact measurements were made of how much had been built each week, and the men paid accordingly, and as no one was exempt from this treatment, even the engineer's pay was scrutinized.[75] A contract could be varied only with the agreement of both sides, and the Order was particularly reluctant to allow any changes as these would normally have involved it in more expense.[76] These contracts, and in particular the records of the payments made under them, are incomplete and cannot form the basis for a calculation of the cost of the fortifications. Moreover, the payments to the craftsmen were but one item in the total construction costs. The other major expense was for building material. Admittedly, there were no problems in obtaining building stone; an ample supply was available locally so that no heavy shipping costs were incurred. Under some of the contracts the craftsmen agreed to provide common building stone (*franka*) themselves, but this was not always so. More specialized stone, even that quarried on the island, such as *żonqor*, was supplied by the Order. Most of the other materials – wood, iron, pozzolana, mortar – had to be imported. This naturally added to their cost and they were carefully guarded by the commissioner of works and his assistants, who had to account for their use. There is not a great deal of information available as to the cost of materials, but what there is suggests that they were a major item of expenditure; for instance, in a six-month period in 1690 and 1691, out of a sum of 5,102 scudi being spent on alterations to St. Elmo, building supplies (including *żonqor*) accounted for almost three quarters of the total (3,597), and the wages of craftsmen only one quarter (1,505).[77] This may have been exceptionally high, although in the 1640s the engineer Buonamici calculated material, excluding stone, as a quarter of his costs.[78] The Order was obviously anxious to economize wherever possible in the use of materials, and Floriani recounts proudly how he had saved about 25,000 scudi by using ordinary earth as a binding agent rather than more expensive lime.[79]

Another item of expenditure which it is almost impossible to quantify is the amount paid in compensation to proprietors whose land was compulsorily purchased to make way for fortifications. Sometimes the owners received no financial compensation but were given instead

---

75 AOM 116, f. 263 (16 September 1649); it was found that Buonamici had received an excess of 230 scudi in the course of three years.

76 In 1728 the contractors at fort Manoel claimed that they could not fulfil the original conditions (Clerkenwell, MS. O 1, item 15).

77 AOM 1016, p. 6.

78 AOM 6402, f. 147.

79 Chigi, R I 25, ff. 336-7.

plots of equivalent area and value out of existing stocks of public land.[80] Although at first the Order was unwilling to pay any compensation for buildings or trees which happened to be on the land, claiming that it derived no benefit from them, by the eighteenth century a change of heart had taken place and the engineer Marandon can be found busily surveying property in great detail and assessing its value down to the last cupboard.[81] Probably inevitably, disputes arose over the amount and nature of compensation. The Order did, however, attempt to act equitably in this matter, and such purchases of land added to the cost of the fortifications.[82]

The workforce engaged on building the fortifications naturally included unskilled labourers as well as craftsmen. The craftsmen paid their own company of workers, but in addition there was an army of men employed directly by the Order in digging ditches and transporting materials. Although this provided a large force of several thousand men, it proved less costly to the Order than might have been thought, for many of the labourers were not paid wages, being either Maltese performing labour service, convicts, or slaves, and the only charge made on the *cassa della fortificazione* was for the bread and rice with which each worker was provided.[83]

Any estimate as to how much the Order was spending on fortification is bound, through the limitations of the sources, to be tentative. At certain times we may know how much was being made available for use in the fortifications; on other occasions we are told how much has been spent; and (probably the most unreliable information) we also have estimates of how much certain works were to cost.

The amounts assigned by the common treasury to the fortifications varied depending mainly on the volume and nature of the work being undertaken. The treasury allocated 200 scudi a month to Floriana at a time when work was progressing at a steady, but not exceptional, rate, and this was later augmented by an additional 100 scudi a month for a four-month period.[84] The low level of activity can also be seen from three accounts of the period which indicate that the

80 AOM 113, f. 113v. (27 February 1641); AOM 114, ff. 59 (22 January 1643) and 222v. (24 January 1644); AOM 482, f. 280v. (1 October 1670).

81 Clerkenwell, MS. O 1, item 24 (1757).

82 The records of the litigation are kept in the Archives of the Superior Courts, Valletta, and in the Notarial Archives, Valletta.

83 AOM 296, f. 165 (1631); AOM 256, f. 129 (5 March 1635); AOM 116, ff. 6v. (7 April 1647) and 262v. (16 September 1649); RML MS. 676, f. 280 (9 November 1648).

84 AOM 260, ff. 20 (8 November 1657) and 128v. (6 June 1662).

200 scudi limit was respected.[85] The contributions from the common treasury gradually increased in the 1660s from copper valued at 500 scudi per week in 1666 to 500 silver scudi in 1668, which perhaps reflects the growing anxiety over the situation in Crete, which the Order believed was a preliminary to an attack on Malta.[86] The allocation had risen by 1715 when, as an economy measure, it was cut back to its former level.[87] This proved unrealistic, and a limit of 300 scudi a week was set in 1723.[88] The Turkish threat in 1761 resulted in increased expenditure, but with a return to more peaceful times, the contribution of the treasury to the fortifications reverted to its 'accustomed' level of 12,000 scudi per annum, which showed a slight reduction from the provisions of the 1720s despite the fact that costs were rising.[89] The sum of 12,000 scudi a year was confirmed by the chapter general in 1776, and remained the standard allocation until 1795 when, in a desperate attempt at economy, it was halved.[90]

These sums represent the amount which the treasury was prepared to spend in routine maintenance and minor repairs and modifications. It was when an extensive new building project was under construction that the Order reverted to extraordinary means of fund raising, such as taxes on the knights and the Maltese. The two periods for which we have detailed knowledge of regular expenditure, one at the beginning, the other at the close of the eighteenth century, both show spending keeping more or less to the prescribed limits. A maximum of 300 scudi a week was set in 1723, and the engineer Mondion reported an average weekly expenditure of between 250 and 350 scudi in the years 1724 to 1731.[91] His report records only fairly routine work, the major item being the addition of barrack rooms to St. Elmo, for fort Manoel which was then under construction was being financed by the grand master. After a somewhat discouraging year in 1765 when expenditure rose to 36,000 scudi, three times the permitted level, an investigation was ordered, and the congregation of fortification gradually managed to reduce its spending to approximately

85 The commissioners of fortification spent the following amounts: between 1 November 1657 and 7 May 1661, 11,297 scudi (AOM 121, f. 191v.); 2,002 scudi in the last ten months of 1662 (AOM 260, f. 144); and 2,400 scudi in the year 1662-3 (AOM 6397, f. 229).

86 AOM 261, ff. 59 (29 October 1666) and 97 (1 March 1668).

87 AOM 266, f. 162 (6 June 1715).

88 AOM 267, f. 203 (4 June 1723).

89 AOM 272, f. 28 (18 July 1765).

90 AOM 309, f. 158 (1776); AOM 1015, p. 441 (14 September 1795).

91 Clerkenwell, MS. O 1, item 20.

12,000 scudi a year.[92] In fact the annual average expenditure in the ten years before 1788 was 12,765 scudi, although the actual yearly totals fluctuated between 6,118 scudi in 1780 and 15,987 in 1785.[93] However, the treasury was prepared to offer additional funds to cover any work beyond the routine – to the tune of 6,000 scudi in 1788 to repair the dilapidated coastal batteries of Gozo and western Malta.[94] It remains the case that to confound further any attempt at calculating the total cost of the fortifications, even in this comparatively well documented period, the value of supplies issued by the commissioner of works was excluded from the 12,000 scudi.[95]

Any estimate of the true extent of the Order's financial commitment to the fortifications must always take into account the large sums which were spent in the initial years of any project while enthusiasm and fear were driving forces. Once the immediate danger had passed, or the grand master had died, funds became more restricted, the level of activity tended to subside, and the undertaking to drag on interminably. This pattern can be seen clearly in the building of Floriana, Sta. Margherita and Cottonera; on the other hand, the first flush of enthusiasm carried the work on Valletta to the point in 1571 where it was feasible to transfer the convent, so ensuring its completion. For the cost of Valletta itself there are only estimates, such as the one made in 1568 that the work then completed had cost 200,000 scudi, and that the fortifications would require another 100,000 and the public buildings likewise 100,000 scudi, a considerable sum when compared to the same author's calculation that the total annual revenues of the Order amounted to 116,732 scudi.[96] Another measure of the scale of expenses may be obtained by considering the towers built by Alof de Wignacourt in the first two decades of the seventeenth century.[97] Although forts St. Lucian (1610), St. Thomas (1614), and St. Mary on Comino (1618) show great similarity in design, their costs varied, being 11,745, 13,450 and 18,628 scudi respectively. As no breakdown is available one cannot say what proportion, if any, of the increase can be

---

92 AOM 1015, p. 52 (25 February 1766); the sums spent in the following years were: 26,255 scudi in the year ending 30 April 1767 (AOM 272, f. 88v.); 20,304 in 1768 (*ibid.*, f. 151v.); 17,226 in 1769 (*ibid.*, f. 198v.); 17,719 in 1770 (*ibid.*, f. 232v.); 15,171 in 1771 (*ibid.*, f. 249); 16,755 in 1772 (*ibid.*, f. 251); 15,717 in 1773 (AOM 273, f. 20).

93 Average figures – Bosredon; actual figures – AOM 273, f. 254 (1780) and AOM 274, f. 88 (1785).

94 AOM 159, f. 273 (3 December 1777); AOM 274, f. 136 (7 July 1788).

95 AOM 159, f. 273 (3 December 1777).

96 Urb. Lat. 833, ff. 192 and 183v.

97 AOM 6385, ff. 192-4v.

ascribed to rising prices rather than to a more elaborate design. The other two forts, St. Paul (1609) and Sta. Maria delle Grazie (1620) were smaller structures altogether, costing only 6,748 and 4,948 scudi respectively.

In the early years large sums were also spent on the Floriana lines, a total of 39,965 scudi being paid out under contract to master craftsmen in the first year of operations and another 32,102 in the following seven months.[98] The late 1640s show a marked decline with only 25,815 scudi being paid to craftsmen over a seventeen-month period, but even this compares favourably with 2,400 scudi per annum which the common treasury was allocating in 1657.[99] In the meanwhile the Order had diverted its interest and money to the construction of the mezzalunas outside the Porta Reale of Valletta; these in 1642 were reported as consuming over 67,000 scudi out of a total of 83,000 scudi.[100] The estimates as to how much Floriana was to cost differed widely depending upon whether one was in sympathy with Floriani's plans or not. The lowest sum quoted was 72,000 scudi calculated on the basis that the perimeter measured 12,000 canes and that the works had been contracted out at six scudi per cane,[101] but even Floriani always talked in terms of a larger cost than that, and estimated that 125,000 scudi would be needed to complete the project in two years.[102] This was disputed by his critics, two of whom claimed, probably with justice, that 200,000 to 300,000 scudi would be nearer the mark,[103] for after all, Floriana was an ambitious project built on difficult virgin terrain. Moreover, as the Order's income was then about 300,000 a year,[104] this highest estimate still represented a smaller percentage of its resources than the 400,000 estimate for the building of Valletta.

Examples of the divergence between estimates and actual expenditure are hardly surprising. What is more startling is the apparent accuracy of Philippe de Vendôme's claim that 40,000 scudi would suffice for his scheme to defend the coast by means of batteries and redoubts.[105] Indeed, in the years 1715 and 1716 41,561 scudi were paid

98 AOM 111, f. 276v. (29 November 1636); AOM 112, f. 45v. (20 June 1637).

99 AOM 116, f. 263 (16 September 1649); AOM 260, f. 20 (1657).

100 AOM 257, f. 114v. (13 June 1642) – it does not state the exact period covered by the account.

101 Borg, p. 34; Floriani claimed the cost was five scudi a cubed cane (Barb. Lat. 6697, f. 79) but neither figure represents the true cost.

102 Barb. Lat. 6689, f. 364 (6 October 1635).

103 AOM 6402, f. 365, and Chigi, R I 25, f. 306.

104 Barb. Lat. 5035, f. 13v.

105 AOM 6556, p. 91 (1715).

out to the contractors working in sites on the east coast from Marsaxlokk to the Gozo Channel and on Gozo and Comino.[106] It is possible that this sum represents the major outlay on these defences, for 1,000 scudi seems to have been an acceptable contemporary estimate for the construction of a battery, and besides, it was later claimed that these works had been poorly, perhaps thereby implying cheaply, built.[107]

By 1716, however, the Order had succeeded in accumulating a backlog of so many unfinished schemes that even to complete the works around the harbours would, it was estimated, cost 221,750 scudi, of which 146,950 represented urgent work.[108] The recommendations made at this time by Tigné seem to have been carried out, but at what cost we do not know. A report written only six years later lists still further work necessary to complete the same forts, with a projected expenditure of 55,800 scudi.[109] Thus in 1722 it was estimated that the perfection of the harbour fortifications, the most recent of which had been commenced in 1670, would cost as much as the construction of fort Manoel.[110]

The Order's financial state, however, exerted remarkably little influence over the timing of building operations. Valletta was built when the treasury was empty, and as late as 1793, after the confiscation of the French properties, fort Tigné was constructed. Any outburst of intensive activity can usually be traced to rumours of an imminent Turkish attack, for it was only after such a threat was acknowledged by the Order that it would mobilize its financial resources and activate the extraordinary sources from which it could raise sums of the magnitude required to initiate any substantial new project. Thus, the nature of the funds available for the construction of fortifications ensured that work commenced only when danger seemed very close at hand. Fortunately the threats never materialized: the Turks never descended on the islands in force after 1565. Once the emergency had passed, immediate interest in defence subsided, the extraordinary methods of fund raising were allowed to lapse, and a backlog of unfinished projects began to accumulate until the next

106 AOM 6543.

107 RML MS. 1301, p. 175, report by Tigné, 1716. AOM 267, f. 147 (25 September 1722).

108 RML MS. 1301, pp. 165-77; the total breaks down thus: Valletta–13,300 scudi, Floriana–37,300, Senglea–6,900, Birgu–24,800, Sta. Margherita–81,000, Cottonera–47,500, Ricasoli–10,950.

109 AOM 1011, f. 43 (8 July 1722).

110 RML MS. 1301, p. 169; estimated cost of fort Manoel was 28,000 scudi; there is evidence that it cost more than this (Clerkenwell, MS. O 1, item 15) but this was paid by the grand master.

scare, when the same pattern was repeated. Changing ideas about the most efficient design of fortifications undoubtedly caused the Order to embark on new building schemes. By 1635 Valletta was considered old fashioned because it possessed no outworks, and in the eighteenth century the Order decided to change its strategy and oppose any enemy on the beaches, but without the pressure of an external threat it is doubtful if work would ever have been begun. After all, the earliest proposal to build a new city on Sciberras was made in 1524, forty-two years before the first stone was laid. At the end of the eighteenth century, the only period for which there are reliable accounts, the importance attached to military matters, at a time when the Order's original role as protector of Christendom had lost credibility, is clearly illustrated: out of a total of 1,285,334 scudi the navy consumed 474,943, land defence, including fortifications, 195,339, and hospitaller activities 123,109.[111] In 1796 the percentage of the total spent on defence had risen; the navy cost 429,221 scudi, land defence 143,264, and hospitaller activities 146,481, while the total expenditure had fallen to 1,138,442.[112] It may be said therefore, that the Order was able to finance fortification schemes when the need arose, and although it might claim to be under financial strain as a result of its building programmes, military necessity always overcame financial difficulties.

---

111 Thornton, p. 10; these figures are the annual average between 1779 and 1788.
112 Thornton, p. 26.

Chapter 12

The Final Collapse

The final collapse of the Order in Malta may in one sense be considered a military collapse. The Order was dispossessed of the Maltese islands by a hostile army which forced a surrender by its superiority in both numbers and ability. The French landed about 40,000 troops against the knights' total force of 17,000 men.[1] The defenders, however, were hardly put to the test; the Order was not defeated in battle because it made no concerted attempt to fight the French. Although the invaders encountered sporadic resistance it could scarcely be claimed that they were vigorously opposed. What caused the knights to surrender to the French revolutionary army with barely a shot being fired? It was not that the fortifications were inadequate; Napoleon wrote in his memoirs 'the place certainly possessed immense physical means of resistance';[2] the fault lay rather in the knights' lack of resolve, and, above all, in the lack of leadership; to quote Napoleon again, he perceived that the place had 'no moral strength whatever'. In seeking to explain the final collapse of the Order in Malta one must look therefore beyond the military situation and consider the condition of the Order and its position in late-eighteenth-century Europe.

One of the primary aims of the Order was to fight the infidel. By the 1790s this was not a simple proposition. In any case diplomatic alliances no longer respected the division of Europe into a Moslem and a Christian camp. As early as 1535 France had concluded a peace treaty with the Turks which was renewed in 1581, 1597, 1604, 1673

1 Ryan, p. 279.
2 Quoted by Cavaliero, p. 231.

and 1740. The French obtained trading rights in the Ottoman Empire and an ally ideally situated to assist in their struggle against the Hapsburgs. By the eighteenth century France was even prepared to intervene openly on behalf of the Turks in disputes with the Order. In 1751 Louis XV secured the release of Pasha Mustapha and ten years later purchased the *Ottoman crown* (which had been sailed to Malta by its mutinous Christian crew) from the knights and restored it to the sultan.[3] Even the Barbary corsairs were no longer considered the universal enemy of Christendom, and the French and English were rarely molested in the eighteenth century largely on account of their naval strength which forced the corsairs to respect treaty agreements.[4] The smaller states followed the lead given by the great trading nations and concluded treaties with the Barbary states. By 1750 a whole series of agreements had been concluded whereby, in return for tribute, the corsairs guaranteed not to attack a nation's shipping.[5] Although the legal problems surrounding the *corso* (as the pursuit of corsair activity was known) became more complex the Order continued to pursue Barbary vessels. Even so the activity of the navy, and of corsair ships sailing under the flag of the Order or of the grand master, fell during the eighteenth century,[6] so that it became hardly possible for the knights to claim that they were attacking the infidel wherever they encountered him, or that they were any longer undertaking the task of protecting Christendom.

In the course of the Order's rule Malta became an important trading centre. In the eighteenth century its value was recognized as a staging-post for Levantine trade. Merchants stored bonded goods in the quayside warehouses which sprang up, and many ships found Malta a convenient port at which to fulfil their quarantine requirements.[7] Once again the crusading instincts of the Order came into conflict with more mundane practical considerations. There was for example a significant volume of trade between the island and the north-African Regencies; so much so that in 1735 the Bey of Tunis appealed to the knights to help him exterminate the corsairs who were using Sfax and Tunis harbours to disrupt his commerce.[8] Moreover, it was the French, by then established as the traditional allies of the Sultan,

---

3 Cavaliero, pp. 141-2.
4 Earle, p. 41.
5 Earle, p. 265.
6 Earle, pp. 121-2 and 267-70.
7 Blouet, p. 136; for details of the quarantine see P. Cassar, *Medical history*, pp. 285-301.
8 Blouet, p. 136; Cavaliero, p. 119.

who made extensive use of Malta as a half-way house for their Levantine trade. By far the greatest numbers of ships completing their quarantine in Malta were French.[9] Malta was essential to the supremacy of French commerce in the Levant and long before its conquest the island was virtually a French colony in many respects.[10] Many of the traders on the island were Frenchmen and much of the islands' trade was with France, so that the Order could not afford to offend the French king. In 1750 Pinto claimed that France more than any other nation profited from the services of the Order.[11] It was very much to the advantage of France for Malta to be able to defend herself, and there was never any question of the knights being denied military supplies even when France herself was at war.[12] The two nations even mounted combined operations against the north-African Regencies in 1728 and 1741.[13] Although no subsidies were paid to the Order, France was anxious that it should remain financially solvent, and it received favourable treatment when it stood to lose a considerable amount after the catastrophic collapse of John Law's financial schemes.[14] The decision in 1765 to allow the Maltese to enjoy the rights of citizens before French civil, criminal and commercial tribunals recognized the special relationship between the two countries.[15]

This dependence on France accorded badly with the Order's claims to be an independent, neutral body, and the close relations between the two did not go unnoticed. The general opinion in England was that Malta was a French naval base, which was perhaps somewhat unfair since the knights scrupulously provided the same facilities to all Christian powers, even to the Protestants.[16] In order to prevent a large war fleet sheltering in the harbours and thereby endangering its pretensions to neutrality, in 1758 the Order decreed that only four warships at a time could enter port.[17] Even so the Spaniards complained to Rome about the extent to which the Order was being governed according to the wishes of the French king,[18] but this was

---

9 Godechot, pp. 72-4.

10 Godechot, p. 67. Godechot probably overestimates the extent to which Malta was under French influence.

11 Godechot, p. 70.

12 Cavaliero, p. 49.

13 Cavaliero, p. 48.

14 Cavaliero, pp. 49 and 275.

15 Godechot, p. 71; A.O.M. 272, 61v.-64 (dated 12 July 1765).

16 Cavaliero, p. 48.

17 Godechot, p. 70; A.O.M. 271, f. 90.

18 Godechot, p. 71.

largely a case of 'sour grapes', for Spain had undoubtedly lost its position of protector which as suzerain of the islands it enjoyed in the sixteenth and for part of the seventeenth century. The islands' dependence on Sicily as a supplier of grain had traditionally allowed the Spaniards a measure of influence over the Order. The War of Spanish Succession, which eventually placed Bourbons on the thrones of Parma, Naples and Spain, in addition to that of France, led to greatly increased French presence and power in the Mediterranean, so that the Spaniards feared, and rightly so, that the Order was becoming French dominated. France provided by far the largest number of knights – 400 out of a total of 600 in 1789, and 200 out of the 332 knights present in Malta in 1798. This had always been the case, but in the eighteenth century the preponderance of French knights combined with growing French interest in the island itself to threaten the independent position of the Order at the very time when its attitude to the concept of crusade was becoming equivocal. The importance of France to the Order was reflected in the revenue which was derived from the lands in Europe. In the 1780s nearly half the responsions, 580,406 scudi, came from France, while the rest of Europe (Spain, Italy, Portugal, Germany and Bavaria) raised 648,390 scudi.[19] It was because of such overdependence on one country that the Order found itself in so serious a financial situation once this source had been cut off in 1792.

By the late eighteenth century the fate of the Order had become inextricably linked with that of France, and France experienced a revolution. Even before 1789 a number of the French knights had proved troublesome to Grand Master de Rohan. They were supporters, whether or not they were publicly declared members, of the Auvergnat Club which had been founded in 1776 by a group of knights belonging to the langue of Auvergne, who were determined to challenge De Rohan's authority and his manner of government which they considered autocratic.[20] The arena of conflict in 1776 was the chapter general which De Rohan, secure, in the possession of a papal bull forbidding all discussion of the grand master's status, summoned to sanction a rise in the responsions, but which his opponents hoped would overhaul the machinery of government. The reformers proposed that the chaplains and servants-at-arms, supporters of De Rohan, should be disenfranchised, but the Auvergnats were overruled, the chaplains and servants-at-arms voted, the responsions were raised, but no major reforms in

19 Bosredon de Ransijat's accounts, A.O.M. 6406.
20 Cavaliero, pp. 164 and 171-4.

government were authorized. Despite his victory, De Rohan realized that the events of 1776 foreshadowed future troubles, and for the last years of its life in Malta the Order was plagued by internal dissensions, often trivial in themselves, but undermining morale and making the vow of obedience meaningless. They did nothing to improve the image of the Order abroad; the knights' role as crusaders was now discredited, and the Order was seen by its opponents as a body enjoying privileges which it did nothing to earn.

Thanks to the inaptitude of the ambassador in Paris, it was not long before the Order was attacked in the National Assembly, and early in 1790 a pamphlet appeared questioning its value: *A quoi bon l'Ordre de Malte?*[21] to which the author gave the reply 'the Order of Malta is good for nothing'. The Order's defenders pointed out its services to French commerce, the nursing care that it had provided for sailors and the shelter which it had afforded to French ships. Despite attempts to establish its position as a sovereign body independent of the French clergy, the Order finally suffered the confiscation of its property in September 1792. Suitable pensions from public funds were to be given to members of the Order and their tenants provided they remained in France.[22] This action was hardly unexpected but there was no way in which the blow could be softened. The Order had lost almost half its revenues, and the influx of penniless refugees into Malta requiring financial support was increasing the demands on the common treasury. Although economies were made, these could not tackle the fundamental problem, which was that the whole financial basis of the Order had been shattered. Worse was to come, for as the revolutionary armies marched triumphantly eastwards and southwards, commanderies in the Rhineland, Switzerland and Italy were lost, so that by 1797 the income of the common treasury had dropped to a third of its former level.

It was hardly surprising that the Order which had leant so heavily on French revenues and support should now look elsewhere for a protector to fill the gap. Russia in particular was beginning to show an interest in Malta,[23] and the grand master had also allowed Maltese sailors to enlist on a British warship.[24] With his grandiose plans for conquest in the east, Napoleon could not allow the strategically placed

---

21 Published Paris, 1790; Cavaliero, p. 183.
22 Ryan, p. 208; Cavaliero, p. 200.
23 See A. P. Vella, *Malta and the Czars* (Malta, 1965).
24 Cavaliero, p. 208.

island to fall into hostile hands. Realizing that Malta, with its strongly fortified storm-free harbours and its weak government, was too rich a prize not to be coveted by his rivals, Napoleon planned a conquest on his way to Egypt. The very fortifications on which the knights had expended so much of their substance provoked an attack, for now the island could no longer be ignored as a barren rock, albeit with safe anchorages. It was now a strongly fortified, but weakly defended, citadel which no sensible commander could afford to leave in his rear, for fear it might be taken by his enemies and turned to their advantage. The Order had become so weak, partly as the result of events beyond its control, that its claims to neutrality could no longer be respected.

Napoleon certainly believed the possession of Malta to be important. In May 1797 he wrote 'the island of Malta is of major interest for us. The grand master [De Rohan] is dying and it looks as though his successor will be a German... Valletta has 37,000 inhabitants who are very well disposed towards the French; there are no longer any English in the Mediterranean; why should not our fleet or the Spanish, before going into the Atlantic, sail to Valletta and occupy it? There are only 500 knights and the regiment of the Order is only 600 strong. If we do not, Malta will fall into the power of the king of Naples. This little island is worth any price to us.'[25] Although the islands appeared to be under-garrisoned, Napoleon realized that if the knights put up a spirited resistance, he might be forced to undertake a prolonged siege which would allow the other interested powers time to appear on the scene. It was necessary, therefore, to take Malta peacefully or, if force were needed, swiftly. The French therefore cultivated contacts in the island. Napoleon had been furnished with a list of discontented French knights by the Maltese Vincenzo Barbara who had been exiled in 1797 for his part in an obscure plot to seize arms from the arsenal in Qormi.[26] A French agent after sounding the French knights reported that Napoleon could count on the support of only about twenty out of two hundred, and that there were many émigrés on the island who could be assumed to be implacably opposed to the aims of the revolution. On the other hand, he found that there was a possibility of support from the Maltese who could see no advantage in remaining under the rule of the Order.[27] A further report which indicated

---

25 J. E. Howard, *Letters and Documents of Napoleon* (London, 1961), I, 191.
26 Cavaliero, p. 216; Ryan, p. 255.
27 Howard, I, 201; Cavaliero, p. 217.

that the Maltese could be expected to welcome Napoleon was received from Admiral de Brueys in March 1798.[28]

The decision to conquer Malta was taken by the Directory on 12 April 1798.[29] The decree justified the action on the grounds that the grand master had refused to recognize the French Republic; that he had welcomed *émigrés*; that he had allied himself with the Republic's enemies and appeared to be contemplating surrendering the island to them. There seems no doubt that Grand Master Hompesch was warned of the coming attack, but he did nothing to prepare the island.[30] Indeed the inadequate state of the defences had already been demonstrated in March when De Brueys appeared off Malta with seventeen French warships. Only a third of the men considered necessary to defend the island had been mustered,[31] but there was little that could be done to increase the numbers in view of the Order's financial situation. Instead Hompesch had to hope that Russia or Austria would act to prevent Malta falling to the French. Hompesch was not the man to lead the Order in time of crisis; he failed to give a firm lead and such resistance as took place was not coordinated or executed according to any plan.

A scheme did exist for the defence of the islands which had been drawn up in the early years of the century, endorsed by the French engineers in 1761, and finally updated in 1797. This plan proposed that the enemy should first be actively resisted as he landed, and then as he marched across the country to take up siege positions around the main fortresses. The resources in manpower which this plan required will be appreciated when it is realized that there were forty-four possible landing places along a coastline of thirty or forty miles. The second line of defence was a line of entrenchments running through Naxxar, which divided the northern part of Malta from the harbour fortresses. Finally if this line could not be held, the troops were to withdraw into Valletta and prepare for a siege. Despite the opposition of the engineer Tousard, the congregation of war refused to change the plan of defence, and would not accept his advice, and the advice of others, to concentrate the forces available to defend the harbour fortresses.

One reason which Hompesch put forward for not withdrawing into the fortresses was that he feared that the Maltese, once within the walls, might turn against the Order, for he thought that they had

---

28 Cavaliero, p. 219; Ryan, p. 265.
29 Decree published Howard, I, 233.
30 Cavaliero, pp. 221-2; Ryan, p. 263.
31 Cavaliero, p. 219; Ryan, p. 265.

perhaps been infected by revolutionary ideas. Whether for this reason, or because of the terrifying tales that they had heard of the revolutionary soldiery, there were good grounds to believe that the islanders would not put up a resolute defence against the French.

At first, however, Hompesch was prepared to make a show of resistance. When Napoleon requested that his fleet be allowed to take on water, the grand master, backed by the council, insisted on the old formula for preserving neutrality: he would allow only four ships to enter at a time. This was scarcely a practical proposition with a fleet the size of Napoleon's, five to six hundred vessels. Napoleon therefore issued instructions for an attack on the island on 10 June.[32] Four days earlier the Order had made its dispositions for defence. The forces were divided into some twenty-eight separate minor commands each in the charge of a knight.[33] In accordance with the agreed plans these were scattered around the island and not concentrated in the fortress. Napoleon, knowing that the conquest had to be swift before any assistance could reach the knights, landed an overwhelming force of 40,000 men against the Order's 17,000. The landing at Marsaxlokk was unopposed; at St. Julian's bay the Malta regiment soon retreated and the only counterattack came from some boats commanded by the knight De Soubiras under the covering fire of fort Tigné. The French under General Vaubois marched to the Città Vecchia where the inhabitants decided resistance was futile and surrendered once their freedom had been guaranteed. The force which landed at St. Paul's bay captured all the defences overlooking that bay and Mellieħa bay. In Gozo alone the French met spirited resistance, but by the end of the day the Gozitans, deserted by their commanding knight, had surrendered with promises of personal and religious liberty.

The congregation of war had failed in its task of maintaining the islands' defences in a state of readiness, having undoubtedly been hampered by the reluctance of the Order to allocate sufficient funds except in an emergency. The artillery was old and unreliable; the munitions and powder had not been distributed correctly; the entrenchments along the coasts had never been completed; and, in the years immediately before 1798, the expenditure on the fortifications had been cut back as an economy measure, so that the standard of maintenance, never beyond reproach, fell even further.

---

32 Howard, I, 235.

33 Description of the French landing is taken from Ryan, pp. 279-83. For the separate commands set up see Miège, III, 39-41.

Thus by the evening of 10 June 1798 all Malta and Gozo except the harbour forts were held by the French. Although the Order's scheme to defend the islands by opposing any landing had failed disastrously, the knights were not in an impossible situation. Because there had been so little fighting they had not lost many men and they had now consolidated their forces within the fortresses, and it might well have been possible to hold out for a week or so in the hope that some relief might arrive. But even the appearance of such succour might pose problems, for it was most likely to materialize in the form of either the British or the Russian navy, neither of which powers was Catholic, and both of which, despite the recent formation of a Russian priory, had ulterior motives, besides the well-being of the Order, for wishing to prevent the island falling under French control.

There was no simple solution to the situation in which the Order now found itself. Militarily it was in a defendable position, but future prospects were bleak. Aid, if it did come, could well threaten the whole concept of the Order as an international neutral body subject only to the pope and dedicated to fight only the infidel and never a Christian power. Moreover, the Order had outlived any usefulness which it had had as part of the defence of Europe against Moslem expansion. The whole concept of the Order was an anomaly in eighteenth-century Europe. The powers might tolerate the knights' possession of Malta while it suited their purpose, but by 1798 it was apparent that the Order could survive only under the wing of a protector. The island was such a strong fortress, strategically situated in the middle of the Mediterranean, that the question of who controlled the Order and Malta was of great importance especially to the naval powers.

Hompesch, however, was faced with a complex problem. He was besieged and although he could hold out for some time, any country which came to his aid might impose conditions which would jeopardize the Order's claim to be an independent sovereign body. He was afraid of dissension within the Order and he was convinced that the Maltese were not prepared to fight to maintain the Order's position. Indeed, in the face of the French attack, some of the Maltese militia had mutinied and murdered two knights who had been their officers.[34] Other officers deserted their posts, reporting to the council tales of flight and disobedience by their men. The knight Bosredon de Ransijat declared that he had undertaken to fight the infidel, and could not

34 The description of the events of 10-12 June is taken from Ryan, pp. 284-308 and Cavaliero, pp. 226-33.

fight his fellow countrymen, the French; he was imprisoned in St. Angelo. Overall the situation within the fortifications was confused; hearing only rumours, as no reliable information was available, neither the islanders nor many of the knights knew what was happening. In fact, although the council was in permanent session, neither it nor the grand master was providing any positive lead. Finally, when a deputation from the Maltese appeared on the evening of 10 June to plead that an armistice be arranged with Napoleon, the council decided to request one, and a twenty-four hour truce was agreed while the surrender of the islands was negotiated.[35]

The French Republic was granted rights of ownership and sovereignty over Malta;[36] in return the French would try to obtain for the grand master at the Congress of Rastadt a German principality of equal value. In the meantime he would be paid an annual pension of 300,000 francs. French knights present in Malta who had not actually fought against the Republic could return to France and receive a pension of 700 francs a year if under sixty years of age, and one 1,000 if over sixty. On 13 June the knights were expelled from Malta. Those over sixty who were not subjects of a power at war with France were allowed to remain; of the others only those who had been of use to Napoleon were allowed to stay. The list of those so exempted included Bosredon de Ransijat, De Fay the commissioner of fortifications, and Tousard the engineer,[37] although there is no evidence of the specific service which had been rendered either by De Fay or by Tousard. There does not in fact seem to have been a plot to undermine the defences of the island. Tousard had opposed the war plan which required that the enemy be resisted in the open, and, from the events which took place, his opposition can be seen to have been based on sound military judgement. De Fay and Tousard left soon afterwards as part of the French army of the east; the latter served with distinction in the campaigns of 1806, 1807, 1808 and 1809 in Prussia, Russia and Austria.[38] The grand master never obtained a German principality. Although the Treaty of Amiens provided that Malta, then in British hands, should be returned to the Order, the provision was never implemented. The island, which the British captured from the French in 1800, remained a British colony until independence was granted in 1964.

---

35 Howard, I, 236.
36 Convention published Howard, I, 236-7.
37 Cavaliero, p. 230; Ryan, p. 316.
38 Miège, III, 36.

When the attack by a hostile power, for which the Order had so long prepared by constantly adding to and modifying the fortifications, finally materialized, the enemy was France. Although the fate of the Order was of little consequence in the general struggle between the European powers, possession of its fortress stronghold was of vital importance. The loss of the French properties and those in the lands invaded by the French had left the Order in a desperate financial state, and even with the most drastic economies it was doubtful if it could have continued as an independent sovereign body. Although the knights had maintained their hospital and medical services, these had been curtailed after the loss of the French revenue. Their other major activity, pursuing Moslems, had dwindled into insignificance as the eighteenth century wore on. Here again they were restrained by cost but even more by the increasingly complex system of alliances between Christian and Moslem powers. Although there was still scope for the knights to act as hospitallers, by the end of the eighteenth century there was little opportunity for them to fulfil their now anachronistic role as a military crusading order. Undoubtedly the collapse of morale highlighted in the behaviour of Hompesch, was in part brought about by the disappearance of their military role. The Order of St. John of Jerusalem had by 1798 not reorientated itself sufficiently to be able fully to devote its energy to hospitaller and charitable deeds. Instead life in Malta had an aimless and purposeless, if often pleasant, character. It was, however, above all the deplorable lack of leadership in the crisis and the lack of the will to fight which led to the surrender of the stronghold of Valletta, Floriana and the Three Cities, before the French had made any attempt at assault. These fortifications were never tested. How long the revolutionary army with its backbone of veterans, could have been resisted by a determined garrison is a matter for speculation. Although the plan of defence based on opposing the enemy on the beaches (and therewith the system of redoubts, batteries and entrenchments built to execute the scheme) was discredited, the same could not be said of the major fortresses. Their contribution to the defeat was in the political sphere: the islands offered such strongly fortified harbours and military facilities that for any interested power to leave them in the hands of the debilitated Order was too great a risk; the islands had indeed to be conquered quickly before the Order joined the enemy camp.

Conclusion

The failure of the Order to put up a spirited resistance to Napoleon did ensure that the fortifications survived more or less intact. Even during the later lengthy blockade by the British they did not suffer unduly because the British hoped to force surrender through starvation rather than bombardment. The method by which the knights sought to up-date their defences, adding successive rings of fortifications, reveals the stages in the development of the vast system which still exists today. Although Malta was never a major European power, her fortifications are a fine example of the bastioned system of defence popular in Europe between the sixteenth and the eighteenth centuries. The defence of the island was a major concern of the knights and one to which they were prepared to devote money, energy and time. Although somewhat remote geographically from the rest of Europe, the knights were determined that their island defences should be in the mainstream of European development, allowing for modifications to suit local conditions and building materials. To this end they resolutely obtained the services of an expert from abroad whenever a new project was in the air. Whatever disadvantages ensued from the system whereby the designing engineer often in the space of a few weeks had his first sight of the island, drew up a scheme, supervised the initial stages of construction and then departed, they were thought to be outweighed by the excellence of the designs obtained. Perhaps the Order suspected that Malta was too isolated, and the opportunities for making one's reputation too restricted to attract as resident engineer a man of the calibre they required.

The knights saw themselves in the forefront of the Christian struggle against the infidel, although by the late eighteenth century their part in such of the contest as still continued had degenerated into little more than skirmishing with opposing piratical powers. The fortifications were primarily defensive, constructed to repel an invader or to withstand a siege. The offensive actions of the Order – the exploits in the Morea, the campaigns against the north-African states, the harassment of Moslem shipping – touched the fortifications only in so far as they excited retaliation against the home base of the troublesome knights. Yet the threat of such an assault produced a defensive reaction. The fabric, the design, the artillery, the provisioning and the garrisons of the fortifications were constantly inspected, while, on occasion, large and costly new works were initiated. Once the hope of reconquering Rhodes had been abandoned, the material and financial rewards accruing from the Order's aggressive foreign policy were far offset by the ever increasing cost of maintaining the fortresses, towers, redoubts, batteries and entrenchments, and of providing the islands with an adequate garrison. It could be argued that had the Order ceased its provocative behaviour, the vast investment of energy and money in the defences would no longer have been necessary. Leaving aside the fact that the aggression was not one-sided, the entire abandonment of a military role would have completely changed the nature of the Order, for its institutions had been built around its dual origin as a hospitaller and military organization. Any fundamental challenge to its crusading ideals, even if these were wearing somewhat thin, would have severely shaken the whole foundations and *raison d'être* of the Order. In the delicate international diplomatic intricacies of the eighteenth century there was no alternative military employment to which the knights could turn without jeopardizing their supranational status.

The construction of the fortifications impinged upon most aspects of the Order's existence in Malta. The commitment to fortify the island seems to have become an obsession, driving the knights to undertake schemes which, in retrospect, can be seen to have been beyond their powers to complete, maintain or man, and these vast undertakings had repercussions outside the purely military sphere. Indeed, in the history of the Order after 1565 the effectiveness or otherwise of the fortifications as defences is of remarkably little significance. The array of fortifications may have deterred the casual raider, but Malta's freedom from serious assault between 1565 and 1798 can perhaps be ascribed to the growing weakness of the Turkish empire and the Order's assumption of the role of French protégé. The Order was undoubtedly an anachronism in eighteenth-century Europe, and its military instincts, no longer able to find satisfaction in relentless pursuit of the infidel, may have found an outlet in building forts. Already in the construction of Cottonera in the late seventeenth century, the prestige of the grand master appears to have been of greater importance than the strategic value of the works.

Yet throughout their stay in Malta the knights clearly felt their military position to be insecure. Ambitious building programmes were undertaken on the grounds of military necessity regardless of the state of the Order's finances. What is remarkable is the way in which money could be raised when the occasion demanded it. Valletta was built, with some but not overwhelming outside help, when the Order's fortunes were at a very low ebb, and despite constant pleas of poverty vast works were erected in the course of the seventeenth century. The Order had, in fact, large resources of wealth in its European properties but the problem lay in mobilizing these resources. Where the knights failed was in sustaining their effort once the emergency had passed. Thus certain schemes took many years, and several emergencies, to complete, and in between bursts of activity the fortifications were starved of funds. As the complex of defences grew the demands for maintenance became greater, at the very time when the revenue reaching Malta appears to have been falling. But the fortifications, even although underfinanced in many ways, still consumed a huge sum and undoubtedly this drain contributed to the financial difficulties of the Order.

It was not only in the financial sphere that the fortifications left their mark. Their design and construction were issues of crucial importance to the knights. Schemes were considered and criticised, arguments ensued and opposing positions were adopted. The internal tensions of a supranational Order at a time of growing national awareness are revealed in the disputes over the merits and faults of the various projects. The increasing French domination of the Order, and the transfer from the Imperial into the French orbit of influence (as well as the growing prestige of French engineers) is shown by the choice of French engineers in the eighteenth century. At the same time the declining influence of the papacy is seen in its unwillingness, or inability, to intervene in the affairs of the island. The grand master became ever more autocratic, no longer seeking a papal brief before imposing taxes upon the Maltese.

Although the Maltese were undoubtedly justified when they complained that the demands of the fortifications imposed heavy burdens on them, they did also benefit from the works. It cannot be denied that they profited from the primary purpose of the defences: they were better protected than they had been in the past. Indeed the desire to be able to shelter the islanders was an important consideration in adopting the schemes of Floriani and Valperga. As rulers of the islands the grand masters had a duty to defend their subjects, but there were also more mundane considerations involved. As the French engineer François Bachelieu commented, men would not fight well if worried about the security of their families.[1] The Order felt obliged to protect the Maltese (even those of no military use) and their animals. Indeed, on occasion the Order deferred to the wishes of the islanders, and, for instance, abandoned plans to demolish the Città Vecchia and Castello after resistance from the inhabitants.

By the eighteenth century there were areas, such as Cottonera and Floriana, into which the country dwellers could retire when an attack was threatened. But the benefits from the increase in fortified area were to some extent offset by the growth in population. In 1760 it is estimated that there were 66,000 persons in Malta alone, and by 1798 there were probably 100,000 in the three inhabited islands. Despite the continual additions and improvements which the Order made to the defensive system of the islands, the remoter parts never became completely secure. The danger of a corsair attack persisted into the eighteenth century. People remained reluctant to settle in the northern part of Malta or around the coasts, and instead the large villages such as Qormi, Birkirkara, Żebbuġ and Żejtun grew up at the expense of smaller settlements. Above all, new towns grew up around the Grand Harbour and Marsamxett, close to, if not within, the encircling fortifications. Within the new harbour fortresses the knights attempted to create a planned urban environment, laying out regular grid-iron street plans, issuing building regulations and exercising what supervision they could.[2] In Gozo, which suffered even more than Malta from raids, the development of rural settlements was delayed until the eighteenth century, by which time the dangers of corsair attack had become less. Although the Order's strategy in the eighteenth century stressed

---

1 A.O.M. 6552, f. 44v. (1715).

2 J.Q. Hughes, 'Give me time and I will give you life: Francesco Laparelli and the building of Valletta, Malta', *Town Planning Review*, XLIX (1978), 61-74; E. Sammut, 'L'officio delle case ed i regolamenti per la fabbrica della Valletta (1556-1629)' in *Atti del XV Congresso di Storia dell'Architettura: l'architettura a Malta dalla preistoria all'ottocento* (Rome, 1970), pp. 387-99; B. Blouet, 'Town planning in Malta 1530-1798', *Town Planning Review*, XXXV (1964), 183-93; S.R. Borg Cardona, 'The Officio delle Case and the housing laws of the early grand masters', *Law Journal* (Malta, 1951).

the importance of defending the coasts and preventing a landing, it is unlikely that this changed strategy was of any direct benefit to the villagers. The increasing security of the country dwellers was the result of a general decrease in corsair activity rather than the fruit of the deterrent value of the entrenchments, batteries and redoubts built to repulse a landing force.

Malta undoubtedly gained some financial benefits from the construction programmes. Extra money was drawn in from abroad to pay for the works and this filtered into the economy in general. The principal building material, limestone, was available locally and quarrying businesses prospered. Some commodities, such as wood, had to be imported but, as far as possible, building techniques were adapted to suit those materials obtainable locally. The Order employed Maltese craftsmen to build and maintain the fortifications and the arrival of the knights led to a rapidly expanding construction industry, in answer to both civil and military needs. Some islanders, therefore, profited considerably from the many building contracts which the Order issued, and the craftsmen were but one example of the growing number of Maltese who, under the rule of the knights, became engaged in non-agricultural trades and pursuits. Apart from stone, however, Malta had few resources and armaments, munitions and other military supplies had to be imported. The extent to which the whole fortification entreprise stimulated the economy can, in any case, be overstated. Malta's growing prosperity in the eighteenth century depended largely on cotton; wealth was generated through commerce and not by the building of the fortifications.[3] Indeed, military activities and naval cruises often *caused* financial problems and tempted the Order to resort to expedients such as the issuing of copper coins, which actually harmed trade. If the endless expansion of the fortification network seemed to signal continuing hostility to the Moslem powers, in practice, at least where trading was concerned, attitudes had softened a good deal.

The schemes for fortification impressed themselves on the Maltese through two principal demands – for their labour and their money. The islanders did not submit without protest, but at times their resistance to the burdens imposed by the fortifications seems to have been symptomatic of a general resentment at what they considered the Order's high-handed methods of government. Without outside support this resistance failed and the Maltese were forced to rely on the

3 A. Luttrell, 'Eighteenth-century Malta: prosperity and problems', *Hyphen*, III (1982), 43-6.

paternalistic benevolence of the Order. The knights, however, were concerned primarily with the well-being of their own Order, and, while they did not exploit the Maltese ruthlessly, the needs of the islanders inevitably took second place. Increasingly in the course of the eighteenth century the Maltese showed their resentment of the Order's rule. Doubts as to the loyalty of the islanders made Hompesch reluctant to concentrate his forces within the harbour fortresses for fear that they might mutiny. He followed instead the strategy laid down in the early years of the century of opposing an invader in the field – a strategy totally inappropriate given the troops under his command. The island was not, however, lost simply because of a mistaken strategy or because of a failure to maintain the fortifications adequately. The heavy defence burden borne by the Order of St. John, which by the late eighteenth century was far beyond its means, was unable in the final analysis to compensate for the growing social and moral decay, the increasing failure of nerve and doubt as to mission which were such a feature of its leadership during the Napoleonic period.

Appendices

Appendix i

Currency and Measurements

On taking possession of Malta the Order of St. John insisted on obtaining authority from Charles V to mint its own coinage, believing this to be essential in establishing *de facto* independent sovereignty. The practice, established at Rhodes, of minting gold, silver and copper coins was continued in Malta. Everyday transactions within the island were conducted in silver coins (tari and multiples of tari) and in fractional currency both silver and copper, made up of carlini, cinquine, grani and piccioli, while for larger dealings the gold zecchino, similar to the Venetian ducat, was available [see Table I]. The carlino and cinquina were originally silver coins but after 1622 the latter was minted only in copper and a century later the carlino suffered the same fate. Although the Sicilian scudo was employed as the unit of account, it was not until the rule of Vilhena that a Maltese silver scudo coin, equivalent to twelve tari, was issued.

To ease problems arising from delay in receiving revenues from the priories, the knights occasionally issued fiduciary copper coinage to be redeemed when monies were remitted from Europe, not only in small denominations but also in two and four tari pieces. Silver and copper coins of the same denomination were nominally of equal value; in practice, however, the holder of copper was liable to lose up to thirty per cent of its value on converting it to silver. Even the value of the gold and silver coins varied depending as it did on fineness and weight.

This meant that each coin had to be weighed prior to any commercial transaction.

The exchange rates between Maltese and foreign currencies naturally fluctuated and this created tremendous problems for the Order, which drew so much of its income from abroad. Devaluation, depreciation and other economic factors could and did lead to rapid changes in the relative values of currencies, and those lists of exchange rates which do survive are valid only for their date of compilation. It is not therefore possible to make general comparisons between costs in Malta and elsewhere. With the introduction of Maltese scudi coins in the eighteenth century, the Order appears to have abandoned the Sicilian scudo as a unit of account and adopted a local scudo unit. This change was probably prompted by the increasing divergence in value between the Maltese and the Sicilian scudo, the latter being worth twice the former by the mid-eighteenth century. There is certainly no evidence of any significant discrepancy between the value of the scudo coin and the scudo accounting unit during the Order's closing years in Malta.

When the British arrived in 1800 they fixed the exchange rate at six shillings and eight pence to the zecchino and at one shilling and eight pence to the scudo. Although the Order's copper coinage was withdrawn in 1827 the silver and gold currency was allowed to circulate freely until 1886. Even after its withdrawal the memory of the old coinage survived and before the decimalisation of 1972 old names continued to denote certain values. Thus 2½d. was referred to as *tliet karnijet* [*karlinijiet*] (three carlini), half a crown as *tmintax irbiegħi* (eighteen tari) and 1s. 3d. as *disa' rbajja'* (nine tari).'[1]

The relative value of the zecchino and the scudo varied according to intrinsic value.

Table I: Maltese money

6 piccioli or dinieri	1 grano
5 grani	1 cinquina
2 cinquine	1 carlino
2 carlini	1 taro
12 tari	1 scudo
30 tari	1 oncia or pezza

1 For further details of the Order's monetary system, see H. Calleja Schembri, *Coins and Medals of the Knights of Malta* (London, 1908; reprinted 1966); J. C. Sammut, 'The coinage of the Order of St. John in Malta', Thirteenth Council of Europe art exhibition: *The Order of St. John in Malta* (Malta, 1970), pp. 47-52; M. Sant, 'Minting and attempted recalling of fiduciary copper coinage in Malta', *Melita Historica*, VI (1972), 60-80; Hoppen, 'The finances of the Order'; F. Restelli and J.C. Sammut, *The Coinage of the Knights in Malta*, 2 vols. (Malta, 1977).

As a small efficiently administered state, Malta enjoyed a standardized system of weights and measures throughout the rule of the knights. The standard unit of linear measurement was the cane which was that normally employed by the engineers whatever their country of origin. While in Malta they normally conformed to local usage, stating their measurements in canes and palms [see Table II]. The Maltese measurement for land area, the salma, was not, however, employed in calculating the dimensions of the fortifications. Occasionally an engineer would use a foreign unit, more often than not omitting to mention either its value or its precise provenance. Where an equivalent can be calculated, or an informed guess made as to the value, this has been given in the text. Because both British and Maltese units were standardized as early as the sixteenth century, the equivalent values should remain constant throughout the period under consideration. However, as the style of many of the engineers' reports makes it more than possible that their measurements were merely approximate, and that adjustments were made on the ground, any effort at precise conversion may give a spurious impression of accuracy and inflexibility on the part of their authors.

The Maltese also used a foot measurement (*piede*) equivalent to 11.167 inches. The toise used can be identified as the standard French unit equivalent to 6.395 feet or 1.949 metres.

Table II: Measurements

Linear

12 inches (*pulzieri*)	1 palm (*xiber*)
8 palms (*xbar*)	1 cane (*qasba*)

Maltese	*British*	*Metric*
1 inch	.859 inches	.02183 metres
1 palm	10.312 inches	.26190 metres
1 cane	2.292 yards	2.09500 metres
Square		
1 salma	4.444 acres	1.798 hectares

Appendix ii

Visiting Engineers Employed in Malta

*Name**	*Date(s) of visit(s)*	*Place of Origin*	*Full-time Employer*	*Membership of the Order (if any)*
(?) Piccino	1532-35	Florence		
Antonio Ferramolino	1535 1541	Bergamo	Viceroy of Sicily	
Pietro Prato	1552	Italy	Viceroy of Sicily	
Bartolomeo Genga	1558	Cesena	Duke of Urbino	
Baldassare Lanci	1562	Urbino	Duke of Florence	
Francesco Laparelli	1566-68 1569-70	Cortona	Pope	
Gabrio Serbelloni	1566	Milan	King of Spain	knight of justice
Giorgio Palearo, Il Fratino	1566	Italy	King of Spain	
Giovanni Luigi Vitelli, Marquis of Cetona	1565	Città di Castello	King of Spain	
Scipio Campi	?1566 1576	Pesaro	King of Spain	
Pompeo Floriani*	1576	Macerata	King of Spain	
Giovanni Rinaldini*	1599	Ancona	King of France	
Pietro Paolo Floriani*	1635-36	Macerata	Pope	knight of honour
Jardin	1636-?38	France	Landgrave of Hesse Darmstadt	
Vincenzo Maculano da Firenzuola	1638	Firenzuola	Pope	
Giovanni de' Medici, Marquis of St. Angelo	1640	Florence	Grand Duke of Tuscany	
Blaise François, Count de Pagan*	1645	France	King of France	
Louis, Viscount d'Arpajon	1645	France	King of France	
Louis Nicolas de Clerville	1645	France	King of France	knight of justice
Giovanni Bendinelli Pallavicino	1645	Italy		knight of justice

Domenico Guazzo	1645-46	Italy	Grand Duke of Tuscany	
Antonio Maurizio, Count Valperga*	1670	Turin	Duke of Savoy	
Carl Grunenberg	1681 1687 1689-90	Flanders	Viceroy	knight of honour
Claude de Colongues	1703	France	King of France	knight of grace
Johan Hecker	1708	Sweden	Pope	
Rougemont	1714-15	France	King of France	
René Jacques de Tigné	1715 1716 1723	France	King of France	knight of grace
Victor-Hyacinthe d'Artus	1715	France	King of France	
Philippe de Vendôme	1715	France	King of France	knight of justice
André de Tressemane	1715	France	King of France	knight of justice
Jean Charles de Folard*	1715	France	King of France	
Philippe Maigret*	1715-16	France	King of France	
François Charles Count de Bourlamaque	1761	France	King of France	
Pontleroy	1761	France	King of France	
Thomas de Comtes Masino Valperga di Caluso	1761	Turin		

*An asterisk against a man's name indicates that he published at least one work.

Appendix iii

Engineers Abroad Consulted by the Order

*Name**	*Date of Consultation*	*Place of Origin*	*Employer*
Lelio Brancaccio*	1636, 1638	Naples	Spain
Ansaldo de Mari	1638	Genoa	
Niccolò d'Este	1638		Genoa
Bartholomeo Bianco	1638	Como	Genoa
Orazio Grassi	1638	Savona	Savoy
Count Carlo Castellamonte*	1638	Piedmont	Savoy
François Lecamus	1638	France	France
? Capponi	1638	France	France
Henri de Nogaret d'Eperon, Duke of Candale	1638	France	France
Giovanni de Garay	1638		Spain
Count Ferrante Bolognino Attendolo	1638	Milan	Spain
Giuseppe Baracca	1638	Milan	Spain
? Bracelli	1638		Florence
Giovanni Francesco Cantagallina	1638	Borgo S. Sepolcro	Florence
Claudio Riccardo	1639		Spain
Giovanni Rudolfo Vertmiller	1639		
? Montbrun, Marquis of St. André	1670	France	Venice
Gaspare Beretta	1670	Milan	Spain
Count Verneda	1671		Venice
Sébastien Le Prestre de Vauban	1681	France	France
François Blondel*	1681	France	France
François de Beaufort	1681	France	France
François Houssaye	1681	France	France
Pierre Mallel	1681	France	France
Charles de Sauvage de la Boissière	1681	France	France
Alain Manesson Mallet*	1681	France	France
Jean Baptiste Favart	1716	France	France
Antoine Le Prestre de Vauban	1716	France	France
Charles Guy de Valory	1716	France	France

Antoine de Montaigut	1734		Spain
Marquis Giuseppe Palmieri*	1753	Martignano	Naples
Juan Martin Zermeño	1753	Spain	Spain
Charles Louis Auguste Fouquet, Duke of Belleisle	1753	France	France
Giuseppe Francesco Ignazio Bertola	1753	Piedmont	Spain

*An asterisk against a man's name indicates that he published at least one work.

Appendix iv

Resident Engineers Employed in Malta

Name	*Period Employed*	*Rank*	*Place or Country of Origin*	*Whether a Member of the Order*
Nicolò Bellavanti	1554-?	resident	Italy(?)	
Evangelista Menga	1560-67	resident	Brindisi	
Girolamo Cassar	1560 1567-92	capomastro resident	Malta	donat
Vittorio Cassar	1590-1607	resident	Malta	servant-at-arms
Francesco Buonamici	1635-59	resident	Lucca	knight of grace
Mederico Blondel	1659-98	resident	France	knight of grace
Romano Fortunato Carapecchia	1706-38	architect and water supply engineer	Rome	servant-at-arms
Johan Wespert Godfried Person	1707-09	second engineer	Mainz	
François Bachelieu	1713-?15	second engineer	France	
Charles François Gion de Mondion	1715-19 1720-33	resident resident	France	knight of grace
Francesco Marandon	1727-34 1734-62	second engineer resident	Turin	
Stephen de Tousard	?1793-98	resident	France	servant-at-arms

Appendix v

Grand Masters of the Order of St. John of Jerusalem in Malta

Philippe Villiers de l'Isle Adam	French	1530-34
Pietro del Ponte	Italian	1534-35
Didier de St. Jaille	French	1535-36
Juan Homedes	Aragonese	1536-53
Claude de la Sengle	French	1553-57
Jean de la Valette-Parisot	French	1557-68
Pietro del Monte	Italian	1568-72
Jean l'Evêque de la Cassière	French	1572-81
Hugues Loubens de Verdalle	French	1581-95
Martin Garzes	Aragonese	1595-1601
Alof de Wignacourt	French	1601-22
Luis Mendez de Vasconcellos	Portuguese	1622-23
Antoine de Paule	French	1623-36
Jean-Paul de Lascaris-Castellar	French	1636-57
Martin de Redin	Aragonese	1657-60
Annet de Clermont-Gessan	French	1660-60
Rafael Cotoner	Aragonese	1660-63
Nicolas Cotoner	Aragonese	1663-80
Gregorio Carafa	Italian	1680-90
Adrien de Wignacourt	French	1690-97
Ramon Perellos y Roccaful	Aragonese	1697-1720
Marcantonio Zondadari	Italian	1720-22
Antonio Manoel de Vilhena	Portuguese	1722-36
Ramon Despuig	Aragonese	1736-41
Manoel Pinto de Fonseca	Portuguese	1741-73
Francisco Ximenes de Texada	Aragonese	1773-75
Emmanuel de Rohan	French	1775-97
Ferdinand von Hompesch	German	1797-98

Glossary

Banquette An infantry fire-step built behind a parapet.

Bastion An artillery platform projecting from the main curtain wall in order to provide flanking fire; normally a four-sided work consisting of two faces and two flanks.

Braye A continuous outwork shielding the main enceinte and separated from it and from the counterscarp by ditches.

Caponier A protected passageway providing communication between the main enceinte and an outwork.

Cavalier A raised artillery platform sited within the main enceinte usually in the centre of a bastion.

Cordon The continuous rounded stone moulding running around a fort below the revetment of the parapet.

Counterguard A detached work standing in front of a bastion.

Counterscarp The side of the ditch opposite the main fort.

Covert-way A path outside the ditch sunk below the crest of the glacis to afford protection.

Crownwork An outwork composed of two long branches on either side and front consisting of a bastion and two demi-bastions.

Curtain A length of rampart between two bastions.

Demi-bastion A half bastion of one face and one flank.

Embrasure An opening made through a parapet or wall to allow a cannon to fire through the thickness.

Enceinte The principal, continuous perimeter of a fort.

Enfilade Firing coming from the flank in such a way that the effect is felt along the length of a fortification.

Fascines Bundles of sticks used in the construction of earth works.

Fausse-braye A parapet built between the base of the rampart and the ditch.

Glacis The slope between the covert-way and the open country designed to afford the attacker no cover.

Hornwork An outwork composed of two long branches on either side and a front consisting of two demi-bastions joined by a curtain.

Lunette A small outwork in the form of a little detached bastion.

Mezzaluna A detached outwork placed in front of a curtain. By the seventeenth century the term is interchangeable with 'ravelin'.

Orillion A protecting shoulder of a bastion intended to cover the guns and defenders on the flank.

Parapet A wall placed along the forward edge of fortifications, especially on a rampart, to afford protection to the defenders.

Place of Arms An enlarged area of the covert-way where troops can assemble.

Platform A level site for mounting an artillery battery.

Rampart A thick wall of earth, stone or masonry, which forms the main defence of a fortress, and is normally supported by a terraplein at the rear.

Ravelin A detached outwork placed in front of a curtain, usually triangular with two faces.

Redoubt (a) An outpost well in front of the main enceinte, enclosed on all sides. (b) A small fort placed at a strategic site.

Retrenchment An interior defence.

Revetment A retaining wall.

Sally port A small gate usually set in a curtain which permits troops to leave on a sortie.

Scarp The side of the ditch nearer the fort.

Tenaille A detached oblong outwork in the ditch usually in front of, and parallel to, a curtain.

Terraplein The backing behind a rampart; in Malta usually constructed of stone.

Traverse A bank or wall, usually at right angles to the main alignment of the work, which protects defenders from enfilade.

Bibliography

A. Guides to Sources

BONNICI, A., 'Due secoli di storia politico-religiosa di Malta nel Fondo Barberini Latino della Biblioteca Vaticana', *Melita historica, IV (1967), 229-56.*

DONALDSON, G., *Handlist of manuscripts in the British Isles relating to Malta* (Malta, 1950).

HELLWALD, F., *Bibliographie méthodique de l'ordre souverain de St-Jean de Jérusalem* (Rome, 1885; reprinted Farnborough, Hants., 1968).

Inventory (general) of the records and registers of the Maltese tribunals for the period 1531-1814 kept in the superior archives of His Majesty's Courts of justice (Malta, 1932).

List of volumes and other documents of the Order of St John of Jerusalem and of the municipal institutions known as the Università preserved in the government treasury (Malta, 1932).

MANGION, G., *Melitensia 1900-1975: Catalogue of the exhibition held at St. John's Annexe, Valletta, June 3-15, 1975* (Malta, 1975).

MICHEL, E., 'I manoscritti della Biblioteca Vaticana relativi alla storia di Malta', *Archivio storico di Malta, I (1929), 152.*

__________*'I manoscritti della Biblioteca Nazionale di Parigi relativi alla storia di Malta',* Archivio storico di Malta, II (1931), 76.

__________ 'I manoscritti delle biblioteche di Roma relativi alla storia di Malta', *Archivio storico di Malta, III (1932), 115-42.*

MIZZI, J., 'A bibliography of the Order of St. John of Jerusalem, 1925-1969', Thirteenth Council of Europe art exhibition, *The Order of St. John in Malta* (Malta, 1970), pp. 108-204.

OCCHINI, P. L., *Un grande italiano del '500, Francesco Laparelli a Malta* (Arezzo, 1937).

ROSSI, E., *Aggiunta alla Bibliographie méthodique de l'ordre souverain de St Jean de Jérusalem di Ferdinand de Hellwald* (Rome, 1924; reprinted Farnborough, Hants., 1968).

SCICLUNA, H. P., *List of manuscripts and other records preserved amongst the various collections of the Archivio Apostolico Vaticano bearing on the history of Malta...* (Malta, 1932).

ZAMMIT GABARRETTA, A., *et al.*, *Catalogue of the records of the Order of St. John of Jerusalem in the Royal Malta Library*: published to date (Malta): Vols. I (1964), II (1970, 1973, 1978 and 1979), III (1965 and 1966), IV (1964), VII (1964), VIII (1967), X (1969), XI (1969), XII (1968), XIII (1967).

B. Original Sources

I. Manuscript Material

England

Cambridge
Trinity College Library
MS. R 46. Volume of Italian tracts.

London
British Museum (now the *British Library*)
Harleian MS. 6794. Contains sixteenth-century description of the fortifications.
Add. MS. 48133. Contains sixteenth-century description of the fortifications.
Add. MS. 48146. Contains sixteenth-century description of the fortifications.
Library of the Order of St. John, St.John's Gate, Clerkenwell
MS. O 1. Notes on the fortifications of Malta (now shelved at H 1).
MS. P 4. 'Catalogo estima delli priorati baliaggi e commende, 1583'.
Public Record Office
War Office, MS. 55, 1555. Observations on the defence of Malta, 1681-1879.
Lambeth Palace Library
MS. 490. Italian papers.

Oxford
Bodleian Library
Tanner MS. 231. Contains report on the fortifications.
Western MS. 3031. Contains report on the fortifications.

ITALY

Florence
Countess Laparelli-Pitti
Codex Laparelli.

Rome
Vatican Secret Archives
a. Apostolic Secretariate
Arm. XLII, 26. Minutes of briefs.
b. Secretariate of State
Miscellanea Arm. II, 81.
Miscellanea Arm. II, 88.
Miscellanea Arm. XV, 53.
Lettere di particolari 15.
c. Fondo Pio.
MS. 246. Miscellaneous.
Vatican Library
a. Fondo Barberini Latino
MS. 5036. 'Relazione della Religione Gerosolimitana di Malta'.
MS. 5325. 'Miscellanea di documenti'.
MS. 6689. Various letters, 1623-36.
MS. 6697. Various letters, 1635-70.
MS. 9296. Letters from P. P. Floriani to Francesco Barberini.
MS. 9905. Plans of fortifications.
b. Fondo Chigi
MS. A I 3. Letters from Fabio Chigi to 1636.
MS. A I 4. Letters from Fabio Chigi, 1636-9.
MS. A III 57. Various letters to Fabio Chigi, 1636-7.
MS. N III 57. Papers on the fortification of Malta.
MS. N III 61. Papers on the fortification of Malta.
MS. N III 77. Papers on the fortification of Malta.
MS. Q III 69. Papers on the fortification of Malta.
MS. R 1 25. Reports on Maltese affairs.
c. Fondo Trivulziano
MS. 1467. Miscellaneous.
d. Fondo Urbinate Latino
MS. 826. Miscellaneous.
MS. 833. Miscellaneous.
MS. 854. Miscellaneous.
e. Fondo Vaticano Latino
MS. 7776. Miscellaneous.

MALTA

Valletta
Royal Malta Library (now the *National Library of Malta*).
a. Archives of the Order of Malta
MS. 61. 'Lettere d'Italia', 1552-1762.

MS. 70. Charter of Charles V granting Malta to the Order.
MSS. 84-167. 'Libri conciliorum', 1522-1797.
MSS. 255-78. 'Libri conciliorum status', 1623-1798.
MSS. 286-315. 'Sacra capitula generalia', 1526-1776.
MSS. 410-624. 'Libri bullarum', 1522-1798.
MSS. 644-62. 'Registri dei decreti della camera de tesoro', 1653-1798.
MSS. 692-9. 'Libri mastri di cassa di conservatoria', 1781-96.
MSS. 737-74. 'Libri dei contratti del tesoro', 1620-1794.
MS. 1011. 'Diversi relazioni, discorsi e sentimenti militari de' ingegneri su le fortificazioni 1689-1722'.
MS. 1012. 'Varie materie relative a Fort Chambray'.
MS. 1013. 'Forte Ricasoli: mandate di lavori'.
MS. 1015. 'Registro delle deliberazioni, progetti, relazioni e visite della Veneranda Congregazione di Guerra e Fortificazione, 1759-98'.
MS. 1016. 'Registro delle risoluzione della Veneranda Congregazione della Fortificazione, 1690-1705'.
MSS. 1017-25. Petitions to the congregation of war, 1714-95.
MSS. 1026-31. Accounts of the congregation of war, 1782-90.
MS. 1054. 'Memoria sulla securezza di Malta', c. 1789.
MSS. 1215-19. Letters from the Order's ambassador to the French court to the grand master, 1689-1724.
MSS. 1264-7. Letters from the Order's ambassador to the Holy See to the grand master, 1635-9.
MS. 1320. Letters from the Order's ambassador to the Holy See to the grand master, 1708.
MSS. 1414-17. Registers of Italian letters sent by the grand master, 1635-8.
MS. 1469. Register of Italian letters sent by the grand master, 1708.
MSS. 1561-3. Registers of French letters sent by the grand master, 1705-22.
MS. 1918. 'Consume dei materiali, 1764-77'.
MSS. 6383-6408. Miscellaneous.
MS. 6519. 'Memoire général sur l'isle de Malte, 1761'.
MS. 6543. 'Retrenchement des côtes des Isles de Malte et du Goze, 1715-16'.
MS. 6546. 'Spesi e pagamenti per le trinci e fornelli di S. Giuliano, 1767-70'.
MS. 6551. 'Discorsi e pareri sopra le fortificazioni, 1633-81'.
MS. 6552. 'Brogliardo di varie deliberationi seguite nella Veneranda Congregazione di Guerra... 1700-15'.
MS. 6553. 'Decreti del Venerando Consiglio in materia di Guerra, 1554-1645'.
MS. 6554. 'Discorsi sopra le fortificationi, 1633-98'.
MS. 6555. 'Memoire général sur l'Isle de Malte, 1761'.
MS. 6556. 'Raccolta di differenti disegni e memorie su lo stabilimento delle coste marittime dell'Isola di Malta e sue adiacenze, 1714-17'.
MS. 6557. 'Memoire sur les fortifications, 1761'.

MS. 6558. 'Copie di diverse memorie e notizie su materie esaminate provedute dallaa Veneranda Congregazione di Stato e Guerra, 1761'.
MS. 6560. 'Memoire historique sur les fortifications de Malte'.
MS. 6565. 'Memoire sur la defence de Malte et Gozo'.
MS. 6571. 'Relationi diverse'.

b. Treasury Documents

MS. A 23. Manoel foundation.
MS. A 104. 'Prova e generale descriptione di tutti li fondi e stabili appartenenti alla Veneranda Congregazione di Guerra, 1766'.
MS. A 105. 'Administrazione di guerra, 1779-97'.
MS. A 106. 'L'introiti... alla cassa delle fortificationi', 1768-73.
MS. A 110. 'Libro di tutti gl'introiti della Veneranda Congregazione di Guerra, 1725-33'.
MS. A 111. 'Registro delle gabelle et affitti di terreni botteghe, etc., 1737-96'.
MS. A 113. 'Brogliardo degl'affitti e gabelle...'

c. Royal Malta Library Manuscript Collection

MS. 140. Miscellaneous reports, eighteenth century.
MS. 186. 'Trattato del commun tesoro del Prior Caravita'.
MS. 290. 'Memoire sur les fortifications, 1715.'
MS. 438. Extracts from the registers of the Università, 1486-1648.
MS. 676. 'Decreti del consiglio'.
MS. 698. 'Bilancio della Religione, 1640'.
MS. 742. 'Decreti provisionali del conseglio in materia di guerra, 1554-1645'.
MS. 1219. 'Siège de Malte'.
MS. 1301. 'Mémoire historique sur les fortifications de Malte', 1715-17.

d. Università Manuscripts

MS. 3. Privileges of the Università.
MS. 11. Register of the Università of Notabile, 1450-98.
MSS. 95-8. 'Spese per le fortificazoni', 1722-48.

II. Printed and Calendared Material

BORG, V., *Fabio Chigi, apostolic delegate in Malta (1634-1639)* (*Studi e Testi*, no. 249, Vatican City, 1967).

Colección de documentos inéditos para la historia de España, ed. M. de Pidal, M. Salva *et al.* 112 vols. (Madrid, 1842-95).

COLLURA, P., 'La difesa militare di Malta nella seconda metà del secolo XVI', *Archivio storico di Malta*, XI (1940), 177-203.

DONNA D'OLDENICO, A., *Redditi e spese dell'Ordine Militare Gerosolimitano di Malta nel 1587* (Ciriè, 1964).

ELLUL, G. V., 'The French invasion of Malta: an unpublished account', *Hyphen: Journal of the Upper Secondary School, Valletta*, III (1978), 1-20.

FERRAMOLINO, A., *Le fortificazioni di Palermo nel secolo XVI*, ed. V. di Giovanni (Società Siciliana per la Storia Patria: Documenti per servire alla storia di Sicilia, serie 4, vol. IV, Palermo, 1896).

GIAMBRUNO, S., & GENUARDI, L., *Capitoli inediti delle città demaniali di Sicilia approvati sino al 1458* (Palermo, 1918).

HOWARD, J., *Letters and documents of Napoleon* (London, 1961).

LEOPARDI, E. R., 'Bandi of the XV century', *Melita historica*, II (1957-9), 122-35, 186-95, 248-62.

MALLIA-MILANES, V., 'Scipione Campi's report of the fortifications of Valletta, 1576', *Melita historica*, VIII (1983), 275-90.

PAULI, S., *Codice diplomatico del Sacro Militare Ordine Gerosolimitano, oggi di Malta*, 2 vols. (Lucca, 1733-7).

VELLA BONAVITA, R., 'A sixteenth-century proposal for a fort on "Manoel" island', *Melita historica*, VI (1973), 141-52.

C. Contemporary and Nearly Contemporary Works

ABELA, G.F., *Della descrizione di Malta* (Malta; 1647).

BALBI, F., *The siege of Malta*, trans. H. Balbi (Copenhagen, 1961).

BLONDEL, F., *L'art de jetter les bombes* (Paris, (1683).

___________*Nouvelle manière de fortifier les places* (Paris, 1683).

BOSIO, G., *Istoria della Sacra Religione Militare di S. Giovanni Gerosolimitano*, 3 vols. (Rome, 1594-1620).

BRAUN, G., & HOGENBERG, F., *Civitates orbis terrarum*, 6 vols. (Cologne, 1572-1618; reprinted in 3 vols. Cologne, 1965).

BRYDONE, P., *A tour through Sicily and Malta, in a series of letters to W. Beckford, Esq.*, 2 vols. (London, 1791).

FLORIANI, P. P., *Difesa et ofesa delle piazze* (Macerata, 1630).

FLORIANI, POMPEO, *Discorso della Goletta et del forte di Tunisi* (Macerata, 1574).

___________*Discorso all'isola di Malta e di ciò che porrà succedere tentando il Turco dal impresa* (Macerata, 1576).

FOLARD, J. C. DE, *Histoire de Polybe traduite du Grec par Dom V. Thuillier... avec un commentaire ou un corps de science militaire... par M. de Folard*, 6 vols. (Paris, 1727-30).

FOREST DE BELIDOR, B., *La science des ingénieurs dans la conduite des travaux de fortification et d'architecture civile* (Paris, 1729).

MAGGI, G., & CASTRIOTTO, G., *Della fortificatione delle città* (Venice, 1564).

MAIGRET, P., *Traité de la sûreté et conservation des états par le moyen des forteresses* (Paris, 1725).

MARCHI, F., *Della architettura militare* (Brescia, 1599).

PAGAN, B. F., *Les fortifications* (Paris, 1645).

PEREZ D'ALECCIO, M., *I veri ritratti della guerra e dell'assedio dati alla Isola di Malta dall'armata Turchesa l'anno MDLXV* (Rome, 1582); reprinted as: *The true depiction of the investment and attack suffered by the island of Malta in 1565*, trans. and ed. D. Calnan and G. Testaferrata Abela (Malta, 1965).

POZZO, B. DAL, *Historia della Sacra Religione Militare di S. Giovanni Gerosolimitano, detta di Malta* (Vol. 1, Verona, 1703; Vol. II, Venice, 1715).

RINALDINI, G., *Conclusione che non si devono fare le piazze basse ne' fianchi delle fortezze* (Messina, 1610).

SCAMOZZI, V., *Dell'idea dell'architettura universale*, 2 vols. (Venice, 1615).

SPECKLE, D., *Architectura von Festungen* (Strasbourg, 1589).

VALPERGA, A. M., *Essercitio militare a beneficio del nuovo soldato* (Naples, 1653).

__________*Indirizzo del nuovo soldato diviso in due parti* (Naples, 1655).

VASARI, G., *Lives of the painters, sculptors and architects*, ed. W. Gaunt, 4 vols. (London, 1927).

VENUTI, F., *Vita del Capitano F. Laparelli da Cortona* (Livorno, 1761).

VERTOT, R., *Histoire des Chevaliers Hospitaliers de St. Jean de Jérusalem*, 4 vols. (Paris, 1726).

D. Modern Works

AGNELLO, S.L., 'Michelangelo Buonamici architetto del secolo XVII', in *Atti del XV Congresso di Storia dell'Architettura: l'architettura a Malta dalla preistoria all'ottocento* (Rome, 1970), pp. 465-6.

AUGOYAT, M., *Aperçu historique sur les fortifications, les ingénieurs et sur le Corps du Génie en France*, 3 vols. (Paris, 1860-4).

AVANA, L.R., & MANUCY, A., *The building of Castillo de San Marcos* (St. Augustine, Florida, 1977).

AYALA, M.D', 'Degl' ingegneri militari italiani dal secolo XIII al XVIII', *Archivio storico italiano*, IX (1869), 71-110.

BLANCHARD, A., *Les ingénieurs du "roy" de Louis XIV à Louis XVI: étude du corps des fortifications* (Montpellier, 1979).

BLOMFIELD, R., *Sébastien le Prestre de Vauban, 1633-1707* (London, 1938; reprinted 1971).

BLOUET, B.W., 'Town planning in Malta 1530-1798', *Town planning review*, XXXV (1964), 183-93.

__________*Story of Malta* (London, 1967).

BOISGELIN, L. DE, *Ancient and modern Malta*, 2 vols. (London, 1805).

BORG CARDONA, S.R., 'The Officio delle Case and the housing laws of the early grand masters 1531-69', *Law Journal* (Malta, 1951).

BOSCARINO, S., 'Catania: le fortificazioni alla fine del seicento ed il piano di ricostruzione dopo il terremoto del 1693', *Quaderno dell' Istituto Dipartimentale de Architettura ed Urbanistica,* Università di Catania, VIII (1976), 69-102.

BOSHER, F., *French finances, 1770-95* (Cambridge, 1970).

BOXER, C.R., & AZEVEDO, A. DE, *Fort Jesus and the Portuguese in Mombasa* (London, 1960).

BRADFORD, E., *The great siege: Malta 1565* (London, 1961).

BRAUDEL, F., *The Mediterranean and the Mediterranean world in the age of Philip II*, trans. S. Reynolds, 2 vols. (London, 1972 and 1973).

BRESC, H., 'The "Secrezia" and the royal patrimony in Malta: 1240-1450' in *Medieval Malta: studies on Malta before the knights*, ed. A.T. Luttrell (London, 1975), pp. 126-162.

BUTLER, L., 'The Maltese people and the Order of St. John in the sixteenth century', *Annales de l'Ordre Souverain Militaire de Malte*, XXIV (1966), 95-101.

CAPEL, H., GARCIA, L., MONCADA, J-O., *et al. Los ingenieros militares en España siglo XVIII repertorio biográfico e inventario de su labor científico y espacial* (Barcelona, 1983).

CARTER, F.W., *Dubrovnik (Ragusa): a classic city-state* (London, 1972).

CASSAR, P., 'The Maltese corsairs and the Order of St. John of Jerusalem', *Catholic historical review*, XLVI (1960), 137-56.

CASSAR, P., *Medical history of Malta* (London, 1964/5).

CAVALIERO, R., *The last of the crusaders* (London, 1960).

CLARK, G. N., *War and society in the seventeenth century* (Cambridge, 1958).

CLAUSETTI, E., 'Pietro Paolo Floriani, ingegnere militare, 1585-1638', *Palladio* III (1939), 153-62.

COURCELLES, CHEV. DE, *Dictionnaire historique et biographique des généraux français depuis le onzième siècle jusqu'en 1821*, 9 vols. (Paris, 1820-3).

COUTURA, J., *et al. La citadelle de Blaye* (Paris, 1978).

DEBONO, J., 'The wine trade of Malta in the eighteenth century', *Melita historica*, IX (1984), 74-92.

DE LA CROIX, H., 'The literature on fortification in Renaissance Italy', *Technology and culture*, IV (1963), 30-50.

DE LUCCA, D., 'The Maltese "perit" in history', *Melita historica*, VI (1975), 431-6.

__________ 'French military engineers in Malta during the 17th and 18th centuries', *Melita Historica*, VIII (1980), 23-33.

__________ 'The contribution of François de Mondion in the architectural developement of 18th century Malta', in *Proceedings of History Week 1981*, ed. M. Buhagiar (Malta, 1982), pp. 76-81.

Dictionnaire de biographie français (Paris, 1933–).

Dizionario biografico degli italiani (Rome, 1960–).

DUFFY, C., *Fire and stone: the science of fortress warfare, 1660-1860* (Newton Abbot and London, 1975).

__________ *Siege warfare: the fortress in the early modern world, 1494-1660* (London, 1979).

__________ *The fortress in the age of Vauban and Frederick the Great, 1660-1798* (London, 1985).

EARLE, P., *Corsairs of Malta and Barbary* (London, 1970).

EICKHOF, E., *Venedig, Wien und die Osmanen, 1645-1700* (Munich, 1971).

[ENGELS, F.], 'Fortification', in *The new American cyclopaedia*, ed. C. A. Dana and G. Ripley, 16 vols. (New York, 1858-63).

FIORINI, S., 'Status Animarum I: a unique source for the 17th and 18th century Maltese demography', *Melita historica*, VIII (1983), 325-44.

__________ 'The resettlement of Gozo after 1551', *Melita historica*, IX (1986), 203-44.

FORTI, L.C., *Le fortificazioni di Genova* (Genoa, 1971).

__________ 'The fortifications of Genoa', *Fort*, IX (1981), 7-11.

GABRIEL, A., *La cité de Rhodes*, 2 vols. (Paris, 1921).

GALEA SCANNURA, C., 'The building of the Cottonera fortifications: a Maltese protest against taxation', *Hyphen*, III (Malta, 1982), 185-96.

GIUFFRÈ, M., 'Palermo città murata dal XVI al XIX secolo', *Quaderno dell' Istituto Dipartimentale di Architettura ed Urbanistica*, Università di Catania, VIII (1976), 41-68.

GODECHOT, J., 'La France et Malte au XVIIIe siècle', *Revue historique*, CCVI (1951), 67-79.

HALE, J. R., 'The argument of some military title pages of the Renaissance', *Newberry Library bulletin*, VI (1964), 91-102.

__________ 'The early development of the bastion' in *Europe in the late Middle Ages*, ed. J. R. Hale, J. R. L. Highfield and B. Smalley (London, 1965), pp. 466-94.

__________ 'Armies, navies and the art of war', in *New Cambridge modern history*, III, *The Counter-Reformation and the price revolution, 1559 1610'* ed. R. B. Wernham (Cambridge, 1968), pp. 171-208.

__________ 'Francesco Tensini and the fortification of Vicenza', *Studi veneziani*, X (1968), 231-89.

__________ 'The military education of the officer class in early modern Europe', in *Cultural aspects of the Italian Renaissance*, ed. C.H. Clough (Manchester, 1976), pp. 440-61.

__________ *Renaissance fortification: art or engineering?* (London, 1977).

HALL, A. R., *Ballistics in the seventeenth century* (Cambridge, 1952).

HOOK, J., 'Fortifications and the end of the Sienese state', *History*, LXII (1977), 372-87.

HOPPEN (BUCHAN), A., 'The fortification of Malta by the Order of the Hospital of St. John of Jerusalem, 1530-1798' (Ph.D. thesis, University of St. Andrews, 1970).

__________ 'The finances of the Order of St. John of Jerusalem in the sixteenth and seventeenth centuries', *European studies review*, III (1973), 103-19.

__________ 'The Knights Hospitallers and the defence of Malta', *Annales de l'Ordre Souverain Militaire de Malte*, XXXV (1977), 30-7.

__________ 'Military engineers in Malta, 1530-1798', *Annales of science*, XXXVIII (1981), 413-33.

__________ 'Military priorities and social realities in the early modern Mediterranean: Malta and its fortifications', in *Hospitaller Malta 1530-1798: Studies in early modern Malta and the Order of St. John of Jerusalem* ed. V. Mallia-Milanes (Malta, 1993), pp. 399-428.

HUGHES, J. Q., *The building of Malta, 1530-1795* (London, 1956).

__________ *Fortress: architecture and military history in Malta* (London, 1969).

__________ 'The defence of Malta', *Quaderno dell'Istituto Dipartimentale di Architettura ed Urbanistica*, Università di Catania, VIII (1976), 1-40. Reprinted in *Fort*, IV (1977), 13-52.

__________ 'Give me time and I will give you life: Francesco Laparelli and the building of Valletta, Malta, 1565-1569', *Town planning review*, XLIX (1978), 61-74.

__________ *Malta: a guide to the fortifications* (Liverpool, 1985).

JONES, H. D., 'Memoranda and details of the mode of building houses in the island of Malta', *Papers on subjects connected with the duties of the corps of Royal Engineers*, V (1842), 196-205.

LAVEDAN, P., *Histoire de l'urbanisme: Renaissance et temps modernes* (Paris, 1941).

LAZARD, P., *Vauban, 1633-1707* (Paris, 1934).

LEOPARDI, E. R., 'The island of Gozo, 1432-53', *Melita historica*, III (1962), 77-80, IV (1964), 67-71.

LUTTRELL, A. T., 'Approaches to medieval Malta', in *Medieval Malta: studies on Malta before the knights*, ed. A. T. Luttrell (London, 1975), pp. 1-70.

_________ 'Eighteenth-century Malta: prosperity and problems', *Hyphen*, III (Malta, 1982), 37-51.

MALLET, M., & HALE, J.R., *The military organization of a Renaissance state: Venice c. 1400-1617* (Cambridge, 1984).

MALLIA-MILANES, V., 'In search of Vittorio Cassar: a documentary approach', *Melita historica*, IX (1986), 247-70.

MANGION, G., 'Girolamo Cassar architetto maltese del cinquecento', *Melita historica*, VI (1973), 192-200.

MARCONI, P., 'I progetti inediti della Valletta: dal Laparelli al Floriani', in *Atti del XV Congresso di Storia dell' Architettura: l'architettura a Malta dalla preistoria all' ottocento* (Rome, 1970), pp. 353-86.

MELI, F., 'Degli architetti del senato di Palermo nel secolo XVII e XVIII' *Archivio storico per la Sicilia [Archivio storico siciliano]*, IV-V (1938-9), 305-470.

MIÈGE, *Histoire de Malte*, 3 vols. (Paris, 1840).

MIFSUD, A., 'Un cenno al 1565 nel 1915', *Archivum melitense*, II (1915), 229.

_________ 'Papi, fortificazioni e tasse nel passato di Malta', *Archivum melitense*, III (1919), 399-430.

_________ 'La milizia e le torri antiche di Malta', *Archivum melitense*, IV (1920), 55-100.

MURRAY, J., 'The Maltese islands with special reference to their geological structure', *Scottish geographical magazine*, VI (1890), 449-88.

MUSCAT, J., 'Visitatio Turrium', *Melita historica*, VIII (1981), 101-108.

Nuovo dizionario istorico, 27 vols. (Naples, 1791-4).

PEPPER, S., & ADAMS, N., *Firearms and fortifications: military architecture and siege warfare in sixteenth-century Siena* (Chicago, 1986).

PORTER, W., *The history of the fortress of Malta* (Malta, 1858).

PROMIS, C., 'Gl' ingegneri militari della Marca d'Ancona che operarono e scrissero dall' anno MDL all' anno MDCL' in *Miscellanea di storia italiana*, VI (Turin, 1865), 241-356.

_________ 'Gl' ingegneri militari che operano o scrissero in Piemonte dal 1300 al 1650' in *Miscellanea di storia italiana*, XII (Turin, 1871), 411-646.

_________ 'Biografie dei ingegneri militari italiani dal secolo XIV alla metà del XVIII', *Miscellanea di storia italiana*, XIV (Turin, 1874).

RESTELLI, F., & SAMMUT, J. C., *The coinage of the knights in Malta*, 2 vols. (Malta,1977).

RILEY-SMITH, J., *The knights of St. John in Jerusalem and Cyprus, 1050-1310* (London, 1967).

ROBERTS, M., 'The military revolution, 1560-1660', in *Essays in Swedish history* (London, 1967), pp. 195-225.

RYAN, F., *The house of the Temple* (London, 1930).

SAMMUT, E., 'L'officio delle case ed i regolamenti per la fabbrica della Valletta (1556-1629)', in *Atti del XV Congresso di Storia dell'Architettura: l'architettura a Malta dalla preistoria all'ottocento* (Rome, 1970), pp. 387-99.

SAMMUT, J. C., 'The coinage of the Order of St. John in Malta', Thirteenth Council of Europe art exhibition, *The Order of St. John in Malta* (Malta, 1970), pp. 47-52.

SANT, M., 'Minting and attempted recalling of fiduciary coinage in Malta', *Melita historica*, VI (1972,), 60-80.

SCHEMBRI, H., CALLEJA, *Coins and medals of the knights of Malta* (London, 1908).

SPITERI, S.C., *Discovering the fortifications of the Order of St. John in Malta* (Malta, 1988).

THORNTON, W. H., *Memoir on the finances of the Order* (Malta, 1836).

TONNA, J., & DE LUCCA, D., *Romano Carapecchia: studies in Maltese architecture*, I (Malta, 1975).

VELLA, A. P., *Malta and the czars* (Malta, 1965).

WETTINGER, G., 'The militia list of 1419-20', *Melita historica*, V (1969), 80-106.

__________ 'Early Maltese popular attitudes to the government of the Order of St. John', *Melita historica*, VI (1974), 255-78.

__________ 'Lost villages and hamlets in Malta', in *Medieval Malta: studies on Malta before the knights*, ed. A.T. Luttrell, (London, 1975), pp. 181-217.

ZABARELLA, C. S., *Lo assedio di Malta* (Turin, 1902).

ZASTROW, A. DE, *Histoire de la fortification permanente*, trans. Neuens, 2 vols. (Liège, 1846).

Index